THE DOMESTIC SOURCES OF AMERICAN FOREIGN POLICY

THE DOMESTIC SOURCES OF AMERICAN FOREIGN POLICY

Insights and Evidence

Third Edition

Edited by
Eugene R. Wittkopf and
James M. McCormick

ROWMAN & LITTLEFIELD PUBLISHERS, INC.
Lanham • Boulder • New York • Oxford

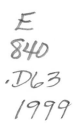

ROWMAN & LITTLEFIELD PUBLISHERS, INC.

Published in the United States of America
by Rowman & Littlefield Publishers, Inc.
4720 Boston Way, Lanham, Maryland 20706

12 Hid's Copse Road
Cumnor Hill, Oxford OX2 9JJ, England

British Library Cataloguing in Publication Information Available

Library of Congress Cataloging-in-Publication Data

The domestic sources of American foreign policy : insights and
   evidence / edited by Eugene R. Wittkopf, James M. McCormick.—
   3rd ed.
      p. cm.
   Includes bibliographical references and index.
   ISBN 0-8476-8749-X (cloth : alk. paper).—ISBN 0-8476-8850-X
(pbk. : alk. paper)
    1. United States—Foreign relations—1945–1989. 2. United States—
Foreign relations—1989– 3. United States—Foreign relations—
Decision making. 4. United States—Foreign relations
administration. I. Wittkopf, Eugene R., 1943– . II. McCormick,
James M.
E840.D63   1998
327.73'009'045—dc21   98-21010
                                         CIP

Printed in the United States of America

∞ ™ The paper used in this publication meets the minimum requirements of
American National Standard for Information Sciences—Permanence of Paper for
Printed Library Materials, ANSI Z39.48—1984.

Contents

ACKNOWLEDGMENTS

"The Erosion of American National Interests" by Samuel P. Huntington. Reprinted by permission of *Foreign Affairs* 76 (5, September/October 1997): 28–49. Copyright 1997 by the Council on Foreign Relations, Inc.

"The Domestic Core of Foreign Policy" by Ronald Steel. © 1995 by Ronald Steel, as first published in *The Atlantic Monthly*.

"Public Opinion and Foreign Policy: The People's Common Sense" by John Mueller. Reprinted with permission. © *The National Interest,* No. 47, Spring 1997, Washington, D.C.

"The Politics of Military Base Closures" by Genevieve Anton and Jeff Thomas. Adapted from a series of articles that appeared in the *Colorado Springs Gazette Telegraph.* Reprinted with permission. © 1995 Freedom Communications, Inc.

"The New China Lobby" by Richard Bernstein and Ross H. Munro. From *The Coming Conflict with China* by Richard Bernstein and Ross H. Munro. Copyright © 1997 by Richard Bernstein and Ross H. Munro. Reprinted by permission of Alfred A. Knopf, Inc.

"The CNN Effect: Myth or Reality?" by Warren P. Strobel. Reprinted by permission of *American Journalism Review.*

"The Electoral Cycle and the Conduct of American Foreign Policy" by William B. Quandt. Reprinted with permission from *Political Science Quarterly* 101 (5, 1986): 825–837. This article was revised and updated for this book.

"Presidential Management of the Executive Bureaucracy" by Geoffrey Kemp. From Robert J. Art and Seyom Brown, *United States Foreign Policy: The Search for a New Role.* Copyright © 1993. All rights reserved. Reprinted/adapted by permission of Allyn & Bacon.

"Globalization and Diplomacy: The View from Foggy Bottom" by Strobe Talbott. Reprinted with permission from *Foreign Policy* (Fall 1997): 69–83. Copyright 1997 by the Carnegie Endowment for International Peace.

"Civil-Military Relations: Causes of Concern" by Eliot A. Cohen. © 1997 by Eliot A. Cohen. Reprinted with permission.

"Information Age Intelligence" by Bruce D. Berkowitz. Reprinted with permission from *Foreign Policy* 103 (Summer 1996): 35–50. Copyright 1996 by the Carnegie Endowment for International Peace.

"Trade Policy Decisionmaking: Competing Explanations" by Stephen D. Cohen, Joel R. Paul, and Robert A. Blecker. Originally published as "Decisionmaking Explained: The How and Why of Policymakers' Behavior," in Stephen D. Cohen, Joel R. Paul, and Robert A. Blecker, *Fundamentals of U.S. Foreign Trade Policy.* Copyright © 1997 by Westview Press. Reprinted by permission of Westview Press.

"How Could Vietnam Happen? An Autopsy" by James C. Thomson Jr. Copyright © 1968 by James C. Thomson Jr. Reprinted with permission.

"Tribal Tongues: Intelligence Consumers, Intelligence Producers" by Mark M. Lowenthal. Reprinted from *The Washington Quarterly* 15:1 (Winter 1992): 157–168 by permission of the MIT Press. © 1992 by the Center for Strategic and International Studies (CSIS) and the Massachusetts Institute of Technology.

"Policy Preferences and Bureaucratic Position: The Case of the American Hostage Rescue Mission" by Steve Smith. This article first appeared in the Winter 1984–85 issue of *International Affairs* (61:1): 9–25, the quarterly journal of the Royal Institute of International Affairs, London, and is reproduced with permission.

"Are Bureaucracies Important? A Reexamination of the Accounts of the Cuban Missile Crisis" by Stephen D. Krasner. © 1972 by Stephen D. Krasner. Reprinted with permission.

"NATO Expansion: The Anatomy of a Decision" by James M. Goldgeier. Reprinted from *The Washington Quarterly* 21:1 (Winter 1998): 85–102 by permission of the MIT Press. © 1998 by the Center for Strategic and International Studies (CSIS) and the Massachusetts Institute of Technology.

Introduction

Over a decade has passed since the fall of the Berlin Wall and the collapse of the Cold War principles that shaped American foreign policy for over two generations. In their wake, two competing global processes have accelerated change and enhanced the domestic–foreign nexus in American policymaking. *Globalization*—political, economic, and social forces that are drawing peoples together regardless of state boundaries—has pulled the international community and American foreign policy in one direction. *Fragmentation*—political, economic, and social forces driving peoples apart within and across states—has pushed the world's political actors and American foreign policy in another direction. As a consequence, domestic politics and foreign policy are increasingly inseparable. Thus, the need to understand the domestic sources of American foreign policy is more compelling than ever. Such is our purpose in this book.

The process of globalization across a variety of policy arenas has accelerated since the end of the Cold War, directly affecting the very fabric of the contemporary state system and reshaping the contours of the world political landscape as we approach the millennium. The rapid development and expansion of new regional trading organizations (e.g., the North American Free Trade Agreement and the Asia-Pacific Economic Cooperation forum); the transformation of existing or birth of new military and political organizations with increasingly larger memberships (e.g., the North Atlantic Treaty Organization, the Organization for Security and Cooperation in Europe, and the ASEAN Regional Forum); and the explosion of media and communications worldwide (e.g., CNN, the fax machine, and the World Wide Web) reflect the remarkable changes occurring at the end of the twentieth century. These and other developments epitomize the "end of geography" and the "death of distance" in the global system, knitting peoples and states together and clouding the distinction between domestic and foreign affairs as never before.

Fragmentation in the global community coexists alongside globalization. Widespread ethnopolitical conflict evident in Rwanda, Bosnia, Chechnya,

Mexico, and elsewhere has shifted the focus of world politics from conflicts between states to conflicts within them, thus challenging the principle of sovereignty on which the state system itself rests. The collapse of financial institutions in Korea and Japan, followed by a currency collapse in Indonesia and financial instability elsewhere, demonstrate the dark side of globalization, often causing dislocations and economic hardships on people within and across state boundaries. In the security sphere, concerns about the proliferation of nuclear, biological, and chemical weapons of mass destruction reveal the differences that continue to divide states and peoples. Similarly, fears of climate change stimulated by global warming and of social dislocations and unrest tied to human rights violations and the increased number of migrants and refugees continue to fragment the global community.

Globalization and fragmentation have affected American foreign policy as profoundly as they have shaped world politics since the Berlin Wall fell. First, they have fueled a continuing domestic debate not only over *how* the United States should be involved in the world, but also over *whether* it should be involved at all. With its victory in the Cold War, some analysts argue that the United States should take advantage of its position as the "sole remaining superpower" to pursue a strategy of "primacy," urging that the aspirations of emerging challengers to its power and position be thwarted and recommending that the United States expend whatever treasure may be required to meet the challenge. Others believe that the United States should reduce its global involvements, seek a more narrowly defined set of interests, and insulate itself as much as possible from the competing forces of globalization and fragmentation. Still others see the divergent forces in world politics as presenting the United States with little choice but to remain engaged—actively but selectively—seeking to manage and control them for the benefit of the nation.[1]

Second, these twin processes have helped to alter the potency of participants in the policy process. Ironically, the intensification of U.S. interdependence with the world political economy that accompanies globalization increases domestic pressures on the nation's foreign policies and policymaking processes. As the experience of other nations confirms, interdependence compromises the sovereign autonomy of the state, blurs the distinction between foreign and domestic politics, and elevates the participation of domestically oriented government agencies in the policy process. Many recent economic changes accelerated by the forces of globalization, for example, produce clear winners and losers within the American polity. Each group vigorously appeals to government officials seeking either policy continuity or policy change to meet its concerns. The upshot of their actions is a further "domestication" of American foreign policy.

The fragmentation of the international system has had a similar effect. Unlike the Cold War years, when the threat of Soviet-inspired communism and the fear of nuclear war led to the dominance of a single security issue, none of the multiple challenges now facing the United States commands primacy of place among policymakers or the public, and none suggests policy positions that unite policymakers' preferences and public sentiments like the communist threat did. Instead, as suggested, they divide the American people much as they do the international community. As a consequence, various bureaucracies, members of Congress, differing interest groups, and the public at large seek to weigh in on their preferred issue and policy prescription.[2]

Furthermore, the nature of the issues in the current era have encouraged domestic sources to play a larger role in shaping American foreign policy. Today's issues, generated by the demands of globalization and fragmentation, are increasingly perceived less as crisis issues, ones that characteristically require prompt attention and action. More often they are seen either as strategic issues or as structural issues. Strategic policy issues "specify the goals and tactics of foreign policy" (e.g., the development of "constructive engagement" toward China or "dual containment" toward Iran and Iraq). Structural policy issues, on the other hand, dictate "how resources are used," such as "procuring, deploying, and organizing military personnel and material" or "which countries will receive aid, what rules will govern immigration, and how much money will be given to international organizations."[3] Since neither strategic nor structural policy issues require the kinds of rapid responses crises demand, and since neither confines the locus of decision making solely to the executive branch, more domestic participants have the opportunity to influence the outcome.

Domestic Politics and Foreign Policy

The proposition that domestic politics explains foreign policy stands in sharp contrast to the realist tradition in the study of foreign policy. Political realism, a perspective that enjoyed widespread acceptance among policymakers and scholars during the Cold War and before, argues that foreign policy is primarily a function of what occurs outside national borders. In this tradition, states are the principal actors; power and national interests are the dominant policy considerations; and maintaining the balance of power among states is the principal policy imperative. Furthermore, all states—democratic and nondemocratic—operate on the same assumptions and respond similarly to changes in the international system. In short, from a realist perspective, domestic politics exerts little if any impact on state behavior.

While political realism provides valuable insights into the motivations and actions of states, it surely underestimates the effects of the domestic environment both historically and in the current era. Even the Greek philosopher Thucididyes, perhaps the first political realist, recognized the importance of domestic politics in shaping the external behavior of Athens and Sparta. In language with a decidedly contemporary ring, he observed that the actions leaders of Greek city-states directed toward one another often sought to affect the political climate within their own polities, not what happened between them.

Centuries later Immanuel Kant observed in his treatise *Perpetual Peace* that democracies are inherently less warlike than autocracies because democratic leaders are accountable to the public, which restrains them from waging war. Because ordinary citizens would have to supply the soldiers and bear the human and financial costs of imperial policies, he contended, liberal democracies are "natural" forces for peace. History has been kind to Kant's thesis: Democracies rarely fight one another. The reasons may be more complex than Kant suggested, but nothing argues more persuasively for understanding the nexus between domestic politics and foreign policy than this empirical regularity.

In the early twentieth century V.I. Lenin hypothesized that the domestic economic structures of states were also critical explanations of states' foreign policies. Drawing on the ideas of Karl Marx and others, he reasoned that capitalism as an economic system within states was pivotal in explaining warfare between them. Capitalist states had to expand to find raw materials and new markets; hence warfare with other capitalist states became "inevitable." While the evidence supporting Lenin's proposition is less persuasive than that supporting Kant's, nevertheless, it, too, points to the centrality of the domestic arena in understanding foreign-policy behavior.

Policymakers in the post–Cold War decade have highlighted the absence of war between democratic states, using the "democratic peace proposition" to rationalize the spread of democratic market economies as good for business as well as for peace. But the impact of domestic politics on foreign policy manifests itself in other ways. For example, it is difficult to explain Britain's reluctance to join the European Union's monetary union without understanding its insular mentality and the historical significance of its currency, the pound sterling. Japan's protectionist trade policy is deeply rooted in its political culture and its long tradition of protecting domestic agricultural and industrial interests. New Zealand's aversion to nuclear weapons, and nuclear power generally, can only partly be understood in terms of the actions of other states; instead, partisan divisions and widespread antinuclear public sentiment are more persuasive explanations. Finally, the actions of Bosnia's political leaders cannot be understood without reference to the religious and ethnic divisions that have long rended the Balkans.

Domestic Politics and American Foreign Policy

America's post–Cold War foreign policy is rife with examples of how domestic politics shape and restrain its actions abroad. At the outset of his administration in 1993, President Clinton consciously chose to focus on a domestic agenda, not a foreign-policy one. As the demands of the external environment increasingly intruded on his priorities, however, Clinton changed directions, but he did so in a way that reflected the primacy of domestic politics. His decision to delink the granting of most favored nation (MFN) status to China from its abysmal human rights record reflected domestic economic considerations; his reluctance to use force in Rwanda turned in part on public apprehension over further U.S. involvement in UN peacekeeping activities; his embrace of NATO expansion drew both inspiration and support from ethnic groups with ties to Central Europe; and his position on the global warming treaty fell between the strong environmental stance advocated by Vice President Al Gore and business and industrial interests' persistent lobbying against limitations on fossil fuel consumption. Indeed, one assessment attributed the Clinton administration's "strategic void" in foreign policy to "the primacy Clinton gives to political calculations."[4]

The Republican Congress, which first came to power in 1994 after forty years "in exile" as the minority party, proved to be equally sensitive to domestic pressures. This was most evident in its effort to reduce or eliminate America's involvement in UN peacekeeping operations and in its unwillingness to fund other international activities, including those of international financial institutions with a special interest in coping with the dark side of economic globalization. In short, both ends of Pennsylvania Avenue responded to the imperatives of domestic politics in shaping America's foreign policy at the dawn of the new millennium.

Given the nation's historical roots, the constraints domestic politics impose on American foreign policy should hardly be surprisingly. Since its founding, the United States has perceived itself as a different, indeed, an exceptional nation, one whose foreign policy is driven more by domestic values than by the vagaries of international politics. Analysts who have examined the views of Thomas Jefferson and others among the Founders conclude that they believed that "the objectives of foreign policy were but a means to the end of posterity and promoting the goals of domestic society."[5] That belief still permeates the political process. In fact, satisfying the requirements of domestic politics in foreign policy has arguably become more acute with the end of the Cold War than at other times in this century. Whether that is cause for concern may be debated. Still, it raises questions about the ability of a democratic society to pursue a successful foreign-policy strategy. As the French political sociologist Alexis de Tocqueville observed over 150 years ago, "Foreign politics demand scarcely any of those qualities which a democracy possesses; they require, on the contrary, the perfect use of almost all those faculties in which it is deficient."

Although there may be broad agreement that domestic imperatives sometimes shape foreign policy, there is less agreement about the particulars and how they manifest themselves in the political process. For analytic purposes, we can begin our inquiry into the domestic sources of American foreign policy by grouping them into three broad categories: (1) the societal environment of the nation; (2) its institutional setting; and (3) the individual characteristics of the nation's decisionmakers and the policymaking positions they occupy.

Figure 1 illustrates the relationship between each of the domestic explanatory categories and American foreign policy and their interrelationships with one another. The figure posits that domestic policy influences are inputs into the decisionmaking process that converts policy demands into foreign policy. (We can define foreign policy as the goals that the nation's officials seek to realize abroad, the values that give rise to them, and the means or instruments used to pursue them.) Conceptualized as the output of the process that converts policy demands into goals and means, foreign policy is typically multifaceted, ranging from discrete behaviors linked to specific issues to recurring patterns of behavior that define the continual efforts of the United States to cope with the environment beyond its borders. Noteworthy, however, is that neither discrete events nor broad policy patterns are likely to be explained adequately by reference to only one explanatory factor.

It is easy to identify many of the discrete variables that make up the domestic source categories, but the lines between the categories themselves are not always clear-cut. To help draw these larger distinctions as well as explicate the smaller ones, it is useful to think of the explanatory categories as layers of differing size and complexity.

The Societal Environment

The broadest layer is the societal environment. The political culture of the United States—the basic needs, values, beliefs and self-images widely shared by Americans about their political system—stands out as a primary societal source of American foreign policy. Minimally, those beliefs find expression in the kinds of values and political institutions American policymakers have sought to export to others throughout much of its history. Included is a preference for democracy, capitalism, and the values of the American liberal tradition—limited government, individual liberty, due process of the law, self-determination, free enterprise, inalienable (natural) rights, the equality of citizens before the law, majority rule, minority rights, federalism, and the separation of powers.

With roots deeply implanted in the nation's history, elements of the political culture remain potent forces explaining what the United States does in its foreign policy. However, as the processes of globalization and fragmentation deepen, the domestic roots of foreign policy may increasingly be found elsewhere. On globalization issues, for instance, industry, labor, and environmental interests can be expected to respond differently, as they try to place their

FIGURE 1
The Sources of American Foreign Policy

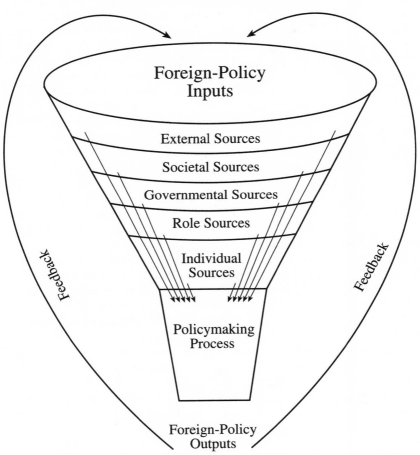

Source: Charles W. Kegley Jr., and Eugene R. Wittkopf, *American Foreign Policy: Pattern and Process,* 5th ed. (New York: St. Martin's Press, 1996), 15.

own stamp on U.S. responses. On fragmentation issues, disagreements are often found among ideological and ethnic groups, who try to impose the imprint of their viewpoints on policy positions. In short, domestic divisions obfuscate a clear and consistent U.S. foreign-policy response to the issues that today populate the global agenda.

American public opinion toward foreign policy reveals these divisions, much as interest group activities do. While American policymakers and opinion leaders remain overwhelmingly internationalist in orientation, there are signs that the American public at large has wearied of the burdens of leadership. The majority of Americans continues to support active U.S. involvement in the world, but nearly two in five now prefer a retreat from globalism and a return to the isolationist posture of the pre–Cold War era.[6] Even many internationalists would prefer to direct attention to domestic priorities rather than international ones.

The rapid globalization of the world political economy has fueled Americans' introspection about the U.S. role in world affairs. Many of them believe that they have been victimized by an international economic system in which capital and production are highly mobile, but labor is not.[7] They also worry about the influx of immigrants, who not only take jobs paying lower wages than many Americans find acceptable but also bring with them ideas from their homelands that challenge what many believe to be fundamental American values. Many Americans have also become wary of the costs of leadership, particularly in conflict situations that may threaten the lives of U.S. soldiers. Indeed, it is now axiomatic that public opinion will not tolerate large numbers of American casualties in pursuit of foreign-policy objectives.

Historically, American leaders have been able to define the parameters of American involvement in the world and to count on public support for their choices. Especially important was the so-called Establishment consisting of (largely male) leaders drawn from the corporate and financial world and later supplemented by faculty members from the nation's elite universities. With roots in the early twentieth century, the Establishment was a major force defining key elements of American foreign policy prior to World War II and in the decades of Cold War conflict that followed. Its role is consistent with the *elitist* model of foreign-policy making, which says that public policy is little more than an expression of elites' preferences—and the interests underlying them.

The notion that public opinion will not tolerate large losses of life in situations involving American troops is consistent with another tradition known as *pluralism*. Whereas the elitist model sees the process of policy making as one flowing from the top downward, pluralism sees the process as an upward flowing one. Mass public opinion enjoys greater weight in this model. It finds expression through interest groups, whose ability to shape foreign policy has been enhanced in the current environment.

The media figure prominently but quite differently in these competing policymaking models. From the elitist perspective, the media are largely the mouthpieces of elites, providing the conduit through which mass public opinion is manipulated and molded to fit elite preferences. From the pluralist perspective, on the other hand, the media comprise an independent force able to scrutinize what the government is doing and provide an independent assessment of its policies. Thus, the media appear less conspiratorial in the pluralist than in the elitist model, but their role is potent nonetheless. Indeed, to some the media are public opinion. Minimally, the media help to set the agenda for public discussion and often lay out for the American people the range of interpretations about foreign-policy issues from which they might choose. Thus, the media help to aggregate the interests of more discrete groups in American society.

Political parties also aggregate interests. In the two-party system of the United States, political parties are broad coalitions of ethnic, religious, economic, educational, professional, working-class, and other sociodemographic groups. One of the most important functions these broad coalitions serve is the selection of personnel to key policymaking positions. They can also serve as referenda on past policy performance.

What role foreign-policy beliefs and preferences play in shaping citizens' choices on these broad issues is difficult to determine. On the one hand, most citizens are motivated not by foreign-policy issues, but by domestic ones. Their electoral choices typically reflect those preferences, something especially evident in the presidential elections in this decade. Arguably, Bill Clinton's success in 1992 and again in 1996 was made possible because the end of the Cold War contest with Soviet communism had effectively removed foreign-policy concerns from voters' calculations. On the other hand, and at crucial moments, foreign and national security policy issues can figure uppermost in some Americans' minds; for them foreign-policy issues may be critical when they enter the voting booth. Among the 8 percent of voters who indicated that foreign policy determined their vote in 1992, for example, George Bush held an 11–1 advantage over Bill Clinton.[8] In an environment where a few thousands of votes in a few electoral precincts can mean the difference between a candidate's victory or defeat, foreign policy may indeed matter.

As these ideas suggest, the political culture, the foreign-policy beliefs and preferences of leaders and masses, and the role of the media, interest groups, and elections as expressions of (or the absence of, as the case may be) political attitudes and preferences may be potent explanations of what the United States does in the world. The eight chapters in Part I of this book explore these ideas in greater depth.

The Institutional Setting

As we peel away the societal environment as a source of American foreign policy, a second category is revealed: the institutional setting, consisting of the various branches of government and the departments and agencies assigned responsibility for decisionmaking, management, and implementation. The category incorporates the diverse properties related to the structure of the U.S. government that limit or enhance the foreign-policy choices made by decision makers and affect their implementation, thus revealing the linkages between the substance of foreign policy and the process by which it is made.

The structure of the American "foreign affairs government" encompasses a cluster of variables and organizational actors that influence what the United States does—or does not do—abroad. Most striking in this regard is the division of authority and responsibility for foreign-policy making between the Congress and the president. The Constitution embraces the eighteenth-century belief that the abuse of political power is controlled best not through centralization but by fragmenting it in a system of checks and balances. Hence, because authority and responsibility for American foreign policy is lodged in separate institutions sharing power, the Constitution is an "invitation to struggle."[9]

The struggle for control over foreign-policy making is not confined to the executive and legislative branches. Many executive branch departments and agencies that grew in size during nearly a half-century of Cold War competition with the Soviet Union also struggle to imprint American foreign policy. The growing interdependence of the United States with the world political economy reinforces these developments, as several executive branch departments seemingly oriented toward domestic affairs (e.g., Agriculture, Commerce, Justice, and Treasury) now also have bureaucratic stakes in the foreign-policy game. At the same time, the sheer size and complexity of the foreign affairs government often promote policy persistence, not innovation. Thus, it is not surprising that many of the basic parameters that defined America's Cold War foreign policy remain intact.

With growth, complexity, and competition has come fragmentation of authority over policy making within the executive branch itself. That characterization takes on a special meaning when we consider the often overlapping roles performed by the White House and National Security Council staffs, the State Department, the Defense Department, the Treasury Department, the Central Intelligence Agency, and other decisionmaking units. As more agencies have achieved presence in the foreign affairs government, and as the domestic political support they enjoy has solidified, the management of policy making by the president, whose role in the conduct of foreign affairs is preeminent, has become more difficult. To many, blame for the incoherence and inconsistency sometimes exhibited in American foreign policy lies here. Ironically, however, efforts to enhance presidential control of foreign-policy making by centralizing it in the White House have sometimes exacerbated rather than diminished incoherence and inconsistency by encouraging competition and conflict between the presidency, on the one hand, and the executive branch departments and agencies comprising the permanent foreign affairs government, on the other.

In sum, understanding the institutional setting as a source of American foreign policy requires an examination of the responsibilities of numerous institutions and their relations with one another: the institutionalized presidency, the Congress, and the cabinet-level departments and other agencies with foreign affairs responsibilities. These, then, will be our concerns in Part II.

Decisionmakers and Their Policymaking Positions

When we peel away the institutional setting as a domestic source of American foreign policy, the people who make the policies, their policymaking positions, and the bureaucratic environments in which they work become the focus of our attention. The underlying proposition is that the personal characteristics of individuals (personality traits, perceptions, and psychological predispositions), the role responsibilities that the individual assumes within the decision process (as president, national security advisor, or secretary of the treasury), and the differing bureaucratic environments (the National Security Council versus the Central Intelligence Agency, for instance[10]) in which individuals operate affect the policy choices that result. Still, and despite the combination of these forces, it is important to keep in mind that the individual decisionmaker is the ultimate source of influence on policy, the final mediating force in the causal chain linking the other domestic sources to the ends and means of American foreign policy.

There are several ways personality and perceptual factors may impinge upon foreign-policy making. Ideas about communism and the Soviet Union instilled early in life, for example, may subsequently affect the attitudes and behaviors of those responsible for negotiating with the leaders of the post–Soviet states. Similarly, policymakers' orientation toward decision making may profoundly affect the nation's foreign-policy strategies. It has been suggested, for example, that twentieth-century American leaders can be characterized as either crusaders or pragmatists. The hallmark of a crusader is a "missionary zeal to make the world better. The crusader tends to make decisions based on a preconceived idea rather than on the basis of experience. Even though there are alternatives, he usually does not see them." The pragmatist, on the other hand, "is guided by the facts and his experience in a given situation, not by wishes or unexamined preconceptions. . . . Always flexible, he does not get locked into a losing policy. He can change direction and try again, without inflicting damage to his self-esteem."[11] Woodrow Wilson is the preeminent twentieth-century crusader, and Harry S Truman the personification of the pragmatist.

Personality factors also help to explain how presidents will choose to manage the conduct of foreign affairs. A president's approach to information processing, known as his or her cognitive style; orientation toward political conflict, and sense of political efficacy, are all important in understanding how he or she will structure the policymaking system and deal with those around the chief executive.[12] In this case personal predispositions form a bridge between the institutional setting of American foreign-policy making and the process of decision making itself.

Presidents sometimes engage in foreign-policy actions not for their effect on the external environment but to influence domestic politics. Foreign policy can be used to mobilize popular support at home (the "rally 'round the flag" effect), to increase authority through appeals to patriotism, and to enhance prospects for reelection. Nothing better illustrates the connection between domestic politics and foreign policy.

Although policymakers doubtless use foreign policy for domestic purposes, it is unclear whether they do so because of who they are or because of the positions they occupy. Because of the frequency with which policymakers in the United States and other countries alike allegedly engage in this type of behavior, it seems that leaders' role requirements, not their personal predilections, explain this behavior. Policymakers' positions thus appear to stimulate certain predictable patterns of behavior. Conversely, the position an individual holds may constrain the impact of personality on policymaking behavior. Institutional roles thus reduce the influence of idiosyncratic factors on policy performance.

Individuals can, of course, interpret the roles they occupy differently. That fact blurs the distinction between decisionmakers and their policy positions as competing rather than complementary explanations of American foreign policy. Clearly, however, policymaking positions, or roles, severely circumscribe the freedom and autonomy of the particular individuals who occupy them, and thus diminish the range of politically feasible choices. Hence, we must understand the relationship between the person and the position and how each separately and in combination affects policy outcomes. Nowhere is that conclusion illustrated more clearly than with a simple aphorism drawn from bureaucratic politics: "Where you stand depends on where you sit."

In sum, a focus on decisionmakers and their policy positions as a category of domestic influences on American foreign policy draws attention to the capacity of individuals to place their personal imprints on the nation's conduct abroad, while simultaneously alerting us to the need to examine the forces that constrain individual initiative. Principal among these are the role-induced constraints that occur within bureaucratic settings. Because the making and execution of American foreign policy is fundamentally a group or organizational enterprise, we can surmise that these constraints are considerable. The essays in Part III will focus on these and on the capacity of individuals to transcend them.

Notes

1. See Richard N. Haass, *The Reluctant Sheriff: The United States After the Cold War* (New York: Council on Foreign Relations, 1997), 49–77, and Barry R. Posen and

Andrew L. Ross, "Competing U.S. Grand Strategies," in Robert J. Lieber, ed., *Adrift: American Foreign Policy at the End of the Century* (New York: Longman, 1997), 100–134, for discussions of several alternate grand strategies for the new era.

2. For a cogent analysis of the impact of the post–Cold War order on domestic politics and institutions, see Daniel Deudney and G. John Ikenberry, "America After the Long War," *Current History* 94 (November 1995): 364–369.

3. James M. Lindsay and Randall B. Ripley, "How Congress Influences Foreign and Defense Policy," in Randall B. Ripley and James M. Lindsay, eds., *Congress Resurgent: Foreign and Defense Policy on Capitol Hill* (Ann Arbor: The University of Michigan Press, 1993), 19.

4. Moises Naim, "Clinton's Foreign Policy: A Victim of Globalization?" *Foreign Policy* 109 (Winter 1997–98): 35.

5. Robert W. Tucker and David C. Hendrickson, "Thomas Jefferson and American Foreign Policy," *Foreign Affairs* 69 (Spring 1990): 139. For views of other Founders on foreign policy, see pp. 143–146.

6. Andrew Kohut, *America's Place in the World II* (Washington, D.C.: The Pew Research Center for the People & The Press, 1997), 15.

7. One indicator of the dislocations for American workers produced by NAFTA is that 142,884 workers have been certified as eligible for the transitional adjustment assistance program because of imports from Mexico or Canada or the shift in American production to those countries. See *North American Free Trade Agreement: Impacts and Implementation.* Statement by Jay Etta Z. Hecker, Associate Director, International Relations and Trade Issues, National Security and International Affairs Division. Washington, D.C.: United States General Accounting Office, September 11, 1997.

8. William Schneider, "The New Isolationism," in Robert J. Lieber, ed., *Eagle Adrift: American Foreign Policy at the End of the Century* (New York: Longman, 1997), 30.

9. Edwin S. Corwin, *The President: Office and Power* (New York: New York University Press, 1940), 200.

10. Interestingly, Laura Tyson, chair of both the Council of Economic Advisers and the National Economic Council during the Clinton administration, comments on how differently the National Security Council and the National Economic Council operated, despite the fact that both are part of the Executive Office of the President. See "Tyson Discusses Life Inside the Beltway" and "Some Excerpts from Tyson's Talk," *Public Affairs Report* 39 (January 1998), 3.

11. John G. Stoessinger, *Crusaders and Pragmatists: Movers of Modern American Foreign Policy* (New York: Norton, 1985), xiii–xiv.

12. Alexander L. George, *Presidential Decisionmaking in Foreign Policy: The Effective Use of Information and Advice* (Boulder, Colo.: Westview Press, 1980).

Part I

The Societal Environment

The popular aphorism "Politics stops at the water's edge" may have accurately described the societal context of American foreign policy during the height of the Cold War,[1] but surely it no longer does. American foreign policy has always been colored by domestic considerations as policymakers sought to maintain their power base at home, but, for several reasons, the societal environment has become a particularly acute constraint in the post–Cold War era of globalization and fragmentation.

First, public attitudes toward foreign affairs are changing. While the public generally supported an activist and interventionist foreign policy for over two generations, and while it continues to support active U.S. involvement in the world, its commitment to internationalism has taken on a new coloration. The public now embraces an internationalism that seeks to promote American economic and social interests in its foreign-policy actions, rather than supporting what has been called "non-self-interested" activities in global affairs.[2] Pursuing foreign-policy objectives that protect American jobs, control illegal immigration, stop illicit trafficking in drugs, and reduce the U.S. trade deficit, for example, are more likely to be supported by the public than promoting human rights, advancing democracy, or supporting allies abroad.[3] As political analyst Michael Mandelbaum observes, "Without an overarching principle to guide the nation's foreign relations . . . the promotion of domestic interests is the default strategy of American foreign policy."[4]

The reluctance of Americans to support the use of U.S. forces abroad reflects this more cautious, interest-based internationalism, as the American people now shy away from foreign encounters that risk American lives. Ironically, the swift and (in terms of casualties) nearly costless victory of the United States in the Persian Gulf War contributed to this timidity, making it more difficult for political leaders to place American troops in harm's way to promote and protect U.S. interests.

Some analysts draw on what they call the "public's prudence" to explain variations in support for military intervention. They argue that public support

1

for interventionism is greatest when force is used to coerce "foreign policy restraint" by an adversary engaged in aggressive actions against the United States or its allies. The Persian Gulf War is a premier example. Alternately, they argue that public support is at its least when force is used to engineer "internal political change" within another country. Operation Restore Hope in Somalia falls here. Yet, in a fragmenting world, the frequency of interventionist choices that involve internal change is unlikely to diminish, thus continuing to divide public sentiment and constraining the use of force as an instrument of foreign policy.[5]

Second, partisanship and ideology also divide Americans' foreign-policy sentiments. The partisan and ideological character of foreign-policy making is not a new phenomenon, having been especially evident since the Vietnam War, which pitted conservatives against liberals, Republicans against Democrats in bitter and fractious dispute. The fractiousness continued throughout the remaining Cold War years as other foreign-policy issues came to the fore. The end of the Cold War might have been expected to mute these differences; instead, competing ideological visions of the proper role of the United States in world affairs have been fueled by the forces of globalization and fragmentation that now animate world politics.

The fusion of ideology and partisanship has reinforced these fissures. Increasingly, Democrats are likely to be foreign-policy liberals, as southern conservatives switch to the Republican party; and Republicans are likely to be foreign-policy conservatives, as moderate or liberal northern Republicans vanish from the scene. Without the cross-pressures of competing ideologies *within* the two major parties, compromise and accommodation *across* the parties are difficult, further fueling domestic discord on foreign-policy issues.

Third, the emergence of a broader array of issues coupled with a growing cadre of assertive interest groups has also contributed to the domestic disputes that surround foreign policy. Both traditional security and newer strategic and structural (economic and environmental) issues portend more, not less, partisan, ideological, and interest conflicts. These differing sets of issues also stimulate greater interest group activity than before, as we noted in the introduction.

Consider the debate over a traditional security issue such as U.S. intervention in Bosnia. In December 1995 the Clinton administration brokered the Dayton Accords designed to stop years of violence and "ethnic cleansing" in the former Yugoslavia. It then proposed sending 20,000 American troops to Bosnia as part of a larger NATO force. The public was skeptical: 54 percent of the American people disapproved the plan. Furthermore, differences among supporters and opponents were sharply drawn along party lines, with 67 percent of Republicans opposing the action and 57 percent of Democrats approving it.[6] Congress reflected this tepid public support as well as its undercurrents. Resolutions were introduced in Congress that expressed support for American troops in Bosnia, but not support for the president's policies there. Not surprisingly, Democrats opposed them, while Republicans supported them. Indeed, it increasingly appears that Republicans oppose foreign military interventions, while Democrats favor them, something not true when the Republicans occupied the White House.

The domestic dispute over the wisdom of expanding NATO (the North Atlantic Treaty Organization) reveals the emerging ideological and interest differences over foreign-policy issues today. An ethnically based interest group, the Central and Eastern European Coalition, weighed in heavily in favor of NATO expansion, seeing expansion as one way of ensuring security for countries in the region, while Establishment foreign-policy elites raised a skeptical eye toward this proposal, seeing expansion as a challenge to Russia and possibly reigniting the Cold War.[7] Although partisan differences were less sharply drawn in this instance compared with Bosnia, the debate over NATO expansion does confirm how a crucial foreign-policy security issue may now become a source of domestic dispute.

Arguably, strategic and structural foreign-policy issues provoke domestic debate to a greater extent than security ones, since these issues affect various segments of the American public differentially and thus create the conditions for more active interest group involvement. During the debate over the North American Free Trade Agreement (NAFTA), for instance, labor groups and environmentalists with one set of ideological and interest positions lined up on one side of the debate, and business and industrial groups lined up on the other. All of these groups sought to shape the agreement in a way consistent with the views of their domestic constituents. Indeed, the congressional votes approving the agreement revealed sharp divisions as well, with northern, rustbelt Democrats less likely to support this accord and western, sunbelt Republicans more likely to do so. Granting most favored nation (MFN) status to China also elicited involvement by domestic interest groups, with the conservative Christian Coalition, concerned about the treatment of Christians in China and human rights generally, seeking to stop this presidential action; and business lobbies, such as Boeing and Motorola, who worried about their access to the vast Chinese market, seeking to promote it. Congressional involvement reflected these ideological divisions as well with liberal Democratic Congresswoman Nancy Pelosi of California leading the fight to stop MFN, and conservative Speaker of the House Newt Gingrich supporting the president's action.

The pervasiveness of the media has helped to sharpen our view of this new, more contentious American foreign-policy environment. The public's quick and ready access to foreign-policy information via television, the fax machine, and the Internet has helped to erode the distinction between the domestic and foreign-policy arenas. Access to information also contributes to the ability of domestic participants, especially interest groups, to respond rapidly to issues when they arise.

Understanding American foreign policy in the new era thus requires a fuller understanding of the domestic political and social environment. In particular, we should ask: What are the competing societal forces shaping America's responses abroad? Which among them play pivotal roles in shaping the direction of foreign policy? How are they likely to fare in the post–Cold War era?

The Societal Environment as an Influence on American Foreign Policy

We begin our search for answers to these questions with two broad-ranging assessments of the domestic priorities and challenges to the dominant political culture that face the United States at the dawn of the new millennium. In the first chapter, "The Erosion of American National Interests," the distinguished Harvard University professor Samuel P. Huntington, a longtime foreign-policy analyst and policy practitioner himself, worries that today's challenges to the nation's traditional values threaten to undermine its global role. While the Cold War fostered "a common identity between American people and government," Huntington argues that the end of the Cold War has eroded that bond.

Two interrelated trends are the cause of that erosion: "changes in the scope and sources of immigration and the rise of the cult of multiculturalism." In their wake, we have witnessed "the displacement of national interests by commercial and ethnic interests" and a "foreign policy of particularism." The former reflects "the domesticization of foreign policy," while the latter reveals how powerful interest-based calculations have become in the shaping of America's foreign policy. Alarmed by these developments, Huntington calls for "a policy of restraint and reconstitution aimed at limiting the diversion of American resources to the service of particularistic subnational, transnational, and nonnational interests." He contends that sound foreign policy in the new era can only be maintained by looking beyond particularistic interests and by focusing on the traditional values and interests of the nation as a whole.

In contrast, Ronald Steel in "The Domestic Core of Foreign Policy" raises serious questions about the wisdom of continuing the expansive role in world politics that characterized Cold War American foreign policy. Instead, Steel believes that the United States should now focus on its domestic needs. "With our old enemy tamed and communism repudiated, foreign policy often seems to have become nearly irrelevant," he argues, especially in light of a domestic agenda that is "a pressing, and indeed a depressing, one." Poverty, illiteracy, crime, infant mortality, homelessness—these are the key issues for the United States in the new era; they should shape America's foreign-policy priorities, not the other way around, as during the Cold War. Indeed, Steel contends that

"A nation that seeks not only to protect the world but also to inspire other countries with its values and achievements must be able to offer at least as much to its own people as to those it seeks to guard." Furthermore, according to Steel, domestic values, a clear sense of the national interest, and selective involvement only in areas where the United States can make a difference should be the guiding principles of American foreign policy.

Deciding on these priorities, however, and building a consensus on what to do at home and abroad will depend critically on the thinking and attitudes of the American people and policy influentials. The emergence of a new, post–Cold War era raises important questions about the nature of those attitudes. Indeed, Steel begins his analysis with the premise that the international ethos that guided American foreign policy throughout the Cold War is on the wane. Could it be that Americans' thinking about foreign-policy issues will move in radically new directions and take on sharply different forms in the years ahead?

In their chapter, "The Political Foundations of Elites' Domestic and Foreign Policy Beliefs," Ole R. Holsti and James N. Rosenau seek an answer to that question by examining the attitudes of American opinion leaders. Drawing inspiration from the elitist model of public policy making, which assumes that elite attitudes and preferences are crucial determinants of the foreign-policy beliefs and preferences of society as a whole, Holsti and Rosenau ask, first, how similar elites' current views (foreign and domestic) are compared with the Cold War years and, second, whether their attitudes on domestic and foreign-policy issues are explained by their partisan attachments and ideological predispositions.

Dividing leaders' foreign-policy preferences along two internationalist dimensions, one that emphasizes the militant aspects of American foreign policy and a second that emphasizes its cooperative elements, Holsti and Rosenau are able to place leaders into one of four categories that define their foreign-policy beliefs. The evidence drawn from their analyses reveals that some redistributions have occurred among the four foreign-policy belief systems (internationalists, accommodationists, hardliners, and isolationists) compared with earlier findings. More striking, however, is the degree to which leaders' beliefs have remained constant. Indeed, American leaders as a whole remain extraordinarily committed to an internationalist role in foreign policy today, just as during the Cold War era.

Holsti and Rosenau also probe the relationship between opinion leaders' foreign and domestic policy beliefs. During the Cold War era these two sets of attitudes were not always in sync; liberals on domestic policy might be conservatives on foreign policy, and foreign-policy conservatives might be domestic liberals. President Kennedy, for example, was a committed cold warrior, but he pursued a liberal agenda at home. However, since the Vietnam War foreign and domestic policy beliefs seem increasingly to have become aligned with one another,[8] a fact that helps explain the persistent partisan and ideological discord underlying policy making generally.

Holsti and Rosenau show considerable consistency in leaders' foreign and domestic policy beliefs. They first divide American leaders into four identifiable domestic policy groups and then compare them with the four foreign-policy groups. They note that there is a "strong . . . relationship between foreign-policy orientations [among the leaders] and preferences on economic and social/value domestic policy issues." Similarly, they report, "there are also large . . . differences on foreign-policy goals when opinion leaders are grouped according to their domestic policy orientations."

Furthermore, their analysis reveals that partisanship and ideology are important predictors of leaders' beliefs and that the structure of leadership opinion has remained markedly stable over the past two decades, even in the face of profound change at the international level. In sum, foreign and domestic policy opinion are tightly linked, and partisanship and ideology bridge them in consistent, predictable ways.

Our next chapter draws on the pluralist rather than the elitist tradition. John Mueller's chapter titled "Public Opinion and Foreign Policy: The Peoples' Common Sense'" considers the foreign-policy views of the American public as a whole. Drawing on an array of public opinion polls, he deduces ten provocative propositions that purport to describe how average Americans relate to foreign-policy issues. While Mueller argues that the public typically pays little attention to foreign policy, its responses to global events are "fairly sensible" and generally internationalist in outlook, a conclusion that parallels Holsti and Rosenau's research on elite attitudes. He also notes that the American people typically provide presidents with considerable leeway to undertake global involvements as long as they do not affect their lives directly. But the public is mobilized when costs rise, especially when American troops are endangered and casualties are incurred, as we noted earlier. Nonetheless, Mueller reports that foreign-policy successes or failures are now less likely to affect the public's assessment of presidents or of presidential contenders than in the past. Furthermore, he concludes (much as Steel urges) that foreign-policy issues are now less likely to be the focus of attention than domestic issues.

The American military establishment has long been regarded as a powerful influence on American foreign policy as a consequence of its extensive ties with people and institutions throughout American society. Indeed, dating from President Eisenhower's 1961 farewell address, in which he warned of the prospect of "unwarranted influence, whether sought or unsought, by the military-industrial complex," the proper role of the military has been a source of often heated debate. The usual assumption is that the Pentagon's influence arises from its strong ties to industry and to members of Congress, whose constituents benefit from military contracts awarded to companies in members' districts or states.

Military bases also provide economic benefits, thus helping to build and sustain support for the military establishment within local communities spread throughout the country. Ironically, with the end of the Cold War and the need to redesign America's military strategy and force structure for the new era, the Defense Department now finds itself faced with the necessity of closing many military facilities, thus raising the ire of communities who fear they will suffer greatly. Already large numbers of bases have been closed, and the Clinton administration's Quadrennial Defense Review of May 1997 called for additional closures in the coming years.

While opening and closing military bases has a long tradition in American society, dating from the earliest days of the Republic, national and local politics usually were pivotal in determining where bases would be located and whether they would be maintained. However, Genevieve Anton and Jeff Thomas show in "The Politics of Military Base Closures" that traditional political tactics failed to protect the bases during the successive rounds of closures that took place in the years immediately following the end of the Cold War. Instead, the changing international political environment and the demands of federal budget-balancing proved more important. The development of a new decisionmaking mechanism—the independent commission—designed to insulate the Congress and the executive branch from local constituency pressures was also crucial.

First proposed by Congressman Dick Armey in 1989, the BRAC—the Defense Base Closure and Realignment Commission—made a single decision on base closures, subject only to outright acceptance or rejection by the executive and legislative branches. Hence the president and members of Congress were cross-pressured into considering both the efforts to restructure the military and the demands of local constituencies. The former proved more compelling than the latter. As Anton and Thomas note, even a city with a well-orchestrated campaign to keep its base open, such as Charleston, South Carolina, did not succeed. "You can do everything right, and still end up with your base being closed," lamented one South Carolina official. On this issue, particularistic interests no longer seem as potent as previously; instead, national concerns appear to have carried the day.

While local organized interests may not have succeeded in this instance, the increasing pervasiveness of foreign-policy interest groups, a more open foreign-policy process, and the emergence of new issues have enhanced the opportunities for such groups to have an impact. As foreign-policy issues have moved from crises to strategic and structural issues, as noted in the introduction of this book, interest groups are increasingly advantaged since these issues encourage greater access to Congress. In particular, interest group activities undertaken or supported by foreign countries (e.g., Japan or Russia) or by new ethnic lobbies (e.g., Cuban-Americans or African-Americans) have proved quite successful in influencing American foreign policy in the new era.

In "The New China Lobby," Richard Bernstein and Ross H. Munro illustrate foreign lobbies' newfound influence. In particular, they document the various mechanisms that China has used to influence American foreign policy and illustrate its relative success in shaping American trade policy in its favor. Notice the variety of individuals and measures that China has employed in its efforts to affect policy: reliance on threats of economic retaliation for those who disagree with it; denial of access for those officials, businesspeople, and academics who are critical of its policy; and reliance on influential former American officials and businesses to make supporting statements on its behalf. The result is a "New China Lobby," a loosely connected group of individuals and companies within the United States that "advances the cause of Beijing . . . and has become ever more active." An offshoot of this lobby, the "China Normalization Initiative," currently seeks to extend MFN permanently to China and ensure its full entry into the World Trade Organization. With an established record of success, the New China Lobby may well succeed in these endeavors, thus affirming the ability of an organized, determined interest group to shape American foreign policy.

Yet another group of societal participants that has come under closer scrutiny are the media. A former newspaper journalist observed recently that "the debate on the relationship between foreign policy and the news media is often cast in one of two ways. The media either take foreign policy out of the hands of the elite and open the process to the ill-informed public or they are indentured servants of the foreign policy elite."[9] Now, however, with the pervasive growth of the electronic media, arguments are rife that the media have become important actors in shaping policy directly. That viewpoint is captured in the phrase the "CNN Effect."

Because the media now have the power to portray global events vividly and to send their images around the world instantaneously—with the CNN (Cable News Network) Effect serving as a caricature for the power of the media as a whole—some argue that the media have the ability to force policymakers to respond to events that they might otherwise prefer to ignore. The case of Somalia in the early 1990s is often used to illustrate the media's new power. The argument is that the media's ability to draw attention to horrific conditions in Somalia forced the Bush administration to take action, leading to the humanitarian intervention known as Operation Restore Hope.[10]

In Chapter 7, Warren Strobel, a former White House and State Department correspondent for the *Washington Times,* raises serious doubts about the accuracy of this assessment of the media in "The CNN Effect: Myth or Reality?" If the CNN Effect means "a loss of policy control on the part of policymakers because of the power of the media, a power that they can do nothing about," Strobel challenges its influence. If the CNN Effect means that it "changes governance, shrinks decision making time and opens up military operations to public scrutiny," the effect occurs, but those kinds of changes are "not the same as saying that it determines policy." Instead, as one policymaker interviewed by Strobel noted, "Policymakers are becoming more adept at dealing with the CNN factor." That is, they can use the media for their own ends, they can still decide what policies are on the agenda and what policies to pursue, and they can develop well-grounded and well-supported policies to weaken the presumed effect. In short, Strobel judges that "the CNN Effect is narrower and more complex than the conventional wisdom holds" and that "the struggle between reporters and officials continues as before—just at a faster pace."

The concluding essay in Part I takes a broad look at how the American electoral system itself impacts on the foreign-policy performance of a president. Where a president is in the election cycle, William B. Quandt suggests in his "The Electoral Cycle and the Conduct of American Foreign Policy," shapes the prospect of undertaking foreign-policy initiatives and achieving success. Noting the constitutional requirements that congressional elections be held every two years and presidential elections every four, Quandt concludes that "presidents have little time during their incumbency when they have both the experience and the power needed for sensible and effective conduct of foreign policy."

Quandt also points out that "a reelected president in his second term faces a somewhat different problem." While the "first year and half [of the second term] may be the best time for taking foreign-policy initiatives" by a reelected president, he or she is likely quickly to become a "lame-duck." Foreign leaders will now be less eager to deal with the president fearing that domestic support will dwindle and that a successor will soon fill the president's seat in the Oval Office. Furthermore, "the opposition party has little incentive to help the outgoing president win any foreign-policy victories, and within the president's own party the struggle for succession may weaken his or her base of support." Thus, second-term presidents, and especially when they are in their final two years in office, inevitably will find it difficult to realize foreign-policy successes.

In the final analysis, then, Quandt's perspective on the electoral process reinforces the judgment that the nature of American society and its political system may have untoward policy consequences: "The price we pay [for the structure of the electoral cycle] is a foreign policy excessively geared to short-term calculations, in which narrow domestic political considerations often outweigh sound strategic thinking, and where turnover in high positions is so frequent that consistency and coherence are lost."

Notes

1. For some evidence, see James M. McCormick and Eugene R. Wittkopf, "Bipartisanship, Partisanship, and Ideology in Congressional-Executive Foreign Policy Rela-

tions, 1947–1988," *The Journal of Politics* 52 (November 1990): 1077–1100, and Eugene R. Wittkopf and James M. McCormick, "The Cold War Consensus: Did It Exist?" *Polity* 22 (Summer 1990): 627–653.

2. See William Schneider, "The New Isolationism," in Robert J. Lieber, ed., *Eagle Adrift: American Foreign Policy at the End of the Century* (New York: Longman, 1997), 27–28.

3. Recent data on support for these foreign policy goals may be found in John E. Reilly, ed., *American Public Opinion and U.S. Foreign Policy 1995* (Chicago: Chicago Council on Foreign Relations, 1995), esp. at p. 15.

4. Michael Mandelbaum, "Foreign Policy as Social Work," *Foreign Affairs* 75 (January/February 1996): 16–32.

5. See Bruce W. Jentleson, "The Pretty Prudent Public: Post Post-Vietnam American Opinion on the Use of Military Force," *International Studies Quarterly* 36 (March 1992): 49–74; Bruce W. Jentleson, "Who, Why, What, and How: Debates Over Post-Cold War Military Intervention," in *Eagle Adrift: American Foreign Policy at the End of the Century,* Robert J. Lieber, ed. (New York: Longman, 1997), 39–70; John R. Oneal, Brad Lian, and James H. Joyner, Jr., "Are the American People 'Pretty Prudent?' Public Responses to U.S. Uses of Force, 1950–1980," *International Studies Quarterly* 40 (June 1996): 261–280.

6. George Gallup Jr., *The Gallup Poll: Public Opinion 1995* (Wilmington, Del.: Scholarly Resources, 1996), 192.

7. See, for example, Dick Kirschten, "Ethnics Resurging," *National Journal,* February 25, 1995; and Michael E. Brown, "The Flawed Logic of NATO Expansion," *Survival* 37 (Spring 1995): 34–52.

8. For empirical evidence, see Bruce Russett and Elizabeth G. Hanson, *Interest and Ideology: The Foreign Policy Beliefs of American Businessmen* (San Francisco: Freeman, 1975), esp. 130–138; and Eugene R. Wittkopf, *Faces of Internationalism: Public Opinion and American Foreign Policy* (Durham, N.C.: Duke University Press, 1990).

9. Bill Kovach, "Do the News Media Make Foreign Policy?" *Foreign Policy* 102 (Spring 1996): 171.

10. For a careful analysis that casts doubt on the media's impact on the decision to intervene in Somalia, see Steven Livingston and Todd Eachus, "Humanitarian Crises and U.S. Foreign Policy: Somalia and the CNN Effect Reconsidered," *Political Communication* 12, 4 (1995): 413–429.

1

The Erosion of American National Interests

Samuel P. Huntington

The Disintegration of Identity

The years since the end of the Cold War have seen intense, wide-ranging, and confused debates about American national interests. Much of this confusion stems from the complexity of the post–Cold War world. The new environment has been variously interpreted as involving the end of history, bipolar conflict between rich and poor countries, movement back to a future of traditional power politics, the proliferation of ethnic conflict verging on anarchy, the clash of civilizations, and conflicting trends toward integration and fragmentation. The new world is all these things, and hence there is good reason for uncertainty about American interests in it. Yet that is not the only source of confusion. Efforts to define national interest presuppose agreement on the nature of the country whose interests are to be defined. National interest derives from national identity. We have to know who we are before we can know what our interests are.

Historically, American identity has had two primary components: culture and creed. The first has been the values and institutions of the original settlers, who were Northern European, primarily British, and Christian, primarily Protestant. This culture included most importantly the English language and traditions concerning relations between church and state and the place of the individual in society. Over the course of three centuries, black people were slowly and only partially assimilated into this culture. Immigrants from western, southern, and eastern Europe were more fully assimilated, and the original culture evolved and was modified but not fundamentally altered as a result. In *The Next American Nation,* Michael Lind captures the broad outlines of this

---

Note: Notes have been deleted.

evolution when he argues that American culture developed through three phases: Anglo-America (1789–1861), Euro-America (1875–1957), and Multi-cultural America (1972–present). The cultural definition of national identity assumes that while the culture may change, it has a basic continuity.

The second component of American identity has been a set of universal ideas and principles articulated in the founding documents by American leaders: liberty, equality, democracy, constitutionalism, liberalism, limited government, private enterprise. These constitute what Gunnar Myrdal termed the American Creed, and the popular consensus on them has been commented on by foreign observers from Crevecoeur and Tocqueville down to the present. This identity was neatly summed up by Richard Hofstadter: "It has been our fate as a nation not to have ideologies but to be one."

These dual sources of identity are, of course, closely related. The creed was a product of the culture. Now, however, the end of the Cold War and social, intellectual, and demographic changes in American society have brought into question the validity and relevance of both traditional components of American identity. Without a sure sense of national identity, Americans have become unable to define their national interests, and as a result subnational commercial interests and transnational and nonnational ethnic interests have come to dominate foreign policy.

Loss of the Other

The most profound question concerning the American role in the post–Cold War world was improbably posed by Rabbit Angstrom, the harried central character of John Updike's novels: "Without the cold war, what's the point of being an American?" If being an American means being committed to the principles of liberty, democracy, individualism, and private property, and if there is no evil empire out there threatening those principles, what indeed does it mean to be an American, and what becomes of American national interests?

From the start, Americans have constructed their creedal identity in contrast to an undesirable "other." America's opponents are always defined as liberty's opponents. At the time of independence, Americans could not distinguish themselves culturally from Britain; hence they had to do so politically. Britain embodied tyranny, aristocracy, oppression; America, democracy, equality, republicanism. Until the end of the nineteenth century, the United States defined itself in opposition to Europe. Europe was the past: backward, unfree, unequal, characterized by feudalism, monarchy, and imperialism. The United States, in contrast, was the future: progressive, free, equal, republican. In the twentieth century, the United States emerged on the world scene and increasingly saw itself not as the antithesis of Europe but rather as the leader of European-

American civilization against upstart challengers to that civilization, imperial and then Nazi Germany.

After World War II the United States defined itself as the leader of the democratic free world against the Soviet Union and world communism. During the Cold War the United States pursued many foreign policy goals, but its one overriding national purpose was to contain and defeat communism. When other goals and interests clashed with this purpose, they were usually subordinated to it. For 40 years virtually all the great American initiatives in foreign policy, as well as many in domestic policy, were justified by this overriding priority: the Greek-Turkish aid program, the Marshall Plan, NATO, the Korean War, nuclear weapons and strategic missiles, foreign aid, intelligence operations, reduction of trade barriers, the space program, the Alliance for Progress, military alliances with Japan and Korea, support for Israel, overseas military deployments, an unprecedentedly large military establishment, the Vietnam War, the openings to China, support for the Afghan mujahideen and other anticommunist insurgencies. If there is no Cold War, the rationale for major programs and initiatives like these disappears.

As the Cold War wound down in the late 1980s, Gorbachev's adviser Georgiy Arbatov commented: "We are doing something really terrible to you—we are depriving you of an enemy." Psychologists generally agree that individuals and groups define their identity by differentiating themselves from and placing themselves in opposition to others. While wars at times may have a divisive effect on society, a common enemy can often help to promote identity and cohesion among people. The weakening or absence of a common enemy can do just the reverse. Abraham Lincoln commented on this effect in his Lyceum speech in 1837 when he argued that the American Revolution and its aftermath had directed enmity outward: "The jealousy, envy, avarice incident to our nature, and so common to a state of peace, prosperity, and conscious strength, were for a time in a great measure smothered and rendered inactive, while the deep-rooted principles of hate, and the powerful motive of revenge, instead of being turned against each other, were directed exclusively against the British nation." Hence, he said, "the basest principles of our nature" were either dormant or "the active agents in the advancement of the noblest of causes—that of establishing and maintaining civil and religious liberty." But he warned, "this state of feeling must fade, is fading, has faded, with the circumstances that produced it." He spoke, of course, as the nation was starting to disintegrate. As the heritage of World War II and the Cold War fades, America may be faced with a comparable dynamic.

The Cold War fostered a common identity between American people and government. Its end is likely to weaken or at least alter that identity. One possible consequence is the rising opposition to the federal government, which is, after all, the principal institutional manifestation of American national identity and unity. Would nationalist fanatics bomb federal buildings and attack federal agents if the federal government was still defending the country against a serious foreign threat? Would the militia movement be as strong as it is today? In the past, comparable bombing attacks were usually the work of foreigners who saw the United States as their enemy, and the first response of many people to the Oklahoma City bombing was to assume that it was the work of a "new enemy," Muslim terrorists. That response could reflect a psychological need to believe that such an act must have been carried out by an external enemy. Ironically, the bombing may have been in part the result of the absence of such an enemy.

Georg Simmel, Lewis A. Coser, and other scholars have shown that in some ways and circumstances the existence of an enemy may have positive consequences for group cohesion, morale, and achievement. World War II and the Cold War were responsible for much American economic, technological, and social progress, and the perceived economic challenge from Japan in the 1980s generated public and private efforts to increase American productivity and competitiveness. At present, thanks to the extent to which democracy and market economies have been embraced throughout the world, the United States lacks any single country or threat against which it can convincingly counterpose itself. Saddam Hussein simply does not suffice as a foil. Islamic fundamentalism is too diffuse and too remote geographically. China is too problematic and its potential dangers too distant in the future.

Given the domestic forces pushing toward heterogeneity, diversity, multiculturalism, and ethnic and racial division, however, the United States, perhaps more than most countries, may need an opposing other to maintain its unity. Two millennia ago in 84 B.C., after the Romans had completed their conquest of the known world by defeating the armies of Mithradates, Sulla posed the question: "Now the universe offers us no more enemies, what may be the fate of the Republic?" The answer came quickly; the republic collapsed a few years later. It is unlikely that a similar fate awaits the United States, yet to what extent will the American Creed retain its appeal, command support, and stay vibrant in the absence of competing ideologies? The end of history, the global victory of democracy, if it occurs, could be a most traumatic and unsettling event for America.

Ideologies of Diversity

The disintegrative effects of the end of the Cold War have been reinforced by the interaction of two trends in American society: changes in the scope and sources of immigration and the rise of the cult of multiculturalism.

Immigration, legal and illegal, has increased dramatically since the immigration laws were changed in 1965. Recent immigration is overwhelmingly from Latin America and Asia. Coupled with the high birth rates of some immigrant groups, it is changing the racial, religious, and ethnic makeup of the United States. By the middle of the next century, according to the Census Bureau, non-Hispanic whites will have dropped from more than three-quarters of the population to only slightly more than half, and one-quarter of Americans will be Hispanic, 14 percent black, and 8 percent of Asian and Pacific heritage. The religious balance is also shifting, with Muslims already reportedly outnumbering Episcopalians.

In the past, assimilation, American style, . . . involved an implicit contract in which immigrants were welcomed as equal members of the national community and urged to become citizens, provided they accepted English as the national language and committed themselves to the principles of the American Creed and the Protestant work ethic. In return, immigrants could be as ethnic as they wished in their homes and local communities. At times, particularly during the great waves of Irish immigration in the 1840s and 1850s and of the southern and eastern European immigration at the turn of the century, immigrants were discriminated against and simultaneously subjected to major programs of "Americanization" to incorporate them into the national culture and society. Overall, however, assimilation American style worked well. Immigration renewed American society; assimilation preserved American culture.

Past worries about the assimilation of immigrants have proved unfounded. Until recently immigrant groups came to America because they saw immigration as an opportunity to become American. To what extent now, however, do people come because they see it as an opportunity to remain themselves? Previously immigrants felt discriminated against if they were not permitted to join the mainstream. Now it appears that some groups feel discriminated against if they are not allowed to remain apart from the mainstream.

The ideologies of multiculturalism and diversity reinforce and legitimate these trends. They deny the existence of a common culture in the United States, denounce assimilation, and promote the primacy of racial, ethnic, and other subnational cultural identities and groupings. They also question a central element in the American Creed by substituting for the rights of individuals the rights of groups, defined largely in terms of race, ethnicity, gender, and sexual preference. These goals were manifested in a variety of statutes that followed the civil rights acts of the 1960s, and in the 1990s the Clinton administration made the encouragement of diversity one of its major goals.

The contrast with the past is striking. The Founding Fathers saw diversity as a reality and a problem: hence the national motto, *e pluribus unum*. Later political leaders, also fearful of the dangers of racial, sectional, ethnic, economic, and cultural diversity (which, indeed, produced the biggest war of the century between 1815 and 1914), responded to the need to bring us together, and made the promotion of national unity their central responsibility. "The one absolutely certain way of bringing this nation to ruin, of preventing all possibility of its continuing as a nation at all," warned Theodore Roosevelt, "would be to permit it to become a tangle of squabbling nationalities . . ." Bill Clinton, in contrast, is almost certainly the first president to promote the diversity rather than the unity of the country he leads. This promotion of ethnic and racial identities means that recent immigrants are not subject to the same pressures and inducements as previous immigrants to integrate themselves into American culture. As a result, ethnic identities are becoming more meaningful and appear to be increasing in relevance compared with national identity.

If the United States becomes truly multicultural, American identity and unity will depend on a continuing consensus on political ideology. Americans have thought of their commitment to universal values such as liberty and equality as a great source of national strength. That ideology, Myrdal observed, has been "the cement in the structure of this great and disparate nation." Without an underlying common culture, however, these principles are a fragile basis for national unity. As theories of cognitive dissonance suggest, people can change their ideas and beliefs relatively quickly and easily in response to a changed external environment. Throughout the formerly communist world, elites have redefined themselves as devoted democrats, free marketeers, or fervent nationalists.

For most countries, ideology bears little relation to national identity. China has survived the collapse of many dynasties and will survive the collapse of communism. Absent communism, China will still be China. Britain, France, Japan, Germany, and other countries have survived various dominant ideologies in their history. But could the United States survive the end of its political ideology? The fate of the Soviet Union offers a sobering example for Americans. The United States and the Soviet Union were very different, but they also resembled each other in that neither was a nation-state in the classic sense of the term. In considerable measure, each defined itself in terms of an ideology, which, as the Soviet example suggests, is likely to be a much more fragile basis for unity than a national culture richly grounded in history. If multiculturalism prevails and if the consensus on liberal democracy disintegrates, the United States could join the Soviet Union on the ash heap of history.

In Search of National Interests

A national interest is a public good of concern to all or most Americans; a vital national interest is one which they are willing to expend blood and treasure to defend. National interests usually combine security and material concerns, on the one hand, and moral and ethical concerns, on the other. Military action against Saddam Hussein was seen as a vital national interest because he threatened reliable and inexpensive access to Persian Gulf oil and because he was a rapacious dictator who had blatantly invaded and annexed another country.

During the Cold War the Soviet Union and communism were perceived as threats to both American security and American values; a happy coincidence existed between the demands of power politics and the demands of morality. Hence broad public support buttressed government efforts to defeat communism and thus, in Walter Lippmann's terms, to maintain a balance between capabilities and commitments. That balance was often tenuous and arguably got skewed in the 1970s. With the end of the Cold War, however, the danger of a "Lippmann gap" vanished, and instead the United States appears to have a Lippmann surplus. Now the need is not to find the power to serve American purposes but rather to find purposes for the use of American power.

This need has led the American foreign policy establishment to search frantically for new purposes that would justify a continuing U.S. role in world affairs comparable to that in the Cold War. The Commission on America's National Interests put the problem this way in 1996: "After four decades of unusual single-mindedness in containing Soviet Communist expansion, we have seen five years of ad hoc fits and starts. If it continues, this drift will threaten our values, our fortunes, and indeed our lives."

The commission identified five vital national interests: prevent attacks on the United States with weapons of mass destruction, prevent the emergence of hostile hegemons in Europe or Asia and of hostile powers on U.S. borders or in control of the seas, prevent the collapse of the global systems for trade, financial markets, energy supplies, and the environment, and ensure the survival of U.S. allies.

What, however, are the threats to these interests? Nuclear terrorism against the United States could be a near-term threat, and the emergence of China as an East Asian hegemon could be a longer-term one. Apart from these, however, it is hard to see any major looming challenges to the commission's vital interests. New threats will undoubtedly arise, but given the scarcity of current ones, campaigns to arouse interest in foreign affairs and support for major foreign policy initiatives now fall on deaf ears. The [Clinton] administration's call for the "enlargement" of democracy does not resonate with the public and is belied by the administration's own actions. Arguments from neoconservatives for big increases in defense spending have the same air of unreality that arguments for the abolition of nuclear weapons had during the Cold War.

The argument is frequently made that American "leadership" is needed to deal with world problems. Often it is. The call for leadership, however, begs the question of leadership to do what, and rests on the assumption that the world's problems are America's problems. Often they are not. The fact that things are going wrong in many places in the world is unfortunate, but it does not mean that the United States has either an interest in or the responsibility for correcting them. The National Interests Commission said that presidential leadership is necessary to create a consensus on national interests. In some measure, however, a consensus already exists that American national interests do not warrant extensive American involvement in most problems in most of the world. The foreign policy establishment is asking the president to make a case for a cause that simply will not sell. The most striking feature of the search for national interests has been its failure to generate purposes that command anything remotely resembling broad support and to which people are willing to commit significant resources.

Commercialism and Ethnicity

The lack of national interests that command widespread support does not imply a return to isolationism. America remains involved in the world, but its involvement is now directed at commercial and ethnic interests rather than national interests. Economic and ethnic particularism define the current American role in the world. The institutions and capabilities—political, military, economic, intelligence—created to serve a grand national purpose in the Cold War are now being suborned and redirected to serve narrow subnational, transnational, and even nonnational purposes. Increasingly people are arguing that these are precisely the interests foreign policy should serve.

The Clinton administration has given priority to "commercial diplomacy," making the promotion of American exports a primary foreign policy objective. It has been successful in wringing access to some foreign markets for American products. Commercial achievements have become a primary criterion for judging the performance of American ambassadors. President Clinton may well be spending more time promoting American sales abroad than doing anything else in foreign affairs. If so, that would be a dramatic sign of the redirection of American foreign policy. In case after case, country after country, the dictates of commercialism have prevailed over other purposes including human rights, democracy, alliance relationships, maintaining the balance of power, technology export controls, and other strategic and political considerations described by one administration official as "stratocrap and globaloney." "Many in the administration, Congress, and the broader foreign policy community," a former senior official in the Clinton Commerce Department argued . . . "still believe that commercial policy is a tool of foreign policy, when it should more often be the other way around—the United States should use all its foreign policy levers to achieve commercial goals." The funds devoted to promoting commercial goals should be greatly increased; the personnel working on these goals should be upgraded and professionalized; the agencies concerned with export promotion need to be strengthened and reorganized. Landing the contract is the name of the game in foreign policy.

Or at least it is the name of one game. The other game is the promotion of ethnic interests. While economic interests are usually subnational, ethnic interests are generally transnational or nonnational. The promotion of particular businesses and industries may not involve a broad public good, as does a general reduction in trade barriers, but it does promote the interests of some Americans. Ethnic groups promote the interests of people and entities outside the United States. Boeing has an interest in aircraft sales and the Polish-American Congress in help for Poland, but the former benefits residents of Seattle, the latter residents of Eastern Europe.

The growing role of ethnic groups in shaping American foreign policy is reinforced by the waves of recent immigration and by the arguments for diversity and multiculturalism. In addition, the greater wealth of ethnic communities and the dramatic improvements in communications and transportation now make it much easier for ethnic groups to remain in touch with their home countries. As a result, these groups are being transformed from cultural communities within the boundaries of a state into diasporas that transcend these boundaries. State-based diasporas, that is, trans-state cultural communities that control at least one state, are increasingly important and increasingly identify with the interests of their homeland. "Full assimilation into their host societies," a leading expert, Gabriel Sheffer, has observed in *Survival,* "has become unfashionable among both established and incipient state-based diasporas . . . many diasporal communities neither confront overwhelming pressure to assimilate nor feel any marked advantage in assimilating into their host societies or even obtaining citizenship there." Since the United States is the premier immigrant country in the world, it is most affected by the shifts from assimilation to diversity and from ethnic group to diaspora.

During the Cold War, immigrants and refugees from communist countries usually vigorously opposed, for political and ideological reasons, the governments of their home countries and actively supported American anticommunist policies against them. Now, diasporas in the United States support their home governments. Products of the Cold War, Cuban-Americans ardently support U.S. anti-Castro policies. Chinese-Americans, in contrast, overwhelmingly pressure the United States to adopt favorable policies towards China. Culture has supplanted ideology in shaping attitudes in diaspora populations.

Diasporas provide many benefits to their home countries. Economically prosperous diasporas furnish major financial support to the homeland, Jewish-Americans, for instance, contributing up to $1 billion a year to Israel. Armenian-Americans send enough to earn Armenia the sobriquet of "the Israel of the Caucasus." Diasporas supply expertise, military recruits, and on occasion political leadership to the homeland. They often pressure their home governments to adopt more nationalist and assertive policies towards neighboring countries. Recent cases in the United States show that they can be a source of spies used to gather information for their homeland governments.

Most important, diasporas can influence the actions and policies of their host country and co-opt its resources and influence to serve the interests of their homeland. Ethnic groups have played active roles in politics throughout American history. Now, ethnic diaspora groups proliferate, are more active, and have greater self-consciousness, legitimacy, and political clout. In recent years, diasporas have had a major impact on American policy towards Greece and Turkey, the Caucasus, the recognition of Macedonia, support for Croatia, sanctions against South Africa, aid for black Africa, intervention in Haiti, NATO expansion, sanctions against Cuba, the controversy in Northern Ireland, and the relations between Israel and its neighbors. Diaspora-based policies may at times coincide with broader national interests, as could arguably be the case with NATO expansion, but they are also often pursued at the expense of broader interests and American relations with long-standing allies. Overall, as James R. Schlesinger observed in a 1997 lecture at the Center for Strategic and International Studies, the United States has "less of a foreign policy in a traditional sense of a great power than we have the stapling together of a series of goals put forth by domestic constituency groups . . . The result is that American foreign policy is incoherent. It is scarcely what one would expect from the leading world power." . . .

The displacement of national interests by commercial and ethnic interests reflects the domesticization of foreign policy. Domestic politics and interests have always inevitably and appropriately influenced foreign policy. Now, however, previous assumptions that the foreign and domestic policymaking processes differ from each other for important reasons no longer hold. For an understanding of American foreign policy it is necessary to study not the interests of the American state in a world of competing states but rather the play of economic and ethnic interests in American domestic politics. At least in recent years, the latter has been a superb predictor of foreign policy stands. Foreign policy, in the sense of actions consciously designed to promote the interests of the United States as a collective entity in relation to similar collective entities, is slowly but steadily disappearing. . . .

Particularism vs. Restraint

American foreign policy is becoming a foreign policy of particularism increasingly devoted to the promotion abroad of highly specific commercial and ethnic interests. The institutions, resources, and influence generated to serve national interests in the Cold War are being redirected to serve these interests. These developments may have been furthered by the almost exclusive concern of the Clinton administration with domestic politics, but their roots lie in broader changes in the external and internal context of the United States and changing conceptions of American national identity. . . .

The alternative to particularism is . . . not promulgation of a "grand design," "coherent strategy," or "foreign policy vision." It is a policy of restraint and reconstitution aimed at limiting the diversion of American resources to the service of particularistic subnational, transnational, and non-national interests. The national interest is national restraint, and that appears to be the only national interest the American people are willing to support at this time in their history. Hence, instead of formulating unrealistic schemes for grand endeavors abroad, foreign policy elites might well devote their energies to designing plans for lowering American involvement in the world in ways that will safeguard possible future national interests.

At some point in the future, the combination of security threat and moral challenge will require Americans once again to commit major resources to the defense of national interests. The *de novo* mobilization of those resources from a low base, experience suggests, is likely to be easier than the redirection of resources that have been committed to entrenched particularistic interests. A more restrained role now could facilitate America's assumption of a more positive role in the future when the time comes for it to renew its national identity and to pursue national purposes for which Americans are willing to pledge their lives, their fortunes, and their national honor.

2

The Domestic Core of Foreign Policy

Ronald Steel

During the Cold War, foreign policy was the nation's highest priority. Almost any sacrifice could be, and often was, justified in its name. But today, with our old enemy tamed and communism repudiated, foreign policy often seems to have become nearly irrelevant. Almost any sacrifice in its name is viewed as an intolerable burden. When, as in Somalia and Haiti, American troops are put in harm's way—a normal occupational hazard for those who choose to enter the Armed Forces—the public demands their immediate withdrawal.

Asked its view on foreign commitments, the public prefers them to be minimal. An extensive survey conducted in 1993 showed overwhelming support for a domestic agenda in preference to an international one. In this poll the public rejected some of the reigning shibboleths of the foreign-policy establishment. It opposed promoting democracy abroad if that risked electing an unfriendly government, and promoting human rights abroad if that was likely to antagonize friendly nations with different traditions. Only one person in ten believed that the United States should be the single global leader, and only one in six favored self-determination for ethnic groups if that risked breaking up established states into warring regions.

Clearly there is a chasm between a foreign-policy establishment mesmerized by notions of American leadership and "global responsibilities" and an American public concerned by drug trafficking and addiction, jobs, illegal aliens, crime, health-care costs, and the environment. Not since the early days of the Cold War, when that establishment rallied the public to a policy of global activism under the banner of anti-communism, has there been such a gap between the perceptions of the foreign-policy elite and the realities of the world in which most Americans live.

This is a problem even on foreign economic issues. The average working American does not share the view of the elites, particularly economists, that global free trade and market efficiency should take precedence over unemployment and other presumably "parochial" local issues—or that it makes no difference if Japan and the European Union become richer and more powerful than the United States, so long as global trade increases. The angry debate over the North American Free Trade Agreement in the fall of 1993 went beyond partisan politics. It illustrated the conflict between those concerned with efficiency and global markets, and those worried about jobs in declining industries.

The domestic agenda is a pressing, and indeed a depressing, one. We suffer from some of the highest rates of illiteracy, malnutrition, infant mortality, violent crime, homelessness, imprisonment, and poverty in the industrialized world. Our country is hobbled by debt, weakened by fears for personal safety, suspicious of its leaders, and increasingly divided between the skilled and the unskilled, the jobholders and the unemployable.

Despite a growing economy, the median household income is less than it was twenty years ago. The gap between rich and poor grows steadily. According to a 1994 Census Bureau report, the share of the total national household income obtained by the population's lowest fifth has been dropping for years, and fell from 4.2 percent in 1968 to 3.6 percent in 1993. In the same period the share of the top fifth rose from 42.8 percent to 48.2 percent. Nearly 40 million Americans were without health insurance in 1993. More than 15 percent of the population fell below the poverty line—an annual income of $14,763 for a family of four.

By many measures of social well-being we fall inexorably behind our trading partners, just as each new generation of Americans trails its parents in income and opportunity. We put a higher proportion of our people in prison than does any other country except Russia. We murder one another at a rate that astounds the world. Whole sections of our great cities resemble parts of the Third World. As in Latin American countries, an affluent elite hides behind walls, alarm systems, and security guards. Outside these walls the growing ranks of the uneducated poor become more violent and more threatening.

We have created a class of people that has jobs but is nonetheless impoverished. We call these people the working poor. They are untrained in modern technologies, sometimes homeless, and everywhere ignored by the political system. Although we live in an ever more stratified social structure, we are loath to call it by its proper name. Indeed, it is considered unseemly, perhaps unpatriotic, to point out that a class society exists.

We hold our nation up as an example to the world, which in many ways it is. But virtually no country in Western Europe has a multigenerational underclass. None is plagued by the gun culture that has infected American cities and has now spread even to small towns. No other mass culture so extols violence. In no other Western nation is the civil society so much a hostage to unrestrained and seemingly unrestrainable violence. Indeed, violence may be the single greatest difference between American culture and European or Japanese culture, and the major reason that Europe and Japan no longer look to the United States as a model and a leader.

Our domestic troubles are not in a realm separate from our foreign policy. They are an integral part, even a product, of it. A nation that seeks not only to protect the world but also to inspire other countries with its values and achievements must be able to offer at least as much to its own people as to those it seeks to guard. Yet at home, even more than in our foreign policy, we have failed abjectly.

Although domestic policy and foreign policy were put into separate compartments during the Cold War, they are integrally related. The nation's economic health, social well-being, and political cohesion are also foreign-policy issues. The kind of division that has been made between the two realms is entirely artificial. A sick civil society is the mark of a weak nation. Gun control and public investment to train and educate the underclass and restore American cities to health may be the most important foreign-policy initiatives that the government can take.

A nation prey to drugs, guns, and violence, increasingly stratified by social class, torn by racial tension, and riven by insecurity, will be a weak player on the world stage. It may also be a threatened democracy—its people disillusioned with traditional political parties, vulnerable to the rantings of talk-show demagogues and politically motivated television evangelists, and sympathetic to vote-seeking messiahs inundating the airwaves with promises of deliverance from conventional politics. It is not easy to see what lessons in democracy the United States can offer the world when Americans themselves increasingly seem to believe that democracy is not working in this country.

For this reason a valid foreign policy must be geared to the needs of American society. It cannot indulge in flights of rhetoric, dedicating itself to the pursuit of vague objectives like "democracy" and "pluralism" in lands inhospitable to these values and posing no threat to the United States, without inviting the failure of our efforts and the alienation of a public asked to support such quixotic goals.

The unreality of current notions of the national interest was dramatized by the President's national-security adviser at the time of the American occupation of Haiti [in 1994]. Enemies of the United States, he declared in a flurry of rhetoric, include "extreme nationalists and tribalists, terrorists, organized criminals, coup plotters, rogue states and all those who would return newly free societies to the intolerant ways of the past." After thus lining up the United States for a crusade against most of the world, the Clinton Administration, unsurprisingly, has had to retreat in one area after another, upon discovering that it was standing alone.

Having emerged from decades of foreign-policy "crises," the country is in no mood for costly adventures in redeeming the world. Leaders who set such agendas are doomed to failure and will be repudiated. The result may well be to discredit not only their more grandiose projects but also their necessary ones, such as cooperation with other major powers to dampen regional conflicts. That is the price paid for lacking a sense of proportion.

The End of Allies

As the Cold War led to the domination of foreign policy, so in this post–Cold War period domestic policy has become paramount. This is natural and entirely proper. It is what happens after every war, and it marks the restoration of a normal balance. Our foreign policy should flow from our domestic society, from the needs and values of the American people. Reflecting its emphasis on economics, the Clinton Administration has declared that the obsolete containment doctrine should be replaced with an "enlargement of the world's free community of market democracies." The assumption behind this is that free markets require free societies, and that democracies rarely go to war against one another. But a glance at the world, beginning with the fast-growing "tigers" of Southeast Asia, reveals that there is no necessary correlation between market success and democracy. The idea that there is one is at best wishful thinking, and at base a provincial conceit, a delusion rather than a policy.

Most emerging countries—even Japan and other advanced industrial ones—do not use economic growth primarily to expand domestic consumption, as does the United States. They use it to expand production, penetrate foreign markets, acquire assets abroad, and increase their power. Economic power is the foundation of military power. As China grows richer, to take one case, it may or may not become less authoritarian. But, as its ever growing military budgets indicate, it will be stronger and more assertive. The notion that Japan should have military potential commensurate with its economic power is no longer a taboo topic in Tokyo.

Tomorrow's America will not be dealing with a world it dominates. It will be part of a complex of market economies, some of which will be democratic and some not—but all of which will be energetic competitors with their own agendas. The days of deference by allies to American military power are over. Indeed, the days of allies are over. In a world without a single menacing enemy, alliances are deprived of meaning. And in trade wars, unlike military confrontations, there are no allies, only rivals.

Even the centerpiece of our Cold War alliance structure—NATO—is sliding into atrophy in the absence of an enemy. Its major functions today are bureaucratic and psychological rather than military. It provides a purpose for general staffs that have no military duties, and it gives the illusion of security against enemies that are now nonexistent. . . . The ritualistic preservation of outworn structures is an evasion that puffs up our vanity and keeps us from the necessary work of re-evaluating our interests.

A new American diplomacy—one that leaves Cold War thinking behind—will pose practical questions. It will ask what responsibilities the nation has to itself and to the welfare of its citizens. For what causes should we use our power to intervene militarily, and what price is worth paying? Should we operate alone, or only in conjunction with others? At what point does a humanitarian act—such as feeding the hungry or separating victim from executioner—become a political one, such as creating and policing a nation? What is the place of morality in foreign policy?

Morality Tempered by Realism

This last question is particularly difficult for Americans. More than any other people, we believe that our foreign policy should have a moral component. The glue that bound together the anti-communist consensus was in part a moral one. Since the end of the Cold War and the disappearance of any serious security threat, decisions about intervention have often involved the issue of morality. What constitutes moral behavior on the part of a nation? When is interference in another country's affairs morally justified? These are not easy questions to answer. Well-meaning people can disagree on the morality of a given situation. The inability of the Clinton Administration to forge a consensus on the Bosnian war rightly caused it to retreat from its original impulse to intervene. What seemed like a moral outrage to some was to others merely a Balkan civil feud that outsiders could not resolve. [The United States did finally intervene in Bosnia along with its NATO allies following the Dayton agreement reached in December 1995.—Eds.]

Under what circumstances should the United States intervene against other nations? There would seem to be two general justifications: morality and self-interest. In the category of morality, most Americans would agree that intervention is justified to alleviate extraordinary and severe human suffering, such as in famine, plague, and drought. This was the rationale in Somalia before the mission became compromised by grandiose notions of "nation building." And acts of genocide cannot be tolerated by the community of civilized nations. When people are being exterminated because of their ethnicity, race, or social class, outside powers have not only the right but the duty to intervene. Ideally they should do so in concert, whether through the United Nations or simply by joint agreement. It was shameful that the United States did not intervene in Rwanda . . . to stop the slaughter of half a million Tutsi by the rival Hutu tribe. France was the only Western country to send troops to end the bloodshed. It was no less shameful that in the late 1970s not a single Western nation moved against the Khmer Rouge, who killed some two million of their countrymen in a drive to "purify" Cambodia for communism. Finally neighboring Vietnam entered the killing fields to stop the genocide.

If armed intervention was justified in Rwanda and Cambodia, why not in Bosnia or Haiti? Here, as in all political distinctions, the lines cannot be drawn with precision. But there are major differences that are crucial. Bosnia was the scene of a civil war in which civilians were targeted because of their ethnicity, in which people were displaced from their homes to create "ethnically cleansed" zones, and in which terrible human-rights abuses occurred. But this took place in the context of a traditional war over territory, and neither the intention nor the result was the systematic eradication of a people, which is the strict definition of genocide. The suffering resulted from the decision of a state to secede from the country of which it was a part, and unilaterally declare its independence. This is not an issue in which the United States has any responsibility to intervene.

In Haiti significant human-rights abuses have taken place for generations, as a ruling elite used intimidation and terror to enforce its authority over an impoverished peasantry. This is deplorable. But it is also the condition under which much of the world lives. To insist that the United States must intervene to overthrow repressive regimes around the globe, or even in this hemisphere, is to set an agenda that would lead to perpetual and ruinous wars of righteousness. It is a policy that could not be honored, and would rightfully be repudiated by the American people.

The lesson of these examples is not that the United States must never intervene for reasons of morality. There are times when it should and must: in cases in which it has the power to stop the horror quickly, as in Rwanda and Cambodia, and in cases in which the horror is on such a scale as to undermine the foundations of Western civilization itself, as in the genocidal madness of Nazi Germany.

But if a foreign policy is to be effective, it must have the support of the American public. And if it is to gain that support, it cannot be quixotic or simply utopian. It cannot seek impossible ends, such as the democratization of the world, or the attainment of a beneficent "world order" that will somehow be pleasing to revolutionaries and conservatives alike. It will avoid grandiose rhetoric precisely so that it can act in those cases—few but critical—in which it can at acceptable cost achieve its ends, and in which the degree of suffering or injustice that it addresses greatly exceeds the customary or the tolerable. This is not a formula that will satisfy zealots or crusaders, and it is also more than some others may be willing to support. But it is one that accords with the moral values of the American people and has limitations realistic enough to win their support.

Balance of Power

The major justification for the use of force will continue to be, as it has been in the past, self-interest. In a democracy the interests of the people are, or at least should be, coterminous with those of the state. In practice, as we have seen as recently as the Vietnam War, leaders sometimes have fantastical ideas of the national interest and can do incalculable harm to their nation. In such a case the only remedy is to elect new leaders.

The United States might be driven to use force in the pursuit of self-interest for a number of reasons: to protect vital natural resources; to quell regional disorder that might threaten American security; to defend the nation's borders from, for example, drug traffickers, illegal aliens, or terrorists; to block a hostile power from conquering a critical area such as Western Europe; to ward off nuclear or ecological threats to our national well-being.

Admittedly, this is a long list, but it is not an indiscriminate one, and in matters of military intervention discrimination is all. The list does not include intervention to establish a democracy, or to make the world a better place, or to combat uncongenial ideologies and religions. It does not set the United States the impossible and self-destructive task of correcting all the world's wrongs or converting all the world's peoples to the blessings of our way of life. It does not reflect a policy subject to spasms of self-intoxication and to crusades of self-righteousness.

As an act of hostility or aggression, the denial of any vital resource to a nation is traditionally a cause of war. A great power must defend its interests whether they concern oil or any other commodity (although in the case of oil, the United States must also reduce its imports by reforming its wasteful practices).

Where serious political disorder, particularly near our shores, threatens our stability or that of areas we consider vital to our interests, we cannot, as a great power, abjure the right to intervene. This does not mean that we should behave like a global fire brigade. Rather, such interventions to maintain order, where necessary, should be almost entirely within our geographic region: North America and the Caribbean.

A nation that cannot control its own borders will have difficulty controlling the direction of its national life. Since we are an immigrant nation, our policies toward political refugees must be liberal and compassionate—but not impotent and anarchic. And we have a duty to protect ourselves, by appropriate means, from those who seek to do us harm, such as drug dealers and terrorists.

The concept of "balance of power" may have a nineteenth-century ring, but it remains a reality. The United States intervened three times in this century—in the two world wars and the Cold War—to prevent any single nation from controlling the European continent, and the maintenance of a European balance remains an American interest. If diplomatic means to ensure balance fail, force may once again be a necessary recourse.

Finally, and most obviously, threats to our very survival—whether from rogue states, terrorist groups armed with nuclear weapons, or states or powerful corporations that imperil our natural habitat through pollution and the destruction of irreplaceable resources—may in certain circumstances be controllable only through the use of force. It is not power, after all, that is evil but only its abuse or misapplication.

The How of Force

If force is to be used, *how* shall it be done? Four possibilities present themselves: the United States can act alone, as the world's single most powerful state; it can form alliances with weaker nations, as it did during the Cold War; it can organize temporary coalitions, as it did during the Persian Gulf conflict; or it can try to operate through a multilateral organization, such as the United Nations, or a regional one, such as the Organization of American States.

The approach, of course, should depend on the circumstances. Yet it is clear that since the disappearance of our sole serious enemy, formal alliances have declined in relevance and usefulness, and are kept alive largely through bureaucratic inertia. Temporary coalitions tend to depend on the willingness of a single major nation to organize the action and carry the brunt of the burden, as the United States did during the Gulf War. Multilateral action through the UN or other organizations diffuses responsibility, and is likely to be invoked increasingly in the future. But it is workable only when it accords with the joint interests of all the major powers. . . .

The current enthusiasm for multilateralism results in large part from the unwillingness of states to make serious sacrifices to establish order in remote and peripheral areas. The consequent failure of an organization of states to act upon its grandiose ambitions necessarily lessens its credibility even in areas where it is capable of action. A further result is to inhibit crisis-dampening by regional powers that have a direct and vital stake in the outcome. The world for the most part stood by during the war in Bosnia, because the European states vitally concerned were not sufficiently organized to take action, while the United States, which had the power, lacked sufficient interest.

What this anomaly suggests is that regional disturbances that do not threaten the world power balance should be dealt with by the major powers of the region, ideally with the endorsement of the international community. Instead of seeking an ephemeral global security, we should . . . accept the reality of the long-standing tradition of spheres of influence—a tradition that we scrupulously insist upon in the Western Hemisphere under our unilaterally imposed Monroe Doctrine.

Now that many major regional powers are democratic, like the United States and the European Union, or moving toward democracy, like Russia, such a policy should be more tolerable to those concerned about the equality of all states. With the Cold War behind us, a benign spheres-of-influence policy becomes far more feasible than it was in the past. It is also more realistic than any alternative.

"Splendid Isolation"

The recent past should have taught us that regional powers may be the only ones willing to deal with regional breakdowns. Uganda's murderous Idi Amin was deposed by neighboring Tanzania, not by the UN or the distant great powers. Vietnam put down the Khmer Rouge's genocide in Cambodia, and India stopped the Pakistani army's extermination campaign in East Bengal. Civil war and violence ravaged Lebanon for years until Syria stepped in to end it. The United States intervened to impose what it considered a desirable order in Grenada, Panama, and Haiti. Only Russia has either the interest or the capacity, whether by bribery or cruel force, to pacify warring ethnic groups in the Caucasus. It was a blind refusal to recognize the reality of China's sphere of influence that drew the United States into its disastrous adventure in Indochina.

A spheres-of-influence policy is the basis of our relationships with Canada, Mexico, and the Caribbean, just as it is of Russia's with the states of the former Soviet Union, and of China's with Southeast Asia. Such a policy no doubt seems unjust to those who believe in a global community of equal states, none able to impose any authority on the others. But it is also an alternative to anarchy. And it is a reality of the world we live in. It avoids indiscriminate globalism on the one hand, and utopian visions that cannot be translated into reality on the other.

Utopianism is as unrealistic, and as dangerous, as isolationism. We have never truly been an isolationist power, and we certainly cannot be one in a world integrated economically and technologically. But we also cannot afford to indulge in lingering Cold War conceits of military omnipotence and unlimited global responsibilities. Such fantasies are doomed to failure, and they breed distrust of democratic government.

We have won a victory, of sorts, and now that war is over. We enjoy a time of peace, of sorts, although the peace is not everywhere, and the time certainly will not last forever. Our task today is not so heroic as fighting a war, but it is no less difficult, and in the end it may be as important: to recognize our limitations, to reject the vanity of trying to remake the world in our image, and to restore the promise of our neglected society.

America today is hobbled by self-doubt about its political system and by "crises" abroad that in fact pose little danger. Yet the nation enjoys an unparalleled freedom of action in foreign policy. Like Britain at the height of its power, in the mid-nineteenth century, we live in a world where we are not unchallenged but are unquestionably first among only potential equals. We have no serious enemies and require no allies. This is our equivalent of what the British called their period of "splendid isolation."

The term has been much abused in recent years. It does not mean that the British were isolated, any more than we are today. Quite the contrary: they were never more engaged in the world. But the engagement was on their terms. Lord Palmerston, their leading statesman at the time, declared, in words that are often quoted, that Britain had no eternal allies and no permanent enemies, but its interests were eternal and its duty was to follow those interests. The British lived in a world of other major and aspiring powers, which did not always wish them well but learned to respect their strength, their diplomatic agility, and their values. . . .

As we have left the Cold War behind us, so have we left the American century. The war gave us a sense of purpose, and without it we feel trapped by domestic troubles from which we can find no escape in parades, drum rolls, and demonstrations of resolve. The self-confidence that has always been one of our most attractive national characteristics has been sapped, leaving our nation confused and even embittered. For a long time foreign policy was a useful evasion.

It cannot be that anymore. We have to accept our domestic problems as requiring the painful compromises that they do. And we must return to foreign policy not as an escape or a salvation but merely as a means of making our way, without illusions but also without cynicism, in a world of usually competing, sometimes cooperating states.

This is not a heroic task. But it is an important one, for on its success hinges our ability to preserve and enlarge the noble vision that has justly been called the promise of American life.

3

The Political Foundations of Elites' Domestic and Foreign-Policy Beliefs

Ole R. Holsti and James N. Rosenau

In 1984, well before the end of the Cold War, three perceptive foreign affairs analysts asserted that "For two decades, the making of American foreign policy has been growing far more political—or more precisely, far more partisan and ideological" (Destler, Gelb, and Lake, 1984, p. 13). Is their assessment still valid several years after the disintegration of the Soviet Union? Alternatively, have some mitigating factors reduced the impact of partisan and ideological cleavages on the conduct of American diplomacy? At least two possibilities come to mind. First, as the dividing line between domestic and foreign-policy issues has eroded, have positions on domestic issues dampened partisan-ideological divisions by creating cross-cutting rather than overlapping cleavages? Second, although there are some data showing a systematic correlation between attitudes on domestic and foreign policy, most of them were derived from the Cold War period. Have the dramatic international events of the period since the Destler-Gelb-Lake analysis altered political attitudes sufficiently to render their verdict obsolete? This chapter addresses these questions, focusing on American opinion leaders. After examining the relationship between domestic and foreign-policy beliefs over a twelve-year period (1984–1996), the analysis probes the partisan and ideological foundations of political beliefs espoused by American opinion leaders.

Before turning to the evidence it may be useful to summarize briefly some findings on the relationship between attitudes on domestic and foreign-policy issues. Even a cursory survey reveals that a definitive answer is elusive. These questions—part of a larger controversy about the strength of ideological thinking and structural coherence in American public opinion—are the focus of a vigorous debate. Much of the early evidence on the issue was derived from analyses of data generated either by panel studies of the American electorate or by Gallup and other surveys of public opinion. At first glance it appears that virtually all of the findings point toward the conclusion that attitudes about issues in the domestic and international arenas are independent rather than systematically linked. In their study of the 1948 election, Berelson and his colleagues (1954, pp. 197–198) found a limited correlation between domestic "position [economic] issues" and either civil rights or international "style issues." "The dilemma is that the two contemporary axes of liberalism-conservatism, the one economic-class and the other ethnic-international, vary independently of each other. . . . To know, for example, that someone supported the New Deal on economic issues provided no indication of his international or civil rights opinions." Similar findings emerged from several other studies of the electorate. Campbell and his colleagues (1964, p. 113) reported, "Across our sample as a whole in 1956 there was no relationship between scale positions of individuals on the domestic and foreign attitudinal dimensions." Partisanship characterized responses to domestic issues but not to foreign-policy issues. Key (1961, p. 158) uncovered a similar finding. Assessing the relationship between internationalism—a willingness to tolerate international involvement—and domestic liberalism, he concluded, "The lines of cleavage in the two policy areas did not coincide." Converse's (1964) frequently cited analysis of belief systems among elites and the general public reported correlations among responses to domestic and foreign-policy issues. He came to the same conclusion. Among the general public, the degree of policy consistency, whether on domestic issues, foreign-policy issues, or across the two issues areas, was quite low.

However, the apparent consensus represented by the Converse findings has also generated considerable controversy. Some analysts found a greater ideological consistency among the general public during the turbulent era of the 1960s and 1970s, but they, too, have encountered criticism. This is not the place to provide a blow-by-blow account of these extensive debates. Excellent summaries of the vast literature may be found in Kinder (1983), Kinder and Sears (1985), Sniderman and Tetlock (1986), and Sniderman (1993).

For present purposes, the more directly relevant question concerns the degree of consistency of views across domestic and foreign-policy issues among persons who can be described as opinion leaders by virtue of their positions in a wide range of major American institutions. Many analysts have found that, compared with the general public, elites are more likely to hold policy views that are consistent—that is, that their beliefs are held together by some underlying ideological principles. Converse (1964) found that correlations among responses to both domestic and foreign-policy issues were consistently higher for Congressional candidates than for the public at large. Russett and Hanson (1975, p. 138) surveyed military officers and business leaders, and they found "dovish [international] and liberal [domestic] attitudes consistently together on the one hand, and conservative [domestic] and hawkish [international] attitudes regularly together on the other." Similar results emerged from an analysis of a 1984 survey of American opinion leaders (Holsti and Rosenau, 1988), as well as from a panel study of elites (Murray, 1996).

This chapter extends the previously cited analysis of 1984 data with evidence from subsequent surveys of opinion leaders in 1988, 1992, and 1996. The Foreign Policy Leadership (FPLP) surveys, initiated in 1976 and replicated every four years since, provide the primary evidence. Because the first two of these studies (1976 and 1980) included few domestic policy questions, the analyses that follow focus on the four surveys conducted between 1984 and 1996. Each of the FPLP surveys was conducted by means of a long questionnaire mailed to samples of approximately 4,000 opinion leaders whose names had been drawn from such general sources as *Who's Who in America,* and *Who's Who of American Women,* as well as more specialized directories listing leaders in occupations that are underrepresented in *Who's Who,* including media leaders, politicians, military officers, labor leaders, State Department and foreign service officers, foreign-policy experts outside government, and the like. In two cases—chief editorial writers of high circulation newspapers and students at the National War College—the entire population of the groups rather than samples were included in the survey. Return rates for the FPLP surveys have ranged between 53 and 63 percent. In 1996, 2,141 opinion leaders filled out and returned the questionnaire for a return rate of 54 percent.

The four most recent FPLP surveys encompass strikingly different international settings, especially in the range of relations between Washington and Moscow. The 1984 survey took place at the height of "Cold War II" when vitriolic rhetoric and arms racing had overtaken any manifestations of détente. Only four years later, President Reagan and Chairman Gorbachev were meeting regularly, had signed an unprecedented arms control agreement, and referred to each other as friends rather than as leaders of "evil empires." Startling as the changes between 1984 and 1988 were, they paled in comparison with those of the next eight years, which witnessed not only the end of the Cold War but also of the Soviet Union, a war against Iraq, as well as internal conflicts that resulted in the deployment of American troops to Somalia, Haiti, and Bosnia. To summarize very briefly, then, the four most recent FPLP surveys spanned the Cold War and its end, the transition to the post–Cold War era, and almost a decade of an era in which opposition to the Soviet Union no longer provided a beacon to guide American foreign policy. Findings that persist through such dramatic changes would appear to be very robust.

The analysis in this chapter will proceed in three stages. The first describes an analytical scheme that is used to classify opinion leaders into one of four categories on the basis of their responses to fourteen foreign-policy questions. Answers to a dozen domestic policy questionnaire items are used to construct a second typology. The next step examines the strength of the relationship between the domestic and foreign-policy belief systems. The final stage of the analysis assesses the degree to which domestic and foreign-policy beliefs of the opinion leaders are rooted in partisan and ideological differences. The conclusion assesses the contemporary validity of the previously cited assertion by Destler, Gelb, and Lake in light of the evidence, as well as some policy implications of the findings.

Findings

Foreign-Policy Beliefs

Much of the research during and immediately after World War II measured public opinion on a single isolationist-to-internationalist scale, but most of the recent studies have shown that attitudes on foreign affairs are better described in multidimensional terms. (Wittkopf, 1990; Hinckley, 1992; Chittick, Billingsley, and Travis, 1996). A series of studies of public opinion by Wittkopf (1990, 1996) has demonstrated that there are two "faces of internationalism." Attitudes toward two dimensions—support for or opposition to *militant internationalism* (MI) and *cooperative internationalism* (CI)—are necessary for describing the beliefs structures of both elites and the general public. Dichotomizing and crossing these two dimensions yields four types, with quadrants labeled as *hard-liners* (support MI, oppose CI), *accommodationists* (oppose MI, support CI), *internationalists* (support both MI and CI), and *isolationists* (oppose both MI and CI). Analyses of the five FPLP surveys conducted between 1976 and 1992, although using somewhat different methods and questions than those employed by Wittkopf, revealed that the MI/CI scheme is an effective way of classifying opinion leaders' foreign-policy beliefs; knowing how respondents are classified provides powerful predictors of their attitudes on a broad array of international issues (Holsti and Rosenau, 1993; Holsti, 1996).

Seven questions from the FPLP questionnaires represent various dimensions of an MI orientation toward world affairs, including an emphasis on a conflictual world; the expansionist policies of adversaries that constitute a major threat to the United States; the necessity of being prepared to use force, including the CIA, to cope with the threats; the dangerous consequences, as postulated by the "domino theory," of failing to meet international challenges; and a zero-sum view of international relations. The seven items on the CI scale emphasize international cooperation and institutions; "North-South" issues, including global hunger and the standard of living in less developed nations; arms control; foreign aid; and the role of the United Nations.

When responses to the MI are aggregated, attitudes on that scale remained stable during the four-year period ending in 1996. However, this overall result masks some pronounced changes on specific questions. The willingness to "take all steps including the use of force to prevent aggression by any expansionist power" declined, although a majority of opinion leaders still approve such an open-ended commitment. Other changes of more than marginal magnitude include a less benign view of Russia's foreign policy goals and reduced support for a military policy of "striking at the heart of the opponent's power." The results indicate that, in the aggregate, respondents are almost exactly at the midpoint of the MI scale, as they were in 1992.

The trend on cooperative internationalism is more easily summarized. Although each of the FPLP surveys has shown an overall favorable attitude toward CI, support for all seven items constituting that scale declined in 1996 from the levels recorded four years earlier. The importance attributed to such foreign-policy goals as strengthening the United Nations and combating world hunger fell especially sharply. From a longer range perspective, however, the 1996 results on the CI scale are about in line with those of the four FPLP surveys prior to 1992.

Each respondent was scored on both the MI and CI scales, with 0.00 serving as the cutting point between supporters (those with a score greater than 0.00) and opponents (those with a lower score). Table 3.1 reveals the distribution of opinion leaders when they were classified according to the MI/CI scheme. Accommodationists and internationalists, the two groups defined as supporting cooperative internationalism, accounted for about three-fourths of the entire leadership group, as they did in the surveys conducted between 1984 and 1988. But, as suggested by the results summarized in Table 3.1, the opponents of CI—the hard-liners and isolationists—gained at the expense of the interna-

TABLE 3.1
The Distribution of American Leaders Among Four Categories of
Foreign Policy Beliefs, 1984–1996 (percentages)

	Cooperative Internationalism			
	Oppose		Support	
Militant Internationalism				
	Hard-Liners		Internationalists	
Support	1984	17	1984	25
	1988	16	1988	25
	1992	9	1992	33
	1996	13	1996	29
	Isolationists		Accommodationists	
Oppose	1984	7	1984	51
	1988	8	1988	52
	1992	5	1992	53
	1996	10	1996	48

Note: Percentages for each year may not add up to 100 due to rounding.

tionalists and accommodationists when the 1996 results are compared with those four years earlier.

Domestic Policy Beliefs

As noted earlier, in contrast to the decades immediately following World War II, one of the features of public opinion during the post–Vietnam period has been a tendency for attitudes on domestic and foreign policy to converge along partisan and ideological lines. That trend has some important implications, for example, regarding efforts to create foreign policy coalitions that cut across differences on domestic issues, as both the Truman and Eisenhower administrations were often able to do. The question to be addressed in the next section is whether the trend toward overlapping rather than cross-cutting cleavages has abated. A brief examination of attitudes toward several domestic issues will lay the groundwork for that analysis.

The FPLP surveys since 1984 have included a cluster of items asking opinion leaders to express their views on a dozen economic and social/value issues. The economic issues scale included items on tax increases to balance the federal budget, tuition tax credits, environmental regulations, defense spending, nuclear power and income redistribution. Those on the social/value scale focus on several of the controversial and emotion-laden issues of recent decades: school busing, abortion, the Equal Rights Amendment, school prayer, gay rights, and the death penalty.

Responses to the economic issues reveal some significant changes between 1992 and 1996 toward more conservative positions—there was increasing opposition to balancing the budget by raising taxes, and growing support for increasing the defense budget—and rather small ones on income redistribution and tuition tax credits for parents who send their children to private or parochial schools. The other two issues yielded changes in opposing directions, with greater support for easing environmental regulation, but declining agreement on reducing restrictions on nuclear power plants.

In contrast, responses to the items on the social/value scale remained quite stable during the four-year interval between the 1992 and 1996 surveys; none of the changes exceeded 5 percent. Reduced support for school busing and the Equal Rights Amendment, policies often favored by liberals, were somewhat offset by slight gains for the prochoice position on abortion and declining agreement that gay teachers should be banned from public schools.

Responses to these items were used to construct a domestic issues classification scheme analogous to the MI/CI typology for foreign-policy issues. The rationale underlying the domestic issues typology is that a single liberal-to-conservative dimension is insufficient to capture some important differences between economic and social/value issues and, therefore, that it is useful to distinguish between them. For example, being a fiscal conservative does not necessarily mandate a single position on the Equal Rights Amendment, school prayer, or capital punishment; and the bitter debates, even among avowed conservatives, between prochoice and prolife advocates underscore the point even more dramatically. The terms "liberal" and "conservative" have varied sufficiently in meaning that their contemporary content cannot be considered self evident. For present purposes, on economic issues liberals were assumed to favor:

- an active role for government in regulating the economy
- an active role for government in regulating activities that may threaten the environment
- taxation for purposes of income redistribution, while opposing tax policies that provide benefits mainly for the more affluent

On social issues, it was assumed that liberals support:

- an active role for government in promoting the interests of those who have traditionally been at a disadvantage owing to race, class, gender, or other attributes
- a ban on the death penalty, at least in part because it has been inflicted disproportionately upon some traditionally disadvantaged groups

In contrast, conservatives were assumed to favor the following positions on economic issues:

- removing or reducing governmental restrictions on economic activity
- reducing taxes
- a large defense budget to ensure a strong national defense

On social issues, conservatives were assumed to oppose:

- an active role for government in attempting to legislate equality between classes, sexes, races, or other groups
- an active role for government in support of those who challenge "traditional values"

These premises were incorporated into scoring responses to the twelve items on economic and social/value issues. Each respondent was then given two scores, the first based on responses to the six economic issues and the second derived from preferences on the six social issues. A cutting point of 0.00 was used for each of the scales. The two scores were then used to classify each respondent into four groups: *liberals* (liberal on both scales), *conservatives* (conservative on both scales), *populists* (liberal on economic issues, conservative on social ones), and *libertarians* (conservative on economic issues, liberal on social ones). The distribution of those taking part in the four FPLP surveys since 1984, displayed in Table 3.2, reflects the increasing conservatism on economic issues in 1996 and the resulting gains among conservatives and libertarians. In contrast, responses to the social issues showed little change in 1996; gains among conservatives were offset by a decline in populists.

Linkages Between Domestic and Foreign-Policy Beliefs

Previous FPLP surveys revealed not only strong correlations among various measures of foreign-policy attitudes, but also among opinions on domestic and foreign policy. The 1996 results indicate that these connections have persisted rather than changed. The links can initially be explored by examining how the opinion leaders, when classified according to their foreign-policy orientations, responded to questions on domestic issues. The next step is to reverse this procedure, analyzing appraisals of foreign-policy goals by leaders when they are grouped according to their domestic policy orientations.

As indicated in Table 3.3, there is a consistently strong and statistically significant relationship between foreign-policy orientations and preferences on both economic and social/value domestic policy issues. The accommodationists and hard-liners usually have the most liberal and most conservative policy preferences, respectively, whereas the populists and libertarians are typically found in between them. Even on the issues that find all four groups on the same side—school busing, abortion, protectionism, drug legalization,

TABLE 3.2
The Distribution of American Leaders Among Four Categories of Domestic Policy Beliefs, 1984–1996 (percentages)

Social Issues	Economic Issues			
	Liberal		Conservative	
	Liberals		Libertarians	
Liberal	1984	45	1984	7
	1988	48	1988	7
	1992	47	1992	7
	1996	45	1996	9
	Populists		Conservatives	
Conservative	1984	15	1984	33
	1988	17	1988	28
	1992	19	1992	27
	1996	11	1996	35

TABLE 3.3

Domestic Policy Issues Assessed by Foreign Policy Beliefs, 1996 (percentages)

This question asks you to indicate your position on certain domestic issues. Please indicate how strongly you agree or disagree with each statement.

	All Respondents (N=2,141)	*Respondents Who Agree Strongly or Agree Somewhat*			
		Isolationists (N=217)	Hard-Liners (N=288)	Accommodationists (N=1,020)	Internationalists (N=616)
Busing children to achieve school integration	34	19	8	49	25
Reducing federal budget deficits by raising taxes	50	42	22	66	40
Relaxing environmental regulation to stimulate economic growth	28	37	61	13	34
Providing tuition tax credits to parents who send children to private or parochial schools	42	46	71	29	48
Leaving abortion decisions to women and their doctors	82	82	60	89	80
Reviving the Equal Rights Amendment	49	42	15	61	47
Permitting prayer in public schools	46	47	73	29	62
Reducing the defense budget to increase the federal education budget	54	44	14	72	45
Barring homosexuals from teaching in public schools	25	30	54	11	32
Easing restrictions on the construction of nuclear power plants	38	43	64	27	42
Redistributing income from the wealthy to the poor through taxation and subsidies	41	29	11	58	31
Banning the death penalty	34	20	9	51	21

Note: Difference among group on all items significant at the .001 level.

and reducing Medicare/Medicaid growth—the gaps across the groups are quite large; for example, agreement that the government should stay out of abortion decisions ranges from 60 percent to 89 percent.

There are also large but somewhat less striking differences on foreign-policy goals when opinion leaders are grouped according to their domestic policy orientations. Three of the goals listed in Table 3.4 resulted in broad agreement across all four groups: preventing nuclear proliferation is uniformly the top priority, defending allies rates as moderately important, and there is little enthusiasm for promoting democracy abroad. For the remaining foreign policy goals, however, the dominant pattern is one of very large differences between liberals and conservatives, with populists and libertarians arrayed in the middle. The largest gaps are on such goals as protecting the environment, international economic cooperation, combatting hunger, arms control, strengthening the United Nations, improving the standard of living in developing countries, and human rights—all most highly ranked by the liberals—and military superiority, fighting drug trafficking and illegal immigration, goals that are given much higher priority by the conservatives.

The relationship between the militant/cooperative internationalism and the domestic policy classification schemes is displayed in Table 3.5. As in the previous three surveys, the 1996 results indicate a strong and persisting pattern of overlapping rather than cross-cutting cleavages, especially among hard-liners and accommodationists. Notice how those who support militant internationalism and oppose cooperative internationalism (the hard-liner category) are largely classified as conservatives on the domestic scale. A similar interpretation may be used to compare the other foreign-policy categories with the domestic ones. One modest change worth noting is the increased number of domestic liberals—from 23 percent to 29 percent—among the internationalists. Some liberals, who typically had opposed American military interventions during the Cold War, have come to support such actions in recent years; prominent examples include Arthur Schlesinger (1995) and *New York Times* columnist Anthony Lewis. At the same time, the isolationists include an increasing number of conservatives. These modest changes notwithstanding, the dominant pattern of persisting linkages between attitudes toward domestic and foreign policy is evident.

Partisanship and Ideology

Respondents in each of the FPLP surveys were asked to provide some standard socio-demographic information, including party preference and placement on a "very liberal to very conservative" ideology scale. Analyses of the five surveys prior to 1996 revealed that deep cleavages on both domestic and foreign-policy issues were rooted in partisan, ideological and, to a lesser degree, occupational differences. In contrast, neither gender nor generation

TABLE 3.4

Foreign-Policy Goals Assessed by Domestic Policy Beliefs, 1996 (percentages)

Please indicate how much importance should be attached to each goal.

		Those Responding "Very Important"			
	All Respondents (N=2,141)	Liberals (N=953)	Populists (N=239)	Libertarians (N=201)	Conservatives (N=748)
Preventing the spread of nuclear weapons	83	86	85	80	80
Worldwide arms control	60	73	65	58	43
Strengthening the United Nations	26	40	24	16	11
Protecting weaker nations against foreign aggression	18	21	18	15	14
Fostering international cooperation to solve common problems, such as food, inflation, and energy	56	72	59	46	37
Protecting the global environment	47	67	53	38	22
Combatting world hunger	36	50	38	29	19
Helping to improve the standard of living in less developed countries	28	41	26	24	14
Securing adequate supplies of energy	52	44	57	58	61
Protecting the jobs of American workers	29	25	38	24	32
Protecting the interests of American business abroad	19	12	17	22	30
Stopping the flow of illegal drugs into the United States	58	44	68	59	71
Controlling and reducing illegal immigration	33	16	41	29	51
Promoting and defending human rights in other countries	24	35	24	16	11
Helping to bring a democratic form of government to other nations	15	17	16	11	14
Defending our allies' security	36	34	39	39	37
Maintaining superior military power worldwide	40	19	38	45	64
Containing communism	15	5	16	13	27

Note: Differences among groups significant at the .001 level for all items except numbers 1 (spread of nuclear weapons), 15 (bringing democracy to others), and 16 (defending allies' security).

TABLE 3.5
Relationship Between Foreign and Domestic Policy Beliefs, 1984–1996

Militant Internationalism

		Cooperative Internationalism									
		Oppose					**Support**				
		Hard-Liners					Internationalists				
		1984	*1988*	*1992*	*1996*		*1984*	*1988*	*1992*	*1996*
Support	Liberals	7	8	8	5	Liberals	21	23	23	29
	Conservatives	74	70	71	82	Conservatives	51	42	42	44
	Populists	13	16	13	6	Populists	20	27	26	16
	Libertarians	6	6	7	7	Libertarians	8	8	9	10
		Isolationists					Accommodationists				
		1984	*1988*	*1992*	*1996*		*1984*	*1988*	*1992*	*1996*
Oppose	Liberals	40	41	31	31	Liberals	71	73	70	68
	Conservatives	33	34	41	46	Conservatives	10	8	8	14
	Populists	17	17	17	11	Populists	13	13	16	9
	Libertarians	10	8	11	12	Libertarians	6	6	6	9

Note: Cell entries are percentages. Columns may not add up to 100% due to rounding.

	1984	1988	1992	1996
Correlations between international and domestic belief systems (phi)	.60	.61	.56	.55

proved to be especially powerful sources of opinion differences. (Holsti, 1996, chapter 5). Many surveys of the general public have found that education is closely linked to international attitudes, but the FPLP samples are so heavily skewed toward the high end of educational attainment—virtually all respondents have had a college degree and about three-fourths of them have also earned a graduate degree—that differences grounded in levels of education are likely to be quite modest.

The figures in Table 3.6 provide a summary overview of partisan and ideological foundations of foreign-policy orientations, as measured by the MI/CI classification scheme, in the 1996 FPLP survey. Among hard-liners, Republicans outnumbered Democrats by an overwhelming margin of 8–1, whereas a very solid majority of accommodationists were Democrats. To a less dramatic extent, internationalists and isolationists preferred the GOP to the Democratic

TABLE 3.6
Foreign Policy Beliefs and Partisan and Ideological Attachments 1996
(percentages)

Militant Internationalists	*Cooperative Internationalism*			
	Oppose		Support	
Support	Hard-Liners ($N=270$) Self-identification		Internationalists ($N=585$) Self-identification	
	Republicans	72	Republicans	47
	Independents	19	Independents	21
	Democrats	9	Democrats	32
	Conservative	82	Conservative	47
	Moderate	14	Moderate	32
	Liberal	4	Liberal	21
Oppose	Isolationists ($N=191$) Self-identification		Accommodationists ($N=946$) Self-identification	
	Republicans	51	Republicans	19
	Independents	24	Independents	24
	Democrats	25	Democrats	57
	Conservative	52	Conservative	18
	Moderate	32	Moderate	29
	Liberal	15	Liberal	53

Note: Totals for each year may not add up to 100% due to rounding. Table excludes 81 respondents who did not express a party preference and 99 who did not place themselves on the ideology scale.

Correlations (phi): foreign policy beliefs and party: .42, foreign policy beliefs and ideology: .50.

Party. The correlation between party and foreign-policy orientation is a strong .42.

The relationship between orientations on the MI/CI typology and ideology is even stronger, as summarized in the correlation coefficient of .50. Once again the most striking differences are between the hard-liners, more than 80 percent of whom identified themselves as conservative, and the strongly liberal accommodationists. The ideological self-identifications of the internationalists and isolationists also tended to tilt toward the conservative end of the ideological self-identification scale.

Table 3.7 provides comparable data on the partisan and ideological correlates of the domestic issues typology. The pattern of relationships is quite similar to that in the previous table in that party and ideology are strongly linked to policy positions; the major difference is that the correlations on domestic issues are even higher than they were on foreign-policy issues. Respondents whose policy positions placed them in the liberal category of the

TABLE 3.7
Domestic Policy Beliefs and Partisan and Ideological Attachments, 1996
(percentages)

	Economic Issues			
	Liberals		Conservatives	
Social Issues				
	Liberals (*N* = 892) Self-identification		Libertarians (*N* = 182) Self-identification	
	Republicans	9	Republicans	45
	Independents	21	Independents	32
Liberals	Democrats	70	Democrats	23
	Conservative	6	Conservative	39
	Moderate	28	Moderate	43
	Liberal	66	Liberal	18
	Populists (*N* = 215) Self-identification		Conservatives (*N* = 705) Self-identification	
	Republicans	34	Republicans	73
	Independents	29	Independents	19
Conservatives	Democrats	36	Democrats	8
	Conservative	37	Conservative	79
	Moderate	49	Moderate	18
	Liberal	14	Liberal	3

Note: Columns may not add up to 100% due to rounding. Table excludes 81 respondents who did not express a party preference and 99 who did not place themselves on the ideology scale.

Correlations (phi): foreign policy beliefs and party: .66, foreign policy beliefs and ideology: .75.

domestic issues typology are overwhelmingly liberal Democrats according to their self-identifications. Similarly, well over 70 percent of the leaders who expressed policy preferences that led to their placement in the conservative quadrant of the domestic issues classification scheme identified themselves as Republicans and conservatives. In contrast, the partisan and ideological preferences of the libertarians and populists is much more mixed. A plurality of both groups placed themselves in the middle of the ideology spectrum and neither political party claimed a majority of leaders in either group.

As the evidence in Tables 3.6 and 3.7 suggests, the correlation between party and ideology in 1996 was exceptionally high (phi = .75) as increasing numbers of Republicans (78 percent) identified themselves as conservatives, while Democrats were predominantly on the liberal side (68 percent) of the ideology scale; conservative Democrats (6 percent) and liberal Republicans (4 percent) are a vanishing breed among the rosters of American leaders.

Although partisan cleavages are evident on a very large majority of issues broached in the 1996 survey, there are also some interesting exceptions. Eastward expansion of NATO received strong support across the political spectrum, with three-fourths of Republicans, Democrats, and independents expressing their approval. A more general pattern that emerges from the data is bipartisan agreement among opinion leaders on most trade issues. A strong majority of respondents opposed erecting trade barriers; rated protecting jobs and the interests of American businesses abroad as foreign-policy goals of limited importance; and approved major steps toward trade liberalization, including NAFTA, GATT, and the World Trade Organization agreements. The grant of most favored nation trade status to China divided opinion leaders almost evenly, but the cleavages cut *across* rather than along party lines. Finally, bipartisan agreement on trade liberalization appears to arise from widespread belief—shared by Republicans, Democrats, and independents—that economic competition, whether with Europe or Japan, does not constitute a threat to the United States. It should be noted that the absence of partisan divisions on trade issues in 1996 represents continuity rather than change in the view of opinion leaders. None of the earlier surveys uncovered much evidence of support for protectionism among leaders, whether Democrats, Republicans, or independents.

Compared to partisan divisions, those rooted in ideology are even broader on most questions. Yet, within an overall pattern of deep ideological cleavages, there are also indications of occasional convergence between the most liberal and most conservative opinion leaders. The point is illustrated in responses to a cluster of questions asking respondents to assess several recent U.S. foreign and defense policy decisions. On most issues there was a steady increase or decrease in support as one moves across the ideological spectrum, and the gaps are typically quite large. For example, the Haiti intervention received overwhelming support from liberals and far less from conservatives, whereas exactly the opposite was the case with respect to increasing trade sanctions on Cuba and reducing the American contribution to the United Nations budget. But on five of the issues a quite different pattern emerged, wherein the strongest approval for U.S. decisions was found in the ideological middle, and the most liberal and most conservative respondents were the least supportive. Further, each of these issues deals with trade policy: MFN status for China, NAFTA, pressure on Europe and Japan to open their markets, GATT and the World Trade Organization, and support for American firms doing business in China. Thus, whereas trade issues remain relatively free of partisan differences, they tend to pit leaders in the center of the ideological spectrum against those on both ends. This pattern tends to conform rather closely to debates in Congress on such issues as NAFTA several years ago, and the coalitions that emerged on China's trade status in 1997, in which such liberals as Dick Gephardt were aligned with the Christian right in opposing the president and Republican congressional leaders, all of whom supported renewal of MFN.

Conclusion

This chapter began with the Destler-Gelb-Lake lament about the impact of partisanship and ideology on the conduct of American foreign relations. The evidence summarized above indicates that the strong relationship between domestic and foreign-policy beliefs uncovered in response to the 1984 FPLP survey has persisted through the end of the Cold War and well into the post–Cold War era. The *structure* of both domestic and foreign policy beliefs has remained quite stable across a period of almost unprecedented international change. No doubt one reason for this stability is that both clusters of beliefs continue to be systematically grounded in ideology and partisanship. Although the evidence has identified some areas of agreement among opinion leaders—preferences for liberalizing rather than restricting trade is a notable example—it has also uncovered considerable evidence of deep partisan and ideological cleavages. Even the trade issue is not without controversy, as it has given rise to exceptionally deep differences between opinion leaders and the general public, which has generally expressed stronger support for protectionist policies. These cleavages encompass both general positions on the merits of trade liberalization as well as opinions on such specific undertakings as the North American Free Trade Agreement (NAFTA).

The survey data also revealed striking partisan and ideological cleavages among opinion leaders on many domestic issues. Disagreements on domestic and foreign-policy issues have been the exception rather than the rule in American politics; in that sense, the data presented here hardly represents a break from earlier eras. What may be new is the extent that the cross-cutting cleavages created by domestic and international issues during the two decades following World War II have given way to overlapping divisions that, in turn, have powerful ideological and partisan foundations. The end of the Cold War has done little to alter this trend. The tenor of political debates during the first five years of the Clinton administration would appear to sustain the continuing relevance of the Destler-Gelb-Lake diagnosis in this respect. The broader implications of these tendencies will vary according to one's normative vision. Those who have criticized American politics and parties for lacking ideological coherence will no doubt be pleased, whereas those who find merit in the more pragmatic style of politics made necessary by cross-cutting cleavages are less likely to applaud.

References

Berelson, Bernard R., Paul F. Lazarsfeld, and William N. McPhee. 1954. *Voting: A Study of Opinion Formulation in a Presidential Campaign.* Chicago: University of Chicago Press.

Campbell, Angus, Philip E. Converse, Warren E. Miller, and Donald E. Stokes. 1964. *The American Voter.* New York: John Wiley.

Chittick, William O., Keith R. Billingsley, and Rich Travis. 1995. "A Three-Dimensional Model of American Foreign Policy Beliefs." *International Studies Quarterly* **39:** 313–31.

Converse, Philip E. 1964. "The Nature of Belief Systems in Mass Publics." In David E. Apter, ed., *Ideology and Discontent.* New York: Free Press.

Destler, I.M., Leslie H. Gelb, and Anthony Lake. 1984. *Our Own Worst Enemy.* New York: Simon and Schuster.

Hinckley, Ronald H. 1992. *People, Polls, and Policy-Makers: American Public Opinion and National Security.* New York: Lexington Books.

Holsti, Ole R. 1996. *Public Opinion and American Foreign Policy.* Ann Arbor: University of Michigan Press.

Holsti, Ole R., and James N. Rosenau. 1988. "The Domestic and Foreign Policy Beliefs of American Leaders." *Journal of Conflict Resolution* **32:** 248–94.

Holsti, Ole R., and James N. Rosenau. 1993. "The Structure of Foreign Policy Beliefs Among American Opinion Leaders—After the Cold War." *Millennium* **22:** 235–78.

Key, V.O. Jr. 1961. *Public Opinion and American Democracy.* New York: Knopf.

Kinder, Donald R. 1983. "Diversity and Complexity in American Public Opinion." In Ada W. Finifter, ed., *Political Science: The State of the Discipline.* Washington: American Political Science Association.

Kinder, Donald R., and David O. Sears. 1985. "Public Opinion and Political Action." In Elliott Aronson and Gardner Lindzey, eds., *Handbook of Social Psychology,* 3rd ed. New York: Random House.

Murray, Shoon. 1996. *Anchors Against Change: American Opinion Leaders' Beliefs After the Cold War.* Ann Arbor: University of Michigan Press.

Russett, Bruce M., and Elizabeth C. Hanson. 1975. *Interest and Ideology: The Foreign Policy Beliefs of American Businessmen.* San Francisco: Freeman.

Schlesinger, Arthur Jr. 1995. "Back to the Womb?" *Foreign Affairs* **74** (July-August): 2–8.

Sniderman, Paul M. 1993. "The New Look in Public Opinion Research." In Ada W. Finifter, ed., *Political Science: The State of the Discipline II.* Washington: American Political Science Association.

Sniderman, Paul M., and Philip E. Tetlock. 1986. "Interrelationship of Political Ideology and Public Opinion." In Margaret G. Hermann, ed., *Political Psychology.* San Francisco: Jossey-Bass.

Wittkopf, Eugene R. 1990. *Faces of Internationalism: Public Opinion and American Foreign Policy.* Durham, N.C.: Duke University Press.

Wittkopf, Eugene R. 1996. "What Americans Really Think About Foreign Policy." *Washington Quarterly* **19:** 91–106.

4

Public Opinion and Foreign Policy: The People's "Common Sense"

John Mueller

A few years ago international politics experienced the functional equivalent of World War III, only without the bloodshed. In a remarkably short time, virtually all the major problems that haunted international affairs for a half century were solved. The Cold War evaporated, the attendant arms race was reversed, intense disagreement over Eastern Europe and the division of Germany was resolved, and the threat of expansionist international communism simply withered away. In the wake of this quiet cataclysm, we have entered an extraordinary new era: If we apply conventional standards, the leading countries are today presented at the international level with minor, immediate problems and major long-range ones—but no major immediate problems or threats.

Some international relations scholars and writers have been trying . . . to refashion constructs and theories originally designed for an era with compelling threats to fit one that lacks them. Despite their efforts, however, a policy consensus seems to be emerging among those who actually carry out international affairs in the leading countries. It stresses as a primary goal economic enrichment through open markets and freer trade (rather than through empire or triumph in war as in days of old); it allows for the inclusion into the club of those less developed countries that are able to get their acts together; and it seeks cooperatively to alleviate troubles in other parts of the world if this can be done at low cost (particularly in lives), and to isolate and contain those troubles that cannot be so alleviated.

In this new world dominated by unthreatened wealth seekers, public opinion will play its role in U.S. foreign policy, and as always it will be an important one. Many have rued this condition, . . . but looked at over time, the general

Note: Most notes have been deleted.

sense of the American public on core issues of foreign policy has often been rather coherent and reasonable—sometimes more so than that shown by the country's elites.

There is a considerable cache of good data about public opinion on foreign policy, some of it sufficiently consistent in design over time to show reliable patterns. Such data do not, of course, announce their own interpretations, but their meaning can be teased out. Based on extensive analysis of this data . . . I offer here ten propositions about American public opinion that bear important implications for the practice of foreign policy in our new era. . . .

Proposition 1

Two facts are central: The public pays little attention to international affairs, and nothing much can be done about it; this, however, does not mean that Americans have become, or are becoming, isolationist.

Even in an age in which international interdependence is supposedly increasing by the minute, Americans principally focus on domestic matters. From time to time their attention can be diverted by major threats, or by explicit, specific, and dramatic dangers to American lives. But once these troubles vanish from the scene, the public returns to domestic concerns with considerable alacrity. So strong is the evidence on this score that it must be accepted as a fact of life that no amount of elite cajoling or uses of the bully pulpit will ever change.

According to the data, over the last sixty years the few events that have notably caused the public to divert its attention from domestic matters include the Second World War, the Korean War, the Vietnam War, and certain Cold War crises before 1963. Also included in this list, fleetingly at least, were the Iran hostage crisis of 1979–81, perhaps embellished by concern over the Soviet invasion of Afghanistan; the apparent prospect in the early to mid-1980s of nuclear war; and the Gulf War. That's about it; at no time since the 1968 Tet Offensive have foreign policy concerns outweighed domestic ones in the public eye—even in the midst of the Gulf War.

Nevertheless, the data suggest that the public has not become newly isolationist—it is about as accepting of involvement in foreign affairs as ever. That the American public has been able to contain its enthusiasm for sending American troops to police such trouble spots as Bosnia and Haiti does not mean that it has turned isolationist. Americans were willing, at least at the outset, to send troops to die in Korea and Vietnam because they subscribed to the view that communism was a genuine and serious threat to the United States that needed to be stopped wherever it was advancing. But polls from the time make clear that they had little interest in risking American lives simply to help out beleaguered South Koreans or South Vietnamese. Moreover, poll questions designed directly to measure isolationism find little change in the wake of the Cold War. In other words, the public does not pay much attention to foreign affairs most of the time, but it seems ready to care about foreign affairs if there is a clear, obvious reason to do so. This trait has been fairly consistent over many years.

Proposition 2

The public undertakes a fairly sensible cost-benefit accounting when evaluating foreign affairs and, not unreasonably, the key to its definition of cost is the high value it places on American lives.

Public opinion analysis generally supports the proposition that the American people will tolerate a substantial loss of American lives if the enemy is seen to be powerful and set on jeopardizing vital American interests. But the notion that Americans should die to police a small, distant, perennially troubled, and unthreatening place has always proved difficult to sell. Nor has it been possible to generate much support for the notion that American lives should be put at risk in order to encourage democracy abroad.

After Pearl Harbor the American public had no difficulty accepting the necessity, and the human costs, of confronting the threats posed by Germany and Japan. And after the war, it came to accept international communism as a similar source of threat and was willing to support military action to combat it. However, as the Cold War's hot wars progressed in Korea and Vietnam, the data show clearly that the public undertook a continuing reevaluation of these premises, and, as it did, misgivings mounted. The data also suggest that these misgivings were primarily a function of cumulating American casualties, not of television coverage and, in the case of Vietnam, definitely not of antiwar protest.

Policy in the Gulf War was subject to a similar calculus. Many Americans bought George Bush's notion that it was worth some American lives—perhaps one or two thousand, far lower than in Korea or Vietnam—to turn back Saddam Hussein's aggression in Kuwait. But it is clear from poll data that support for the effort would have eroded quickly if significant casualties had been suffered.

While the public's concern about American lives often seems nuanced, there are times when it becomes so obsessive, so unreasonable by some standards, that policy may suffer in consequence. In the case of Vietnam, public opinion essentially supported the war until American prisoners-of-war held by Hanoi were returned; after that burden was eased, the weight of growing misgivings overtook any inclination to press on. Although some might question the wisdom of continuing a war costing thousands of lives to gain the return of a few hundred prisoners, it would be difficult to exaggerate the political potency of this issue. In a May 1971 poll, 68 percent agreed that U.S. troops should be withdrawn from Vietnam by the end of the year. However, when asked if they approved of withdrawal "even if it threatened [not *cost*] the lives or safety of United States POWs held by North Vietnam," support for withdrawal plummeted to 11 percent.

The emotional attachment to prisoners-of-war has been a recurring theme in the politics of U.S. military interventions. It was central to the lengthy and acrimonious peace talks in Korea, and outrage at the fate of American POWs on Bataan probably generated as much hatred for the Japanese during the Second World War as the attack on Pearl Harbor. Saddam Hussein's decision to parade captured American pilots on television early in the Gulf War ranks among his many major blunders. The preoccupation with hostages held by Iran during the crisis of 1979–81, and after that the fate of a few abducted Americans in Lebanon—a concern that helped to generate the Iran-Contra scandal—are also cases in point.

On the other hand, Americans seem quite insensitive to casualties suffered by foreigners, including foreign civilians. During the Gulf War Americans displayed little animosity toward the Iraqi people. However, . . . this view did not translate into sympathy for Iraqi casualties. Extensive coverage of civilian deaths in an attack on a Baghdad bomb shelter had no effect on attitudes toward U.S. bombing policy. Similarly, images of the "highway of death", and early postwar reports that 100,000 Iraqi soldiers had died in the war (a figure too high probably by a factor of more than ten), scarcely dampened the enthusiasm of the various "victory" parades and celebrations.

These basic characteristics of American opinion are also illustrated by the public response to the international mission to Somalia in 1992–93. American policy there has been labeled a "failure" because, although tens and probably hundreds of thousands of foreign lives were saved, a few Americans were killed in the process. In essence, when Americans asked themselves how many American lives peace in Somalia was worth, the answer was rather close to zero.

Proposition 3

The public's attitudes on foreign affairs are set much more by the objective content of the issue and by the position of major policymakers (including the political opposition) than by the media.

The media are not so much agenda setters as purveyors and entrepreneurs of tantalizing information and, like any other entrepreneur, they are suscepti-ble to market forces. If they give an issue big play, it may arrest attention for a while, but this is no guarantee the issue will "take." As with any business enterprise, media moguls follow up on those proffered items that stimulate their customers' interest. In that very important sense, the media does not set the agenda, the public does.

Concern about the Ethiopian famine of the mid-1980s, for example, is often taken to have been media-generated since it was only after the problem received prominent play that it entered the public's agenda. However, the media were at first reluctant to cover the issue because they saw African famine as a dog-bites-man story. Then NBC television decided to buck the consensus and do a three-day sequence on it, and this in turn inspired a huge public response, whereupon NBC gave the crisis extensive follow-up coverage while its television and print competitors scrambled to get on the bandwagon. There is a sense, of course, in which it could be said that NBC put the issue on the public's agenda. But the network is constantly doing three-day stories, and this one just happened to catch on, to strike a responsive chord. It seems more accurate, then, to say that NBC put the item on display—alongside a great many others—and that it was the public that found it there, picked it out, and took it home.

Proposition 4

The "CNN effect" is vastly exaggerated. [See also the essay by Warren Stroebel on the CNN effect, which follows later in this part—eds.] It follows from the above that the argument that television pictures set the public's agenda and policy mood—the so-called CNN effect—is hard to credit. This effect is usually taken to mean that televised images can cause intense interest where there might otherwise be none, and that such interest can have important effects on policy. Sometimes this might be the case, but, on balance, the CNN effect is exaggerated, and some interpretations of it seem well off the mark.

Essentially, believers in the CNN effect contend that people are so unimaginative that they react only when they see something visualized. However, Americans were outraged and quickly mobilized over the Pearl Harbor attack months before they saw any pictures of the event. Less obvious but more important, the Vietnam War was not noticeably more unpopular than the Korean War for the period in which the wars produced comparable American casualties, despite the fact that the later war was a "television war", while the earlier one was fought during that medium's infancy.

The conventional wisdom about the CNN effect amounts to a triumph of myth over matter. After all, for years we were deluged by pictures of horrors in Bosnia and, while these pictures may have influenced the opinion of some editorial writers and columnists, there was remarkably little public demand to send American troops over to fix the problem. Nor did poignant and memorable pictures inspire a surging public demand to do much of anything about Rwanda or Haiti. The reason, it would seem from the data, is disarmingly simple: Whatever the pictures showed, the public saw no serious threat to American security in either of these cases that could justify risking American lives. . . .

Proposition 5

Foreign policy has become less important in judging the performance of the president and of presidential contenders.

During the Cold War, foreign policy was often important in presidential elections, but in its wake the general tendency of the American public to ignore foreign policy in national elections has been given free reign. Banking on his Gulf War success and on his opponent's lack of experience in foreign policy, George Bush tried hard to make foreign affairs a central issue in the 1992 campaign, but failed. His ratings for handling the economy plummeted within days of the end of the war as the public quickly refocused its attention on domestic matters. And when candidate Bill Clinton went out of his way to deliver a few serious foreign policy speeches, he found them generating little public or press attention. As suggested by the 1996 campaign, this phenomenon is likely to continue.

Proposition 6

The advantage to a president of a success in a minor foreign policy venture is marginal; the disadvantage to a president of a failure in such a venture is more than marginal, but still far from devastating unless the failure becomes massively expensive.

If George Bush found little lasting electoral advantage in a large dramatic victory like the Gulf War, smaller accomplishments are likely to be even less rewarding in an era of great foreign policy inattention. America's recent venture into Haiti has been a success by most reasonable standards. Yet, while surely a feather in his cap, this venture . . . garnered Bill Clinton little credit—though it probably helped to diffuse his reputation for foreign policy ineptitude as a potential Republican campaign issue [in 1996]. Something similar could be said for his successes—possibly of historical importance—on the North American Free Trade Agreement and on the General Agreement on Tariffs and Trade.

Although messing up marginal ventures can be politically damaging by contrast, particularly if seen to fall within a pattern of poor performance, the costs need not be high. This stems from the fact that the public has shown a willingness to abandon an overextended or untenable position after American lives have been lost: The deaths of eighteen U.S. soldiers in Somalia in 1993, for example, led to outraged demands for withdrawal, not for calls to revenge the humiliation.

This episode, as well as the withdrawal from Lebanon after a truck bomb killed 241 U.S. Marines in 1983, suggests that when peacekeeping leads to unacceptable deaths, peacekeepers can be readily removed with little concern for saving face. If a venture is seen to be of little importance in terms of serious American interests, a president can, precisely because of that, cut and run without fear of inordinate electoral costs—though it will hardly be something to brag about. U.S. military interventions, then, need not become "quagmires."

Proposition 7

If they are not being killed, American troops can remain in peacekeeping ventures virtually indefinitely with little public criticism; it is not important to have an "exit strategy", a "closed-end commitment", or "a time-certain for withdrawal" except for the purpose of selling an intervention in the first place.

Although there is an overwhelming political demand that casualties be extremely low in ventures deemed of minor importance, there seems to be little problem with keeping occupying forces in place as long as they are not being killed. After the deadly Somalia firefight, the Americans stayed on for several months and, since there were no further casualties, little attention was paid or concern voiced. Similarly, although there was scant public or political support for sending U.S. troops to Haiti, there has been almost no protest about keeping them there since none have been killed. And Americans have tolerated—indeed, hardly noticed—the stationing of hundreds of thousands of U.S. troops in Europe, Japan, and South Korea for decades on end. If they are not being killed, it scarcely matters whether the troops are in Macedonia or in Kansas.

On the other hand, if American troops start to take casualties while on peacekeeping missions, there will be demands to get them out quickly, whatever "date-certain" for withdrawal had been previously arranged. Thus, despite calls for knowing in advance what the endgame will look like, the only real "exit strategy" required is the tactical flexibility to yank the troops abruptly from the scene if things go awry.

Proposition 8

A venture deemed of small importance is best sold not with cosmic internationalist hype, but rather as international social work that can be shrugged off if it goes wrong.

Most of the knotty and dramatic international problems that occupy the headlines are of remarkably little concern to the United States if one applies commonly accepted standards of what constitutes the national interest—and the public seems to be applying exactly those standards. Many problems are, in fact, mainly humanitarian in nature, exercises in what Michael Mandelbaum has called international "social work."[1]

But the notion of the United States doing international social work is not necessarily a non-starter. There is, after all, adequate support for domestic social work. International social work might best be sold in the same way as the domestic variety—as a good faith effort that can be abandoned if the client proves untreatable, rather than wrapped in the false guise of strategic interest. By contrast, in 1995 President Clinton argued that, "If war reignites in Bosnia, it could spark a much wider conflagration. In 1914, a gunshot in Sarajevo launched the first of two world wars"—a historical parallel that was wildly overdrawn, as numerous commentators promptly pointed out. Despite Clinton's claim that a new war in Bosnia "could spread like a cancer throughout the region", the "conflagration" in Bosnia seems, if anything, to have been successfully contained.

In principle, grandiloquent rhetoric can restrict later policy flexibility: If the fate of Europe really does hinge on tiny Bosnia (Clinton: "Europe will not come together with a brutal conflict raging at its heart"), failure there would be disaster. Fortunately, however, the public often seems more sensible on such matters than its leaders. When he sent the Marines to help police Lebanon, Ronald Reagan declared that "in an age of nuclear challenge and economic interdependence, such conflicts are a threat to all the people of the world, not just to the Middle East itself." Despite such an overblown sales pitch, however, the public had no difficulty accepting Reagan's later decision to have the Marines "re-deployed to the sea" after 241 of them were killed by a truck bomb.

The American people clearly do not spend a lot of time musing over public policy issues, particularly international ones. But they *are* grown-ups and, generally, they react as such. Policymakers might do well occasionally to notice this elemental and important fact.

Proposition 9

A danger in peacekeeping missions is that Americans might be taken hostage, something that can suddenly and disproportionately magnify the perceived stakes.

Because of the overriding importance Americans place on American lives, policy in low-valued ventures remains vulnerable to hostage-taking. As noted, peacekeeping missions need not become quagmires because the president can still abruptly withdraw troops from an overextended position with little long-lasting political cost. However, this flexibility can be dramatically compromised if American troops are taken hostage.

This is illustrated by some evidence from the Somalia episode. In the debacle of October 1993, a Somali group captured one American soldier. Polls clearly demonstrated that the public was determined that U.S. forces remain until the prisoner was recovered and only then to withdraw. Some opposition to placing U.S. soldiers on the Golan Heights between Israel and Syria has rested in part upon fear that U.S. personnel might be taken hostage by Syrian-supported Shi'a fundamentalists—and perhaps killed as well, as was the fate of Lt. Col. William Higgins in 1989. While such fears may be exaggerated, and sometimes pressed into political service for ulterior reasons, the concern is by no means baseless.

Proposition 10

Nuclear weapons in the hands of rogue states and international terrorism remain potentially attention-arresting concerns.

In an era free of compelling threats, few concerns can turn the public's attention to foreign affairs. However, polls show that from time to time nuclear weapons do seem to retain some of their legendary attention-arresting aura, and the same may hold for biological and chemical weapons.

While it is not entirely clear what a country like North Korea, Iran, or Iraq would actually do with a nuclear weapon or two—confronted as they are by countries that have thousands of them—alarm over such a possibility can rise to notable levels. In 1994, 82 percent of the public (up from 58 percent four years earlier) identified "preventing the spread of nuclear weapons" as a very important foreign policy goal—putting it in third place in the poll's sixteen-item list. . . . The public's fear of international terrorism is also quite robust. On average, international terrorism kills fewer Americans each year than lightning, or colliding with a deer. But though terrorism is rather unimportant in that literal sense, it generates fear and concern far out of proportion to its objective significance; it was almost as oft-cited a "critical threat" as nuclear proliferation in the 1994 poll.

In the end, it seems, misanthropes and curmudgeons are the only truly happy people: no matter how much things improve, there will always be something to complain about and to worry over. When one problem is solved, another is quickly promoted to take its place. Thus, now that life expectancy has increased to a level that would have tested the credulity of our ancestors a century ago, we, their progeny, worry about the huge budget deficit substantially caused by the fact that people now live so long. Most Americans believe that there has been an increase over the last twenty years in air pollution and in the number of elderly living in poverty, when the reverse is decidedly the case. "Status quo", as Ronald Reagan reportedly liked to put it, "is Latin for 'the mess we're in'", and there is, reliably, always some mess somewhere to be in.

This general phenomenon carries over to international affairs as well. When a peace mission helps peoples in the former Yugoslavia to stop killing each other, pundits are quick to find fault because it is unable to entice them to love each other as well. Thus there is a school of thought that contends that the post-Cold War era is just as dangerous as the one we have left behind, and it counsels keeping commitments and defense spending high, and tolerance for the mischief of others low. So, even in a state of considerable peace the catastrophe quota will always remain comfortably full. Although the chances of a global thermonuclear war—or indeed of any war among major developed countries—have diminished to the point where remarkably few even remember the terror it once inspired, one can concentrate on more vaporous enemies like insecurity, uncertainty, instability, and what one European foreign minister, the late Johan Jørgen Holst of Norway, darkly labeled "unspecified risks and dangers." Or one can declare our new era to be profoundly, even dangerously, "complex" by conveniently forgetting the difficult and painful choices of the Cold War. . . .

In any event, it is clear that alarums about uncertainty and complexity from academics and pensive foreign diplomats will not cure the attention deficit disorder that, as usual, characterizes the American public's approach to international affairs. In an era free of compelling threats, the public is likely to continue happily to focus its ennui and its *Weltschmerz* on parochial matters, not foreign ones—at least until there is good reason for them to do otherwise. Given the record of its generally good sense, that is perhaps not such a tragedy.

Note

1. Michael Mandelbaum, "Foreign Policy as Social Work", *Foreign Affairs* (January/February 1996).

5

The Politics of Military Base Closures

Genevieve Anton and Jeff Thomas

For more than 200 years, Congress has created military bases. For more than 200 years, military considerations have helped determine where to put them. And for more than 200 years, the desire for money that a base brings—and the politics that springs from it—have done just as much to secure a place in the U.S. military's vast empire.

An American Tradition

Military bases have long shaped America. Their names have become history: Bunker Hill, Fort Sumter, Pearl Harbor. Over two centuries, they and hundreds of other posts with less familiar names—Hope and Disappointment, Ranger and Tonto, Ord and Hitchepuckesassa—have made the United States the most heavily fortified nation on Earth. Along the way, they have also pumped life into hundreds of cities, big and small. Sleepy hollows—such as Minot, North Dakota; Mountain Home, Idaho; Junction City, Kansas; and Colorado Springs—that might have dozed through the twentieth century instead of thrived on military jobs and payroll.

None wants to step off the gravy train. Certainly no member of Congress wants to anger voters by throwing thousands of rent-paying, grocery-buying neighbors out of work. Representative Don Dellums (Democrat from California), an opponent of new weapons systems, was extremely upset when the naval bases in his Bay Area district were targeted for closure during the . . . round of [military base] cuts in 1993. Republican Representative Joel Hefley of Colorado Springs, Colorado, a self-proclaimed porkbuster, [pulled] every string he [could] to save Fort Carson in 1995.

The fact is, however, that closing military bases is part of the tradition. The legendary Atlantic forts—Monroe, McHenry, Sumter—ultimately fell to obsolescence. Most frontier Army encampments returned to the prairie. Bases were being closed until the eve of World War II, and once it ended, unfinished

61

barracks were abandoned. Bases again closed by the hundreds after wars in Korea and Vietnam.

Now, this part of the tradition is in full swing again, sparked by the need to cut the federal budget deficit and sustained by the end of the Cold War. As the military gets leaner, faster, and more nimble to land a quick punch to any spot on the globe, it wants to spend less on bases and more on training troops and operating planes, ships, and tanks. Yet the stakes have never been higher for military towns. By the mid-1980s, domestic bases employed more than 1.4 million troops and nearly 1 million civilians, pumping $60 billion a year into cities nationwide. And during an age when a college degree no longer guarantees a stable job, a military base is a prized neighborhood employer—something worth fighting for.

Still the Rule: Location, Location

No one knows precisely where Jean Ribaut and his group of French explorers dropped anchor and waded ashore in May 1562. On an island bordering what they called the New World, they cut some trees and dug some earth to erect the first colonial fortification. They named it Charles Fort, after their king. But its walls could not protect the colonists from hunger, and it was soon abandoned. Today, on the same island, raw recruits from throughout the eastern United States get their first gritty taste of military life at the Parris Island Marine Corps Recruit Depot in South Carolina.

As the number of U.S. military bases has grown and shrunk over the past two centuries, one fact has remained constant: A strategic location is the foremost consideration in the decision of where to put a base. Some of those decisions, made long ago, are felt today. The Army cultivates officers at the spot where rebellious colonists erected a fort to deny British control of the Hudson River Valley, a place called West Point. Norfolk, Virginia, gateway to vital Chesapeake Bay, has had a Navy base as long as there has been a Navy. The Army's First Infantry Division lives and trains at Fort Riley, Kansas, built [more than 140] years ago to help secure the frontier. Since the early days of aviation, the military has flown airplanes at San Diego's North Island, where the weather is almost always perfect for flying. Good ground, deep ports, clear skies—they are some of the reasons why bases are located where they are.

But there are other reasons why we have so many of them:

- There is fear: Forts were built after the War of 1812, as Washington smoldered and Congress realized its pitiful coastal defenses needed more muscle.
- There is growth: From a porous line of Army posts strung from Minnesota to Texas, new forts extended like fingers along the Oregon and Santa Fe trails in the 1840s and 1850s.

- There is trade: By the turn of the century, American interests stretched across the Pacific. Yankee traders sought elbow room among the established European powers. Bases in Hawaii and places around the globe sprouted.
- And, of course, there is war: In 1917 the United States had 200,000 men in uniform. Eighteen months into World War I, it had 2.6 million. The war in Europe prompted the Army to build thirty-two training camps almost overnight. Airplanes, an Army experiment confined to six tiny fields before the war, buzzed over forty-four training fields by 1918. The Navy opened twenty-five naval air stations.

The United States proved it could fire up an awesome war machine. But an important fact has been lost amid all the hand wringing over . . . recent . . . cuts: The United States has, for most of its history, been a nation that would rather close bases than open them.

Having won its independence, the new United States gave Henry Knox, the first secretary of war, only 718 soldiers to defend the vast nation. Having fought to a draw with Britain on home ground, the United States built sturdier coastal forts—but then cut the Army in half as nationalistic fervor waned and the West beckoned. Having closed the frontier, the Army closed its scattered posts and consolidated troops at remaining locations. And after World War I the United States cut the Army manpower three times, to nearly prewar levels. Plans to resume a prewar expansion of the Navy ran aground. By 1939 only a dozen Army airfields remained. The words of George Washington—to assure peace, prepare for war—still had not sunk in completely.

That changed with World War II. The attack on Pearl Harbor led the United States to decide, for the first time, that it needed a huge, permanent military—in wartime and even in peace. The Army created nearly twice as many training camps as it did during World War I. . . . The number of Army Air Force installations grew to nearly 1,500, ranging from searchlight stations to air bases to rented hotels. Naval bases opened in Alaska, Washington, and California.

The United States came out of the war a superpower. Just a half-million strong before World War II, the U.S. armed forces kept about 1.5 million soldiers, sailors, and airmen after the war. They had to live and work somewhere. But in the nuclear age, it did not matter as much where. "You're vulnerable no matter where you are," said retired Admiral Eugene Carroll, former commander of U.S. forces in Europe and the Middle East. So, by 1960 mammoth B-52 bombers were on constant alert in remote, inland places such as Grand Forks, North Dakota, and Gwynn, Michigan—not only distant targets, but well-placed for an over-the-pole trek into Soviet territory. At the height of the Cold War, the Strategic Air Command was the largest segment of the Air Force, operating forty-six domestic bases from Maine to Guam. By the time the BRAC (Defense Base Closure and Realignment) Commission [was] finished [in 1995], only fourteen of those installations [would] remain.

Overall, the Air Force shed eleven of twenty-four wings it had in 1990. The Army went from eighteen divisions to ten; the Navy from 546 combat ships to 346. Most of the remaining forces will be stationed in the United States, ready to move quickly to hot spots around the world. Does that mean troops and planes and tanks will move toward the coasts? Or will they remain at large inland bases, where there is plenty of room to practice? . . . With the BRAC Commission ordered to get rid of some otherwise perfectly good bases in the name of budget cutting, it [found] itself relying on old-fashioned qualities when separating the winners from the losers. After 432 years, we are back to what French explorer Jean Ribaut was looking for when he hit the South Carolina coast: good ground, clear skies, and deep ports.

Military Bases and Politics Travel Hand-in-Hand

The location of military bases has always had as much to do with money as with strategy. The first colonial forts protected merchant ships. Later, they were never far from fur-trading posts. The young U.S. Navy charted the seas, chased pirates, escorted merchant ships, and, with guns very visible, opened trade with Japan. Soldiers cleared the way for commerce. President Jefferson dispatched former officers Lewis and Clark to chart the Northwest, and later, Lieutenant John Fremont to the Rocky Mountains. Soldiers dug canals, cleared roads, protected railroad crews, and built sawmills and blacksmith shops outside their encampments.

Where there was money, politics was close behind. After the Navy's birth in 1794, Secretary of War Knox thought it "just and wise to proportion . . . benefits as nearly as may be to those places of states which pay the greatest amount to its support." Knox established Navy yards in six cities that had supported the Naval Act to build the nation's first six warships. The yard at Philadelphia had long finished its work when Congress ordered new ships with "not less than 74 guns" each. It was a blank check, and the Navy wrote Philadelphia a whopper. For 15 years, Congress winked as the Navy did nothing at the yard but build the world's most bloated gunship—one that barely sailed and was never used.

If pork-barrel excesses continue to cause occasional embarrassment, they also reveal the huge appetite communities have for military installations. And the military has known it for a long time. When the Army looked for a place to put its first major airplane base in 1915, it merely put the word out to local chambers of commerce and waited for the offers to roll in. Seizing the opportunity, several Hampton, Virginia, businessmen locked up thousands of acres and promised to provide a railroad and water. Hampton has prospered ever since. Today, Langley Air Force Base employs more than 11,000 people and pumps an annual payroll of $358 million.

Land for jobs has long been the terms of the deal, the essential transaction of a military base. Colorado Springs, its tourist economy mired in the Great Depression, courted the Army in 1941 for one purpose only: economic salvation. The city had land. The Army had jobs. The negotiations began. The city bought the 5,533-acre Cheyenne Valley Ranch and offered it, along with gas, water, and electricity hookups, to the Army. The Colorado congressional delegation and the assistant secretary of the interior—a Coloradan—twisted arms in Washington. Charles Tutt hosted Army brass at his Broadmoor hotel. The golf was superb, the rare, pre-Prohibition liquor sublime. The Army did not merely appreciate the gestures. The Army expected them. As Fort Carson officials later wrote in a base history: "An Army post has to be wanted— wanted so much that the requesting community must provide countless reasons why it should be built at its doorstep rather than elsewhere. In addition, that community has to guarantee not only the soil on which future soldiers will live and train, but also a lifetime of water, utilities, and a multitude of other necessities."

The Army's final inspection of Colorado Springs was barely finished before the attack on Pearl Harbor sent the United States into World War II. Suddenly more desperate than selective, the Army in one stroke approved the new camps in Colorado Springs and 22 other cities.

After the war Camp Carson's population dropped sharply and bounced up and down with the Army's constant reorganizations until 1970, when the Fourth Infantry Division arrived. Uncertainty was the price of peace. "During wartime, Congress merely asks the services how much they need, then turns them loose," said Paolo Coletta, a retired Naval Academy historian. "When the war's over and it's time to retrench, that's when the problems start." That is when it helps to have friends like Mendel Rivers.

During Rivers's tenure from 1941–1970 representing Charleston, South Carolina, on the House Armed Services Committee, that city's naval yard became a major Atlantic Fleet base and acquired squadrons of destroyers and nuclear submarines. The base added submarine training and maintenance centers, a hospital, supply and weapons depots, and a mine warfare center. An Army depot, Air Force base, Marine air station, Marine recruiting depot, Coast Guard station and veterans' hospital opened. Never was a campaign slogan truer than "Rivers Delivers." "You put anything else down there in your district, Mendel, it's gonna sink," a colleague once told him.

And that was before Rivers became committee chairman. After he did, Charleston's share of the annual Navy construction budget more than doubled. In just two of Rivers' six years as armed services chairman, the base received as much construction money as it had during the ten years before he took control of the committee. "What my people want is prosperity," Rivers said in 1969. "They want jobs. Money. And that's what I've brought them."

Though perhaps more prolific than most, Rivers was just part of a long tradition of congressional interference when it comes to the placement of military bases. Representative Felix Hebert of New Orleans persuaded President Kennedy to twist the arm of Defense Secretary Robert McNamara to preserve the Eighth Naval District headquarters in his city. Senator Henry Jackson of Washington voted in 1972 to accelerated production of the new Trident submarine. In 1973 the Navy announced that the Trident would be based at Bangor, Washington. The Army tried repeatedly to close frontier relic Fort D.A. Russell in Cheyenne, Wyoming. But the chairman of the Senate Military Affairs Committee happened to be Francis E. Warren of Wyoming. Today his name adorns the base.

There is a reason why politicians for so long were so willing to throw their weight around: In the decades after World War II their constituents had become deeply dependent on these bases. "The sheer growth of the military budget injected billions of dollars into local economies in a way that had never been done before," said economist Greg Bischak, executive director of the National Commission for Economic Conversion, which advocates putting military dollars toward other uses. The Pentagon, aided by a Congress eager to earn points by spreading the wealth, ultimately opened installations in all fifty states, a monstrous federal jobs program that voters could support.

At first, military towns considered the money a bonus. But it became a necessity when the postwar economic boom of the 1950s and 1960s faded. "There was more pressure at that point to not remove any of the existing economic foundations from communities," said Robert Pollin, an economist at the University of California at Riverside, where base closures . . . pushed unemployment to about 10 percent.

Not that the Pentagon did not try. The Kennedy administration closed bases, and Congress complained. The Johnson administration closed bases, and Congress demanded—but did not get—a say-so in choosing the doomed. The Carter administration tried to close bases, and Congress finally just shut down the process, requiring time-consuming studies that could be challenged in court. For the next decade, not a single military base closed.

It would take a congressional rookie from Texas, Dick Armey, and his clever invention of the BRAC Commission to finally break the deadlock in 1989. . . . The independent panel [nominated] bases for closure, and Congress and the president [were required to] vote yes or no on the whole list. The system . . . defanged a Congress that historically had bared its teeth when bases were threatened.

Still, the smell of money and politics [remained] in the air. Representative Dellums, who favored cutting funding for the B-2 bomber and the Strategic Defense Initiative, [claimed] that the decision to close five naval installations in his district was "politically driven." Charleston [grumbled] that the Portsmouth Naval Shipyard between New Hampshire and Maine would have been chosen for closure if George Mitchell of Maine did not happen to be the majority leader of the Senate. A newspaper in Florida, where voters supported George Bush in 1992, [observed] that the state [was] losing the Orlando Naval Training Center while Georgia and Louisiana, which voted for Bill Clinton, [would] gain military jobs under the 1993 round of base realignments. . . .

But . . . the charges of politics may just be sour grapes. . . . With the job of closing bases seemingly out of the hands of politicians [under the BRAC Commission system], hundreds of communities across the country [found] themselves threatened. Threatened, too, [was] the tradition that, for more than two centuries, [had] protected so many.

An Idea Gains Momentum

. . . To lawmakers, military bases were not just a collection of pork barrels— they were the whole, sloppy pig farm. They were expected to protect local bases and the jobs they provided—or risk the wrath of voters. Congress had thrown up so many roadblocks over the years it was impossible to shut down any major base, much less dozens of them.

However, [in 1988], [Representative Dick] Armey's crazy base closure idea [became] law—one that continues to reshape not only the U.S. military, but hundreds of local economies. The nation . . . targeted 250 bases for closure over . . . six years, after a decade of not closing a single one. Meanwhile, the Defense Base Closure and Realignment Commission [went] from a few volunteers stuffed in a tiny office to a staff that [swelled] up to 100 people filling the fourteenth floor of a building near the Pentagon. "It is absolutely the most efficient piece of legislation that the United States Congress has ever passed," said base-closure consultant John Allen. "We'll never see anything like it again." Indeed, an array of political agendas needed to come together before politics could be taken out of the messy job of closing bases.

There was an aggressive new congressman who saw closing bases as a way to make his mark on Capitol Hill. There was pressure on Congress to balance the budget. There was the Reagan administration's desire to shift military spending from bases to high-tech projects such as the Strategic Defense Initiative. And there was the Pentagon's long-simmering displeasure with lawmakers who twisted arms to keep hundreds of obsolete installations open. By the mid-1980s the military had some 3,800 facilities in the United States, including 480 major installations that covered an area the size of Virginia. The cost to keep it all running: $20 billion a year—a fourth of which, the Pentagon said, contributed little or nothing to national defense.

Then, suddenly, base closure became the story of the moment. *The New York Times,* which mentioned base closure just once in 1986, ran ten editorials pushing it in 1988. It was as if people had just discovered that Fort Douglas, Utah, built to patrol stage coach routes, was now nothing more than a collection of historic buildings trapped in the middle of the University of Utah's campus. Or that no military ship had docked for decades at the Naval Station Puget Sound in Washington state. Or that the main attribute of Fort Sheridan outside Chicago was its sprawling golf course, a favorite among military retirees.

Those bases were the first to go. But it wouldn't stop there. Armey's Little Bill That Could had cracked open a door that the end of the Cold War would fling wide open.

The Pentagon and Capitol Hill Wrestle for Control

In the days when the Pentagon called the shots, closing bases was easy. Defense Secretary Robert McNamara took on the biggest military housecleaning in history in the early 1960s, shuffling bases and closing more than sixty major installations—without consulting Congress. Near the end of the Vietnam War, hundreds more bases were closed. Congress howled. The Pentagon shrugged. Within a few years, though, lawmakers would wrest control of base closure from the generals in typical congressional fashion: by wrapping the whole process in a huge wad of red tape. After 1977 the Pentagon was required to, among other things, conduct lengthy and litigious environmental impact studies before closing a base. It worked. No base was closed for a dozen years. . . .

To break a decade of the gridlock, two things were needed: Cut the red tape and shield lawmakers from the political pain that the economic pain of closing bases would bring. Armey's idea was the Defense Base Closure and Realignment Commission. It would do the work that Congress seemed incapable of doing. It would provide the president, and then Congress, with a list of bases to be closed. Lawmakers would vote on it, up or down. No picking, no choosing. No heavy thinking. No fear. New sweat.

The Commission's First Hit List

. . . BRAC commissioners waited until after the 1988 elections to visit some forty bases, trying to calm local fears by calling them fact-finding trips. The panel's spokesman—who spent twelve to fourteen hours a day answering panicked calls—typed a one-paragraph response for each commissioner saying a visit did not mean the base was at risk. But everyone knew the truth. A congressman from Oklahoma toted bags stuffed with more than 13,000 letters to the BRAC Commission's office, begging that his local base be spared. A senator from Virginia swept through four bases in his state to check the commission's homework.

The week after Christmas, the BRAC Commission dropped its first bombshell: A recommendation that eighty-six installations be shut down. There were few surprises. Yet, the list provoked banner headlines and protests. Some lawmakers criticized the commission, saying its research was shoddy and savings projections were inflated. However, outside of the two dozen congressional districts affected, there was not much howling—only relief. Many lawmakers who had dodged the BRAC Commission's bullet thought that base closure had come, and now would go. They were wrong.

The End of the Cold War Gives Renewed Life to BRAC

True, the BRAC Commission was never designed to survive. Its job was to save money, not reshape America's military. But then again, when it was created in 1988, the Berlin Wall was standing, Boris Yeltsin was a little-known politician, and the United States was pumping $300 billion a year into its arsenal. The end of the Cold War challenged the Department of Defense as much as the Soviet Union ever did. Generals suddenly found themselves pouring over spreadsheets instead of maps. Within a few years, the military budget was being slashed 40 percent, the number of troops by a third. Around the Pentagon, tough choices became as common as short haircuts. . . . So the Pentagon and Congress agreed to resurrect the BRAC Commission, giving it five years to eliminate the waste that had built up in America's far-flung galaxy of fortresses. . . .

In 1988 no one knew how the BRAC Commission made its decisions. [After BRAC was resurrected], a base's military value . . . , by law, [had] to be given the greatest weight, and all BRAC Commission meetings and documents [had to be made] public. "We bend over backwards to make sure everybody knows where we are and how to reach us," said Jim Courter, the panel's chairman. To some, however, the BRAC Commission's broad reach [was] still troubling. After shutting down 164 more bases in 1991 and 1993—and with the biggest, bloodiest round [yet to come] in 1995 . . .—a backlash . . . emerged. Lawmakers said [the 1995] round would be too painful. That the nation was still suffering from the last recession and could not handle it. That there was not yet proof that closing bases [saved] money. . . . The Clinton administration and key lawmakers pushed to delay any more closings until after the 1996 election. They failed. . . .

Process and Politics

Not so long ago . . . military bases were the currency spread far and wide by the Pentagon to reward its friends in Congress. The common wisdom among voters is that a congressional powerhouse can save any base, as it [had] in the past. But most observers say the BRAC process [was] surprisingly free and often contemptuous of congressional meddling. The BRAC Commission . . . shut down bases in half of the nation's 50 states, casting its net wide enough to snare even the most powerful of political kingfish. The list of losers is illustrative: Speaker of the House, Senate majority leader, ranking members of both armed services committees. Representative Ron Dellums of California, Democratic chairman of the House Armed Services Committee, watched helplessly in 1993 as the naval installations in his district were sunk, taking 10,000 jobs down with them. . . .

If any community [could] brag it did everything right, [it was] Charleston, South Carolina. To preserve its naval installations in 1993, the city spent $1 million. It hired lawyers, public relations specialists, and a former Navy captain turned lobbyist. In eighteen days, a group called "In Defense of Charleston" rounded up 140,000 signatures on petitions. The operation flooded the BRAC Commission with studies, and it choreographed a hard-hitting presentation that one commissioner called "the best I've ever seen." South Carolina's influential congressional delegation went to work, too. Senator Strom Thurmond used his seniority to take over as ranking Republican on the Senate Armed Services Committee. The state's other senator, Democrat Ernest Hollings, a key member of the Appropriations Committee, reportedly took two BRAC commissioners out for tennis while they were in Charleston for a public hearing.

But all the intense lobbying did not help the city's bases. Each BRAC commissioner gave a long, heartfelt apology to the community. They acknowledged that Charleston had some fine naval facilities—then voted to close them, wiping away a third of the region's payroll. "It was simply redundant," commissioner Bob Stuart [said]. "We couldn't find another solution."

The Charleston effort was so impressive that Haidee Clark Stith of the South Carolina Department of Commerce was invited to share the lessons she learned at . . . [a] base-closure conference in Washington. . . . One perspiring person in the crowd asked her the obvious question: If Charleston did such a good job at trying to dodge the heat of the BRAC process, why did it get burned? "You can do everything right, and still end up with your base being closed," Stith [said]. "The reality is there are just too many bases, and even some good ones are going to go down."

The BRAC Commission director [put] it more bluntly. "If we can close Charleston . . . there ain't nothing sacred anywhere." That may be hard to swallow for communities still dependent on the military of the past—the one with the fat checkbook that never ran dry.

6

The New China Lobby

Richard Bernstein and Ross H. Munro

All countries . . . strive to influence public opinion and policy making in the United States. Still, there are four special characteristics to Chinese lobbying and public relations campaigning in the United States that, taken together, make it different from these efforts by other countries.

One of them, the most important, is that China is in so many ways an adversary, a dictatorship, an emerging superpower whose interests are at odds with those of the United States. Second is the ferocity of China's efforts to influence American actions, the tone of virulent aggrievement with which it greets disagreement, and the breadth of its activities in the United States, which include not just propaganda, threats, and bluster, along with intense private lobbying, but also efforts to buy or steal technology and transfer it to China. . . . Third, an extremely influential group of American former high officials have come to dominate the public debate about China even as they profit from the policies that they advocate. And finally, China has used to great effect the threat of economic warfare to enlist behind it one of the broadest business efforts to influence national policy in all of American history.

In the background of most of these efforts is the lure of profit and the concomitant threat to deny profit if China does not have its way. When Prime Minister Li Peng punished Boeing and bought $1.5 billion worth of Airbus Industrie Airplanes in 1996, he couldn't have been more explicit as to the reason. He praised European leaders because "they do not attach political strings to cooperation with China, unlike the Americans who arbitrarily resort to the threat of sanctions or the use of sanctions." The irony is that China itself has effectively used sanctions, or overt promises of economic benefits or threats of economic punishment, as means of exerting pressure on the American government, even as it issues dire warnings against the United

Note: Notes have been deleted.

71

States's doing the same thing, warnings that are repeated in vociferous tones by the businessmen who stand to suffer from Chinese sanctions. The members of what has come to be a powerful new China lobby never acknowledge that it is precisely the linking of economics and politics, the granting and the withholding of profits, that has made China's policy toward the United States so remarkably effective.

With the important exception of strong congressional support for defending Taiwan against Chinese military intimidation—arms sales have continued despite strong Chinese protests—China's multifarious lobbying activities have been very successful. China in particular has managed to force Washington to back down on practically every threat to take action against China for some violation of international norms. Some might cite another exception, having to do with American willingness to impose sanctions on China for the pirating of music CDs, movie videos, and computer software. But, in fact, despite renewed Chinese promises to crack down in this matter, the signs [are] that the billion-dollar pirating industry, well protected by powerful figures in the provinces and in the army, [continues] to thrive.

In any case, on all of the various questions regarding human rights, . . . on poison gas shipments to Iran, on missile sales to Syria and Pakistan, on nuclear help to Iran and Pakistan, and on trade practices that . . . are aimed at maximizing technology transfers to China and the trade deficit in its favor, the United States has threatened and blustered but in the end taken very little real action. There are many reasons for this, but one of the most important is the effectiveness of what could be called the New China Lobby, a multifaceted, loosely correlated network actively encouraged and manipulated by China mainly by promising or withholding money. . . .

The New China Lobby, though based largely on money, is not based only on money. It also has to do with access, which in certain circles leads to the deals that translate into money.

The Chinese for decades have had a word for this: *guan-xi* (pronounced GWAN-she), which means "relationship" or "connection." If somebody has *quan-xi,* it means that he has an advantage. Among the Chinese themselves, this might be because he has a friend or a relative in the right place—the party secretary of the best local school or the head of the neighborhood committee who assigns available apartments or the assistant to the provincial government who controls licenses to create joint foreign-Chinese companies with the right to send hard currency abroad. If you are a foreigner, your *guan-xi* might involve your friendship with Rong Yiren, who is the chairman of the China International Trust and Investment Corporation (CITIC), China's state-run merchant bank, or with Jiang Zemin himself.

A related expression, commonly used in China since the country was taken over by a Communist bureaucracy (but with its roots in imperial China), is *zou-hou-men,* literally "go the back door." The phrase expresses the realistically cynical view that qualifications, skill, and the lower price mean less in China than the ability to skirt the official rules and to slip into the Palace of Power via the rear entrance.

Foreigners able to carry out special activities in China have long benefited when they have had *guan-xi.* In the 1950s and 1960s, for example, foreign access to China was reserved almost exclusively for a small group of foreign writers and journalists who were designated "friends of China"—translation: propagandists for the Communist revolution. . . . The "friends of China" wrote and spoke about China the way Chinese officials wanted to be written and spoken about. They did this because they actually believed what they said or, if a more cynical interpretation of this behavior is correct, because they needed to protect their *guan-xi,* their access to Beijing's bureaucratic pinnacle. Whatever the case, China itself skillfully created an exclusive club of supporters, rewarding them with visas, with travel permits, with meetings inside Zhongnanhai, the walled annex to the old Forbidden City, where Mao and the other revolutionary progenitors lived and worked. When some specially invited guest betrayed the leadership's hospitality, that person would be denounced as a villain and a scoundrel and held up as an example for others. . . .

American scholars and writers who have publicly criticized the Chinese leadership for human rights violations have been denied visas to visit the country or made to enlist the support of famous Americans in a virtual publicity campaign before the visa is granted. . . . There is a contingent of a half dozen or so senior scholars of China whose careers have flourished, in part because of their skills as analysts but also in part because they have been granted access at a high level in China. They consult informally at the White House, escort American corporate or political bigwigs on trips to China, and write scholarly analyses of Chinese politics. These academic specialists bear only a glancing similarity to the likes of Han Suyin or Edgar Snow, who were straightforward apologists for the Chinese regime at a time when it was most dictatorial and brutal. But given the nature of the Chinese government, today's academic experts face the prospect that they will be cut off if they offend the Chinese on certain subjects. It would be unfair to say that Beijing requires flattery from American scholars in exchange for access. China's leaders are more sophisticated than that. The political scientists who maintain excellent contacts with Chinese officialdom also learn how China's leaders think about issues, and that is valuable knowledge. They write useful articles on Chinese politics. But on certain subjects, like the reputation of Chairman Mao or the questions of human rights, China's military intimidation of Taiwan, and Chinese control over Tibet, it is best either to flatter or to remain silent. Beijing pays close attention. Those who play by China's rules continue to meet with vice premiers in Beijing's Great Hall of the People. Those who don't, don't.

That general rule applies more strictly to the world of business than to any other, and here the Chinese have been masterful in using access to influence

American policy. Among the remarkable aspects of this Chinese success is the way in which a politics of accommodation has been urged on the public and the government by the very people most likely to profit from accommodation.

It works like this: Former government officials—the most conspicuous of whom in this regard are former secretaries of state Henry Kissinger and Alexander M. Haig Jr. but include others like former deputy secretary of state Lawrence Eagleburger and former national security adviser Brent Scowcroft—become counselors to companies doing business in China. The job of a counselor is to give advice. But in China, where business enterprise and the licenses needed to do business are controlled by a self-interested and self-perpetuating political elite, a crucial role of outside advisers is to make contacts with that elite.

"If a consultant wants to get a competitive contract for his client—say, the chairman of a major American corporation—part of the deal is that the consultant will speak out for China or that he will deliver congressional or media delegations to China," said James Lilley, a former American ambassador to Beijing. The consultant knows the Chinese leaders; the American company gets a meeting with the relevant ones; the consultant gets paid by the corporation, and in order to solidify his all-important access to Chinese power brokers, he makes public statements supporting the policies that Beijing favors. "It's never explicitly stated in the contract," Lilley said, "but everyone understands the deal."

Within a couple of days of the Tiananmen massacre in 1989, Kissinger issued a series of statements and wrote op-ed articles that put him squarely into the "friend of China" tradition. "I wouldn't do any sanctions," Kissinger told Peter Jennings of ABC, speaking at a time when Congress was calling for sanctions, and the Bush administration was, to a limited extent, going along with that demand. The very day after the massacre Kissinger's syndicated column referred to Deng Xiaoping as "one of the great reformers in Chinese history" and a man "who chose a more humane and less chaotic course" for China. In fact, Kissinger's statement was not wrong, though it did seem a bit sycophantish when the blood was not yet dry on the paving stones of Tiananmen Square. More to the point, Kissinger's advice to President Bush was to avoid taking any measures against China that would jeopardize "vital American security interests." In another syndicated column, Kissinger criticized Congress for approving anti-Chinese sanctions that went beyond those recommended by President Bush. In that column also, he made this extraordinary statement: "No government in the world would have tolerated having the main square of its capital occupied for eight weeks by tens of thousands of demonstrators," a condition of disorder and chaos that made a crackdown "inevitable." China, Kissinger concluded, remains "too important for America's national security to risk the relationship on the emotions of the moment."

Kissinger did express shock at the "brutality" of the crackdown, but his very brief statement along those lines was perfunctory. His analysis did not include the basic idea which everybody in China understood: that the regime's way of dealing with unarmed student demonstrators was intentionally brutal and murderous, a planned means of eradicating once and for all any inclination the intellectuals might have had to threaten the party's power or to cause public disorder. The general trend of his statements was to find excuses for the Chinese authorities. In late July, Kissinger wrote his column recommending against anti-Chinese sanctions. In November, he was in China, meeting with Chinese foreign minister Qian Qichen, who praised the former secretary of state for having "the courage of a statesman and the foresight of a strategist." One of the people Kissinger and his group (he was accompanying a business delegation) met with on that trip was Deng Xiaoping, with whom he exchanged cordial jokes about being private citizens no longer in power. And after returning to the United States, Kissinger had dinner at the White House, where he reported back on his conversations at the highest level.

In a single year, Kissinger may go to China several times, and the door is always open. In September 1990, he met with Li Peng, the man deemed most directly responsible for ordering the Tiananmen assault on students, who gave him and Nancy Kissinger a banquet complete with warm mutual toasts. The next day, Kissinger went to see Jiang Zemin, who noted that Kissinger was making his eighteenth visit to the People's Republic of China. And so it has continued. In April 1996, weeks after China bracketed Taiwan with missiles in an attempt to intimidate voters in the first free presidential election ever held in a Chinese state, Kissinger was in China where he met with Rong Yiren, Jiang Zemin, and Li Peng. Shortly before that, on March 31, Kissinger published a syndicated article in which he briefly mentioned "China's militaristic conduct in the Taiwan Strait," but then spent paragraphs justifying it. The Beijing leaders, he wrote, had to "draw a line" given their discontent over the fact that Taiwan's president Lee Teng-hui had been allowed to travel to the United States; and he warned that China would "fight at any cost" if it felt its sovereignty was at stake.

Kissinger's strategic thinking on China was summed up in an earlier article published in the *Washington Post* in July 1995. Where once China served American interests as a counterbalance to the Soviet Union, he argued, it has become important to the United States in its own right, holding as it does the key to stability in Asia. China is surrounded by countries whose strength is growing and who are not necessarily friendly to it, including Japan, India, and Russia, and it needs the United States to help it prevent any country from achieving hegemony in Asia. Indeed, Kissinger wrote, "Both America and China have their own reasons for opposing the domination of Asia by a single hegemonic power." Therefore, "China wants the United States to help balance its relationship with powerful neighbors . . . at least until it is strong enough to do so on its own."

In our view, Kissinger is conveniently ignoring numerous elements in China's behavior, including the extent of its military buildup, which is aimed, it is true, at preventing domination of Asia by a single power, unless that power is China. Kissinger allows that human rights "must always constitute a central American concern," but that comment, in the absence of any specific recommendations about making that concern central, smacks of lip service. In any event, Kissinger has no reply to those, like us, who show evidence proving that the human rights picture worsened when the United States took the trade pressure off. Kissinger's view of China is . . . almost identical to the view put forward in public statements by China's leaders themselves. We think that they are lying and that he is wrong.

What Kissinger does not say as he expresses his views on American China policy is just how much he stands to profit himself by the very policies he urges the government to adopt. Kissinger's company, Kissinger Associates, represents many American corporations seeking to do business in China, and who pay Kissinger large sums of money at least in part because of his unparalleled access to China's most powerful figures. Kissinger always speaks in the language of the American national interest, and he no doubt believes what he says. In 1988, for example, he called for an easing of American technology transfers to China, characterizing China as a friendly, nonaligned country, a view that was quickly echoed by Rong Yiren. But Kissinger is a major paid consultant to companies that might want to sell technology to China. While wearing his geo-strategist's hat, he might believe that technology transfers are justified in order to build a strategic alliance with China, but he is a potential beneficiary of those transfers when he wears his business consultant's hat. . . .

At the time of his 1989 statements, Kissinger had just formed a limited partnership called China Ventures to carry out joint ventures with the China International Trust and Investment Corporation, headed by his frequent host in Beijing Rong Yiren. In 1988, he formed the China-America Society with several former American presidents on its board. The society hosts banquets for Chinese leaders visiting the United States and sends delegations to China. Among his corporate clients who do business in China are the Chase Manhattan Bank, Coca-Cola, American Express, the American International Group, Continental Grain, H. J. Heinz, Atlantic Richfield, Midland Bank, and S. G. Warburg. According to Scott Thompson of the National Democratic Policy Committee, at least six of these firms "had billions of dollars of investment at risk in the P.R.C., investments which were likely to be jeopardized if President Bush had implemented the sanctions against the Communist Chinese regime that have been proposed by the U.S. Congress."

When John J. Fialka of *The Wall Street Journal* reported on these business interests, he gave Kissinger a chance to respond to the allegations of conflict of interest. It was "outrageous," he quoted Kissinger as saying, that "I would take a public position to curry favor with the Chinese government for clients." A few months later, complaining about criticism of his China dealings, Kissinger called any linking of his views on China with his business interests a form of "McCarthyism." Again, we do not question Kissinger's sincerity. China's approach is not to force people to express opinions that they disbelieve but to give privileged access to those who speak or write favorably about China while keeping any negative views they have to themselves. Still, to label as "McCarthyism" allegations of conflict of interest when such a conflict so clearly exists is excessive. As Scott Thompson put it before the Senate Foreign Relations Committee, "The fact is that [Kissinger] does receive substantial remuneration from corporations with major investments in China, which stood to benefit from adoption of his positions." The fact is also that the special way that China does business, and the willingness of former senior American officials to help it do business, has resulted in a kind of new and powerful China lobby that, perhaps only by coincidence, has declined to criticize Beijing's human rights record, has warned against "confronting" China or imposing sanctions, and has made substantial profits along the way.

. . . Kissinger is only the best known and most prestigious of a group of former senior officials who have been cultivated by China, who profit from a special relationship with China's leaders, and who have consistently advocated the avoidance of conflict, of sanctions, of harming America's "strategic interests," whatever those might be. It is remarkable the extent to which these individuals, highly respected for their views of the American interest, have come to dominate the discourse on China. . . . Indeed, it is worth remarking on the extent to which associates or former associates of Kissinger have used the revolving door to do business in China, to conduct American foreign policy, and to speak out on television and in op-ed articles in major newspapers. Not long after the Tiananmen crackdown, President Bush sent his national security adviser, Brent Scowcroft, and his deputy secretary of state, Lawrence Eagleburger, on a secret fence-mending trip to Beijing. Scowcroft had been deputy director of Kissinger Associates before going into the Bush administration. Eagleburger was its president before becoming Bush's deputy secretary of state. *The New York Times* reported that in 1988, Eagleburger made $674,000 from Kissinger Associates; Scowcroft earned $293,000 as a consultant to the group. As early as 1991, only two years after the Tiananmen massacre, Eagleburger was cautioning trade sanctions. "We firmly believe," he wrote in the *Washington Post*, "that renewing China's MFN waiver—without conditions—provides our best interest for promoting positive change and U.S. interests in China." A full "engagement" with China, he argued, is the best way to get the country back "on the path to freedom."

Among the members of the board of Kissinger's America-China Society are Cyrus Vance, Haig, former secretary of state William Rogers, Robert Mc-Farlane, and Zbigniew Brzezinski. Haig is perhaps the figure who, after Kissinger, has most clearly mixed public positions of the sort that Beijing likes with business dealings in China on behalf of corporate clients. As secretary of state, Haig was the key Reagan administration official responsible for the 1982 Chinese-American Joint Communiqué that is one of the three key statements guiding relations between the two countries. In it, the United States agreed never to pursue a Two Chinas or a One China–One Taiwan policy, to keep arms sales to Taiwan not to exceed, "either in qualitative or in quantitative terms, the level of those supplied in recent years since the establishment of diplomatic relations between the United States and China," and "to reduce gradually its sales of arms to Taiwan, leading over a period of time to a final resolution." Haig left the administration shortly before that agreement was signed. Beijing was grateful for his role in undermining Taiwan. Haig was soon cashing in on that gratitude.

For example, in the mid-1980s, as reported in *The Wall Street Journal,* Haig was paid $600,000 in fees and retainers by the International Signal & Control Group PLC, in part for help in selling weapons fuses to China. He has been for many years a senior consultant to United Technologies of Hartford, Connecticut, a manufacturer of jet engines and elevators, the world's sixteenth-largest industrial company, America's tenth-largest exporter, and a company that had seventeen joint ventures in China as of 1996. Haig frequently accompanies senior executives of the company to Beijing for meetings. In 1996, for example, he and United Technologies president George David met with Li Peng, during which Haig, not at that time an official of the United States government, reiterated "the U.S. commitment to its 'one-China' policy." . . .

Meanwhile, Haig has written op-ed pieces and made statements in which he has opposed attempts to confront China because of its human rights record and urged the United States to find ever greater means of cooperation. In the spring of 1996, one of the congressmen trying to attach conditions to the renewal of MFN for China was Christopher Cox, a fast-rising California Republican. Earlier that year, Cox played a key role in shepherding a resolution through the House declaring that the United States was obliged to come to Taiwan's aid if China took military action against it. The introduction of the resolution on March 7, with eighty Democratic and Republican cosponsors, was instrumental in President Clinton's decision to send a second aircraft carrier task force to the Taiwan area. The day before the MFN vote, Haig called Cox and berated him, accusing him of trying to destroy U.S.–China relations. "Cox was irate," says his aide, Mark P. Legon. "It was an absolutely unsolicited and inappropriate phone call. We wondered who he's paid by, but we couldn't find out."

The comparison in this regard between Kissinger, Haig, and others like

Eagleburger and Scowcroft on the one side and James Lilley, the American ambassador who did not attend that 1989 National Day rite, on the other is instructive. Lilley, a former senior official at the Central Intelligence Agency, has been a critic of China, a believer in the thesis that China's interests clash with those of the United States and that America does have an obligation to protect Taiwan from a forcible takeover by Beijing. Needless to say, it is figures like Haig who are able to gain lucrative access to Li Peng, Jiang Zemin, and Rong Yiren. Does anybody think that, if Lilley decided to go into the consulting business, he would have much success trying to do the same thing?

The argument here is not that Haig's help to United Technologies is wrong, or that there is anything dubious about the company's business in China. United Technologies, it can be assumed, helps the American economy because of that business, and, like other companies, it should use whatever competitive edge it has to make its way in the China market. What is dubious is the double role played by figures like Kissinger and Haig, who use their prestige and influence both publicly and privately to advance policies from which they profit mightily. Most important, perhaps, the New China Lobby fosters a vision of China as an essentially benign, peaceable, and defensive country whose long-term interests and those of the United States are one and the same. "We cannot have a meaningful debate about China policy because almost the entire establishment has, in the final analysis, an interest in the continuation of the status quo," one Senate aide told us.

The words "China lobby," to those with a memory of recent history, recall the likes of Henry Luce and Senator William Knowland, whose purpose was to advance the cause of the Kuomintang on Taiwan as the legitimate government of all of China. The China lobby today advances the cause of Beijing, and since its victory in the MFN debate of 1994, it has become ever more active. It consists of several loosely connected parts, all of them encouraged through the granting of connections, access, or profit to China. The success of the China lobby in delinking human rights with MFN marked a sea change in American China policy. Ever since, the influence of the business community, especially over China policy, has been enormous—certainly greater than its influence over any other aspect of American foreign policy.

Sometimes it's all in the family. Senator J. Bennett Johnston, the Louisiana Democrat who was chairman of the Senate Energy Committee, took his two sons with him on a trade mission to China paid in part by state and federal funds. Both sons were involved in promoting business deals with China. Johnston then wrote a "dear colleague" letter to members of the Senate Foreign Relations Committee asking them to muffle their support for Chinese-occupied Tibet and offering to arrange meetings with China's ambassador to the United States, Li Daoyu. Some congressional staffers refer to Senator Johnston as the "appointments secretary" for the Chinese ambassador, one congressional insider told us.

A secretive and high-level group, headed by Jiang Zemin himself, is the Central Leading Working Group on the United States Congress. Formed late in 1995 to enhance China's influence in American politics, the Working Group answers only to the seven-member Politburo Standing Committee, and it reflects China's larger awareness of the importance of lobbying directly with members of the legislative branch. China, once utterly ignorant of the American political process and therefore inept in its efforts to influence it, has recently made greater and more skillful efforts in this area. In April 1996 alone, Jiang met three separate congressional delegations led by United States senators. The Chinese Embassy increased its number of congressional liaison officers from two to five at the beginning of 1995. And the Chinese Academy of Social Sciences was ordered to study the policy-making process to help Chinese leaders better understand how to influence both the executive and legislative branches.

The Chinese initiative can sometimes be humorously unsuccessful. In January 1996, Liu Huaqiu, a deputy foreign minister and reportedly [later] China's senior official handling relations with the United States, suggested to American senators visiting Beijing that Congress not bring up anything negative about the relationship during the election year. Senator John Glenn of Ohio replied that Liu evidently did not understand how the American government worked, otherwise he would know that no one can order individual congressmen not to bring up something about China. But on other occasions, the China lobby has achieved remarkable and wisely acknowledged power. In 1994, after Secretary of State Warren Christopher's unsuccessful trip to Beijing, during which his demands for human rights concessions from the Chinese were rebuffed, Senator Ernest Hollings told him at a Senate hearing: "Before you even landed [in Beijing], the K-Street crowd down here of lawyers, consultants and special reps told the Chinese: 'Don't worry about him.' "

Other Chinese initiatives are part of the country's long-term effort to influence public opinion. China puts money into several Chinese-language newspapers published in the United States and into Chinese-language cable-television stations, and these media organizations are run almost in the same way as their counterparts inside China itself. (Taiwan also controls its media organizations, but while they take a pro-Taiwan stance, they reflect in style and content the greater democratic freedoms of Taiwan itself.) China has also heard proposals from international public relations companies that have promised to find ways of improving the Chinese image in the United States. "Concurrent with efforts to secure extension of MFN—without conditions—should be activities designed to improve China's overall image in the United States as a valued trading partner with whom we share many common interests" was the way one such proposal, by Hill and Knowlton Public Affairs Worldwide, read.

Most important, however, is the "K-Street crowd," referring to the Washington street where many lobbyists have their offices, led and financed by corporations with the greatest economic stake in China. Among the most prominent (though not the most powerful) organizations involved in lobbying for China are the United States–China Business Council (US–CBC), the Emergency Committee for American Trade, the United States Chamber of Commerce, the National Association of Retailers, and the National Association of Manufacturers. But the most powerful voices on China policy are the chief executive officers of individual companies. "These guys can just pick up the phone and make things happen," one person with close connections to the pro-China organizations told us. A group of these CEOs formed yet another pro-China group early in 1996. It is the China Normalization Initiative and has quickly become the vanguard of the pro-China lobby. It is an ad hoc coalition whose leading members include Boeing, Motorola, Allied Signal, Caterpillar, and American International Group. The China Normalization Initiative operates out of Boeing's lobbying office in Washington, D.C. It appears to have a great deal of money. Among its activities was the distribution of an information packet to educational organizations and to individual teachers around the country. The slick, two-inch-thick package has, for example, reams of data about Pennsylvania's and New Jersey's exports to China, something the written portions of the packet said meant the creation of jobs. It did not mention jobs possibly lost because of imports, however, or the export of American manufacturing operations abroad.

The China Normalization Initiative is one of many signs of increasingly intense lobbying efforts by business. In Chicago in September 1996, for example, a group of corporations including Motorola, United Airlines, Arthur Anderson, Caterpillar, Deere and Company, and others (all with headquarters in the Chicago area) announced the Illinois Coalition to Support U.S.–China Commercial Relations. Motorola's top executive for Asia, Rick Younts, said: "Illinois jobs depend on trade, and trade with China is at the top of the list of future growth opportunities for a wide variety of industries." And in a press release, the group announced that its goal is "to encourage public policy at the federal, state and local level, which supports the normalization of trade relations between the U.S. and China."

What does "normalization of trade relations" mean? First, according to the Illinois group's statement, it is the "permanent extension of China's Most Favored Nation status." Second, it means "China's accession to the World Trade Organization on terms that are commercially acceptable." On this second subject, the group did not specify acceptable to whom, but the reason for Washington's resistance to Beijing's admission to the WTO has been China's trade and tariff policies, which are themselves in part responsible for the [more than] $33.8 billion deficit the United States now has with China. Still, the Illinois group did not exactly hide its sympathies. Its creation came with an announcement that its activities would be kicked off by a reception for China's vice premier and foreign minister Qian Qichen, held on September 20 at the Ritz-Carlton Hotel in Chicago. Qian spoke to the group on that day, and remarkably enough his views corresponded exactly with those of the businessmen. He called for MFN to be "renewed indefinitely." He also added an implicit threat, one that was first raised a few years ago by Deng Xiaoping. He effectively warned that the United States will suffer the consequences if it doesn't grant China better trading terms so that the Chinese economy can continue improving. "A China with a stagnant economy, an impoverished population and even social turmoil that produces massive exodus of refugees will indeed be a threat to world peace and stability," he said.

Not coincidentally, the same argument was being made in Washington by businessmen and members of the National Association of Manufacturers who testified at a House committee hearing held the same week as the Chicago reception. Lawrence Clarkson, senior vice president of Boeing, told the committee that the repeated debate over MFN had created "a lack of predictability" in American China policy that was hurting business: "Europe extends MFN or standard tariff treatment to China, just as it does to the majority of its trading partners on a permanent basis. This contrast in policy has not gone unnoticed in Beijing. And clearly contributed to China's decision to purchase one and a half billion dollars in Airbus aircraft last April." A representative of the National Association of Manufacturers spoke against "demanding immediate social and political change for the privilege of trading with the United States."

The lesson here is that China's efforts to impose its international political agenda on foreign companies doing business in China has shaken up American businessmen. But it hasn't shaken them into leaving China. It has shaken them into doing China's bidding more eagerly than ever.

There is no more dramatic example of this than Boeing, which was selling one of every ten of its planes to Chinese airlines in the 1993–95 period, accounting for about 70 percent of the entire Chinese market. Boeing seems willing to do almost anything for the Chinese government to hold on to that share. In a series of articles in the Seattle *Times* in 1996, Stanley Holmes portrayed Boeing executives frequently reminding Chinese leaders of the political and economic favors they're performing for China and Chinese leaders constantly demanding more.

Holmes reports that the quid pro quo between Boeing and China is crass and clear: "Boeing is not only lobbying to extend MFN for China this year, but also working with other corporate giants to secure 'permanent MFN' status for China. If the aircraft giant doesn't deliver for China, Boeing's chief international strategist, Lawrence Clarkson, conceded, 'we're toast.'" One

Senate staff member, speaking of Boeing's lobbyists, put it this way: "When it comes to China . . . they're everywhere and they're smart. They do it through front organizations, they publish studies on exports, they know where their suppliers are and they put pressure on them."

Speaking about the K Street crowd, one senior senatorial staff member told us that those in the policy-making establishment striving to attach some importance to human rights in China tend to be steamrolled by the increasingly powerful business lobby that fights for China on Capitol Hill. "As more and more businesses have invested in China, we have lost more and more people," the staffer told us. "The business community is spending tens of millions of dollars against us every year."

7

The CNN Effect: Myth or Reality?

Warren P. Strobel

It's May 31, 1995, there's another flare-up in the long-running Bosnia crisis and the Defense Department spokesman, Kenneth Bacon, is sitting in his office on the Pentagon's policy making E Ring. A clock is ticking over his head. On the wall right outside the door to Bacon's inner office is a television. Aide Brian Cullen glances at it from time to time.

On the bottom of the screen is the familiar CNN logo. Above it is the equally familiar figure of Peter Arnett in flak jacket and helmet, reporting breathlessly from Bosnia, analyzing the latest NATO airstrikes and the Bosnian Serbs' retaliation by taking U.N. peacekeepers hostage. Arnett is answering questions for the host and audience of CNN's interactive "Talk Back Live." Some of that audience is in cyberspace, sending in questions via CompuServe. At the top of the hour, Bacon will escort a "senior Defense Department official" to the podium of the Pentagon briefing room to explain to skeptical reporters why the Clinton administration's latest apparent policy change toward Bosnia is not a change at all.

Here it is, the nexus of media power and foreign policy, where television's instantly transmitted images fire public opinion, demanding instant responses from government officials, shaping and reshaping foreign policy at the whim of electrons. It's known as the CNN Effect.

It's a catchall phrase that has been used to describe a number of different phenomena. Perhaps the best definition, used by Professor Steven Livingston of George Washington University, is a loss of policy control on the part of policy makers because of the power of the media, a power that they can do nothing about.

Or is it the best definition? I'm here to ask Bacon that question. Bacon, a former journalist, is a precise man. He wears a bow tie and wire rim glasses, and looks like he doesn't get ruffled easily. On a day like today, his response is telling. "Policy makers," he says, "are becoming more adept at dealing with the CNN factor."

Bacon's opinion is one heard, in one form or another, over and over in the course of nearly 100 interviews during [1995 and 1996] with secretaries of state, spokespersons and everyone in between. I talked with officials from the Bush and Clinton administrations, the United Nations and relief agencies; military officers who have been in Bosnia, Somalia, Haiti and Rwanda; and journalists who have reported from those places. It is possible, of course, that they are all lying (the officials, that is). After all, who would want to admit that their authority has been usurped, their important jobs made redundant? To paraphrase legendary diplomat George Kennan's almost plaintive diary entry from the day U.S. troops landed in Somalia: If CNN determines foreign policy, why do we need administrators and legislators?

But the closer one looks at those incidents that supposedly prove a CNN Effect, where dramatic and/or real-time images appear to have forced policy makers into making sudden changes, the more the Effect shrinks. It is like a shimmering desert mirage, disappearing as you get closer.

A growing body of academic research is casting doubt on the notion that CNN in particular, or television in general, determines U.S. foreign policy the way it might seem from a quick glance at the live broadcasts from Tiananmen Square in 1989 or the image of the U.S. soldier being dragged through the streets of Mogadishu, Somalia, in October 1993. . . . What officials told me closely parallels the findings of Nik Gowing, diplomatic editor for Britain's Independent Television Network, who interviewed dozens of British and American officials for a Harvard University study. Even many military officers, who might be expected to criticize media performance, have found the CNN Effect to be less than it is billed. But no one is arguing that CNN has had no effect on journalists, government officials, and the way both conduct their business.

Virtually every official interviewed agrees that the rise of Cable News Network has radically altered the way U.S. foreign policy is conducted. Information is everywhere, not just because of CNN, but through other developments, such as the increasingly sophisticated media systems in developing nations and the explosive growth of the Internet. "It's part and parcel of governing," says Margaret Tutwiler, assistant secretary of state for public affairs under James A. Baker III. During her days at the State Department podium, Tutwiler knew that the most important audience was not the reporters asking the questions, but the array of cameras at the back of the briefing room, which sent her descriptions of U.S. policy to leaders, journalists and the public the globe over.

Baker says CNN has destroyed the concept of a "news cycle." In his days as a political campaign director, the news cycle was much longer, which meant the candidate had more time to respond to an opponent's charges. Now officials must respond almost instantly to developments. Because miniaturized cameras and satellite dishes can go virtually anywhere, policy makers no longer have the luxury of ignoring faraway crises.

These changes also affect modern U.S. military operations, which increasingly involve peacekeeping or humanitarian activities, and in which there is no vital U.S. interest at stake and thus less rationale for controlling the news media. The journalist-military debate over news media pools and other restrictions that date from Grenada and the Persian Gulf War has been eclipsed by the Somalias and Haitis, where the news media were so pervasive that reporters were often providing information to the military rather than vice versa. U.S. Army Maj. David Stockwell and Col. Barry Willey, the chief military spokesmen in Somalia and Haiti, both described this media presence as alternately helpful and annoying, but in the end an inevitable piece of what the military calls the "operating environment."

But to say that CNN changes governance, shrinks decision making time and opens up military operations to public scrutiny is not the same as saying that it determines policy. Information indeed has become central to international affairs, but whether officials use this or are used by it depends largely on them. The stakes are higher for those who must make policy, but the tools at their command are also more powerful.

How, then, does the CNN Effect really work? One way to answer that question is to look at some common myths about the network, and at what government officials who must deal with it on a daily basis say really happens.

Myth No. 1

CNN makes life more difficult for foreign policy makers.

For those government officials who know how to use it, Ted Turner's round-the-clock video wire service can in fact be an immense boon. This was seen most vividly during the Persian Gulf War, when the Bush White House, knowing that Iraqi President Saddam Hussein's top aides were reluctant to bring him bad news, got into Saddam's living room via CNN. And because CNN carried Pentagon briefings in Saudi Arabia and Washington live, officials were talking directly to the American public for hours on end. A study of commentators featured on the network during the gulf war found that the majority of them were retired military officers or other "elites" who by and large supported the administration's view of the crisis. Saddam, of course, used CNN too, as illustrated by the controversy over Peter Arnett's reporting from Iraq. This challenged the administration—but also provided a useful window into what the man in Baghdad was thinking.

It doesn't take a massive confrontation and half a million U.S. troops in the desert for CNN to perform this favor for officials. "Everybody talks about the

CNN factor being bad," Pentagon spokesman Bacon says. "But in fact, a lot of it is good." If the Pentagon [disagreed] with a report by CNN Pentagon correspondent Jamie McIntyre, [then] Defense Secretary William Perry [could] and [would] call him to try to put his spin on events. In the good old days of the 6 o'clock evening news, officials would have to wait 24 hours. By then it was usually too late. With CNN, they get many chances throughout the day to try to shape public perceptions.

Because of its speed, CNN also provides a convenient way for administration officials to leak new policies in the hope that they'll define the debate before political opponents do. Many a White House reporter knows that CNN's Wolf Blitzer is a frequent recipient of such leaks. Blitzer is on the White House lawn, repeating to the camera what he's just been told by unnamed officials, while newspaper reporters are still fretting over their leads.

The images of strife and horror abroad that are displayed on CNN and other television outlets also help foreign policy officials explain the need for U.S. intervention. CNN may be the last defense against isolationism. The press "makes the case of the need to be involved sometimes more than we can," says Richard Boucher, State Department spokesman under Baker and former Secretary of State Lawrence Eagleburger.

Myth No. 2

CNN dictates what's on the foreign policy agenda.

Somalia, of course, is the prime example cited. There was equal suffering in southern Sudan in 1992, the common wisdom goes, but the Bush administration was forced to pay attention to Somalia because the TV cameras were there.

While journalists undoubtedly were drawn to the drama of the famine in Somalia, they had a lot of help getting there. Much of this came from international relief agencies that depend on TV images to move governments to respond and the public to open its wallets. "We need the pictures. Always the pictures," says on official who works with the U.N. High Commissioner for Refugees (UNHCR). There isn't anything sinister about this. These private and intergovernmental agencies do good work under dangerous conditions. But for that very reason they are seen by many journalists as lacking the motives that most other sources are assumed to have. In the case of Somalia, these organizations were joined by U.S. government relief agencies and members of Congress interested in Africa in a campaign to generate media attention and government action.

One of the leaders of that campaign was Andrew Natsios, then an assistant administrator of the U.S. Agency for International Development, known for his rapport with reporters. Natsios and his aides gave numerous media interviews and held news conferences in Africa and in Washington in early 1992. "I deliberately used the news media as a medium for educating policy makers in Washington and in Europe" about how to address the crisis, Natsios says. And he says he used the media "to drive policy." Once reporters got to Somalia—sometimes with the UNHCR, the International Committee of the Red Cross and others—they of course sent back graphic reports of the famine that increased the pressure on President Bush to do something.

"It started with government manipulating press," says Herman Cohen, former assistant secretary of state for African affairs, "and then changed to press manipulating the government."

A quick look at the patterns of television reporting on Somalia also raises questions about the media's agenda-setting powers. There were very few television reports on Somalia (15 on the three networks to be exact) prior to Bush's August 1992 decision to begin an airlift. That decision resulted in a burst of reporting. The pattern was repeated later in the year when Bush ordered 25,000 U.S. troops to safeguard humanitarian aid. When they weren't following the actions of relief officials or members of Congress, the cameras were following the troops. CNN, in fact, was less likely than the networks to do independent reporting when Somalia was not on the Washington agenda.

Myth No. 3

Pictures of suffering force officials to intervene.

Televised images of humanitarian suffering do put pressure on the U.S. government to act, as was seen in northern Iraq following the gulf war, in Somalia and in Rwanda. Part of the reason for this, officials say, is because the costs of lending a hand are presumed to be low. (The U.S. foreign policy establishment was disabused of this notion in Somalia, an experience that probably permanently shrunk this facet of the CNN Effect.)

But something interesting happens when the pictures suggest an intervention that is potentially high in costs, especially the cost of American casualties. Images of civil wars, no matter how brutal, simply don't have the same effects as those of lines of refugees or malnourished children at a feeding station.

In the summer and fall of 1992 the Bush administration was under intense pressure from Congress and the U.N. to do something to stop the outrages perpetrated against Bosnia's Muslims. In August, *Newsday* reported the existence of a string of detention camps where Bosnian Serbs were torturing, raping and killing. Within a few days, Britain's ITN confirmed the worst when it broadcast images of emaciated men trapped behind barbed wire. Yet by this time President Bush and his aides had concluded that intervening in the Bosnian civil war would take thousands of troops who might be mired down for years. CNN and its brethren did not change this calculation.

"It wouldn't have mattered if television was going 24 hours around the clock with Serb atrocities. Bush wasn't going to get in," says Warren Zimmermann, the last U.S. ambassador to Yugoslavia. Former Secretary of State Eagleburger confirmed this, saying: "Through all the time we were there, you have to understand that we had largely made a decision we were not going to get militarily involved. And nothing, including those stories, pushed us into it. . . . It made us damn uncomfortable. But this was a policy that wasn't going to get changed no matter what the press said."

The pressures that Eagleburger spoke of were very real. But rather than alter firmly held policy, in Bosnia and many other places, officials, in essence, pretended to. They took minimal steps designed to ease the pressure while keeping policy intact. These responses probably account for much of the perception that CNN and television in general change policy. Bush administration concern with the media "only extended to the appearance of maintaining we were behaving responsibly," says Foreign Service officer George Kenney, who resigned publicly to protest the lack of real U.S. action to save Bosnia. Roy Gutman, who won the Pulitzer Prize for his reporting from Bosnia for *Newsday,* concurs. "What you had is a lot of reaction to reports, but never any policy change."

Images of the brutal slaughter of half a million people in Rwanda in 1994 did not move governments to intervene with force. This was true despite the fact that there was more television coverage of the slaughter than there was of Somalia at any time in 1992 until Bush actually sent the troops. According to officials at the Pentagon and elsewhere, once the slaughter in Rwanda ended and the massive exodus of refugees began, what had seemed like an intervention nightmare became a relatively simple logistical and humanitarian problem that the U.S. military was well-equipped to solve.

Interestingly, the public reacted the same way as the Pentagon did. According to a top relief representative, private relief agencies "got virtually no money whatsoever" from the viewing public when television was broadcasting images of Rwandans who had been hacked to death. Contributions began to pour in when refugees flooded across Rwanda's borders and there were "pictures of women and children . . . innocents in need."

Myth No. 4

There is nothing officials can do about the CNN Effect.

To the contrary, whether or not the CNN Effect is real depends on the actions of government officials themselves. As ABC News' Ted Koppel puts it, "To the degree . . . that U.S. foreign policy in a given region has been clearly stated and adequate, accurate information has been provided, the influence of television coverage diminishes proportionately." In other words, the news media fill a vacuum, and CNN, by its reach and speed, can do so powerfully and quickly.

But this gives officials a lot more sway than Kennan thinks they have. The officials I interviewed did not identify a single instance when television reports forced them to alter a strongly held and/or well-communicated policy. Rather, the media seemed to have an impact when policy was weakly held, was already in the process of being changed or was lacking public support.

There is little doubt that the image of a dead U.S. soldier being desecrated in October 1993 forced President Clinton to come up with a rapid response to calls in Congress for the withdrawal of U.S. troops from Somalia. Often forgotten, however, is that by September 1993 the Clinton administration already was making plans to extract U.S. troops. Just days before the images of the dead soldier were aired, Secretary of State Warren Christopher had told U.N. Secretary General Boutros Boutros-Ghali of Washington's desire to pull out. Congress had withdrawn its approval, and public support for the mission, documented in opinion polls, began falling well before the gruesome video started running on CNN.

What was most important about the imagery, however, was that it could not be explained by U.S. foreign policy makers. The Clinton administration had casually allowed the mission in Somalia to evolve from humanitarian relief to nation-building without explaining to the public and Congress the new costs, risks and goals. The images were the coup de grace. "The message was not handled properly from the administration," says one U.S. military officer who served in Somalia. The images were "a graphic illustration of the futility of what we were doing."

This ability of CNN to alter a policy that is in flux was graphically demonstrated again just a few months later in February 1994 when a mortar shell slammed into a marketplace in Sarajevo, killing 68 people and wounding many more. The images of the "market massacre" caused outrage around the world. The United States abandoned a year-old hands-off policy toward the Balkans and, a few days later, persuaded NATO to declare a zone around Sarajevo free of Bosnian Serb heavy weapons.

But what looks like a simple cause-effect relationship looked different to those making the policy. Here again, just days before, Christopher had presented to his senior government colleagues a plan for more aggressive U.S. action in Bosnia. He and others had become alarmed at the way U.S.-European disputes over Bosnia were debilitating NATO.

A senior State Department official was in a meeting on the new Bosnia policy when the mortaring occurred. He recalls worrying that the new policy would be seen, incorrectly, as a response to the massacre. The images did force the Clinton administration to respond quickly in public and ensured that an internal policy debate that might have lasted for months was telescoped into a few days. But the episode also provides additional evidence that CNN helps officials explain actions they already want to take. The images provided a moment of increased attention to Bosnia that could help justify the administration's policy response. "It was a short window. We took advantage of it. We moved the policy forward. And it was successful," then-White House spokeswoman Dee Dee Myers recalls.

Myth No. 5

The CNN Effect is on the rise.

Sadly, there is at least preliminary evidence that the public and officials are becoming inoculated against pictures of tragedy or brutality coming across their television screens. "We are developing an ability now to see incomprehensible human tragedy on television and understand no matter how horrible it is, we can't get involved in each and every instance," says White House spokesman Michael McCurry. "We are dulling our senses."

When a mortar again struck the Sarajevo marketplace in August 1995, the images were familiar: pools of blood and shredded limbs. For that reason, McCurry says, they had less impact. The policy response—bombing Bosnian Serbs—was driven instead by NATO's pledge a few weeks earlier to use air power to protect remaining U.N.-declared safe areas. NATO knew it had to make good on the pledge if it was to have any credibility left at all. McCurry's point about the dulling of our senses can be heard in what a viewer told an NBC audience researcher: "If I ever see a child with flies swarming around it one more time, I'm not going to watch that show again."

As with any new technology, people are learning over time to adapt to real-time television. While the danger remains that officials will respond to instant reports on CNN that later turn out to be wrong, several current and former spokespeople say that governments are becoming more sophisticated in dealing with time pressures. "As often as not, we buy ourselves time when things happen," Boucher says. "If we think we need the time to decide, we take the time to decide."

Pentagon spokesman Bacon says, "We do not have a big problem with saying, 'Yeah, this looks really awful, but let's find out what the facts really are.'" . . .

On that day [in May 1995] when I interviewed Bacon, media images had not pushed the United States further into the Balkan tangle. Rather, NATO bombing and the prospect that U.S. troops might go to Bosnia to rescue U.N. peacekeepers had sent journalists scurrying back to Sarajevo. The story was heating up again.

The CNN Effect is narrower and far more complex than the conventional wisdom holds. In a more perfect world, the news media—especially television—would be a more independent force, pointing out problems and helping set the public agenda. In reality, CNN and its brethren follow newsmakers at least as frequently as they push them or make them feel uncomfortable. The struggle between reporters and officials continues as before—just at a faster pace.

8

The Electoral Cycle and the Conduct of American Foreign Policy

William B. Quandt

Two hundred years ago, when the Constitution was taking shape, the conduct of the new nation's foreign affairs was not central to the concerns of the founders. Once independence was achieved, it was widely believed, the United States would be able to remain comparatively uninvolved with the rest of the world. A wide ocean separated it from the messy politics of Europe and permitted the first president to imagine the United States could remain unentangled in the affairs of the rest of the world.

The Founders did, of course, make passing reference to the division of powers between the executive and the legislature in such matters as negotiating and ratifying treaties with foreign powers and with raising an army and a navy and directing them in time of war. As elsewhere in the Constitution, on these matters one sees the determination to prevent too much power from being concentrated in any one part of the federal government.[1] Divided responsibility was the key to avoiding abuses of power, and in the domestic arena the wisdom of this philosophical bent has been widely applauded. In the conduct of foreign policy, however, it is much more difficult to argue that the virtues of divided responsibility enhance the common defense or promote the general welfare.

Still, even the most ardent proponent of strong presidential leadership in foreign policy would have a difficult time arguing that the specific provisions of the Constitution regarding foreign policy are at the root of our contemporary problems in world affairs. . . .

The Constitution does not cripple the president in the conduct of foreign policy, at least not because of the definition of powers. These are defined sufficiently broadly and ambiguously so that a strong and popular president

---

Note: Some notes may have been deleted or renumbered.

can provide effective leadership, while a relatively weak and unpopular one will have a difficult time. That is pretty close to what one imagines the intent of the Founders must have been.

The Problem of the Electoral Cycle

But there is still a constitutionally rooted problem that seriously affects the conduct of foreign policy. It derives from the structure of the electoral cycle. Here there is no ambiguity at all in the Constitution. Presidential elections take place every four years; congressional elections every two years; and since the passage of the twenty-second amendment, a president can only be elected twice. In practice, this often means that presidents have little time during their incumbency when they have both the experience and the power needed for sensible and effective conduct of foreign policy. The price we pay is a foreign policy excessively geared to short-term calculations, in which narrow domestic political considerations often outweigh sound strategic thinking, and where turnover in high positions is so frequent that consistency and coherence are lost. . . .

The electoral arrangements for the presidency and Congress have rarely been justified by the contribution they make to sound foreign policy. The rationale is almost entirely domestic. Representatives are supposed to remain closely tied to the wishes of their constituents; hence the two-year term. Senators are expected to take a broader view and thus are given six-year terms. The Senate is supposed to embody a degree of continuity, and, therefore, only one-third of its membership is up for election at any given moment. Presidents fall in between, having to renew their mandate after four years and being obliged to retire at the end of a second term. A pervasive distrust of presidential power can be detected in these arrangements, a distrust that is historically understandable, but which also can have debilitating effects on foreign policy.

In domestic policy it is probably wise to structure the federal system so that presidential authority is limited. After all, the country has so many diverse interests that it is hard to imagine the system working well unless there are strong incentives for compromise and moderation. A certain amount of inconsistency, of vacillation, of changing the calculus of winners and losers is needed to keep this heterogeneous country together. The federal structure and the electoral cycle are all part of the system that allows domestic political issues to be resolved with a minimum of conflict and violence.

Foreign policy is different. Washington speaks for the country as a whole in foreign policy. The president is supposed to be the commander-in-chief of the armed forces. And in the modern world the president literally holds the power of life and death, since he or she has the ultimate authority to decide on the use of nuclear weapons. Such decisions might have to be made in a matter of minutes, and extraordinary measures are taken to be sure that the president is always in a position to act on the basis of the best information available. In the nuclear era there might not be time to consult with Congress, to await declarations of war, or to cultivate public understanding. An enormous responsibility rests with the president, and presumably it is in everyone's interest that matters affecting the nation's welfare and security be handled with skill, expertise, and intelligence. The president electoral arrangements do not contribute to that goal.

The Nature of the Problem

Ideally, one would like to see a president bring wisdom and experience in foreign affairs to the Oval Office. One could hope that he or she, once there, would have the time, the power, and the authority to deal with problems of national security and foreign policy in ways that promote the national interest. But to list these desirable circumstances is to be reminded of how far they are from the recent historical record.

Wisdom is something that a president either has or lacks, and the electoral cycle cannot be held responsible. But experience and power, as well as the time and inclination to deal with foreign affairs, are tied to the rhythms of the electoral cycle. Simply stated, a newly elected president may well have the authority, the power, and the inclination to address foreign policy issues, but rarely has the experience necessary to form sound judgments. Thus, it is common for serious errors to be made in the first year of a presidential term. During the second, and part of the third year, there may be a happy coincidence of sufficient power, experience, and time to deal with the complexities of world affairs. But during the last year or more of a typical first term, a president is drawn into the politics of reelection and rarely has much time or inclination to deal with foreign policy issues unless they seem to hold out the promise of winning votes, which is rarely the case.

A reelected president in the second term faces a somewhat different problem. Experience and authority are likely to be available, but after the midterm elections the lame-duck problem is very likely to set in, making it difficult for a president to conduct foreign policy. Leaders abroad will begin to ask themselves why they should bother to deal with this president when someone else will be in the Oval Office before long, perhaps bringing a change of policy as well. The opposition party has little incentive to help the outgoing president win any foreign policy victories, and within the president's own party the struggle for succession may weaken his or her base of support. In normal times it would be surprising to find major foreign-policy successes in the last phase of a two-term president's incumbency.

This simple descriptive model should not be seen as an absolute guide for how a president will fare in the conduct of foreign policy at different moments of his or her term. Crises can radically change the conventional political calculus, enhancing presidential power and forging a bipartisan base of support. But if a crisis turns into a prolonged, indecisive, costly commitment—as in Vietnam and Lebanon—domestic political considerations are likely to come to the fore again and force a president's hand.

None of this would matter so much if presidents did not really have much to say about foreign policy. In theory, policy might be carried out by the experienced professionals in the bureaucracy on a nonpartisan basis. Or a grand bipartisan consensus might develop that would establish the broad lines of policy, leaving the president relatively free from domestic political considerations as long as he or she operated within that consensus. Those who used to proclaim that "politics stops at the water's edge" were expressing the hope that a nonpartisan foreign policy could be found. But certainly since the mid-1960s and the trauma of Vietnam, there has been no consensus on foreign policy that could insulate a president from the impact of domestic politics and the electoral cycle.

First-Term Presidents: The Typical Pattern

A president's assessment of risks and opportunities is generally a product of experience in office and where he or she stands with respect to the electoral cycle. For analytical purposes and at the risk of some distortion of a more complex reality, it is useful to distinguish among patterns in the first year of a presidential term, the second year, the third, and the fourth.

These categories are useful for understanding the typical evolution of policy over a four-year cycle. They alert the observer to the changing weight of domestic political considerations as a presidential term unfolds. The time when presidents decide to do something is heavily influenced by this cycle, unless they are reacting to a foreign-policy crisis.

If presidents and their advisers are inattentive to the political cycle, they are apt to make serious mistakes. A learning process seems invariably to take place in the course of a four-year term. By the end, most presidents recognize that some of what they tried early in their term was unrealistic; they have become more familiar with the limits on their power; they aim lower and pay more attention to the timing of their major moves.

Skillful presidents will make use of the political cycle to enhance the chances of success in foreign policy. Careless ones will probably pay a high price for ignoring domestic realities. Events, of course, can get out of control, as they did for Jimmy Carter with the Iranian hostage crisis in 1979. It was particularly bad luck for him that this happened just as an election year was beginning. By contrast, Ronald Reagan managed to terminate the controversial American military presence in Lebanon just before his reelection campaign began in 1984, and the issue seemed to do him no political harm at the polls. Luck and skill go hand in hand in successful political careers.

Looking back on their time in office, presidents and their advisers usually decry the intrusion of domestic politics so heavily into the foreign-policy arena. Former Secretary of State Cyrus Vance has argued that the only solution to the problem is to elect a president for one term of six years.

From experience in the making of foreign policy in several administrations, I have concluded that a four-year presidential term has serious drawbacks, especially when it comes to foreign affairs. It takes each new president from six to nine months to learn his job and to feel comfortable in the formulation and execution of foreign policy. For the next eighteen months the president can operate with assurance. But during the last year or so, he is running for reelection and is forced to divert much of his attention to campaigning. As a result, many issues are ignored and important decisions are deferred. Sometimes bad decisions are made under the pressures of months of primary elections. And at home and overseas, we are frequently seen as inconsistent and unstable.[2]

Others have tried to address the problem by pleading for bipartisanship, the removal of foreign policy from the domestic political agenda. Zbigniew Brzezinski, President Carter's national security adviser, has written:

Every Administration goes through a period of an ecstatic emancipation from the past, then a discovery of continuity, and finally a growing preoccupation with Presidential reelection. As a result, the learning curve in the area of foreign policy tends to be highly compressed. Each Administration tends to expend an enormous amount of energy coping with the unintended, untoward consequences of its initial, sometimes excessive, impulses to innovate, to redeem promises, and to harbor illusions. In time, preconceptions give way to reality, disjointedness to intellectual coherence, and vision to pragmatism. But by the time this happens, the Presidential cycle is usually coming to an end. That the four-year election process has a pernicious influence on foreign policy is evident, but it is also clear that this structural handicap is not likely to be undone.[3]

The Pattern of the First Year

Presidents and their advisers often begin their term with relatively little background in foreign-policy issues. This lack of background is especially important if the president has been a Washington outsider and if there has been a change of the party in control of the White House. But even in the case of a Washington insider, such as a senator with experience on the Foreign Relations Committee or a vice president moving up to the presidency, there is little reason to expect more than the faintest familiarity with most foreign policy issues.

Presidents are not allowed the luxury of taking no position on issues until they have learned enough to make sensible judgments. Instead, on issues that evoke strong public interest, such as the Middle East or arms control, candidates for the presidency will be expected to have a position and may even devote a major speech to the topic.

These first definitions of a president's position, often taken in the midst of the campaign, are typically of considerable importance in setting the administration's initial course. They are likely to reflect general foreign-policy predispositions . . . and will generally imply that the previous administration was on the wrong track and that things will soon be put straight. (This, of course, assumes that the presidency is passing from one party to the other.) In addition to defining a course of action by contrasting it with one's predecessor in office, a newly elected president will have to decide what priority to attach to the main foreign-policy issues on the agenda. Not all issues can be dealt with at once, and a signal of presidential interest or disinterest may be more important in setting the administration's policy than the substantive position papers that inevitably begin to flow to the White House from the bureaucracy.

If an issue is treated as important, and if presidential predispositions are reflected in the charting of the initial course, the early months of the new term are likely to be marked by activism. Having just won a national election, the president will probably be optimistic about the ability to use the office to achieve great results in foreign and domestic policy. If initiatives are decided upon, they tend to be ambitious. It takes time to recognize what will work and what will not.

It also takes time for presidents and their advisers to develop a comfortable working style. A high degree of confusion is not unusual in the early days. Public statements may have to be retracted, and it will take time to know who really speaks for the president among the many claimants to the role. In addition, it will take time for the president and the new secretary of state to develop contacts with various foreign leaders. These encounters will eventually add to their education, but at the outset there is usually only a faint understanding of the foreign players, their agendas, and their strengths and weaknesses.

What all of this adds up to is a first year that is often somewhat experimental, where policy objectives are set in ambitious terms, where predispositions and campaign rhetoric still count for something, and where international realities are only dimly appreciated. Typically, toward the end of the first year it becomes clear that the policy agreed upon in January or February has lost momentum or is on the wrong track. Reassessments are then likely, but not until considerable time and energy have been invested in pursuing false leads and indulging in wishful thinking.

The Pattern of the Second Year

Despite the frequent disappointments of dealing with foreign-policy issues in the first year, presidents rarely decide to turn their attention away from the international arena in their second year. If recent experience is a guide, year two is likely to be marked with considerably greater success, either in promoting international agreement through negotiations or in the skillful management of a crisis.

The difference between the first and the second year shows that experience can be a good teacher. Policies in the second year are often more in tune with reality. There is less of an ideological overlay in policy deliberations. At the same time, goals are likely to be less ambitious. Plans for comprehensive solutions may be replaced by attempts at more modest partial agreements.

By the second year, some of the intrabureaucratic feuding and backbiting is likely to have subsided, or at least a president has had the chance to put it to an end if desired. The gap between the political appointees and the foreign service professionals has also narrowed, and more regional expertise is typically being taken into account during policy discussions. If a senior bureaucrat has survived into the second year, he or she is no longer seen as the enemy and has often been judged a team player. In any case, the failures of year one tend to make the president's appointees less contemptuous of the knowledge of the professionals.

During the second year, presidents also begin to realize that mishandling of foreign-policy issues, especially in the Middle East or concerning U.S.–Russian relations, can be costly. Congressional elections are scheduled for November, and in most cases the party in power has to expect some losses. Such losses make it more difficult for presidents to govern, and thus they have a strong interest in minimizing them. This is no time for controversial initiatives. If initiatives are to be taken, there is a high premium on the appearance of success. The mood in the White House is much less experimental than in the first year. Practical criteria come to the fore. Success may require compromises with principle. This is the year in which presidents realize that the slogan of politics being "the art of the possible" is applicable to foreign as well as domestic policy.

The Pattern of the Third Year

During the third year of a typical presidential term, foreign-policy issues are likely to be assessed at the White House in terms of whether or not they can help advance the incumbent's reelection bid. The tendency, therefore, is to try for an apparent success if an initiative is underway, even if the result leaves something to be desired. The administration will even be prepared on occasions to pay heavily with concessions or with promises of aid and arms to get an agreement.

If the prospects for an agreement do not look good during the third year, the tendency is to cut one's losses and to disengage the president from the diplomatic effort. Above all, the president does not want to be seen as responsible for a foreign policy failure as the election year approaches. And certainly by the end of the third year, if not considerably earlier, the preelection season is likely to be underway.

The rush for success, along with the tendency to abandon controversial and costly policies, means that mistakes are often made in the third year. Opportunities may be lost through carelessness. The price of agreement may become very high as the parties to negotiations realize how badly Washington wants a success. Political considerations tend to override the requirements of steady, purposeful diplomacy. Nonetheless, this is sometimes a year in which genuine achievements are possible, especially if the groundwork in the second year has been good.

The Pattern of the Fourth Year

Most presidents go to great lengths to deny that electoral considerations are allowed to influence their conduct of foreign policy. But as political realists, they all know that they must take politics into account. If nothing else, the extraordinary demands on a presidential candidate mean that little time is left for consideration of complex foreign-policy problems, for meeting with visiting heads of state, or for fighting great battles with Congress over aid or arms sales. Added to this is the desire not to lose the support of constituencies that have particularly strong feelings about specific foreign-policy issues. This can be important in terms of votes as well as in terms of financial contributions to the party and to congressional candidates.

The guidelines for the fourth year with respect to potentially controversial foreign-policy issues are thus fairly simple. Try to avoid taking a position. Steer clear of new initiatives. Stick with safe themes and patriotic rhetoric. Attack your opponent as inexperienced, ill-informed, possibly reckless. If crises are forced upon you, they must, of course, be dealt with, and even in election years presidents have considerable authority in emergencies.

In brief, most presidents recognize that they can hope to achieve little in foreign policy in the midst of an election campaign. Even if a president were prepared to take some bold initiative, foreign leaders would be reluctant to respond positively out of a concern that the president might not be in office the following January. Statesmen are likely to want to know who will be in the White House for the next four years before they make major decisions. This weakens the influence of presidents in their fourth year even when they are not up for reelection.

The Pattern of the Second Term

For presidents in their second term, the four-year pattern changes significantly. The first year and half may be the best time for taking foreign-policy initiatives. At the onset of the new term, a president may decide to change all or some of the foreign-policy team. The president may have asked them to remain through the election to avoid the appearance of disarray, but now has the chance to fashion a team that will work well with him or her. Now the president knows as much about substance as he or she ever will. The reelection has provided the proof that may have been needed that the public is supportive.

Late in the second year, however, domestic considerations begin to intrude on foreign-policy concerns. Midterm elections are likely to be of special importance, for they will determine to a large extent how much power the president has in the last two years. If control is lost over one or both houses of Congress, the legislative agenda will be in jeopardy. Any significant loss for the president's party may speed up the succession struggle and can embolden opponents in Congress. At this point, we can expect to hear a great deal about the virtues of a bipartisan foreign policy.

The idea that presidents who do not have to face reelection will be free to act in a statesmanlike manner in their last two years misses the point. They may be free, but they are unlikely to be taken very seriously as they reach the end of their terms. At some point in the third or fourth year, the lame-duck phenomenon is bound to affect the president.

Whatever a president's intentions in foreign policy, they cannot be very ambitious in these last years. Thus, the third year is likely to have a custodial feel to it. Problems have to be managed without new initiatives. The same normally holds for the fourth year, although here the presidential campaign gets in the way. And the president may want to give a boost to his successor by taking into account his or her concerns. There is, however, a short period after the election in November and the inauguration the next January when an outgoing president can still make decisions and when the electorate has already spoken.

Some Illustrative Examples

In the post–World War II era, only three men, Dwight Eisenhower, Richard Nixon, and George Bush assumed the office of president with some measure of expertise in world affairs. Even for these three, however, there were vast gaps in their knowledge, and a period of on-the-job training was essential. All other presidents—Harry Truman, John Kennedy, Lyndon Johnson, Gerald Ford, Jimmy Carter, Ronald Reagan, and Bill Clinton—had relatively little experience with world affairs by the time they assumed office.

If we leave aside the cases of Truman, who became president in the midst of a war, of Eisenhower, who had to deal with the Korean War in his first year, and Bush, who was exceptionally well prepared for his foreign-policy role and brought with him an experienced team, we can look for typical errors of inexperience especially in 1961, 1977, 1981, and 1993. These are the purest examples of a relatively inexperienced man coming to the Oval Office after having campaigned against the previous incumbent.

Whatever one may think of the brief Kennedy presidency, its first year was not its finest hour. In the spring of 1961 Kennedy stumbled into the Bay of Pigs fiasco. In addition, having campaigned on the basis of a nonexistent missile gap, he had to reverse course and adapt to new realities, but not before he had set in motion a new phase of the arms race.

For Carter, his first year was marked by excessive ambition and awkwardness. He tried to move abruptly away from the arms control guidelines that Gerald Ford and Leonid Brezhnev had laid out at Vladivostok, calling instead for deep cuts in strategic weaponry. The Soviets rejected this new proposal, and precious time was lost before arms negotiations could get back on track. In the Middle East, Carter launched an ambitious peace initiative, but compromised its success by some of his clumsy public diplomacy and by mishandling the surrounding dialogue with the Soviet Union. By fall 1977, he felt that he was paying a heavy domestic political price for his Middle East efforts and told Egypt's President Anwar Sadat that there was little more that he could do. At that point Sadat, perceiving Carter's weakness, set off on his own to deal with Israel directly.

Reagan's first-year errors were in part a product of inexperience. In the Middle East, for example, he lent his weight to a policy of building strategic consensus against the Soviet Union. From this perspective, regional problems such as the crisis in Lebanon and the Arab-Israeli conflict were relatively unimportant. Countries such as Israel, Egypt, and Saudi Arabia, all strongly anti-Soviet, would be encouraged to drop their local quarrels and cooperate in pursuit of anti-Soviet policies. Needless to say, strategic consensus was illusory, and neglecting the problems of Lebanon and the Palestinians set the stage for the explosion that came the following year.

Clinton, who came to the presidency with very little experience in foreign policy, had a troubled first year, particularly in Bosnia. While no one had easy answers to the Bosnian imbroglio, Clinton and his secretary of state compounded the difficulty by switching signals and showing little leadership for the NATO allies. In the Middle East, Clinton's uncertainty about how to proceed with the sensitive Palestinian issue led both Israelis and Palestinians to use an alternative channel for the negotiations, with the welcome result that an agreement was reached in Oslo without much direct American involvement. Clinton's tendency to flip-flop was seen in his early remarks on the possibility of redemption for Saddam Hussein of Iraq, followed shortly thereafter by a policy that seemed aimed at his ouster.

Presidents in the second year have presumably learned something of value from their on-the-job experience. This is a time to look for initiatives that are rooted in realism and crisis management marked by some skill and self-confidence. For Kennedy, the Cuban missile crisis came in the second year and his handling of it won him high marks as a tough but flexible statesman. Nixon's deft management of the Jordan crisis, particularly the mobilization of Israeli power to help deter the Syrians, came in his second year. Carter's Camp David success was similarly timed. Reagan's well-conceived but poorly executed Middle East peace initiative also came late in his second year. Bush's masterful handling of both the unraveling of the Soviet empire and the Gulf crisis in 1990 also came in his second year.

Third years are difficult to characterize. On the one hand, presidents have the power and the experience to do well, but they may feel the need to rush for success or to drop controversial issues before the election year is upon them. Particularly in recent years the reelection campaign seems to begin about midway through the third year. Eisenhower may have been somewhat affected by these considerations in the way he handled the Soviet Union in 1955. Here was a mixture of conciliation—the spirit of Geneva—and confusion—the response to the Soviet arms deal with Egypt. On this latter point, Eisenhower wavered between trying to win Egypt's President Gamal Abdel Nasser away from the Soviets with offers of economic aid for the Aswan High Dam and punishing him for refusing to make peace with Israel and for flirting with the Soviets. Not surprisingly, as the election year arrived, the decision was to punish Nasser. The Aswan offer was abruptly withdrawn; Nasser responded by nationalizing the Suez Canal; and before long Eisenhower faced a full-scale international crisis on the eve of elections.

Kennedy's third year is difficult to judge. He seems to have been on the way toward dealing effectively with the Soviets on arms control. Where he was heading with his policy toward Southeast Asia is difficult to determine.

Carter's third year was a mixed one in foreign policy. It began with the collapse of the Shah's regime in Iran, which caused great confusion in Washington. About the same time, however, Carter threw himself into the final negotiations for [an] Egyptian-Israeli peace treaty and was successful. He also pushed SALT II through to signature. But he dropped the Middle East issue when the Palestinian autonomy negotiations were getting underway, thus ensuring their failure, and he was unable to win Senate ratification for SALT II.

Reagan's record in 1983, his third year, was not distinguished. He presided over a Lebanese–Israeli peace agreement, which went sour almost immediately; he clashed with Syria, without any significant gains; and toward the end of the year seemed to lose interest altogether in the troubled Middle East. Bush, by contrast, in his third year brought the Gulf war to a successful conclusion and, with secretary James Baker's assistance, managed to organize the Madrid Peace Conference on the Middle East. So successful did Bush seem in late 1991 that his reelection seemed assured and most potential Democratic challengers were not interested in running against him. Finally, Clinton, who had little to show for his first two years in foreign policy, began to hit his stride in year three, especially in Bosnia, where a firmer, more consistent policy seemed to yield at least limited results.

Election years rarely witness great success in foreign policy. Carter struggled in frustration with the Iranian hostage crisis. Reagan withdrew ignominiously from Lebanon after more than 250 Marines had died. The great exception to this pattern, of course, was Nixon in 1972. Nixon was an unusual president in many ways. He had served as vice president under Eisenhower for eight years, and thus came to the Oval Office with much more knowledge of world affairs than other presidents. He also had a shrewd sense for timing in politics and seemed to realize that his reelection prospects would be helped if he could demonstrate his skill in foreign policy in the election year. Most other presidents have shied away from foreign policy initiatives as the election drew close. Nixon, however, prepared his biggest moves in near secrecy over the previous years. Then in 1972 he brought the American involvement in Vietnam to an end, he traveled to China, and he signed the SALT I agreement in Moscow. All this took place in the space of several months and in an election year. His Democratic challenger, who had been painting Nixon as a reckless warmonger, never had a chance. Many voters, who felt little personal regard for Nixon, nonetheless had to admit that he was a master at the game of nations. His electoral victory was complete.

Bush's reelection strategy seemed similar to Nixon's, but without the same result. Bush continued to act presidential, pressing for serious movement on Middle East peace, helping ease out a hard-line Israeli government, and continuing to manage the delicate relations with the post-Soviet states of Russia and Eastern Europe. But with the Cold War over, his foreign-policy credentials suddenly counted for less, and his seeming disinterest in domestic issues proved to be his undoing at the polls.

It remains to look briefly at the pattern of recent second terms. Reagan got off to a bad start with the Iran-Contra affair late in 1985. The same year, he let drop a promising initiative on Arab-Israeli peace. Part of the problem seemed to be that no one was really in charge, and perhaps his easy reelection gave Reagan a feeling of invulnerability. Except for a relatively steady course on U.S.-Soviet relations and a successful handling of a Kuwaiti request for reflagging of oil tankers in 1987, Reagan's last years were not impressive. His secretary of state tried to launch a major initiative on the Middle East in 1988, but it was too late. The only surprise here was the decision to begin talks with the PLO, a gift to the Bush administration, and timed to come just after the election in 1988.

Clinton's second term prospects are uncertain. He began with a new team, including an energetic secretary of state, Madeleine Albright. Late in 1997, as tensions rose in the Middle East between Arabs and Israelis, he moved, for the first time, from his very cautious approach and held out the promise of greater engagement. He also moved forward on NATO enlargement, a popular step with uncertain consequences. At best, he would have another year or two to define his foreign-policy legacy before time would run out because of electoral-cycle realities.

Conclusion

The American political system was not designed with the conduct of foreign policy in mind. Checks and balances, frequent elections, and the concept of popular sovereignty were all meant to limit abuses of power, not to make it easy for a president to govern. In foreign policy the constraints are often less than in the domestic area. But in modern times even foreign policy has become highly controversial, and thus subject to all the political forces that limit the power of the president.

To understand how American foreign policy is made, one needs to look carefully at the views of key decisionmakers, especially the presidents and their top advisors. The individuals do matter. But they operate within a political context that has some very regular features. Therefore, if they are to leave their imprint on policy, they will have to understand what the broader constitutional system allows. And they will have to learn much about the world as well.

Presidents do have great power at their disposal. It is often most usable in the midst of crises, when the normal restraints of political life are suspended, at least for a while. Presidents can also usually count on a fairly wide latitude in the conduct of foreign policy in their first two years. But in time the need to appeal to the electorate, to have congressional support, and to prepare for reelection appears to dominate thinking at the White House, regardless of who is the incumbent.

This means that the United States is structurally at a disadvantage in trying to develop and sustain politics that require a mastery of complex issues and call for consistency and a long-term vision to enhance the prospects of success. It is hard for presidents to look beyond the next few months. Consistency is often sacrificed for political expediency. Turnover of personnel in top positions erodes the prospects for continuity.

At the same time, the United States, for these very reasons, rarely pursues a strongly ideological foreign policy for long. There are pressures to pursue a course that has a broad popular support, eschewing extremes of left and right. Pragmatic criteria are a common part of policy debates. Thus, if one course of action has clearly failed, another can be tried. This may be hard on the nerves of other world leaders, but sometimes this experimental approach is needed if a viable policy is to be found. . . .

Realizing the full potential of the office of the presidency is probably the best practical solution to the problems posed for the conduct of foreign policy by the constitutionally designed electoral cycle. But that requires that the American people elect statesmen as presidents, and that cannot be expected in the television era. Thus, we will probably have to live with a system that weakens the ability to conduct an effective foreign policy. Understanding that reality may be small consolation, but it may serve to temper the grandiose notion that the United States, as a great power, can reshape the world in its image. Neither the realities of the world nor those of our political system will allow that.

Notes

1. See James MacGregor Burns, *The Deadlock of Democracy: Four-Party Politics in America* (Englewood Cliffs, N.J.: Prentice Hall, 1963), 8–23, on Madison's concept of checks and balances.

2. Cyrus Vance, *Hard Choices: Critical Years in America's Foreign Policy* (New York: Simon & Schuster, 1983), 13.

3. Zbigniew Brzezinski, *Power and Principle: Memories of the National Security Advisor, 1977–1981* (New York: Farrar, Straus, Giroux, 1983), 544.

Part II

The Institutional Setting

Foreign policy is a product of the actions officials take on behalf of the nation. Because of this, the way the government is structured for policy making also arguably affects the conduct and content of foreign affairs. Thus, we can hypothesize that a relationship exists between the substance of policy and the institutional setting from which it derives. The proposition is particularly compelling if attention is directed not to the foreign-policy goals the nation's leaders select but instead to the means they choose to satisfy particular objectives.

A salient feature of the American institutional setting is that the president and the institutionalized presidency—the latter consisting of the president's personal staff and the Executive Office of the President—are preeminent in the foreign-policy making process. This derives in part from the authority granted the president in the Constitution and in part from the combination of judicial interpretation, legislative acquiescence, personal assertiveness, and custom and tradition that have transformed the presidency into the most powerful office in the world.[1] The crisis-ridden atmosphere that characterized the Cold War era also contributed to the enhancement of presidential authority by encouraging the president to act energetically and decisively when dealing with global challenges. The widely shared consensus among American leaders and the American public that the international environment demanded an active American world role also contributed to the felt need for strong presidential leadership. Although this viewpoint was sometimes vigorously debated in the years following American involvement in Vietnam, the perceived need for strong presidential leadership was generally accepted throughout the Cold War era.

Because of the president's key role in foreign-policy making, it is useful to consider the institutional arrangements that govern the process as a series of concentric circles that effectively alter the standard government organization chart so as to draw attention to the core or most immediate source of the action (see Figure II.1). Thus, the innermost circle in the policymaking process consists of the president, his immediate personal advisors, and such important political appointees as the secretaries of state and defense, the director of central intelligence, and various under- and assistant secretaries who bear

FIGURE II.1
The concentric circles of policy making

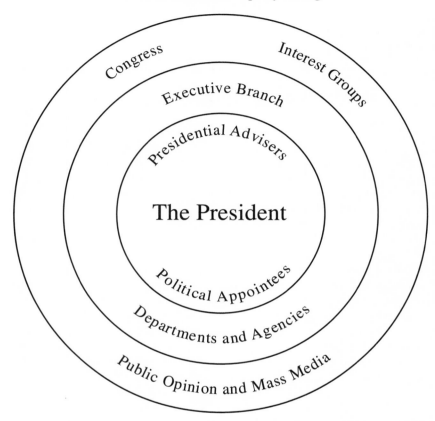

Source: Adapted from Roger Hilsman, *To Move a Nation* (New York: Doubleday, 1967), 541–544.

responsibility for carrying out policy decisions. Here, in principle, is where the most important decisions involving the fate of the nation are made.

The second concentric circle comprises the various departments and agencies of the executive branch. If we exclude from that circle the politically appointed heads of agencies and their immediate subordinates who are more properly placed in the innermost circle, we can think of the individuals within the second circle as career professionals who provide continuity in the implementation of policy from one administration to the next. Their primary tasks—in theory—are to provide top-level policymakers with the information necessary for sound decision making and to carry out the decisions policy-makers reach. As noted in the introduction to this book, the involvement of the United States in a complex webwork of interdependent ties with other nations in the world has led to the involvement in foreign affairs of many organizations whose primary tasks are seemingly oriented toward the domestic environment. The Treasury Department has become especially visible in recent years, as the globalization of the world political economy has increased the salience of economic issues as foreign-policy issues. The Departments of Agriculture, Commerce, and Justice have also figured prominently as globalization has blurred the distinction between foreign and domestic politics and policy. Still, the Departments of State and Defense and the intelligence community continue to command center stage among the dozens of executive-branch departments and agencies now involved in foreign affairs. The State Department's role derives from being the only department charged (in theory at least) with responsibility for the whole range of America's relations with other nations. The Defense Department and the intelligence community, and especially the Central Intelligence Agency (CIA), on the other hand, derived their importance from the threatening and crisis-ridden atmosphere of the Cold War years, in which they often had ready alternatives from which top-level policymakers could choose when diplomacy and negotiation seemed destined to fail. Each may play a diminished role in the post–Cold War world, but both remain principal actors in the foreign affairs government.

Moving beyond the departments and agencies of the executive branch, the third concentric circle consists of Congress. Although technically a single institutional entity, Congress often appears to embrace many different centers of power and authority—ranging from the House and Senate leadership to the various coalitions operative in the legislative branch, and from the various committees and subcommittees in which Congress does its real work to the individual senators and representatives who often vie with one another for publicity as well as power. Of all the institutions involved in foreign-policy making, Congress is least engaged in the day-to-day conduct of the nation's foreign relations, as reflected in its placement in the outermost circle.

The Institutional Setting as an Influence on American Foreign Policy

Does this stylized description of the relative influence of various institutions and actors involved in foreign-policy making continue to hold at the dawn of a new century? Roger Hilsman, who first suggested this institutional conceptualization some three decades ago in his *To Move a Nation,* even then cautioned against a too facile reliance upon this description. Although the institutional setting may affect the form and flow of policy, the politicking inherent in the process by no means conforms to the neatly compartmentalized institutionalized paths implied by Hilsman's framework. What the nation chooses to do abroad is more often the product of an intense political struggle among the prominent players in the policymaking process, the policymaking positions or roles occupied by the key decisionmakers, and the characteristics of those individuals. The changed and changing nature of the international system is also pertinent to the contemporary institutional setting. As the constraints and opportunities in the new era unfold, the character and responsiveness of the institutions steeped in decades of Cold War conflict can be expected to change. It is a hypothesis we examine in the essays in Part II.

Beginning with the innermost concentric circle, a case can be made that the post–Cold War changes in the global environment have had little impact on the presidency and its centrality in the governmental setting. Several years ago, Harvard political scientist Paul E. Peterson argued that the structure and constraints of the international system favor the executive's dominance of foreign-policy making, despite changes in Congress and the growth in the partisan nature of foreign policy after the Vietnam War.[2] In "Presidential Leadership and American Foreign Policy: Implications for a New Era," our first chapter in Part II, Glenn P. Hastedt and Anthony J. Eksterowicz extend this line of inquiry through the Clinton administration and essentially concur with Peterson's viewpoint.

Hastedt and Eksterowicz examine three alternative models of presidential governance and compare their applicability in foreign policy as revealed in presidents' practices since World War II. Each of the presidential governance or leadership models they examine derives from the philosophical views of the Founders of the Republic: The Hamiltonian model of leadership (the presidential government model) calls for a strong executive role in shaping foreign policy; the Jeffersonian model (the party-based model) calls for executive rule, albeit through a strong political party; and the Madisonian model (the executive/congressional model) seeks governance though the collaborative activities of the two branches of government.

From the point of view of domestic politics, each model has its advantages, but Hastedt and Eksterowicz point out that the critical variable affecting presidents' preferences among them is the nature of the international system. Since the end of World War II, when the international system "had become a menacing and ominous environment that held threats of an urgent, immediate and unlimited nature," the presidential government model became presidents' favored leadership style, especially when quick and decisive actions on global affairs were required. Furthermore, Hastedt and Eksterowicz note that Congress has generally acquiesced in that model of governance.

Despite the challenges to the Hamiltonian model in the wake of the Vietnam experience and with the end of the Cold War, presidents have continued to rely on it. Whereas recent presidents have been robbed of clear national security threats to justify reliance on the model, they have successfully "engaged in foreign-policy 'ad hocism' in which periodic understandings with Congress on how to conduct foreign policy are interspersed with presidential attempts to reassert primacy." As a result, the presidential leadership model has continued to prevail, as witnessed most recently in U.S. actions in Somalia, Haiti, and Bosnia. Although Hastedt and Eksterowicz contend that "the new, post–Cold War era provides a necessary, but not sufficient environment" for the emergence of other leadership styles, they maintain that "uncertainty over the direction of post–Cold War international politics propels . . . presidents to continue to rely on [the presidential government model]."

In "Without Restraint: Presidents' Military Initiatives from Korea to Bosnia, "Louis Fisher is equally pessimistic about the prospects of altering the balance of executive–legislative influence in foreign policy, even on issues involving the use of American force abroad. In this critical policy arena, presidents continue to act unilaterally. "Instead of coming to Congress for authority," as the Constitution calls for, "presidents are more likely to justify military actions either on the commander in chief clause . . . or on decisions reached by the UN Security Council and NATO."

President Truman encouraged this process early in the Cold War by first promising to obtain congressional approval for any use of U.S. troops as part of a United Nations operation, but then ignoring Congress when he sent American troops to Korea in June 1950. Presidents Bush and Clinton continued that tradition in the post–Cold War years. "Instead of seeking authority from Congress [to prosecute war against Saddam Hussein], Bush created a multinational alliance and encouraged the [United Nations] Security Council to authorize the use of military force." Even when Bush finally asked Congress to vote on the use of force in the Gulf, "he was asking for 'support,' not authority."

In sending American forces to Haiti and Bosnia, President Clinton followed a similar strategy. To deal with Haiti, he sought and obtained a Security Council resolution authorizing the invasion of Haiti and explicitly denied that he needed congressional support: "I have not agreed that I was constitutionally mandated to obtain the support of Congress." In Bosnia, he invoked authority under Article II of the Constitution and the NATO Treaty to deploy American forces as part of the Dayton Accords of November 1995, and he again denied that he needed congressional approval for his actions.

In all of these cases—Korea, the Persian Gulf, Haiti, and Bosnia—Congress acquiesced in presidential encroachment on its powers. Indeed, Fisher argues that "Congress . . . not only fails to fight back but even volunteers fundamental legislative powers, including the war power and the power of the purse." While partisan politics partially explains Congress's acquiescence, members of both political parties often support presidential prerogatives. In the end, Fisher worries that the process "undermines public control, the system of checks and balances, and constitutional government."

Another important institutional mechanism within the first concentric circle of foreign-policy making is the National Security Council (NSC) system. It consists of the formal NSC Council, the complex of interagency committees that carry on its work, and the NSC staff, which serves the president, his advisers, and the committees making up the NSC system. The NSC staff is headed by the president's assistant for national security affairs, who has assumed a position of prominence in recent decades. Similarly, the NSC system and staff have become crucial mechanisms within the institutionalized presidency used by the White House to ensure its control of policy making and to enhance prospects for policy coherence and consistency according to presidential wishes.

Often the visibility and power of the national security assistant has been cause for conflict with other key participants in the process, notably the secretary of state. That was especially apparent during the Nixon and Carter presidencies. During the Reagan presidency, the role of the NSC staff became more contentious—indeed, infamous—as the staff engaged in the abuse of power: Lieutenant Colonel Oliver L. North undertook covert operational activities designed to divert profits from the sale of arms to Iran to the contras fighting the Sandinista regime in Nicaragua in apparent contravention of congressional prohibitions. Steps were later taken to ensure that the NSC staff would no longer engage in operational activities, and both the Bush and Clinton presidencies were marked by the absence of public squabbles between their respective secretaries of state (James A. Baker for Bush; Warren Christopher and Madeleine Albright for Clinton) and national security advisers (Brent Scowcroft for Bush; Anthony Lake and Samuel Berger for Clinton). Still, Scowcroft, Lake, and Berger were powerful players in the policy process, exercising decisive influence in supporting President Bush's determination to evict Iraqi forces from Kuwait and pressing President Clinton to intervene in Haiti and to support the expansion of NATO.

Geoffrey Kemp, himself a former member of the NSC staff, gives a brief history of the NSC system and explains why the White House dominates foreign and national security policy decision making. As noted in the introduction to this book, personality factors help to explain how presidents choose to manage the conduct of foreign affairs. Kemp acknowledges the importance of presidential style and idiosyncrasies, but he argues that "institutional factors and the policy-making process play a key role in foreign policy decision making, no matter who occupies the Oval Office. This stems from the unique role the United States plays in world politics and the unique system of government in Washington, a system that is very different from those of most other established democracies." These and other institutional realities make "a strong NSC staff . . . necessary."

Having made the case for a strong NSC staff, Kemp turns his attention to the importance of the president's schedule and explains "how the pressure of 'the schedule' influences . . . day-to-day operations, the decision-making process, career incentives, and the lack of coherent long-term planning." He also explains why "managing the media has become one of the most important tasks of the White House staff" and concludes with an assessment of the possibility of orchestrating a foreign policy that looks beyond the short term, "which is frequently measured in hours rather than in days or months." Although Kemp's experience as a member of the Reagan administration's NSC staff dictates his examples, the processes he describes remain timeless.

If the institutions in the innermost (presidential) concentric circle have been seemingly immune to the recent changes in the international environment, the same cannot be said for the institutions depicted in the second and third concentric circles of Figure II.1. Arguably, these institutions have been significantly affected by the forces of globalization and fragmentation that have accompanied the end of the Cold War and by the changes occurring within the institutions themselves. Congress, for example, has undergone significant internal changes in composition and operating procedures since the 1994 congressional elections, with a reduction in the number of committees and subcommittees, enhanced power for committee chairs and their appointment powers, and changes in the role of congressional staff.[3] The Republican-controlled Congress has also sought several important foreign-policy changes, including elimination of the War Powers Resolution, sharp reductions in foreign aid, reorganization of the foreign affairs bureaucracy, and increases in defense spending.

In "End of An Era: Congress and Foreign Policy After the Cold War," James M. Lindsay considers these sources of change as he examines how different Congress is likely to be in the new era. In contrast to Hastedt and Eksterowicz, Lindsay begins by asserting that "the era of undisputed executive preeminence on foreign policy is over." The reason, he argues, is that the demise of the Soviet Union undermined the foreign-policy consensus that gave rise to presidential dominance of foreign affairs. The new environment has "emboldened members of Congress to challenge the White House over the direction of U.S. foreign policy."

Recent congressional initiatives in foreign policy, such as the 1995 foreign aid bill that sought to limit presidential power and to restrict American involvement in United Nations activities, are illustrative of this more assertive posture. Still, Lindsay contends that these actions neither challenge presidential prerogatives in foreign policy nor lead the country toward isolationism. Instead, they simply reassert congressional prerogatives that are well within Congress's constitutional powers (a conclusion consistent with Fisher's viewpoint). Furthermore, recent congressional foreign-policy initiatives rest in part on the belief that the Clinton administration suffered several foreign-policy "missteps," and that the return of Congress to Republican control after four decades out of power ensured that the Democratic president would now be challenged. Nevertheless, fundamental to the congressional change in foreign-policy activism, according to Lindsay, is that "the norms and beliefs that once limited congressional activism are crumbling" now that the United States no longer faces a compelling external threat. As Jeremy Rosner, a State Department official responsible for securing congressional approval for the expansion of NATO, put the dilemma cogently: "Relative peace on earth will tend to mean relatively less peace down the length of Pennsylvania Avenue."[4]

Although sustained congressional activism will not mean the end of presidential leadership, and although activism will surely reveal disadvantages as well as advantages, Lindsay concludes that "U.S. foreign policy is best served when a modest level of tension and conflict pervades executive–legislative relations." Thus, he speaks approvingly in concluding that "post–Cold War presidents will find their leadership skills in foreign policy sorely tested for years to come."

According to the Constitution, the president and Congress are coequal partners in foreign policy making. And both are elected by the American people. In practice, however, the bureaucratic organizations of the permanent foreign affairs government depicted in the second concentric circle in Figure II.1 provide continuity from one administration to the next and through the continuing presidential and congressional electoral cycles. Not surprisingly, then, the organizations comprising the foreign affairs government are often described as "the fourth branch of government."

People who work in the "fourth branch" often spend their entire careers managing the routine affairs that comprise America's relations with other countries. Indeed, these career professionals and the organizations they work for are expected to be the government's "eyes and ears," searching for incipient global changes and assessing American needs and interests abroad. In the new era, then, these key institutions and the people who populate them can be expected to change as global challenges and opportunities change. As the last four chapters in Part II suggest, organizations central to American diplomatic, military, intelligence, and economic policy making are in fact responding to the pressures of a rapidly globalizing world that has altered the tradition mix of security and nonsecurity threats. How well they have adapted is, however, a matter of sometimes contentious political dispute, as the previous chapters dealing with congressional-executive relations suggest.

Strobe Talbott, deputy secretary of state in the Clinton administration and the political appointee with primary responsibility for managing the internal operations of the Department of State, writes persuasively about the need for organizational change in his "Globalization and Diplomacy: The View from Foggy Bottom." Globalization—propelled by "the powerful technological forces of the Information Age [that] have helped to stitch together the economic, political, and cultural lives of nations, making borders more permeable to the movement of people, products, and ideas"—has already begun to transform the lives of people around the world in both positive and negative ways. The challenge for American foreign policy is to respond to globalization in a positive way. And, according to Talbott, the State Department, America's foreign-policy organization responsible for the conduct of U.S. foreign affairs, has an important role to play in shaping this response.

As Talbott notes, the State Department has already undertaken some important changes that are transforming the nature of America's diplomatic operations. New bureaus have been created and others consolidated; greater interactions on global issues are taking place between the State Department and the Departments of Defense, Commerce, and Justice in Washington and abroad. Most importantly, the State Department has sought to implement a strategy of working "multi-multilaterally." That is, its personnel have cooperated with other American agencies, other countries, and numerous governmental and nongovernmental institutions to address issues that cannot be resolved by a single agency, country, or institution—whether it be to ensure water resources in the Middle East or to implement the Dayton Accords in Bosnia. In this way, Talbott argues, the United States and other governments can "leverage scarce resources and improve their ability to address transnational threats."

Finally, and importantly, he also argues that the State Department increasingly reaches out to the American people and to Congress to keep them informed of the diplomatic changes emanating from global interdependence and to seek their support in these endeavors. In this way, American foreign-policy actions arguably will be able to channel "the force of interdependence . . . to the advantage of our own citizens and other nations that share our interests and values."

The American military as a foreign and national security policy institution has hardly been immune from the impact of the end of the Cold War. The Bush administration was initially reluctant to make significant changes in the military establishment and its mission as the Cold War's challenges dissipated. Congress became insistent, helping to spark a reorientation toward what became known as the Base Force. The Base Force concept called for a significantly smaller military establishment, one also designed to respond to different threats than previously.[5] The Clinton administration followed this plan with a Bottom-Up Review that called for a fundamental change in the defense strategy of the United States—from one focused on the Soviet Union to one directed toward the new dangers posed by the spread of weapons of mass destruction and the prospects of increased regional and ethnic conflicts, thus calling for a smaller force with increased mobility and greater reliance on friends and allies in maintaining international peace and security.[6] Two follow-on reviews in 1997, the Quadrennial Defense Review and the Defense Reform Initiative, reiterated the essential theme of this initial review.[7] Both also called for more consolidation and restructuring of the American military.

Eliot A. Cohen in "Crisis in Civil-Military Relations?" takes the need for military restructuring a step further by targeting for reform the officer corps and the policy-making relationship between the civilian and military sectors. In particular, he focuses on the three major problems that have recently developed between the military establishment and civilian leaders. First, the military, and particularly the officer corps, has become increasingly politicized. Although this trend accelerated with the Vietnam War experience (when the military was often vilified), it perhaps reached its apex with the Clinton administration. Because President Clinton did not serve in the military during the Vietnam era and in fact vigorously protested against it, many in the professional military looked askance at his leadership. Second, the military and civilian sectors within American society are becoming increasingly estranged. Officers recruited to the military now come from a comparatively narrow segment of American society—from the families of former military officers and from the military academies. The result is that the values and issues of salience to the military and the rest of society diverge. Furthermore, political leaders often have a limited understanding or appreciation of the role of the military in American society.

Third, Cohen points to the "centralization of military authority" and the enhanced role of a diminished number of military officials in providing policy advice. Since the passage of the Goldwater-Nichols Reorganization Act of 1986, the first major reorganization of the military establishment in many years, "the chairman of the JCS [Joint Chiefs of Staff] serves as a de facto commander of the American armed forces, operating under the supervision of either the president or the secretary of defense." As a result, there has been a diminution in the sources of military advice for civilian policymakers, a reduction in the extent of long-term planning, and a weakening of interservice competition and policy advice. More generally, these decisionmaking changes have increased the policymaking role of military units with the Defense Department at the expense of the Pentagon's civilian leaders.

In Cohen's view, several actions are necessary to alter these trends and to reform civilian-military relations. Among his prescriptions are changing the role of the military service academies in producing officers, recruiting more "citizen-soldiers" (those who would serve for a limited time in the military), improving military officers' understanding of civil-military relations, and instituting greater civilian understanding of the military. Without these changes, Cohen concludes, "the trends in American civil-military relations could breed certain pathologies," perhaps further eroding civilian control of the military.

The intelligence community is the third major foreign policy institution in the second concentric circle of policy making buffeted by recent changes in world politics. While the intelligence community has long come under criticism for its failures in making quality intelligence estimates, perhaps the singular event of the 1990s that most tellingly rocked the intelligence establishment was the revelation that Aldrich "Rick" Ames, a Soviet counter-intelligence agent in the CIA, had been a Soviet (and Russian) "mole" for more than a decade. Ames's espionage provided his foreign patrons hundreds of classified documents and identified countless CIA agents, resulting in the deaths of at least ten.[8] The revelation produced a firestorm of calls for significant reform of the intelligence community, including the elimination of CIA espionage activities.[9]

In "A New Role for the CIA?" Bruce D. Berkowitz contributes to this debate by calling for a fundamental rethinking of how the intelligence community may be restructured to meet the needs of the new era. Critical of the timid efforts of the post–Ames reform initiated by the Clinton administration, Berkowitz suggests a more basic restructuring is necessary if the intelligence community is to remain an effective policymaking voice in the new era, which Berkowitz sees as the "Information Age." He proposes that the community be decentralized, with analysts located closer to the consumer of the intelligence products and given greater latitude in deciding what information to pursue and what mechanisms to use to maximize innovation. Much as American industries have had to retool and refocus their energies to meet the needs of their markets and consumers, Berkowitz argues that the intelligence community must be more innovative if it is to play a useful policymaking role in the new era.

Trade policy already has proven more important since the end of the Cold War, as the globalization of the world political economy has blurred the distinction between foreign and domestic policy. The Clinton administration encouraged globalization as part of an economic strategy designed to enhance American competitiveness overseas. It sought to lower tariff barriers, encourage development of new free trade areas, and expand American investment opportunities in big emerging markets ("The Big Ten"), the world's fastest growing economies.[10]

The Clinton strategy was not always welcomed by domestic constituencies, particularly those who saw themselves as victimized by low-wage labor abroad, causing the presumed export of American jobs to foreign producers. As in the past, these groups, once mobilized, turned to Congress and various executive branch departments and agencies to protect their interests in a globalization process believed inimical to their own well-being.

So how is trade policy made? Is the interest group model discussed in Part I applicable here? Are institutional constraints implied by the second concentric circle of policy making depicted in Figure II.1 more potent? Or is it a combination of the two?

Stephen D. Cohen, Joel R. Paul, and Robert A. Blecker address the questions in our final chapter in Part II. They acknowledge that no simple explanation can account for all policy making in this area, but they also acknowledge that competing explanations of how trade policy is made may usefully be divided between those in which the government is a "reactive decision maker" and those in which it is an "active decision maker."

In the reactive decisionmaker explanation, the government is largely removed from the process. Here, trade policy decisions are the result of the interplay among competing domestic interest groups, competing sovereign states, and the vagaries of domestic and global market conditions. In the active decisionmaker explanation, on the other hand, the government is a central actor. Cohen, Paul, and Blecker conclude that the latter is a more compelling explanation of trade policy making.

To support their analysis, the authors introduce three trade policymaking models: (1) a "presidential fiat" model, which depicts the White House as dominating policy making; (2) a "bureaucratic politics" model, which views policy as the result of competition among executive branch bureaucracies; and (3) an "interbranch" model, which ascribes trade policy to the competition between the executive branch and the legislative branches of government.

Each of these models has explanatory virtues, but Cohen, Paul, and Blecker are unambiguous in their conclusion that the bulk of American trade policy is best explained by bureaucratic politics and the interactions between Congress and the president. Unlike the security sphere, then, and particularly issues relating to the use of force abroad, few decisions fit the presidential fiat model. Such a conclusion has an important implication in that it suggests that the second and third concentric circles of Hilsman's policy-making model will increasingly dominate the trade policy area in the new millennium.

Notes

1. For assessments of legislative acquiescence and judicial tolerance of the executive's dominance of American foreign policy, see Harold Koh, *The National Security Constitution* (New Haven, Conn.: Yale University Press, 1990), and Gordon Silverstein, *Imbalance of Powers: Constitutional Interpretation and the Making of American Foreign Policy* (New York: Oxford University Press, 1997).

2. Paul E. Peterson, "The International System and Foreign Policy," in Paul E. Peterson, ed., *The President, the Congress, and the Making of Foreign Policy* (Norman, Okla.: University of Oklahoma Press, 1994), pp. 3–22.

3. Steven S. Smith and Eric D. Lawrence, "Party Control of Committees in the Republican Congress," in Lawrence C. Dodd and Bruce I. Oppenheimer, eds. *Congress Reconsidered,* sixth edition (Washington, D.C.: CQ Press, 1997).

4. Jeremy D. Rosner, *The New Tug of War: Congress, the Executive Branch, and National Security* (Washington, D.C.: Carnegie Endowment for International Peace, 1995), p. 4.

5. See Paul Stockton, "Congress and U.S. Military Policy Beyond the Cold War," in Randall B. Ripley and James M. Lindsay, eds., *Congress Resurgent: Foreign and Defense Policy on Capitol Hill* (Ann Arbor: The University of Michigan Press, 1993), pp. 235–259, and Paul Stockton, "Beyond Micromanagement: Congressional Budget-

ing for a Post-Cold War Military," *Political Science Quarterly* 110 (Summer 1995): 233–259.

6. Les Aspin, Secretary of Defense, *Report on the Bottom-Up Review,* October 1993.

7. William S. Cohen, *Report of the Quadrennial Defense Review,* May 1997, and "Secretary Cohen Reshapes Defense for the 21st Century," New Release, Office of the Assistant Secretary of Defense (Public Affairs), November 10, 1997. Both are available via the Internet.

8. For an account of the Ames case, see Tim Weiner, David Johnston, and Neil A. Lewis, *Betrayal: The Story of Aldrich Ames, An American Spy* (New York: Random House, 1995).

9. See Roger Hilsman, "Does the CIA Still Have a Role?" *Foreign Affairs* 74 (September/October 1995): 104–116.

10. See Jeffrey E. Garten, *The Big Ten: The Big Emerging Markets and How They Will Change Our Lives* (New York: Basic Books, 1997).

9

Presidential Leadership and American Foreign Policy: Implications for a New Era

Glenn P. Hastedt and Anthony J. Eksterowicz

For the greater part of the Cold War era it has been axiomatic among presidential studies scholars that the nation's chief executive possesses much more leeway and authority in foreign policy than in domestic policy. Even in the realm of foreign policy, however, post–Vietnam presidents have not managed to establish a procedural consensus regarding the proper roles of Congress and the presidency. President Nixon's grand strategy emphasized the emergence of a stable multipolar world guided by the United States. President Carter posited the development of more peaceful and cooperative superpower relationships and a mutually beneficial dialogue with the Third World. President Reagan presented a vision of a fully democratic world reflective of and supporting American values. To this listing, one can now add President Bush's vision of a "New World Order" and President Clinton's "New Internationalism." These presidents have experienced frustration with the Congress over the direction and implementation of their goals and strategies largely due to the failure to establish an interbranch procedural consensus on how to make foreign policy. In two instances this frustration led to constitutional crises, namely, Watergate and the Iran-Contra scandal.

Cold War presidents operated within the context of what James MacGregor Burns first characterized in 1965 as the presidential government model of leadership.[1] Post–Cold War presidents have struggled with this model and exhibited tendencies to experiment, perhaps subconsciously, with elements of other leadership models. The Clinton administration is a case in point. This chapter questions the utility of relying solely upon the presidential leadership model in the face of new and evolving characteristics in the international system and recent trends within Congress. For more than four decades the Cold

War served as a catalyst and source of support for this style of presidential leadership. Its passing thus holds the potential not only for transforming the nature of world politics but also altering the landscape of American politics. The nature of this transformation can be brought into sharper focus by examining alternative models of presidential leadership and how the international environment has helped to shape the presidency.

Models of Presidential Leadership

Presidential Government

Burns describes the presidential leadership model in his book *Presidential Government*. Rooted in Hamiltonian thought, it favors a strong executive because, as Alexander Hamilton stated, "Energy in the executive is a leading character in the definition of good government. It is essential to the protection of the community against foreign attacks."[2] The Constitution's carefully constructed division of authority between the president and Congress concerning war-making powers has contributed directly to the realization of Hamilton's strong, energetic presidency.

While many presidents have conducted business under the presidential government leadership model, most notably Abraham Lincoln and Theodore Roosevelt, the zenith of its practice occurred during the Great Depression–World War II–Cold War eras. In the middle of this period Richard Neustadt published his widely praised work titled *Presidential Power*.[3] No other study of the modern presidency has been more influential. Neustadt's central theme was and is the acquisition, maintenance, and utilization of personal presidential power. He favored activist presidents who acquired and used power to achieve their public policy agendas. These agendas were formulated to move the nation forward while allowing the president, through the concentration of power in the White House, to preserve and protect national security interests during the Cold War era.

Successful leadership required that presidents guard and protect their power, especially from congressional encroachment. For this reason a president's public image and prestige were typically managed through the collection and control of information, because in Washington, those who possess information also possess power. Quite literally image became everything. Presidents surrounded themselves with advisors knowledgeable and skilled in the craft of advertising. Media and public opinion consultants proliferated at the White House level. These advisors exerted major influence on policy.

The attributes of flexibility in action, speed in decision making, control of information, and assertiveness ascribed to the presidential leadership model were valuable and necessary commodities. They were emphasized by those who saw the United States engaged in a protracted Cold War struggle with an inherently hostile and untrustworthy Soviet Union. Having acquired the ability to act, presidents were reluctant to relinquish it. Periods of reduced tension did not bring about a voluntary diminution of presidential power. Instead, they ushered in repeated rounds of interbranch conflict.

Two themes dominated these clashes. The first concerned the wisdom of presidential dominance. Critics pointed to such questionable foreign policy undertakings as Vietnam, Iran-Contra, covert action in Chile and Angola, domestic surveillance of American citizens, and arms sales to the Shah of Iran as evidence of the imperfect fit between presidential monopolization of information and the correctness or success of policy. The second concerned the need for Congress to organize and arm itself with the tools necessary to participate in the foreign policy debate. While the dispersion of power in Congress through the proliferation of subcommittees is widely acknowledged as transforming Congress into an even more unruly body, it also had the effect of increasing Congress's oversight powers. Congressional information and research agencies like the Congressional Budget Office (CBO) and the Congressional Research Service (CRS) were established or refurbished. With the CBO, Congress acquired its own institution for analyzing the president's budget. The net result of these changes, coupled with increases in staff and computer technology, moved Congress in the direction of a more capable force in "codetermining" foreign policy. This was especially the case in areas previously considered sacrosanct by presidents: arms sales, foreign aid, arms control, and defense budgeting. Furthermore, the Congress continued to explore avenues of increasing its voice in the most integral of all presidential foreign-policy powers, namely war-making.

Because of growing doubts about the wisdom of a strong, powerful presidency plus the reality of a stronger and more assertive Congress, a series of conceptual challenges confront advocates of the presidential governance model in the post–Cold War era. First, to what extent is the model compatible with the views of those who crafted the Constitution? The Founders desired a balanced government with each branch sharing powers. But the conventional view of the separation of powers doctrine as separate and compartmentalized powers for each branch of government has never materialized. The Founders were aware that under a strict version of the separation of powers doctrine each branch of government could engage in an abuse of power within its own autonomous sphere. A close reading of James Madison's *Federalist Papers* reveals a more accurate view of the separation of powers doctrine as emphasizing *separate* institutions *sharing* power. This is true even with regard to foreign policy. As Harold H. Koh notes,

> The Framers designed the checks and balances scheme to apply principally in the realm of foreign affairs. The three branches agreed that even governmental decisions regarding covert actions should be conducted through the scheme of

balanced institutional participation mandated by the National Security Constitution—under presidential management, but subject to the checks provided by congressional legislation and judicial review.[4]

Second, in presenting the normative justification for the presidential concentration of power, the presidential governance model draws heavily on the distinction between foreign and domestic policy. Its advocates routinely point to the 1936 Supreme Court ruling in *United States v. Curtiss Wright Export Corporation*. In rendering this decision Justice Sutherland asserted that foreign and domestic policy were inherently different. Sutherland concluded that presidents must be able to act quickly to protect American interests abroad, and that the system of checks and balances was ill-suited for dealing with foreign policy problems. The difficulty today is that the logic underlying Sutherland's position has been steadily eroded by the emergence of a class of policy issues that do not respect the foreign-domestic boundary line. The environment, drugs, immigration, foreign investment in the United States, the national debt, education, investment policy, and military base closings are among the most prominent of these "intermestic" issues. Congress is involved in all of these areas. Furthermore, these issues will most assuredly affect congressional constituencies. It is not self-evident that the proper procedure for dealing with them is through a president freed of the restraints imposed by a system of checks and balances.

Third, because post-Vietnam presidents have had to labor without a societal and elite consensus regarding the proper direction and purpose of American foreign policy, we can question whether the style of leadership inherent in the presidential government model is properly suited for operating under such conditions. Can an enduring societal consensus be imposed by a president? Was this not the central problem demonstrated by the Watergate and Iran-Contra crises? Is this leadership model conducive to the creation of such a consensus? Is it suitable for the cyclical periods of internationalism that many find to be present in American foreign policy but inappropriate for periods of isolationism? Finally, if the absence of an enduring consensus means that a new winning coalition must be created around each successive foreign-policy problem confronting the United States, is the presidential government model best suited for this task? Inevitably, a president will lose valuable political capital building these coalitions.

To the extent that these questions are answered in the negative one must search for a new model of presidential leadership more suited to contemporary realities. There are two leading candidates, a party-based model and an executive/congressional collaboration model.

Executive/Party Model of Leadership

Burns presents in his *Presidential Government* an alternative model of presidential leadership that emphasizes executive teamwork, majority rule, and party responsibility. It is a leadership model with Jeffersonian roots. Thomas Jefferson was wary of a strong presidency. He particularly disliked the possibility of a president being reelected for an indefinite period of time and favored a rotation-of-office provision for the president. Jefferson had an inherent belief in "collective leadership." As president he ruled through a strong political party. This approach enabled him to achieve his goals in the Congress. Unlike the Hamiltonian model of presidential governance, which depended upon the energy and guile of essentially one person, the Jeffersonian model emphasized rule by the majority party. Its goal was to ensure strong leadership with the president as titular head of the party in power. Accordingly, the president could not—and would not—lead alone. Instead, leadership was a collective enterprise, as was political success and failure. Woodrow Wilson was perhaps the last president to rule through a party model of leadership. Notwithstanding its lack of recent usage, the model has been a favorite of American political scientists enthralled with the responsible-party model of governance.

At least in the short run there are a number of problems associated with the Jeffersonian model that prevent it from serving as a credible alternative to the presidential leadership model. First, political parties have declined in power and prestige ever since the Wilson presidency. In part they have been victims of the "good government," antiparty, Progressive reform movement at the turn of the century. Reforms such as the direct primary, initiative, referendum, and recall have all combined to weaken the political party as a public policy facilitator. Second, a comparative analysis of responsible party systems in other countries suggests that, even if instituted, this model would not necessarily generate policies in tune with the public's interest. Third, there has always been an antiparty theme in American politics. Ever since their inception political parties have been viewed as elitist, even nondemocratic institutions. As Jeanne Hahn notes concerning the efficiency implied by the responsible party model, "It would be very efficient government indeed. But accountable to whom? Certainly not the people, from who it would be largely insulated. The people are excluded from the proposed process except in their role as atomized voters—disciplined or required by constitutional directive, to vote a party slate."[5]

A fourth criticism focuses on the difficulties that the responsible party leadership model would face in the current political climate. Two points in particular bear noting. Since the end of World War II, the United States government has been divided more often than not, with the Democratic Party controlling the Congress and the Republican Party capturing the White House. As a result of the 1994 congressional election this situation was reversed, but divided government remains the norm, not the exception. Additionally, a recent Supreme Court ruling (*Rutan v. Republican Party of Illinois,* 1990) appears to strike at the very heart of the responsible party model. The court ruled that federal, state, and local governments cannot refuse to hire, promote, or transfer most employees because of their political affiliations or party activities. Many commentators view this ruling as mitigating the value of, if not outlawing, party patronage, which is essential for strong and effective political parties.

The inadequacies of party-based presidential leadership lead to a consideration of a more collaborative model, one that emphasizes the ideas of neither Alexander Hamilton nor Thomas Jefferson but those of another of the nation's Founders, James Madison.

The Executive/Congressional Leadership Model

The model of governance based on Madisonian premises is the least developed leadership model in Burn's *Presidential Government*. The Madisonian concept of presidential leadership emphasizes four elements: (1) checks and balances among branches of government striving to protect their powers; (2) the protection of minority rights against federal powers; (3) the protection against tyrannical majorities seeking to turn government toward serving their own ends; and (4) the institution of prudent, limited government that would shun rash, undeliberative action. A government could operate only through a popular consensus. All of this implies a model of presidential leadership that stresses the limits imposed on the executive by the Constitution and the Congress. Burns offers the Taft administration as an example of this model in action.

The Madisonian leadership model remains underdeveloped and obscure in part because it has received little support from the academic world (which largely prefers the responsible party model) or from the policymaking community (which prefers the presidential leadership model). It runs counter to the speed, decisiveness, and flexibility promised by the adherents of presidential government and to the centralization of party power in the strong party model. Furthermore, fitting this model to current conditions would require some modifications. Instead of each branch of government striving to protect its powers, a collaborative mode of governance based on Madison's ideas would emphasize separate institutions sharing power. Thus, each branch, while mindful of its own powers, would construct mechanisms or tools to aid interbranch collaboration.

In comparison with the two other models of leadership, the Madisonian model possesses a number of advantages. First, it is probably more in keeping with the constitutional design of checks and balances and the separation of powers that the Founders envisioned. Second, it is more attuned to periods of divided rule, as has become commonplace in recent decades. Third, it would seem to recognize the importance of reaching a consensus through consultation and bargaining among the plethora of interests in any one policy or issue area.

If this model could be instituted it would provide presidents with valuable tools for leadership during periods of divided government. Presidents can no longer realistically hope to freeze Congress out of the decisionmaking process through the denial of information. Breakthroughs in modern communication and transportation technologies simply do not allow this. Real-time communication between the battlefield and national decisionmaking centers provides congressional policymakers with great amounts of information and the opportunity to make their foreign-policy views known. This is true both for a crisis such as that leading to the Persian Gulf War, when senators and representatives were repeatedly asked to comment (but declined to do so for political reasons), and for more slowly evolving foreign-policy issues. For example, legislators from the United States and nearly three dozen other countries meet once a year to make recommendations to the Organization for Security and Cooperation in Europe (OSCE) concerning security questions, human rights, and economics. These recommendations comprise the agenda for annual foreign ministers meetings of the OSCE. Their participation in this largely executive domain implies that members of Congress have a direct role to play in shaping foreign policy within this important transatlantic institution. It may also imply closer executive–congressional collaboration.

Potential structural building blocks for such a model of presidential leadership can be found in the many calls for institutional reform and innovation being put forward in the foreign-policy issue area. Many have argued that meeting the challenges of the post–Cold War will probably require institutional innovations "no less significant" than those put in place in the 1940s, when the CIA, Defense Department, and National Security Council (NSC) were established. The CIA has already begun the process of institutional reform with the creation of a new directorate whose task it is to identify the changing intelligence requirements for the new era. Foremost among these is the perceived need to retool the CIA for economic intelligence. There is no reason to expect that the presidential bureaucracy will be immune from similar pressures for change. One expert in the field of arms control makes the case for appointing a special deputy to the president, who would be in charge of managing rather than controlling the ratification process and creating a special NSC staff committee that would handle relations with Congress and the media.[6]

It is also possible to identify nascent procedural and institutional building blocks on which a Madisonian-based model of presidential leadership might be based. For example, in the area of arms control the Carter administration established the practice of appointing congressional advisors to the SALT II negotiations in Geneva. These advisors were involved in both formal and informal treaty discussions and reviewed the draft of the SALT II agreement. The congressional advisory group continued under the Reagan administration, despite its very different approach to arms control. This type of collaborative arrangement could be extended with the initiation of Executive Congressional Task Forces on arms control issues. The purpose of such task forces would be to better formulate and integrate arms control policy. Other examples of collaborative arrangements include bipartisan congressional representation on the president's team at the annual G-7 summit meetings of the world's leading economic powers to ensure a congressional perspective.

In the area of budget policy the executive-congressional budget agreements of 1990 and 1997 were negotiated by selected congressional and executive budget officials in a summit format. While one may disagree with the substance of these agreements, no one can deny that a collaborative process existed. Perhaps this type of collaboration could be extended by the development of Congressional Administration Support and Evaluation (CASE) task forces for various areas of budget policy. The purpose of such institutions would be to monitor and evaluate support in relation to program budget needs at the department, agency, or program level. Collaboration and compromise would be the goal of such task forces. The National Academy of Public Administration in their report *Beyond Distrust: Building Bridges Between Congress and the Executive* advocated the establishment of institutions such as executive and congressional staff-to-staff working groups to "facilitate interbranch communications during policy development and program implementation."[7]

The foregoing initiatives would be in keeping with the spirit of a Madisonian model of presidential leadership. Another possibility would be to expand use of the type of congressional-executive collaboration implied in the "fast-track" concept that has been used in international trade negotiations. The procedure requires that Congress approve executive-negotiated trade agreements with an up-or-down vote, and not have the opportunity to amend the agreements. Rather than exclude Congress until the details of an agreement are all but worked out, the logic of the fast-track process stresses close executive–congressional collaboration early in the negotiations and throughout the negotiating process. Congressional approval is assured not simply by structuring the ratification vote as an all or nothing affair but by formally presenting Congress with an agreement with which it already concurs. A fast-track procedure in the area of arms control could be useful for ensuring that the technical agreements worked out regarding cuts in weapons systems and verification procedures would have congressional support before they are publicly announced, and that any politically necessary compensatory action, such as increased spending on weapons systems not covered by the agreement, would have congressional approval.

The Presidency and the International System

In presenting our three models of presidential leadership we have alluded to the ways in which changes in the international system exert a powerful influence on the success and failure of any presidential leadership style. With these considerations in mind we can gain further insight into how the presidential government model became dominant by reviewing the American response to the Cold War and the brief flirtation with detente in the 1970s. What we see is that the advantage enjoyed by the president in the realm of foreign policy is not due simply to the fact that it is "foreign policy" but because of the specific types of foreign-policy problems the United States has faced during the past half century. Foremost among these is war and the preparation for war. "War is like the market," writes on prominent analyst. "It punishes some forms of organization and rewards others."[8] The need is for speed and secrecy, neither of which are qualities associated with the workings of legislative bodies or the process of molding a societal consensus through public debate. They are qualities associated with centralized power free from the restraints of competing political forces and the need to make value trade-offs—in short, the presidential governance leadership model.

The historical record affirms this conclusion. With the end of World War II, President Harry Truman moved rapidly to dismantle the bureaucratic structure put into place to fight it. Most notably, Lend-Lease was terminated and the Office of Strategic Services dismantled. But less than four months later Truman reversed himself. On January 22, 1946, he issued a presidential directive creating a National Intelligence Authority comprised of the Secretaries of War, the Navy, and State as well as the president's personal representative, and a Central Intelligence Group to be headed by a director of central intelligence. With the passage of the 1947 National Security Act these agencies were transformed into the National Security Council and the Central Intelligence Agency, respectively. The 1947 National Security Act also created a unified National Military Establishment with three coequal armed services; established the position of the secretary of defense; and officially brought into existence the Joint Chiefs of Staff.

Both Truman's change in thinking about the type of intelligence organization needed and the passage of the 1947 National Security Act can be linked to perceived threats emanating from the international system and judgments about the type of organizational response required. In the former case it was the threat of Soviet expansionism. In the latter it was the reality of Pearl Harbor. These organizational responses and others that would follow did not occur in isolation. They were part of a process by which the United States refined its relationship with the world. The key phrase in this venture was "national security." Significantly for those who employed it, national security not only defined this new relationship, it also suggested the outlines of the proper response.

Central to the concept of national security as it evolved in this period was the view that the international system had changed in four fundamental respects: (1) the European-centered balance of power system had been replaced by global struggle between the United States and the Soviet Union; (2) appeasement or inaction in the face of aggression produced only further aggression; (3) forces in being rather than potentially mobilizable military power were necessary to protect American interests; and (4) the nature of modern technology demanded that the concept of national security integrate thinking about economic and industrial subjects with military concerns. In brief, the international system was no longer seen in benign terms and as holding only marginal relevance to the security interests of the United States. It had become a menacing and ominous environment that held threats of an urgent, immediate, and unlimited nature. These characteristics fitted quite well with the prerequisites of the presidential government leadership model.

Now more than ever the president was regarded as the nation's sole authoritative voice on foreign-policy matters to which Congress came to defer with predictable regularity. The period from 1943–1951 has been characterized as one of accommodation and that between 1955–1965 as one of acquiescence.[9] In neither period was executive-congressional consultation commonplace. In the first period the war-time spirit of bipartisanship muted criticism of the Truman administration's initial handling of the Korean War and "the loss" of China, and provided enthusiastic support for a stepped-up program of foreign aid to stop communist expansionism. In the second, the Cold War policy consensus that had developed around containment effectively reduced most foreign-policy decisions to questions of tactics, something considered well within the preserve of the executive branch. Congressional action consisted largely of passing resolutions (such as those on Formosa, Berlin, and the Tonkin Gulf) that supported presidential foreign policy initiatives. Dissenting voices existed in both these periods, but they remained on its fringes rather than occupying center stage in the executive-congressional dialogue.

Dissension was less evident in the period 1951–1955, which saw the heyday of McCarthyism and the near passage of the Bricker Amendment. While a variety of motives can be ascribed to those who supported either or both of these frontal congressional challenges to presidential preeminence in foreign policy, it is important to note that the nature of the national security threat facing the United States was viewed differently than in the time periods surrounding it. Notwithstanding John Foster Dulles's often harsh rhetoric, it was a period of quiet. By March 1951 fighting in Korea had stabilized around the preinvasion boundary. Stalin died in 1953 and Soviet leaders became embroiled in a succession struggle. In 1955 an Austrian Peace Treaty was signed, a summit conference was held, and Eisenhower spoke of "a new spirit of conciliation and cooperation." In such an environment congressional challenges to presidential foreign-policy initiatives could be more easily made and calls for deference to presidential leadership more easily turned aside.

With the reemergence of threats in 1956 and 1957 meaningful congressional challenges to presidential foreign policy powers ceased. They did not reappear until after the 1968 Tet Offensive in Vietnam. During the war effort in Vietnam, no matter how vocal the opposition of individual legislators, Congress did not act to curtail presidential foreign-policy powers. Only after the war ended and the Watergate scandal unfolded did Congress act to cut off funding for the war, pass such legislation as the War Powers Act and the Case Act, and regularly began to attach "barnacles" to foreign aid and military assistance legislation.

While changes in the internal organization of Congress, the "Vietnam syndrome," and the excessive secrecy associated with presidential leadership and war-making authority contributed greatly to this renewed round of congressional activism, so too did perceived changes in the nature of the international system and the challenges and opportunities it posed to the United States. Foreign-policy challenges continued to confront the United States but once again the specter of war receded into the background. As one groundbreaking study noted, a single set of foreign-policy axioms among the foreign-policy elite no longer existed.[10] From this point forward the dominant foreign policy belief system, Cold War internationalism, would be in competition with other belief systems such as post–Cold War internationalism and even isolationism.

The absence of concrete and agreed upon national security threats robbed post–Vietnam presidents of an important political pillar upon which their preeminent position in the policy process was anchored. This has not caused presidents to change their leadership style. Rather, they have engaged in foreign-policy "ad hocism" in which periodic understandings with Congress on how to conduct foreign policy are interspersed with presidential attempts to reassert primacy.

The cumulative results of foreign-policy ad hocism, however, have been far from satisfactory. Nixon's strategy for dealing with Congress (and the bureaucracy) produced heightened dissensus, and he was forced to resign the presidency in the wake of the Watergate scandal. Carter largely failed in his effort to put into place new codetermination arrangements, and his administration was roundly criticized for its inability to govern. Reagan was unable to lay a firm foundation on which to reassert the principle of presidential primacy in foreign policy making and ultimately resorted to bypassing the Congress and much of the executive branch in conducting such major foreign-policy initiatives as Iran-Contra, the Strategic Defense Initiative (SDI), and his Reykjavik arms control position.

A similar pattern was observable in the Bush administration. A quick accommodation was reached with Congress on Nicaragua, but the administration was unable to use the accord as a point of departure for other foreign-policy initiatives. The most notable failing was with regard to the administration's China policy and the associated issues of aid, human rights policy, and most favored nation status.

Even the Bush administration's greatest success, victory in the Persian Gulf

War, did not relieve it from the practice of foreign-policy ad hocism. Victory in war neither translated into congressional deference to presidential leadership in foreign policy nor enabled it to build a policy consensus on the American role in the new world order. U.S. foreign policy toward the Yugoslavian conflict proceeded in fits and starts, with multiple voices on both ends of Pennsylvania Avenue putting forth policy suggestions. And while the U.S. humanitarian military mission to Somalia was opposed by very few, there was also much disagreement about the scope of the undertaking and its broader implications. Part of the explanation for why the Gulf War failed to lay the basis for a consensus on these missions lies with the fact that the administration's policies were formulated entirely within the purview of the executive branch and that the debate within the administration concerning the goals of the war were kept from Congress and the public.

The Clinton Administration

The pattern of ad hocism described above and the persistent attachment to the presidential government leadership model in foreign affairs continued in the Clinton administration. Bill Clinton was the first president elected after the fall of the Berlin Wall, symbolizing an end to the Cold War, but his administration struggled as it sought to find an appropriate model of presidential leadership. Domestically, Clinton attempted to operate within a party model of leadership best illustrated by the congressional passage of his 1993 economic program. However, he also adopted elements of the presidential model of government during the fight for health care reform in 1994. And in 1997 the president and the Republican-controlled Congress adopted elements of the executive-congressional collaborative leadership model with respect to the 1997 budget negotiations.

Expectations were high that Clinton's would be a presidency in which domestic issues rather than foreign-policy ones dominated. Yet, from the very outset, foreign-policy problems competed for his attention and often forced themselves to the top of the administration's agenda. Clinton embraced the traditional presidential government model of leadership in addressing these issues. Key foreign-policy decisions regarding Somalia, Haiti, and Bosnia were shaped with little systematic input from either Congress or the broader leadership of the Democratic party.

For example, accounts of Clinton's ill-fated decision to send Ranger commandos to Somalia to capture Mohamed Farah Aideed stress two key factors. The first is Clinton himself. It was Clinton who ordered the Rangers to Somalia to capture Aideed in August 1993 following the ambush of U.S. soldiers in Mogadishu, and it was Clinton who, after talking with former President Carter in September, appeared to waiver from the military option to embrace one that contained a political dimension as well. The second key factor in the decision to attempt to capture Aideed is the consensus that developed among his key advisors that such a move was necessary. Press reports stressed the early reluctance to use force on the part of such key Clinton aides as Secretary of Defense Les Aspin, General Colin Powell, General Joseph Hoar (who headed the U.S. Central Command, which had responsibility for Somalia), and National Security Advisor Anthony Lake. There was also a "back channel" that U.S. envoy Robert Gosende and Admiral Jonathan Howe (who was in command of UN forces in Somalia) used to lobby for the use of force.

The wisdom of sending U.S. forces to Haiti to restore democracy was also much debated. Less contentious were Clinton's motivations for sending in U.S. forces. He is widely seen as having responded to two sets of electoral pressures. The first emanated from the Congressional Black Caucus and allied African-American leaders who demanded military action to bring Jean-Bertrand Aristide back to power. The most visible evidence of this pressure was the hunger strike by Randall Robinson, executive director of TransAfrica. The second set of pressures came from Democratic leaders in Florida who were struggling with the surge of Haitian refugees pouring into their state.

One early feature of Clinton's Bosnia policy also bears the imprint of presidential government style leadership. It was the decision to allow Iranian arms to pass through to Bosnian Muslims. Made without congressional input, this decision set off a heated interbranch conflict with many in Congress who argued that they had been deceived by Clinton's decision. Six different congressional committees contemplated investigating the decision. For its part, the Clinton administration invoked the principle of "executive privilege" in responding to congressional demands for information about the decision.

All of these situations deal with issues that fall comfortably within a policy area (the use of force) where strong presidential leadership is expected, so it is not surprising that the Clinton administration adopted a presidential government leadership style. But use-of-force issues were not the only ones that led Clinton to embrace this model of governance. He also did so in attempting to keep his campaign promise to lift the ban on gays in the military. This is a policy issue heavily laden with domestic overtones and one in which congressional deference to executive initiatives was not likely to be forthcoming.

Almost immediately after the election, Senator Sam Nunn, a Democrat from Georgia and Chair of the influential Senate Armed Services Committee, urged Clinton to proceed cautiously. Robert Dole, then Senate leader and later Clinton's Republican presidential challenger, urged the newly elected president to do nothing until a comprehensive review could be undertaken. Secretary of Defense-designate Les Aspin warned Clinton of the need to develop a strategy for heading off the impending fight with Congress. Aspin's aides called for a personal meeting among Clinton, Nunn, Majority Leader George Mitchell, and Senator Ted Kennedy to discuss strategy. No such meeting was ever held, and when Clinton's transition team met with military leaders it was not in a spirit of deciding what to do but only how to minimize the impact of the change on combat effectiveness. Senator Dan Coats, who led the Republican opposition to lifting the ban, complained about the Clinton administration's "in-your-face approach" and the absence of any of the promised hearings and interbranch consultations.

Has Clinton's leadership strategy been successful? Has it contributed to the creation of an effective American foreign policy? Answering these questions is difficult because many factors go into the creation of a successful foreign policy. Alone, a good policy process does not necessarily produce good policy outcomes. There are signs, however, that the presidential government model has not served the Clinton administration well. In 1994 and 1995 Clinton won only half of the foreign policy and national security votes in Congress.[11] This is the worst showing by a president since records were kept some fifty years ago. Moreover, even when successful, the use of a presidential government leadership style did not produce unity behind a foreign-policy initiative. Dole supported Clinton's plan to send troops to Bosnia only when confronted with Secretary of State Warren Christopher's comment that this action would provide "an acid test" of U.S. leadership. Congress openly rebelled against Clinton's 1997 recertification of Mexico as a state committed to stopping drug trafficking. The Congressional Black Caucus broke with Clinton and opposed NAFTA because it felt left out of the decisionmaking process. And in May 1997, Senator Richard Lugar warned that without a major improvement in the administration's congressional lobbying effort, Senate ratification of NATO enlargement was in serious danger.

What of the alternatives? Clinton gave little evidence of seeking to lead on foreign-policy matters through a strategy centered on party unity and collective responsibility, key elements of the Jeffersonian model. Moreover, there is little incentive to try. The presence of divided government undermines the ability of this leadership model to deliver what it promises: coherent policies supported by both branches. Without control of both Congress and the presidency it is not enough to get the leaders of a single party to agree on a foreign-policy initiative. Divided government can also be expected to take its toll on the ability to bring individuals into government who wish to be part of a foreign-policy "team." Upon hearing that Christopher was resigning as secretary of state, Senator Jesse Helms warned Clinton not to nominate Deputy Secretary of State Strobe Talbott for the post. Later, Anthony Lake withdrew his name from consideration as director of Central Intelligence after having undergone intense partisan questioning. Secretary of Defense William Cohen, a Republican who Clinton brought into his second administration in an effort to lay a bipartisan base for his foreign policy is reported to think more like a Republican senator from Maine than a member of the executive branch.

The executive/legislative (Madisonian) model also went largely unused. In fact, Clinton moved away from it in one instance. The Bush administration submitted updated drafts of the NAFTA agreement to the Senate Finance Committee, the Office of Senate Security, the House Committee on Ways and Means, and Majority Leader Richard Gephardt. Ambassador Carla Hills also held briefings by United States Trade Representative (USTR) officials and negotiators for members of Congress and their staffs. And, in February 1992, the USTR led a delegation of eleven members of Congress and twenty-seven private sector representatives to Mexico City where they met with Mexican President Salinas and key Mexican officials. All totaled, more than 350 briefings were given to the 40 congressional advisory committees that were established to oversee the negotiations.

Clinton's support for NAFTA during his first campaign in 1992 had been qualified and made contingent on the signing of side agreements to address oversights in the agreement negotiated by the Bush administration. Once elected Clinton treated these side agreements as executive agreements and not part of the treaty to be voted on by Congress. Rather than work with Congress as a collaborative partner, the Clinton administration fell back upon traditional lobbying strategies that emphasized briefings, personal visits, and pork-barrel politicking in which political favors were given out for the support of key legislators.

In defense of Clinton's switch in leadership style, it can be noted that Bush's approach to winning congressional support for NAFTA was not entirely successful. Richard Gephardt, for example, in spite of all the information made available to him, still publicly spoke out about being "kept in the dark" and the "secret [negotiating] process" that "could seriously undermine the ability of Congress to affirm an agreement."[12] The difficulties Clinton encountered in seeking fast-track authority for negotiating an expansion of NAFTA to include Chile point to the continued presence of high levels of distrust between the two branches that limits the ability of fast-track procedures to serve as a forum for true interbranch collaboration. Absent a policy consensus on the need for a timely agreement, the focus of congressional-executive negotiations on fast-track authority shifted from expediting the process by which American foreign policy is conducted to becoming yet another forum for (pre)determining the content of any agreement. It was a struggle in which each institution sought to dominate rather than collaborate.

Finally, it should be noted that viewed from strictly a political perspective there exists a certain disincentive for presidents to abandon the presidential government leadership model in making foreign policy. It provides them with the opportunity to appear decisive and firm in ways not possible in domestic policy. As Thomas Omestad notes in commenting on the 1996 presidential election, for Clinton foreign policy "became a means of redemption," a forum for refuting Republican charges that he "was feckless and lacked backbone." Yet, as President Bush discovered, the decisive leadership in foreign policy, which he exhibited in the Persian Gulf War, does not provide presidents with lasting political capital to pursue other policy objectives.

Conclusion

The maxim that "politics stops at the water's edge" is an apt descriptor not only of traditional thinking about the relationship between foreign policy and domestic politics, but also of how we have come to think about cause and effect. Students of world politics have looked primarily to international system factors and the defining qualities of the state (its size, geography, military power, and population) for their key explanatory variables, whereas students of domestic politics have focused largely on conditions and political activity within the state. To a degree not appreciated by many, the presidency is an institution whose structure and activities have been shaped by international factors. The most dominating external force in this century has been the Cold War. The ever present national security threat that it came to symbolize provided a rationale and inducement for the concentration of power in the presidency and placed limits on the role that Congress could hope to play in formulating American foreign policy.

The new, post–Cold War era provides a necessary but not sufficient environment for the development and maturation of alternative presidential leadership styles. While it may be clear that the international system foundation on which the presidential government leadership strategy was built no longer exists, uncertainty over the direction of post–Cold War international politics propels today's presidents to continue to rely on it, even while they have experimented with other leadership models in domestic politics. Presidents have discovered that the periodic use of force in areas held to be traditionally vital to American national security interests such as the Caribbean, the Middle East, and Europe provides them with a potent lever to manage and influence their standing with the American people. Heightened levels of public support provide presidents with "a form of political currency that is vital to both the political survival and substantive effectiveness" of their administrations.[13] Thus, when events are properly orchestrated, the inhibiting effect of congressional reforms, changed public attitudes toward war, and economic weakness often disappear for the moment.

Given the issues and concerns raised here, where does this leave us in thinking about the problem of presidential leadership in American foreign policy? Neither of the first two models introduced in this essay provide a solid foundation on which to proceed. Though still favored by presidents, the presidential government leadership model rests upon outmoded assumptions about the nature of world politics and has proven difficult to apply with any consistency. Quite apart from any changes in the nature of world politics, the viability of the executive/party model of leadership is undermined by the inability of the Democratic and Republican parties to serve as unifying forces at the national level and by the increased prominence of divided government. Therefore, whether we like it or not, the Madisonian model of executive/legislative collaboration is the model that offers the most suitable political foundation on which to construct American foreign policy. Utilizing this model as a starting point for developing future foreign-policy initiatives, however, requires that new mechanisms for interbranch decision making be created.

Failing to establish the necessary tools for a model of presidential leadership that is centered on executive-congressional collaboration will almost certainly lead to future stalemates over the direction of American foreign policy. It can also lead to future constitutional crises, failed presidencies, and efforts to bolster presidential popularity through foreign-policy adventurism due to the reliance upon presidential leadership models that are out of tune with domestic and international political realities.

Notes

1. James MacGregor Burns, *Presidential Government: The Crucible of Leadership* (Boston: Houghton-Mifflin, 1965).

2. Clinton Rossiter, *The Federalist Papers* (New York: Mentor Books, 1961), 423.

3. Richard E. Neustadt, *Presidential Power* (New York: John Wiley, 1964).

4. Harold Koh, *The National Security Constitution* (New Haven, Conn.: Yale University Press, 1990), 83

5. Jeanne Hahn, "Neohamiltonianism: A Democratic Critique," in John Manley and Kenneth Dolbeare, eds., *The Case Against the Constitution* (New York: M. E. Sharpe, 1987), 163.

6. Paula Scalingi, "Ratifying Arms Control Agreements," *The Washington Quarterly* 14 (Spring, 1991): 109–124.

7. The National Academy of Public Administration, *Beyond Distrust: Building Bridges Between Congress and the Executive* (Washington, D.C.: The National Academy of Public Administration, 1992).

8. Peter Gourevitch, "The Second Image Reversed: The International Sources of Domestic Politics," *International Organization* 32 (Autumn 1978): 896.

9. Francis Bax, "The Legislative-Executive Relationship in Foreign Policy." *Orbis* 20 (Winter 1977): 881–904.

10. James N. Rosenau and Ole R. Holsti, "US Leadership in a Shrinking World: The Breakdown of Consensus and the Emergence of Conflicting Belief Systems," *World Politics* 35 (April 1983): 368–392.

11. Jim Mann, "Clinton's Foreign Policy Success May Rely on Making Peace With Congress," *The Los Angeles Times,* November 11, 1996, p. 5.

12. George W. Grayson, *The North American Free Trade Agreement* (New York: Foreign Policy Association, 1993), 38.

13. Robin Marra, Charles Ostrom, Jr., and Dennis Simon, "Foreign Policy and Presidential Popularity," *Journal of Conflict Resolution* 34 (December 1990): 588–623.

10

Without Restraint: Presidential Military Initiatives from Korea to Bosnia

Louis Fisher

From 1789 to 1950, military initiatives by the United States were decided primarily by Congress, either by a formal declaration of war or by a statute authorizing the president to use military force. There were some notable exceptions, such as the actions by President James Polk that led to hostilities between the United States and Mexico. Presidents also used military force for various "life and property" actions, but these were typically limited, short-term engagements. By and large, the first century and a half followed the framers' expectations that matters of war and peace would be vested in the government's representative branch, namely, Congress.

The record since 1950 has been dramatically different. Presidents in the second half of the twentieth century have increasingly felt comfortable acting unilaterally when using military force against others. Instead of coming to Congress for authority, they typically have justified resorting to military actions either on the commander in chief clause in the Constitution or on decisions reached by the UN Security Council and NATO. As illustrated by the actions of Presidents Truman, Bush, and Clinton, the impact on constitutional and representative government is profound, extending not only to the war powers but also to the power of the purse.

Constitutional Principles

When the American Constitution was drafted in 1787, the framers were aware that existing models of government placed the war power and foreign affairs solely in the hands of the king. Thus, matters of treaties, appointment of ambassadors, the raising and regulation of fleets and armies, and initiating military actions against other countries had been vested in the king. Accordingly, John Locke and William Blackstone, whose writings deeply influenced the framers, assigned war powers and foreign affairs exclusively to the executive branch.

This monarchical model was expressly rejected at the Philadelphia convention. As revealed in the historical records of the Constitutional Convention,[1] Charles Pinckney said he was for "a vigorous Executive but was afraid the Executive powers of [the existing] Congress might extend to peace & war &c which would render the Executive a Monarchy, of the worst kind, to wit an elective one." Although John Rutledge wanted the executive power placed in a single person, "he was not for giving him the power of war and peace." James Wilson supported a single executive but "did not consider the Prerogative of the British Monarch as a proper guide in defining the Executive powers. Some of these prerogatives were of a Legislative nature. Among others that of war & peace &c." Edmund Randolph worried about executive power, calling it "the foetus of monarchy."

Alexander Hamilton, typically identified as a political realist who supported a strong executive, had no hesitation in rejecting the Lockean and Blackstonian prerogatives in foreign affairs and the war power. While admitting that in his "private opinion he had no scruple in declaring . . . that the British Govt. was the best in the world," he nevertheless proposed that the president would have "with the advice and approbation of the Senate" the power of making treaties, that the Senate would have the "sole power of declaring war," and that the president would be authorized to have "the direction of war when authorized or begun." Those principles are repeated in his private writings, as in Federalist No. 69 and Federalist No. 75.

The framers recognized that the president would need unilateral power in one area: defensive actions to repel sudden attacks when Congress was not in session to legislate. The early draft of the Constitution empowered Congress to "make war." Charles Pinckney objected that legislative proceedings "were too slow" for the safety of the country in an emergency, since he expected Congress to meet but once a year. James Madison and Elbridge Gerry moved to insert "declare" for "make," leaving to the president "the power to repel sudden attacks."

Debate on the Madison–Gerry amendment underscored the limited grant of authority to the president. Pierce Butler wanted to give the president the power to make war, arguing that he "will have all the requisite qualities, and will not make war but when the Nation will support it." Roger Sherman objected: "The Executive shd. be able to repel and not to commence war." Gerry said he "never expected to hear in a republic a motion to empower the Executive alone to declare war." George Mason spoke "agst giving the power of war to the Executive, because not [safely] to be trusted with it; . . . He was for clogging rather than facilitating war."

Similar statements were made at the state ratifying conventions. In Pennsylvania, James Wilson expressed the prevailing sentiment that the system of checks and balances "will not hurry us into war; it is calculated to guard against it. It will not be in the power of a single man, or a single body of men, to involve us in such distress; for the important power of declaring war is vested in the legislature at large." In North Carolina, James Iredell contrasted the limited powers of the president with those of the British monarch. The king of Great Britain was not only the commander in chief "but has power, in time of war, to raise fleets and armies. He has also authority to declare war." The president, however, "has not the power of declaring war by his own authority, nor that of raising fleets and armies. These powers are vested in other hands." In South Carolina, Charles Pinckney assured his colleagues that the president's powers "did not permit him to declare war."

The framers also took great pains to separate the purse and the sword. They were familiar with the efforts of English kings to rely on extraparliamentary sources of revenue for military expeditions. After a series of monarchical transgressions, England lurched into a bloody civil war. The origin of democratic government is directly related to legislative control over the purse.

The U.S. Constitution states that "No Money shall be drawn from the Treasury, but in Consequences of Appropriations made by Law." In Federalist No. 48, Madison explained that "the legislative department alone has access to the pockets of the people." The Constitution empowers Congress to lay and collect taxes, duties, imposts, and excises; to borrow money on the credit of the United States; and to coin money and regulate its value. The power of the purse, Madison said in Federalist No. 58, represents the "most compleat and effectual weapon with which any constitution can arm the immediate representatives of the people, for obtaining a redress of every grievance, and for carrying into effect every just and salutary measure."

In making the president the commander in chief, Congress retained for Congress the important check over spending. Madison set forth this tenet: "Those who are to *conduct a war* cannot in the nature of things, be proper or safe judges, whether *a war ought* to be *commenced, continued,* or *concluded.* They are barred from the latter functions by a great principle in free government, analogous to that which separates the sword from the purse, or the power of executing from the power of enacting laws." At the Philadelphia convention, George Mason counseled that the "purse & the sword ought never to get into the same hands (whether Legislative or Executive.)"

As this brief history shows, the constitutional framework adopted by the framers for foreign affairs, the war power, and the power of the purse is remarkably clear and consistent. Foreign policy would be made jointly, by both branches. The authority to initiate war and vote funds lay with Congress. The president could act unilaterally only in one area: to repel sudden attacks. Throughout the next century and a half, major military actions were either declared by Congress (the War of 1812, the Mexican War of 1846, the Spanish-American War of 1898, World War I, and World War II) or authorized by

Congress (the Quasi-War against France from 1798 to 1800 and the Barbary Wars during the administrations of Thomas Jefferson and James Madison). In either case, presidents came to Congress for authority to take part in offensive actions.

The record since 1950 has been fundamentally different. In that year President Harry Truman sent American troops to Korea, without ever coming to Congress for authority. He based his actions in part on resolutions adopted by the UN Security Council, but nothing in the history of the UN Charter implies that Congress ever contemplated placing in the hands of the president the unilateral power to wage war. Truman's initiative became a model for President George Bush in going to war against Iraq in 1991 and President Bill Clinton in threatening to invade Haiti in 1994. In addition, Clinton cited NATO as authority for air strikes in Bosnia and sending ground troops to that region. But the legislative history of mutual security treaties like NATO shows no intent on the part of Congress to sanction independent presidential war power.

The United Nations and NATO

The UN Charter emerged from a number of deliberate steps, including the Connally and Fulbright Resolutions of 1943, meetings at Dumbarton Oaks in 1944, and the final conference in San Francisco in 1945. At each stage there was close debate about the prerogatives of Congress to authorize, in advance, military initiatives. Two weeks after the end of the meetings at Dumbarton Oaks, President Franklin D. Roosevelt delivered an address in which he anticipated that Congress would grant the president advance approval for responding to military emergencies. He did not claim inherent executive power. Before acting militarily, the president would need explicit authority from Congress.[2] After Roosevelt's death, President Truman sent a cable from Potsdam stating that all agreements involving U.S. troop commitments to the United Nations would first have to be approved by both houses of Congress. He pledged without equivocation: "When any such agreement or agreements are negotiated it will be my purpose to ask the Congress for appropriate legislation to approve them."[3]

By "agreements" Truman meant the procedures that would permit UN military force in dealing with threats to peace, breaches of the peace, and acts of aggression. All UN members would make available to the Security Council, "on its call and in accordance with a special agreement or agreements," armed forces and other assistance for the purpose of maintaining international peace and security. The agreements, concluded between the Security Council and member states, "shall be subject to ratification by the signatory states in accordance with their respective constitutional processes."

After the Senate approved the UN Charter, Congress had to decide the meaning of "constitutional processes." What procedure was necessary, under the U.S. Constitution, to bring into effect the special agreements needed to contribute American troops to UN military actions? That issue was decided by the UN Participation Act of 1945, which stated without the slightest ambiguity that the agreements "shall be subject to the approval of the Congress by appropriate Act or joint resolution." The agreements between the United States and the Security Council would not result from unilateral executive action, nor would they be brought into force only by the Senate acting through the treaty process. Action by both houses of Congress would be required. Presidents could commit armed forces to the United Nations only after Congress had given its explicit consent.

At every step in the legislative history of the UN Participation Act— hearings, committee reports, and floor debate—these elementary points were underscored and reinforced. Executive officials repeatedly assured members of Congress that the president could not commit troops to UN military actions unless Congress first approved.

During this time the Senate also approved the NATO treaty of 1949, which provides that an armed attack against one or more of the parties in Europe or North America "shall be considered an attack against them all." In the event of an attack, member states could exercise the right of individual or collective self-defense recognized by Article 51 of the UN Charter and assist the country or countries attacked by taking "such action as it deems necessary, including the use of armed force." However, Article 11 of the treaty states that it shall be ratified "and its provisions carried out by the Parties in accordance with their respective constitutional processes." The Southeast Asia Treaty (SEATO) of 1954 also stated that the treaty "shall be ratified and its provisions carried out by the Parties in accordance with their respective constitutional processes."

Do these treaties grant the president unilateral power to use military force against other nations? First, it is well recognized that the concept in mutual security treaties of an attack on one nation being an attack on all does not require from any nation an immediate response. Each country maintains the sovereign right to decide such matters by itself. As noted in the Rio Treaty of 1947, "no State shall be required to use armed force without its consent." In the U.S. system, who decides to use armed force?

During hearings in 1949 on NATO, Secretary of State Dean Acheson told the Senate Foreign Relations Committee that it "does not mean that the United States would automatically be at war if one of the other signatory nations were the victim of an armed attack. Under our Constitution, the Congress alone has the power to declare war." Of course he was merely saying what is expressly provided for in the Constitution. However, nothing in the legislative history of NATO gives the president any type of unilateral authority in the event of an attack. That the president lacks unilateral powers under the UN Charter or NATO should be obvious from the fact that both are international treaties entered into by way of a presidential proposal and Senate advice and consent. The president and the Senate cannot use the treaty process to strip from the House of Representatives its prerogatives over the use of military force.

In the words of one scholar, the provisions in the NATO treaty that it be carried out according to constitutional processes was "intended to ensure that the Executive Branch of the Government should come back to the Congress when decisions were required in which the Congress has a constitutional responsibility." The NATO treaty "does not transfer to the President the Congressional power to make war."[4] Those predictions would be eroded by practices during the Clinton administration.

Truman in Korea

With these treaty and statutory safeguards supposedly in place to protect legislative prerogatives, President Truman nonetheless sent U.S. troops to Korea in 1950 without ever seeking or obtaining congressional authority. How could this happen? How could so many explicit assurances to Congress be ignored and circumvented?

On June 26, Truman announced that the UN Security Council had ordered North Korea to withdraw its invading forces to positions north of the 38th parallel and that, "in accordance with the resolution of the Security Council, the United States will vigorously support the effort of the Council to terminate this serious breach of the peace." The next day he ordered U.S. air and sea forces to provide military support to South Korea. It was not until the evening of June 27 that the Security Council actually called for military action. In his memoirs, *Present at the Creation,* Dean Acheson admitted that "some American action, said to be in support of the resolution of June 27, was in fact ordered, and possibly taken, prior to the resolution."

Truman violated the statutory language and legislative history of the UN Participation Act, including his own assurance from Potsdam that he would first obtain the approval of Congress before sending U.S. forces to a UN action. How was this possible? He simply ignored the special agreements that were supposed to be the guarantee of congressional control. Indeed, no state has ever entered into a special agreement with the Security Council—and none is ever likely to do so.

Truman exploited the UN machinery in part because of a fluke: the Soviet Union had absented itself from the Security Council during two crucial votes taken during the early days of the crisis. It is difficult to argue that the president's constitutional powers vary with the presence or absence of Soviet (or other) delegates to the Security Council. As Robert Bork noted in 1971, "the approval of the United Nations was obtained only because the Soviet Union happened to be boycotting the Security Council at the time, and the president's Constitutional powers can hardly be said to ebb and flow with the veto of the Soviet Union in the Security Council."[5]

Truman tried to justify his actions in Korea by calling it a UN "police action" rather than an American war. That argument was suspect from the start and deteriorated as U.S. casualties mounted. The UN exercised no real authority over the conduct of the war. Other than token support from a few nations, it remained an American war—measured by troops, money, casualties, and deaths—from start to finish. The euphemism "police action" was never persuasive. As a federal court concluded in 1953, "We doubt very much if there is any question in the minds of the majority of the people of this country that the conflict now raging in Korea can be anything but war."[6]

Bush in Iraq

Truman's initiative in Korea became a precedent for actions taken by President Bush in Iraq. In response to Iraq's invasion of Kuwait on August 2, 1990, Bush sent several hundred thousand troops to Saudi Arabia for defensive purposes. Over the next few months, the size of the American force climbed to 500,000, giving Bush the capability for mounting an offensive strike.

Instead of seeking authority from Congress, Bush created a multinational alliance and encouraged the UN Security Council to authorize the use of military force. The strategic calculations have been recorded by James A. Baker III, who served as Secretary of State in the Bush administration. In his book, *The Politics of Diplomacy,* Baker says he realized that military initiatives by Reagan in Grenada and Bush in Panama had reinforced in the international community the impression that American foreign policy followed a "cowboy mentality." In response to those concerns, Bush wanted to assemble an international political coalition. Baker notes: "From the very beginning, the president recognized the importance of having the express approval of the international community if at all possible." It is noteworthy that Bush would seek the express approval of other nations but not the express approval of Congress.

On November 20, Bush said he wanted to delay asking Congress for authorization until after the Security Council considered a proposed resolution supporting the use of force against Iraq. About a week later, on November 29, the Security Council authorized member states to use "all necessary means" to force Iraqi troops out of Kuwait. "All necessary means" is code language for military action. To avoid war, Iraq had to withdraw from Kuwait by January 15, 1991. Although the Security Council "authorized" each member state to act militarily against Iraq, the resolution did not compel nor obligate them to participate. Instead, member states were free to use (or refuse) force pursuant to their own constitutional systems and judgments about national interests.

What procedure would the United States follow in deciding to use force? When Secretary of Defense Dick Cheney appeared before the Senate Armed Services Committee on December 3, 1990, he said that President Bush did not require "any additional authorization from the Congress" before attacking Iraq. Through such language he implied that authorization from the UN was sufficient. The UN action, he said, made congressional action not only unnecessary but counterproductive:

> As a general proposition, I can think that the notion of a declaration of war to some extent flies in the face of what we are trying to accomplish here. And what we are trying to accomplish is to marshal an international force, some 26, 27 nations having committed forces to the enterprise, working under the auspices of the United Nations Security Council.

In other words, once presidents assembled an international force and obtained support through a Security Council resolution, Congress had no role except perhaps to pass a resolution indicating its support. Whether it acted or not had no bearing on the president's freedom to move ahead with the multinational force.

The Justice Department argued in court that President Bush could order offensive actions against Iraq without seeking advance authority from Congress. On December 13, 1990, in *Dellums v. Bush,* the court expressly and forcefully rejected the sweeping interpretation of presidential war power advanced by the Justice Department. If the president had the sole power to determine that any offensive military operation, "no matter how vast, does not constitute war-making but only an offensive military attack, the congressional power to declare war will be at the mercy of a semantic decision by the Executive." But, having dismissed the Justice Department's interpretation, the court then held that the case was not ripe for adjudication.

On January 8, 1991, President Bush asked Congress to pass legislation supporting the UN position. Clearly he was asking for "support," not authority. The next day reporters asked whether he needed authority from Congress. His reply: "I don't think I need it. . . . I feel that I have the authority to fully implement the United Nations resolutions." The legal crisis was avoided on January 12 when Congress authorized offensive actions against Iraq. In signing the bill, Bush indicated that he could have acted without legislation: "As I made clear to congressional leaders at the outset, my request for congressional support did not, and my signing this resolution does not, constitute any change in the longstanding positions of the executive branch on either the president's constitutional authority to use the Armed Forces to defend vital U.S. interests or the constitutionality of the War Powers Resolution." Despite his comments, the bill clearly authorized the action against Iraq. A signed statement does not alter the contents of a public law.

In one of his last addresses as president, Bush used a speech at West Point to explain his theory of presidential war power. Referring to President Washington's warning of the dangers of "entangling alliances," and saying that Washington was correct at that point in history, Bush noted that what was "entangling" in Washington's day "is now essential." Congress had a constitutional role in these involvements, but apparently more to offer support rather than to grant authority. Presidential leadership "involves working with the Congress and the American people to provide the essential domestic underpinning if U.S. military commitments are to be sustainable." The word authority appears only in reference to international organizations. In both Iraq and Somalia, Bush said, U.S. forces were "acting under the full authority of the United Nations."

Clinton in Haiti

During the 1992 presidential campaign, Bill Clinton projected himself as a strong leader in foreign affairs and indicated a willingness to resort to military action. Criticizing Bush's foreign policy, he said he would be willing to use military force—in concert with other nations—to bring humanitarian aid to the citizens of Bosnia and Herzegovina. While saying he did not relish the prospect of sending Americans into combat, "neither do I flinch from it."[7] He accused the Bush administration of "turning its back" on "those struggling for democracy in China and on those fleeing Haiti."

Once in office, Clinton's position on what to do about the military regime in Haiti fluctuated from month to month, depending on shifting political pressures. Jean-Bertrand Aristide, the island's first democratically elected president, had been overthrown in a military coup on September 30, 1991. Political repression by the military rulers produced a flood of refugees trying to reach the United States. President Bush maintained that the Haitians were fleeing because of economic conditions, not political persecution, and refused to qualify them for asylum. Refugees were returned to Haiti. Although Clinton had criticized this policy during the 1992 campaign, he reversed course the next year and accepted the policy of the Bush administration.

As the flood of refugees continued, pressure mounted on Clinton to intervene militarily. In October 1993 he sent a contingent of 600 U.S. soldiers to Haiti to work on roads, bridges, and water supplies. A group of armed civilians, opposed to U.S. intervention, prevented them from landing. Lightly armed, the U.S. troops were instructed by their commanders not to use force but to leave the area. The retreat in the face of tiny Haiti was widely interpreted as a humiliation to the United States.

Clinton soon began threatening to use military force. On October 15 he ticked off the telltale signs of an impending U.S. intervention: "First, there are about 1,000 American citizens living in Haiti or working there. Second, there are Americans there who are helping to operate our Embassy. Third, we have an interest in promoting democracy in this hemisphere." He ordered six destroyers to patrol the waters off Haiti and had an infantry company on standby at the Guantanamo Naval Base in Cuba.

In May 1994 Clinton said with regard to Haiti "we cannot afford to discount the prospect of a military option." By late July, rumors began to circulate about an imminent Security Council resolution that would authorize the invasion of Haiti. Dante Caputo, the United Nations' envoy to Haiti, wrote a "confidential" memo to UN Secretary General Boutros Boutros-Ghali describing the political calculations within the Clinton White House. This memo, which found its way into the *Congressional Record,* states that Clinton's advisers believed that an invasion of Haiti would be politically desirable because it would highlight for the American public "the president's decision making capability and the firmness of leadership in international political matters."

On July 31 the UN Security Council adopted a resolution "inviting" all states, particularly those in the region of Haiti, to use "all necessary means" to remove the military leadership in that island. The idea of using the UN as a source of authority for presidential military actions prompted debate in the Senate, which passed a resolution stating the sense of the Senate that the Security Council "does not constitute authorization for the deployment of United States Armed Forces in Haiti under the Constitution of the United States or pursuant to the War Powers Resolution." The Senate amendment passed by a vote of 100 to 0.

At a news conference on August 3, Clinton denied that he needed authority from Congress to invade Haiti: "Like my predecessors of both parties, I have not agreed that I was constitutionally mandated to obtain the support of Congress." In a nationwide television address on September 15, Clinton told the American people that he was prepared to use military force to invade Haiti, referring to the Security Council resolution and expressing his willingness to lead a multilateral force "to carry out the will of the United Nations." No mention at all of the will of Congress.

The public and a substantial majority of legislators assailed the planned invasion. Criticized in the past for currying public favor and failing to lead, Clinton now seemed to glory in the idea of acting against the grain. He was determined to proceed with the invasion: "But regardless [of this opposition], this is what I believe is the right thing to do. I realize it is unpopular. I know it is unpopular. I know the timing is unpopular. I know the whole thing is unpopular. But I believe it is the right thing." Apparently there was no consideration of doing the legal thing, the authorized thing, or the constitutional thing.

Clinton emphasized the need to keep commitments: "I'd like to mention just one other thing that is equally important, and that is the reliability of the United States and the United Nations once we say we're going to do something." But who is the "we"? It was not Congress or the American public. It was a commitment made unilaterally by the executive branch acting in concert with the United Nations.

An invasion of Haiti proved unnecessary. Clinton sent former President Jimmy Carter to negotiate with the military leaders in Haiti. They agreed to step down to permit the return of Aristide. Initially, nearly 20,000 U.S. troops were dispatched to occupy Haiti and provide stability. A resolution was introduced in Congress to provide retroactive authorization for the use of U.S. force in Haiti, but that proposal failed. A remark by Senator Max Baucus, Democrat of Montana, reflected the attitude of many legislators: "The president did not seek my approval for occupying Haiti. And he will not get my approval now." Both houses passed legislation stating that "the president should have sought and welcomed Congressional approval before deploying United States Forces to Haiti."

Intervention in Bosnia

In concert with the United Nations and NATO, the Bush and Clinton administrations participated in humanitarian airlifts in Sarajevo and helped enforce a "no-fly zone" (a ban on unauthorized flights over Bosnia-Herzegovina). In 1993 Clinton indicated that he would have to seek the support and authorization from Congress before ordering air strikes. On May 7 he stated: "If I decide to ask the American people and the United States Congress to support an approach that would include the use of air power, I would have a very specific, clearly defined strategy." He anticipated asking "for the authority to use air power from the Congress and the American people."

Later in the year he began to object to legislative efforts to restrict his military options. He said he opposed any amendment "that affects the way our military people do their business, working with NATO and other military allies." He did not think "we should have an amendment which would tie the president's hands and make us unable to fulfill our NATO commitments." As with the UN resolution authorizing military action against Haiti, "our" commitments would be decided by the president, not by Congress.

Instead of seeking authority from Congress, Clinton now said he would seek from Congress advice and support. He was "fundamentally opposed" to any statutory provisions that "improperly limit my ability to perform my constitutional duties as Commander-in-Chief." He would operate through NATO, even though NATO had never used military force during its almost half century of existence.

In 1994 Clinton threatened air strikes against Serbian militias in Bosnia. Decisions to use air power would be taken in response to UN Security Council resolutions, operating through NATO's military command. There was no more talk about seeking authority from Congress. Curiously, by operating through NATO, Clinton would seek the agreement of England, France, Italy, and other NATO allies, but not Congress. NATO air strikes began in February 1994 and were followed by additional strikes throughout the year and into the next. At the end of August 1995, NATO carried out the war's biggest air raid. Clinton explained that he authorized the air strikes "in conjunction with our NATO allies to implement the relevant U.N. Security Council resolutions and NATO decisions." On September 12, 1995, he regarded the bombing attacks as "authorized by the United Nations." Hence the authorizing body was a multinational organization, not Congress.

The next escalation of U.S. military action was Clinton's decision to introduce ground troops. When reporters asked him on October 19, 1995, if he would send the troops even if Congress did not approve, he replied: "I am not going to lay down any of my constitutional prerogatives here today." Inviting the support of Congress, he denied that legislative authority was necessary. On the basis of what he considered sufficient authority under Article II of the Constitution and under NATO, he ordered the deployment of 20,000 American ground troops to Bosnia without obtaining authority or support from Congress. In an address on November 27, 1995, he said that deployment of U.S. ground troops to Bosnia was "the right thing to do," paralleling his justification for invading Haiti. It was the right thing, even if not the legal thing.

On December 21 Clinton expected that the military mission to Bosnia "can be accomplished in about a year." A year later, on December 17, 1996, he extended the troop deployment for another eighteen months. At the end of 1997 he announced that the deployment would have to be extended again, but this time without attempting to fix a deadline. The administration's initial cost estimate for the Bosnia intervention was $2 billion, a financial commitment made solely by President Clinton. That estimate continued to grow with the lengthened deployment, eventually exceeding $6 billion. In effect, the president had combined the powers of the legislative and the executive branches, exercising both the power of the sword and the power of the purse.

A Failure of Checks and Balances

The framers of the Constitution assumed that each branch of the government would protect its own prerogatives. Efforts by one branch to encroach upon another would be beaten back. As Madison explained in Federalist No. 51: "the great security against a gradual concentration of the several powers in the same department, consists in giving to those who administer each department the necessary constitutional means and personal motives to resist encroachments of the others . . . Ambition must be made to counter ambition." To some extent, this theory has worked well. The president and the judiciary invoke a multitude of powers to protect their institutions.

Congress, on the other hand, not only fails to fight back but even volunteers in surrendering fundamental legislative powers, including the war power and the power of the purse. Members of Congress seem uncertain about the scope of their constitutional powers. Some claim that Congress can limit funds for presidential actions that were taken in the past but never for future actions. There is no constitutional support for that position. The decision to use military force against other nations is reserved to Congress, other than for defensive actions. Members may restrict a president's actions prospectively as well as retrospectively.

Other arguments reinforce the notion that the power of the purse cannot be used to limit the president in military actions. Senator Jacob Javits said that Congress "can hardly cut off appropriations when 500,000 American troops are fighting for their lives, as in Vietnam." The short answer is that Congress can, and has, used the power of the purse to restrict presidential war power. If members of Congress are concerned about the safety of American soldiers, their lives are not protected by voting to continue funding. Terminating appropriations will bring the soldiers home.

Some legislators suggest that a cutoff of funds would leave American soldiers stranded and without ammunition. During debate in 1995 on prohibiting funds from being used for the deployment of ground forces to Bosnia and Herzegovina, Congressman Porter Goss said: "I cannot support a complete withdrawal of funds and support for the United States troops who are already on the ground in the former Yugoslavia. These men and women are wearing the uniform of the U.S. military and obeying orders, and we cannot leave them stranded in hostile territory." Congressman George Gekas added: "I cannot vote under any circumstances to abandon our troops. Not to fund them? Unheard of. I cannot support that. Not to supply them with foods, material, ammunition, all the weapons that they require to do their mission?"[8] Cutting off funds would not have that effect. A funding prohibition would force the withdrawal of whatever troops were in place and prevent the deployment of any other troops to that region.

Congressional acquiescence is explained in part, but only in part, on partisan grounds. Senators and Representatives protect not only their own institutions but often also the presidency, especially when the president is from their party. Depending on the president in office, Senate Majority Leader George Mitchell (D-Me.) took substantially different positions on the allocation of the war power between Congress and the president. In 1991 he strongly challenged President Bush's claim that he could use military force against Iraq without congressional authorization: "the decision to commit the Nation to war should not be left in the hands of one man. . . . if [President Bush] now decides to use those forces in what would plainly be war he is legally obligated to seek the prior approval of the Congress." Two years later he opposed legislative language that would have required President Clinton to obtain advance approval from Congress before sending U.S. forces to Bosnia-Herzegovina. Instead, he supported a nonbinding, sense-of-Congress resolution urging the president to seek congressional authorization. His proposal, he explained, "does not purport to impose prior restraints upon a president performing the duties assigned him under the Constitution." He did not "favor prior restraints. I believe they plainly violate the Constitution."[9] But Mitchell was not averse to using prior restraints on President Bush.

Mitchell's behavior is somewhat understandable in the sense that in 1993 he was balancing two roles: Senate Majority Leader and a key legislator in advancing Clinton's agenda. He was not in a good position to singlemindedly defend Senate prerogatives. More difficult to understand are the statements by Republican leaders in the House and Senate who spoke openly in support of President Clinton's power as commander in chief. Senate Majority Leader Bob Dole (R-Kans.), in objecting to any legislative constraints on Clinton's use of military force in Bosnia, said: "in my view the president has the authority and the power under the Constitution to do what he feels should be done regardless of what Congress does."[10] Senator John McCain, Republican from Arizona, concluded that Congress had no constitutional basis for challenging Clinton: "The president will be sending 20,000 Americans to Bosnia for 1 year, whether we approve or disapprove. . . . The president has the authority under the Constitution to do so, and he intends to exercise that authority with or without our approval."[11]

Here is the fundamental imbalance between the branches and the failure of checks and balances. Presidents do not volunteer their executive powers to Congress. They fight back against encroachments. They do not take steps to defend legislative prerogatives. But legislators from both parties make statements in defense of presidential power, even at the cost of their own institution.

Theories of presidential war power that would have been shocking fifty years ago are now offered as though they were obvious and free of controversy. Instead of the two branches working in concert to create a program that has broad public support and understanding, with some hope of continuity, presidents take unilateral steps to engage the country in military operations abroad. They typically justify their actions not only on broad interpretations of the Constitution but cite "authority" granted by multinational institutions in which the United States is but one of many state actors. This pattern does not merely weaken Congress and the power of the purse. It undermines public control, the system of checks and balances, and constitutional government.

Notes

1. See Max Farrand, ed., *The Records of the Federal Convention of 1787* (New Haven, Conn.: Yale University Press, 1937), especially volume 1, pp. 64–66, and volume 2, pp. 318–319.

2. *Department of State Bulletin,* 11:448 (1945).

3. 91 *Cong. Rec.* 8185 (1945).

4. Richard H. Heindel et al., "The North Atlantic Treaty in the United States Senate," *American Journal of International Law,* 43: 649, 650 (1949).

5. Robert H. Bork, "Comments on the Articles on the Legality of the United States Action in Cambodia," *American Journal of International Law,* 65:81 (1971).

6. *Weissman v. Metropolitan Life Ins. Co.,* 112 *F. Supp.* 420, 425 (S.D. Cal. 1953).

7. *The New York Times,* June 28, 1992, p. 16; *The New York Times,* August 14, 1992, p. A15.

8. 141 *Cong. Rec.* H14820, H14822 (daily ed. December 13, 1995).

9. 137 *Cong. Rec.* S101 (daily ed. January 10, 1991); 139 *Cong. Rec.* S14005 (daily ed. October 20, 1993).

10. 141 *Cong. Rec.* S17529 (daily ed. November 27, 1995).

11. Ibid., p. S17863.

11

Presidential Management of the Executive Bureaucracy

Geoffrey Kemp

Introduction

It is an accepted maxim that the role of the president in making foreign policy and his relationship with the National Security Council (NSC) system and its staff will vary according to his background, temperament, and management style. Jimmy Carter was a "hands-on" president; he became involved in decisions concerning tennis court allocations and the nature of beverages served to White House guests (no hard liquor). Ronald Reagan was very much a "hands-off" president, perhaps unique in recent history. On the other hand, his successor, George Bush, [was] even more activist than Carter. He has been called his "own desk officer." His personal diplomacy during the 1990–1991 Persian Gulf crisis and the attempted Soviet coup in August 1991 confirmed this reputation.

Most recent presidents have been "hands-on," especially in the conduct of foreign policy. Franklin D. Roosevelt, Harry S Truman, and Dwight Eisenhower knew how to use the powers of their office to bypass bureaucracy when necessary. Although they had very different styles, none was as passive as Reagan on matters pertaining to daily management. John F. Kennedy, Lyndon B. Johnson, and Richard M. Nixon likewise controlled foreign policy from the White House and made extensive use of the NSC staff to pursue their particular initiatives. It was under Kennedy that the NSC staff first began to be "noticed" as important players in their own right. Nixon and his national security adviser, Henry Kissinger, made White House control of foreign policy one of the most singular characteristics of the administration. Only during Gerald Ford's short tenure did some semblance of balance emerge in the dis-

---

Note: Some notes have been deleted or renumbered.

tribution of foreign policy decision making. This was due, in large part, to Kissinger's presence at the State Department. Ford certainly had more day-to-day control of the White House than Reagan. It was Ford alone who decided to fire his secretary of defense, James Schlesinger, an action Reagan would never have taken on his own.

Ronald Reagan's tenure can be regarded as something of an aberration concerning the "hands-on–hands-off" debate. Yet the irony is that it was Reagan's meddling in one particular foreign policy issue (that of the Middle East hostages) and his lack of attention to detail that contributed to a major scandal—Iran-contra—and a major review of the presidential management of national security. The Iran–contra affair generated wide publicity about the role of the NSC staff in the management of foreign policy. There were frequent references to "rogue elephant" operations conducted by Oliver North from the White House basement and the Old Executive Office Building. In televised congressional hearings Secretaries of State and Defense George Shultz and Caspar Weinberger described how they were duped by the White House and cut out of the decision-making process. As a result of this crisis, the Tower Commission was established to review the affair. It recommended new guidelines for the NSC staff to ensure closer control on day-to-day operations with an enhanced role for the NSC counsel.[1]

How did it come about that the NSC staff had such power? Could such an operation happen again? What should be the correct relationship between the president, the NSC staff, and other key players in the national security bureaucracy? And to what extent does the entire national security decision-making system need overhaul in view of the new sets of problems facing the United States in both the international and domestic arenas? To answer these questions, I offer a brief history of the NSC system; this is followed by an analysis of why the White House has become, and must remain, the focus of national security decision making; and I then show why it is difficult, although not impossible, for presidents to engage in long-range thinking about foreign policy.

Origins of the National Security Council and Its Staff

During World War II, the Departments of Army, Navy, and State had to cooperate to manage a grand strategy that embraced the entire resources of the nation and the most complicated and politically difficult alliance ever assembled to fight a total war. The United States found itself faced with new global responsibilities at the end of the war. To those in Washington responsible for the new world order, it became clear that institutional changes were necessary to better manage traditionally competitive bureaucracies.

The National Security Council (NSC) was established by the National Security Act, which was signed into law by President Truman on July 26, 1947.

This law also created the position of secretary of defense, to be in charge of a united Department of Defense; the director of Central Intelligence, who was to coordinate all interagency intelligence as well as run the newly created Central Intelligence Agency (CIA); and the Department of the Air Force. It reduced the individual service secretaries to subcabinet rank.

The NSC was to be an advisory body to the president. Truman determined at the time that the body would have no formal policymaking role except in the field of intelligence, for which it was legally responsible under the 1947 act. Early membership of the Council was large and included the president, the secretaries of state and defense, the three service secretaries, the chairman of the National Security Resources Board (NSRB), other cabinet officers, and other advisers and observers. Such a large gathering inevitably diminished the power and authority of the organization, especially that of the secretary of defense, James Forrestal. At Forrestal's insistence, and with Truman's blessing, an amendment to the 1947 act was passed in 1949 and coupled with a new executive order on reforms. The NSC was to be located within the Executive Office of the President. The three service secretaries and the chairman of the NSRB were stripped of membership, but the vice president was added. The chairman of the Joint Chiefs of Staff (JCS) and the Director of Central Intelligence were to be statutory members. The four permanent members have remained so ever since: the president, the vice president, and the secretaries of state and defense. A small staff was created to serve as a secretariat for the NSC. The staff was located in the Executive Office Building, and aside from the executive secretary and his assistant, all other staffers were consultants or detailees from the armed services and the State Department.

The NSC system was used extensively during the Korean War, but its output was of mixed quality, and it could hardly be described as a powerful organization. When Eisenhower became president, he enhanced the power of the NSC and appointed Robert Cutler to be a special assistant to the president for national security affairs, thus institutionalizing a position that had previously been held by personal advisers to the president, such as Colonel Edward M. House and Harry Hopkins.

However, despite these changes, the dominant figures in national security decision making during the Eisenhower administration were the president himself (he chaired more than 90 percent of the meetings) and his secretary of state, John Foster Dulles. Although there was a modest increase in staff, the primary function of the NSC staff was coordination rather than policy formulation.

Under Kennedy, the NSC dramatically changed its function. Kennedy and his special assistant for national security affairs, McGeorge Bundy, rarely used the NSC but instead created a much more personalized system whereby the NSC staff was appointed to serve the president rather than the NSC. The NSC staff was now seen as an independent organization, working directly for the president, and became advocates, rather than brokers, of national security policy. This new approach to managing national security was continued by Johnson and his special assistant, Walt Rostow, and was carried to new heights and much increased staff under Richard Nixon's and Gerald Ford's tenures, with Henry Kissinger playing the key role in managing the growth. This dominance was continued during the Carter presidency, when Zbigniew Brzezinski was national security adviser.

One common characteristic of the NSC system from Kennedy to Reagan was the diminution of the role of the secretary of state as the principal architect of foreign policy. Dean Rusk, William Rogers, and Cyrus Vance were all overshadowed and frequently outmaneuvered by the White House. Both of Reagan's secretaries of state, Alexander Haig and George Shultz, complained bitterly of the undermining of their roles by the White House and other agencies.

During the first year of the Reagan administration, a well-intentioned but totally impractical effort was made to limit the power of the NSC staff in the hope of avoiding the infamous turf battles between the White House and State Department that had been front-page stories during the tenures of NSC advisers Kissinger and Brzezinski. The power of the NSC staff depends largely on the NSC adviser's access to the president and on his relations with the other cabinet officers who deal with foreign policy. Richard Allen, the first of six national security advisers in the Reagan administration, was very well informed on foreign policy but had poor relations with Alexander Haig and the domestic White House staff. He was not permitted direct access to the Oval Office, as his predecessors and successors have been. This "downgrading" of his role reflected on the entire NSC staff. Their ability to deal with interagency counterparts and with domestic White House staff on foreign policy questions was hampered. It led to frequent press speculation that the NSC was "irrelevant" and that it had "lost power." Such reports have a negative impact on staff morale and result in limited access to interagency meetings and diminished effectiveness as senior members of the administration.

Allen was replaced in January 1982 by William Clark. Clark had been appointed deputy secretary of state at the beginning of the Reagan administration to provide some White House "oversight" of Alexander Haig. Clark knew little about foreign policy but had excellent relations with Ronald Reagan, having been his chief of staff when he was governor of California. With Clark's arrival at the White House, things changed for the NSC staff overnight. Clark took the job on condition that he have direct access to the president. This rise in stature had an immediate and positive effect on the NSC senior staff. They not only now had better access to interagency meetings but also were frequently taken into the Oval Office to brief the president and his immediate entourage, including the chief of staff and the vice president.

The Reagan administration's early effort to limit the NSC staff's power failed because a strong managerial structure in the White House is essential to manage the day-to-day conduct of foreign affairs, irrespective of who is president. If the NSC and its staff were abolished by fiat tomorrow, a new institution with very similar authority would have to be put in its place. At the height of the Iran–contra crisis, there were rumblings about making the appointment of the national security adviser subject to congressional approval. No president could accept such constraints on his own staff, and the idea was quickly buried.

Why the White House Dominates National Security Decision Making

Although in no way downgrading the importance of presidential style and idiosyncrasies in the management of national security, institutional factors and the policymaking process play a key role in foreign policy decision making, no matter who sits in the Oval Office. This stems from the unique role the United States plays in world politics and the unique system of open government in Washington, a system that is very different from those of most other established democracies, including those of our close allies.

Three additional institutional issues help explain why process is so important and why, as a result, White House institutions have great power. First, the U.S. executive branch has an increasingly diversified bureaucracy, cutting across many regions and functional interests. Second, the foreign policy agenda is always full. There is never enough time to cover all bases and meet all needs and demands. As a result, presidential time is the most valuable commodity in Washington. Determining how the president allocates his time, including who has access to him and how that access is used, is one of the most important attributes of power. Third, the domestic political and public aspects of foreign policy, including managing the media and relations with Congress, have become dominant, and therefore time-consuming, concerns of the modern White House. This has increased the importance of public diplomacy. There is little time in this day and age of instant communications and hour-by-hour decision making for long-term thinking or . . . "vision."

Because of these institutional realities, a strong NSC staff is necessary. Consider the first reality: the increase in the size and complexity of the bureaucracy and the changing nature of American foreign policy. It used to be that a strong secretary of state, like John Foster Dulles, and a strong president, like Franklin D. Roosevelt or Eisenhower, could determine the basic tenets and guidelines for policy without much reference to other cabinet members (unless defense and financial matters were involved, in which case the secretaries of defense and of the treasury would be consulted). However, as American dominance in world affairs has become more circumspect and as the global economy and environmental issues have become more important components of American foreign policy, more bureaucratic players now have to be consulted on decisions that require the commitment of resources, public policy initiatives, and, occasionally, new legislation. For example, when the Japanese prime minister visits the Oval Office to discuss U.S.–Japanese relations, talking points for the president will be pulled together from position papers solicited from many different agencies. There will usually be strong differences of opinion among the Departments of Commerce, Treasury, State, Defense, and Agriculture and the Special Trade Representative on how to handle the meeting and what points to make.

As more and more bureaucratic players enter the foreign policy field, the primacy of the State Department on day-to-day issues is diminished, and the level of diversity and competition among the executive bureaucracies is healthy, provided there is a workable process to iron out the differences and present the president with alternatives. Depending on the style of the president, an individual NSC adviser—if he or she has stature—may have great leeway to determine which of various opposing cabinet views the president signs off on. For instance, it was very rare for Ronald Reagan to go against the advice of a strong NSC adviser, a fact that two strong secretaries of state, Alexander Haig and George Schultz, both had to face, particularly during William Clark's tenure in the job. There is also the additional factor that the NSC staff's mandate covers all matters relating to national security and intelligence, including issues that frequently fall outside the purview of the State Department.

A second reason why the NSC staff has become more important in recent years has to do with modern communications and crisis management. Because of the intensity of media coverage and the expectation of "instant" news and action, crises have to be managed in "real time"; the president has to respond immediately to a hostage taking, a coup, or a major accident. The White House can find itself actually *following* the crisis agenda of the networks and has to respond to questions about U.S. policy without the luxury of carefully structured analysis, NSC meetings, and interagency intelligence reports. In the nuclear age there is the added necessity of having twenty-four-hour vigilance as part of the national command authority. Crisis decision making is made immediately, usually at White House meetings called at a moment's notice. There is no time for contemplation and careful preparation. Those who have strong visions and express them well at such meetings often carry the day on policy decisions.

The secretary of state and the secretary of defense are the two cabinet members on the National Security Council who have the most day-to-day involvement with foreign and national security policy. However, the nature of their jobs requires that they frequently be out of the country or out of Washington. It is therefore essential that the president have an entourage skilled and knowledgeable about international affairs at his immediate beck and call. A crisis can come and go while the secretary of state is traveling on the other side of the world. Although he has instant communication with Washington, his power to influence crisis decision making is frequently a function of his physical proximity to the president. . . .

A third reason for the importance of the NSC staff concerns the domestic component of American foreign policy, which frequently reflects the diversity of its ethnic population. U.S. policy toward Cuba, South Africa, Israel, or Eastern Europe has to take into account the important domestic constituencies with special interests in these areas. The power of the pro-Israel lobby is well known; in the early 1990s the Eastern European lobbies, especially those for the Baltic countries, have resurfaced as a result of the collapse of Soviet communism; no presidential candidate—especially a Republican—can avoid going to Miami in an election year to denounce Fidel Castro in an appeal for the Cuban-American vote. As different ethnic groups achieve new prominence in the United States, the diversity of foreign policy concerns will increase, and so too will the overlap between foreign policy and domestic issues. Ethnic issues are now paralleled by the growing influence of environmental groups that have important domestic constituents.

In this context, the role of lobbying in U.S. domestic politics is well established, and there are strong supporters as to its effectiveness and impact on the political system. Supporters of the system, including the political action committees (PACs), believe that this is an expression of the democratic process and that the best-organized lobbies are usually the most motivated. The fact that they deliver votes on specific issues reflects their skills, which others, rather than condemning, should try to duplicate. Critics say that the role of the PACs has reached the point now where they have a disproportionate influence on policy. Members of Congress have become highly dependent on the financial support the PACs provide; this is because of new campaign laws that forbid individual donors contributing large sums of money but do permit small amounts of money from individuals being collected by PACs and presented as a package to a candidate.

The most important role the NSC plays in dealing with these lobbies is to ensure that the foreign policy elements of their activities are taken into account. Each lobby uses different techniques, but some—the American Israel Public Affairs Committee (AIPAC), for instance—have the power to influence major policy decisions, especially regarding appropriations, on Capitol Hill.

Although it is easy to become irate about the power of certain lobbies, they can play a role that the White House can exploit. Lobbies are often the repository of intelligence; some of it is scurrilous, some wildly fanciful, but occasionally a useful nugget will turn up. Such information frequently comes in the form of memos, letters, circulars, books, articles, indeed all the paraphernalia of the modern propaganda machine. There is never time to plow through

all the material, but it is useful in keeping track of personalities and in antici-
pating trouble.

For these reasons, the president must have around him people who are sensitive to the linkage between domestic and foreign policy issues and who can
deal with the lobbyists. This means that the NSC staff and the White House
domestic staff must establish good working relations and should, by and large,
be of equal rank. . . .

The Importance of the President's Schedule

Irrespective of the occupant of the Oval Office or the distribution of power
within the White House and between the NSC staff and other government
agencies, perhaps the least understood but intrinsically most important feature
of the modern White House concerns the pressures on the president's time
and how the pressure of "the schedule" influences the day-to-day operations,
the decision-making process, career incentives, and the lack of coherent long-
term policy planning.

Daily priorities are usually determined by morning senior staff members.
Invariably, the key issues will relate to overnight crises or politically sensitive
items in the morning's papers, especially the Washington papers and the *New
York Times*. This sets the agenda for questions that will come up throughout
the day when the president and his senior staff have their encounters with the
White House press corps. There will also be a focused discussion on the meetings scheduled *for that day*. Questions or issues about a meeting—say, with a
foreign minister the following week—will get scant attention. And if anyone
on the staff raises long-term issues—for example, those of ozone depletion or
of the future of the space station, and how the president should be thinking
about these problems with respect to his State of the Union message—that
individual will receive little hearing, unless it is a *very* quiet day.

When a president assumes office, there are dates already marked in his
calendar—for example, that of the annual economic summit with the Western
partners. However, most of the president's calendar is, in theory, clear when
he first takes up residence in the White House. One of the primary tasks of
the chief of staff is to set the calendar. This requires balancing the president's
own personal wishes with the needs of domestic politics and foreign affairs.

Within the foreign policy community, the competition is fierce because
nearly all foreign leaders want to come to Washington, preferably with all the
trappings and ceremony of a state visit. Determining which countries should
receive priority is a fairly straightforward if somewhat contentious process.
The top candidates are, quite naturally, the close allies: Britain, France,
Germany, Italy, Japan, Canada. Mexico and Russia also rank at the top. Increasingly the middle-rank Western European powers are considered impor-

tant—Spain, for instance. From 1989 onward, the new Eastern European leaders have found favor. Problems can arise in the case of Middle Eastern countries. Israel is always near the top of the list, but once Israel is invited, Egypt must follow, or even precede. And if Egypt is invited, Jordan and Saudi Arabia have to be close behind. Invite India, and Pakistan must follow; China also ranks high, as do South Korea and the Philippines. So it is not difficult to set aside all the slots for available state visits for the first two years of an administration without even considering the second-rank countries one wishes to woo or return favors to.

The solution is found in the "working visit," which has all the substance of a state visit but less of the glitz—no White House lawn with the guns and parade, no White House dinner, and therefore less television coverage. For many of the leaders who visit Washington, the coverage back home is extremely important. For the smaller but friendly countries that have no pressing claims on U.S. largesse (like access to military bases) but that are steady, reliable partners, the lack of an invitation to Washington can become an all-consuming issue. Often the primary task of the foreign nation's ambassador is to secure the invitation; his or her future can depend on the whims of the schedule and goodheartedness of a White House staffer. . . .

This is not to say that getting in to see the president is the be-all and end-all of diplomacy in Washington. However, for most visitors the lure and appeal of the White House is obviously a prime concern. It does not matter whether formal policy decisions taken on a particular country are made over on the sixth floor of the State Department by career bureaucrats. Most world leaders want it to be known that they have some personal rapport with the president of the United States. To his credit, Ronald Reagan understood this instinctively in a way that Richard Nixon and Jimmy Carter did not. Reagan was especially generous with the Oval Office photography sessions, the cozy chats, the private lunch and, in the case of the king of Morocco, horseback rides through the national parks. Style and protocol are particularly important when dealing with leaders whose egos and power depend on the perception back home that they are well regarded in Washington. Helping a friendly foreign leader with his or her domestic problems is a natural role for the White House. But it can be very time-consuming.

When the reverse occurs and a U.S. president visits a foreign country, the script of the visit can itself become an extremely important, and at times sensitive, adjunct to the policymaking process. Reagan's much-ballyhooed trip to Germany in May 1985—including the visit to the Bitburg cemetery, which contained the graves of Waffen S.S. troops—absorbed much energy and generated much angst. At the time, the Bitburg controversy dominated the visit. What was planned as a small gesture to support Chancellor Helmut Kohl became the focus of the entire trip.

Trips such as this are planned and controlled by the White House. The advance team that goes out early to set up the logistics relies heavily on the services of the State Department and the local country's protocol offices, but the final decisions are all made by the president's staff, including the Secret Service, which has the final say on security matters. It will also have the last call on who gets to ride in which helicopter, the seating arrangements on Air Force One, and attendance at the state dinners. If handled badly or with malice, these issues can create difficulties, even bad blood, within the overall delegation. It was fighting over such seeming trivia on Reagan's trip to the Versailles summit in June 1982 that convinced William Clark and James Baker that the time had come to replace Alexander Haig as Secretary of State. Bad chemistry can be as detrimental to policy as bad position papers.

Dealing with Unscheduled Events:
Quarrel and Crisis Management

Unscheduled events, by definition, cannot be anticipated, so when they come along, they will disrupt a carefully orchestrated calendar. Unscheduled events usually fall into two categories: major crises that cause the president to drop what he is doing and focus on the immediate issues, and daily Washington quarrels. Crises are the ultimate test of an administration's ability to function effectively. Over the past three decades, one key lesson has emerged. If there is consensus within the executive branch on how to handle a crisis, it will be much easier to manage. The reason is simple: Consensus reduces the prospects for leaks, and leaks to the press and Congress can stymie the ability of the White House to retain control over events. The contrast between the handling of the Lebanon crisis during Reagan's first term and the Gulf crisis was vivid. In the case of Lebanon, there was bitter disagreement among all the key players over what U.S. policy should be, whereas with regard to the Gulf crisis of 1987, operations were carried out with no dissent. The more recent Gulf crisis in the summer, fall, and winter of 1990–1991 was remarkable because of the central role played by President Bush and because of the absence of major leaks to the press concerning disunity over policy.

Three types of Washington quarrels are important: those with the press, which are part of an ongoing, usually healthy, but often antagonistic relationship; those with Congress over legislation; and interagency disputes that may have to be resolved by the president himself.

It is difficult to predict on a day-to-day basis just how many quarrels will have to be dealt with at a particular time. It is on these issues that the skills of the president's staff are put to some of their toughest tests. The press secretary and the assistant for congressional liaison are among the people who can make or break the president's day. Career advancement in the White House and in other agencies frequently comes from being recognized as a good crisis or quarrel manager. Usually, promotions are given to such individuals rather than to the deep strategic thinkers who may have brilliant ideas but who do not help the president get through the next twenty-four hours.

One reason why quarrel management is so important is that, unless handled skillfully, such quarrels escalate into crises and absorb more and more of the president's time. In dealing with the major disputes with Congress, for instance, the president is probably the best quarrel manager, because he can use his authority and stature to broker deals that would not otherwise be possible. However, in doing so, he often has to offer something in exchange for the favor. He also has to take the time to woo on the phone, or meet on a one-on-one basis, those who are opposing him on a particular issue. During the Reagan administration, one of the most time-consuming and bitter quarrels with Congress had to do with the sale of AWACS airplanes to Saudi Arabia. The administration eventually won the fight by focusing great efforts on persuading four senators not to vote against the sale of the plane. From the point of view of the domestic side of the White House, the AWACS fight was a time-consuming burden that far outweighed its foreign policy importance and detracted from more important domestic legislation.

Crisis- and quarrel-management skills seem to come most naturally to men or women of action rather than philosophers or more academic types frequently found in government for short periods of time. John Poindexter and Oliver North received great kudos for their management of the *Achille Lauro* crisis in 1985, when the ship was seized by terrorists, thereby giving Ronald Reagan his first victory over terrorists. During this crisis, North and Poindexter were adroit at getting around the red tape and bureaucratic confusion that normally hamper such operations. *Achille Lauro* did a great deal to propel John Poindexter to the job of national security adviser when Robert McFarlane resigned in December 1985. It was, of course, precisely the talent for bypassing the bureaucracy that got both men into so much trouble with the Iran-contra affair. More [recently], President Bush received high marks for his handling of the Persian Gulf and Soviet crises, in part because he was seen as being in control of his own teams and insisted on loyalty from those who served him.

However, one down side to the "action-oriented" players is that long-term planning and careful deliberation of policy issues have taken a back seat. Since much policy revolves around short-term issues, the strategic thinker, for want of a better word, tends to get cut out of the action. Periodic attempts to reinvigorate the policy planning staff in the State Department and come up with long-term concepts have rarely worked because the policy planning staff finds itself being drawn more and more into crises and day-to-day events, writing speeches, delivering congressional testimony, and getting through the next summit meeting. Furthermore, it must be acknowledged that because "action" is invariably more exciting than concept planning, there is a natural tendency for even those predisposed to strategic thinking to become embroiled in short-term issues. . . .

Using the Schedule to Influence Policy

There are occasions when setting the schedule can become an effective bureaucratic device for focusing, and indeed changing, policy. The example of U.S. policy toward India during the Reagan administration makes the point.

At the beginning of the administration, the priority of the White House was to focus on domestic rather than foreign policy. Within the foreign policy agenda, there was a full list of problems to be tackled in the Caribbean, Europe, and East Asia. For those who believed that the time was right for a reassessment of U.S. policy toward India, which has been largely neglected by the U.S., getting the attention of the president and his topic adviser proved difficult. India was a factor during the major reassessment of policy toward Pakistan in early 1981 but was still peripheral. It was Afghanistan that was the primary concern. Such negligence was not due to ill will. There was agreement, *in principle,* that better relations with India were a good idea. But the United States has global interests, and, as has been pointed out, the agenda is always overflowing with important issues. Therefore, in the absence of some pressing need to bring an item to the top of the president's "in" box, issues that are not at the top of the political agenda become secondary and tend to be ignored. To bring noncrisis issues onto the agenda, it is necessary to have a motivating event. In the case of India, the opportunity arose when it was decided that President Reagan would meet for ten to fifteen minutes with Prime Minister Indira Gandhi at the Economic North–South Summit at Cancun, Mexico, on October 21, 1981.

Once it was agreed—for reasons of protocol as much as for anything else—that the Cancun meeting with Gandhi would take place, it became an official appointment on the president's calendar. It was now possible to send out instructions through the NSC and the State Department to all the agencies saying that "the President will meet with Mrs. Gandhi on October 21st. At that time he will review U.S. policy towards India. We need to prepare talking points for that meeting and, in the process, review where we stand on current relations." As a result of this, the bureaucracy moved into action, interagency meetings were held, papers were written, disagreements were ironed out, discussion points were proposed, briefing books were assembled, and talking points were prepared—and by the time the meeting went ahead, a new alertness to U.S.–Indian relations was under way. Ultimately, this led to much-improved economic ties and increased technical cooperation, including better relations between the Pentagon and the Indian Ministry of Defence.

Short of a crisis, the best way to get the bureaucracy to focus on an issue is to have an event on the calendar. This is why presidential meetings in the White House, or elsewhere, are so important, however brief they may be. Words uttered in the Oval Office, even with the help of prompt cards, take on an importance beyond their apparent face value. When the president speaks or reads a statement about U.S. policy toward Jerusalem or Berlin in the Oval Office, it has an immediate and significant effect on foreign policy. What happens in the meeting itself creates a chain reaction and can set in motion new trends in policy or confirm old trends.

Consequently, the process of getting a president and prime minister together for fifteen minutes not only has a life cycle before the meeting but after the meeting as well, when embellishments and clarifications of policy can be made in background briefings. If the system is working, follow-up becomes an important part of the policy process. If, however, there is confusion and disagreement among the chief players as to what happened in the Oval Office, then more confusion can result. During the Reagan years, there were many times when the president was either ambiguous about or indifferent to follow-up concerning statements he had made in the Oval Office. This meant that those present could each take their own interpretations of events back to their own agencies, and in some cases to the press, and tell different stories as to what happened. It was confusion about what happened in the Oval Office that got the Reagan administration into so much trouble on arms control, relations in the Middle East, and, most tellingly, the Iran–contra affair. President Bush, in contrast, . . . maintained much more coherence about policy, primarily because it [was] he, not his staff, who [had] the last word and who [explained] the policy in detail to the press.

The Media and Public Diplomacy

Managing the media has become one of the most important tasks of the White House staff, in part because of the increased power of television and the vast amounts of raw information that come over the wire services. President Carter's ill-fated "Rose Garden" strategy, adopted at the time the U.S. hostages were first taken in Tehran in November 1979, fell apart because there was no way a president could avoid the daily glare of television and its relentless coverage of the issue. Once a story like the hostage crisis or the Iran–contra affair breaks, the White House's ability to control the news is severely limited. Bad judgment at the beginning of a public crisis can have a disastrous impact on the ensuing drama. The Reagan administration's poor handling of the early days of the Iran–contra nearly toppled the presidency.

It is sometimes not appreciated how far *behind* the news the White House and other agencies of government can be during a crisis. A good example of this occurred on October 6, 1981. News was received in the White House early in the morning that President Anwar Sadat of Egypt had been shot at a national Armed Forces Day parade. There were no details of the shooting. Some reports said that Sadat had suffered minor injuries; others said that his injuries were more serious. Within half an hour a crisis-management team assembled in the White House Situation Room to monitor the events. Throughout the morning there was confusion about what was happening in Cairo. Communications between the U.S. embassy and the State Department were nonexistent, and when messages did come in, they were delayed. Telephone lines were down, and there was no direct contact between the White House and Cairo. Vice President George Bush, as the designated official in charge of crisis management, presided over a group of senior officials in the Situation Room. At one point during the morning this author was called to bring in some briefing papers. He was amazed to find the entire team of senior officials watching ABC news on the Situation Room television monitor. The reason was simple: Television was getting access to real-time intelligence far ahead of the multi-billion-dollar U.S. government network. The White House was, in fact, dependent on television for news all that morning up to the moment when it was announced that Sadat had died.[2]

Dealing with the President's Views

Each president has strong feelings on certain subjects. Sometimes these can emerge as important factors in foreign policy management that are simply not programmable in the normal sense of the word. Controlling surprise presidential remarks is especially difficult if the president misspeaks or speaks out of line with other agency positions. Utterances from the Oval Office take on a life all of their own. The rest of the world still hangs on the news flash from the White House. Given the speed of modern communications and the need to immediately respond to untoward remarks, media management is an increasingly burdensome job; no president has learned how to master it, although some have handled it better than others.

How to Improve Policy Planning and Coordination

This chapter has stressed the impact of process on the White House management of foreign policy. It has been argued that it is difficult to orchestrate policy beyond the short term, which is frequently measured in hours rather than in days or months. But is preoccupation with the short term inevitable, and must it always be at the expense of a carefully articulated strategy?

The office of the presidency is sufficiently powerful that if a strong chief of state, preferably not one up for reelection, were determined to present a long-term agenda to the nation, he or she could probably make some headway.

However, unless there was widespread support in Congress for it, the policy would not get very far. For it is not at all clear that the United States wants a president with "vision" if what is meant by this is a radical departure from the way we currently conduct business. "Visionary" figures in foreign policy conjure up images of a Lenin, a Pol Pot, a Hitler, or a Mao; a Nasser, a Begin, or a Khomeini; a Gandhi, a Sukarno, or a Nkruhmah. In this regard U.S. presidential "doctrines" seem to be more in vogue, though usually this word is applied to some statement codifying existing policy rather than to a dramatic new departure. True, the Truman Doctrine was innovative, but in 1947 the United States could, as a result of its economic strength, reshape the world with new policies. More recent "doctrines"—those of Nixon and Reagan— were less sweeping in their scope and were certainly not new in their content.

What Americans seem to want is not "visions" and "doctrines" but a better sense of how this country is going to solve some very practical and many new foreign policy problems as the year 2000 approaches. How will we reduce the trade deficit? How will we control immigration? How will we compete and cooperate with the new Europe? What to do about the importation of illegal drugs? How do we clean up the environment without collapsing the economy? How much military force do we wish to deploy overseas [now that] the Cold War is over? What should we do about the proliferation of weapons of mass destruction? And how much foreign aid should we provide and to whom, and should it be dispensed bilaterally or multilaterally? The list goes on, and as the world becomes more complex and interactive, it will undoubtedly get longer.

Weaving all these issues together in ways that are both practical and ideologically compatible is not easy. To do this will take "vision" and, for public relations purposes, may even require the added appendage of a "doctrine." But whatever the policy is called, it must deal with the reality of the political process and the competitive pressures of the political marketplace. This cannot be done by wishing on the United States decision-making bodies that resemble the putatively rational approach of the Honda boardroom. Neither can it be done by avoiding painful questions of costs, trade-offs, and taxes. It is the type of policy statement that is tailor-made for a presidential speech—provided, of course, that the occasion is right and the substance is realistic.

The Persian Gulf crisis between August 1990 and March 1991 and the crisis in the Soviet Union in the closing days of August 1991 are vivid reminders that a new world order, democracy, and universal human rights are not yet established norms in international relations. Reliance on the use of force to change the status quo, or to restore it, remains a fact of life. Therefore, although many newly emerging problems face American foreign policy, the basic structure of the international system has not changed sufficiently to make the postwar national security system obsolete. Rather, it needs to be modified to take into account the new issues.

As more and more of these new elements in international relations become institutionalized on a global basis, the necessary bureaucratic structure to support U.S. policy on these issues will have to be created. For instance, if an annual global conference on the environment were established, similar to the annual international economic summits between the seven key industrial powers, more focused attention on environmental issues in the White House would be inevitable.

In sum, the best way to bring the new elements of national security and foreign policy into the day-to-day planning process is to ensure that formal meetings that require regular presidential participation take place. Once it is established that the president will meet every year, or whenever, with foreign leaders to focus on a specific topic, active White House involvement will be ensured. This will lead to the injection of more structured thinking on the new sets of issues that face the nation. Even though long-range policy planning analogous to that adopted by successful multinational businesses will never sit well with the American body politic, the existing policy process can be used to inject more coherent planning and, one hopes, more successful policies.

Notes

1. For a detailed and tendentious but nevertheless useful study of the role of the White House in the Iran-contra crisis, see Theodore Draper, *A Very Thin Line: The Iran-Contra Affair* (New York: Hill & Wang, 1991).

2. Further examples of the frantic and confused life of one NSC staffer can be found in the following review article about the Reagan White House: Geoffrey Kemp, "As the World Turns," *The New Republic,* 21 November 1988.

12

End of an Era: Congress and Foreign Policy after the Cold War

James M. Lindsay

Commentators who predicted that U.S. foreign policy would become more tumultuous after Republicans won control of Congress in the 1994 elections were not disappointed. The first Republican majority on Capitol Hill in forty years challenged the Clinton administration on a broad array of issues, ranging from spending on defense and foreign aid to relations with China and Russia to the organization of the State Department. The seemingly radical nature of many of these proposals in turn spawned a litany of complaints that Congress was usurping the president's powers in foreign policy and seeking to return the United States to its isolationist past.

Despite the frequency of these two criticisms, neither is accurate. Most of the proposals being debated today in Congress involve the assertion of well-established congressional powers and most are more accurately described as internationalist than isolationist. More important, the standard criticisms of Congress miss the true significance of its activism: The era of undisputed executive preeminence on foreign policy is over. Put simply, the collapse of the Soviet Union made obsolete the foreign-policy consensus on which presidential leadership in foreign affairs rested for four decades and emboldened members of Congress to challenge the White House over the direction of U.S. foreign policy. Because the change we are witnessing in executive–legislative relations is systemic rather than temporary, Congress and the White House now face the difficult task of developing a new accommodation that respects the authority of both branches while still promoting American interests.

The Constitution, Foreign Policy, and the U.S. Congress

Critics frequently complain that Congress is overstepping its place in the making of foreign policy. Secretary of State Warren Christopher complained in

May 1995 that the foreign aid bill then on the floor of the House waged "an extraordinary onslaught on the president's constitutional authority to manage foreign policy."[1] President Clinton subsequently endorsed Christopher's attack, accusing members of Congress of launching "nothing less than a frontal assault on the authority of the president to conduct the foreign policy of the United States."[2] Outside of government, Anthony Lewis of the *New York Times* argued that "the Republicans who control Congress are trying to move us back toward the Articles of Confederation."[3] Even Republican officials joined the attack; former Secretary of State Lawrence Eagleburger warned that "the restrictions and demands on the President are an absolute attack on the separation of powers."[4]

Although complaints that Congress is usurping the president's constitutional duties are commonplace, they have little merit. As even a cursory reading of the Constitution makes clear, Congress possesses extensive powers to shape foreign policy. Article 1, Section 8 assigns Congress the power to "provide for the common Defence," "To regulate Commerce with foreign Nations," "To define and punish Piracies and Felonies committed on the high Seas," "To declare War," "To raise and support Armies," "To provide and maintain a Navy," and "To make Rules for the Government and Regulation of the land and naval Forces." Article 2, Section 2 specifies that the Senate must give its advice and consent to all treaties and ambassadorial appointments. And Congress's more general powers to appropriate all government funds and to confirm cabinet officials provide additional means to influence foreign policy.

Because Congress and the president *both* claim authority in foreign affairs, the two branches are, in Richard Neustadt's oft-repeated formulation, "separated institutions *sharing* power."[5] The question of which branch should prevail when their powers conflict has been disputed ever since Alexander Hamilton and James Madison squared off two centuries ago in their famed Pacificus-Helvidius debate. And while the president exercises some foreign-affairs powers that are off limits to Congress—with the power to negotiate on behalf of the United States being perhaps the most prominent—the fact that the Constitution grants Congress extensive authority in foreign policy means that instances in which legislators are usurping powers belonging solely to the executive are rare.

This is precisely the case today. Whatever the wisdom of Congress's foreign-policy proposals, almost all of them involve the exercise of well-established congressional powers. The most popular is the appropriations power, which while not unlimited in scope, is nonetheless quite broad. (The Supreme Court has never struck down any use of the appropriations power as an unconstitutional infringement on the president's authority to conduct foreign policy.) Thus, while one might doubt the wisdom of congressional proposals to cut foreign aid, withdraw U.S. troops from Bosnia, and impose sanctions on companies that trade with terrorist states, all of these actions lie well within Congress's established constitutional authority.

At the same time, the vigorous exercise of congressional prerogatives in foreign policy has ample precedent. Throughout the 1980s, for instance, Democratic majorities in Congress enacted numerous provisions that sought to block what Presidents Reagan and Bush hoped to accomplish overseas. When these Republican presidents denounced what they saw as an imperial Congress, Democratic leaders defended congressional prerogatives. Now that divided government cuts the other way, Republicans have a point when they argue that they are merely giving as good as they got.

Accuracy aside, it makes sense for presidents, be they Democrat or Republican, to cast their foreign-policy battles with Congress in constitutional terms. By portraying members of Congress as trying to usurp presidential authority, presidents (and their defenders) may succeed in shifting the debate from the realm of partisan politics to ground that is ostensibly policy neutral and thus more politically defensible. Nonetheless, what lies at the heart of almost all current disputes between the White House and Capitol Hill is not how the Constitution allocates authority between the two branches but rather disagreements over the substance of foreign policy.

A Return to Isolationism?

Besides complaining that Congress is usurping presidential authority, critics also take Congress to task for embracing isolationism, the idea that the United States can maintain its security and prosperity while disengaging politically from world affairs. In May 1995 President Clinton denounced the House foreign-aid bill for containing "the most isolationist proposals to come before the United States Congress in 50 years."[6] Deputy Secretary of State Strobe Talbott made the same point more colorfully several months later when he warned that legislators were trying to "turn the American eagle into an ostrich."[7] Yet while such charges are politically powerful—most American politicians fear being labeled isolationist—they misrepresent the substantive issues that separate the administration from its congressional critics.

To be sure, isolationist sentiment resonates on Capitol Hill today to an extent not heard for more than a half century. When members of Congress defend legislation they support by arguing, as Rep. Dana Rohrabacher (R-Calif.) did, that is about "America-comes-first as policy," it is hard not to hear echoes of the America First movement that helped keep the United States on the sidelines as World War II began in Europe.[8] Moreover, this isolationist sentiment runs through both political parties. Indeed, it was Democrats and not Republicans who led the opposition to the North American Free Trade Agreement (NAFTA) and the Uruguay Round of the General Agreement on Tariffs and Trade (GATT), and who in 1997 succeeded in blocking legislation that would have expanded President Clinton's authority to negotiate international trade agreements.

The resurgence of isolationist sentiment on Capitol Hill helps explain why Congress cut spending on international affairs programs from $20.6 billion in FY 1993 to less than $19 billion in FY 1998, a cut that is more sizable once you factor in the effect of inflation. Isolationist sentiment also helps explain the strident criticisms some members of Congress have leveled against international organizations such as the United Nations and against proposals to have U.S. troops serve as part of international peacekeeping missions. Some Democrats and Republicans do believe that the United States should disengage from world affairs.

Nonetheless, isolationists remain (at least for now) a minority on Capitol Hill and in both political parties. Cuts in the international affairs budget owe less to isolationism and more to the intense pressure to find politically painless ways to cut federal spending, the well-documented shortcomings of America's foreign-aid programs, and the absence of a compelling rationale for aid in the absence of the Soviet threat. Congressional efforts to force reform on the United Nations have gained momentum less because members of Congress want to turn their backs on the world than because of widespread agreement that the organization is bloated, inefficient, and all too often ineffective. (Indeed, in 1997, Kofi Annan, the new UN Secretary General, said publicly that "The United Nations is not working as well as it should."⁹) And congressional attacks on UN peacekeeping owe as much if not more to the obvious ineffectiveness of UN peacekeepers in places such as Somalia and Bosnia as to a desire to disengage from the world.

The weakness of isolationists on Capitol Hill can be seen in the fact that much of the foreign-policy legislation Congress considers carries a decidedly internationalist cast. However ill-considered it might be to expand membership in NATO, to recognize Tibet as an occupied sovereign country, to halt aid to countries that sell weapons to terrorist states, and to impose sanctions on companies that trade with Cuba and Iran, these are not proposals aimed at disengaging the United States from world affairs.

The crux of many of the conflicts today between the White House and Capitol Hill, then, is not *whether* the United States should be involved in international affairs but rather *how* it should be involved. Throughout his first term in office, President Clinton favored a multilateral approach that emphasized collective action through international institutions such as the United Nations. In contrast, many congressional Republicans preferred a unilateral approach to foreign policy. They believed that international organizations too often reflect, as Robert Dole put it before launching his failed presidential bid, "a consensus that opposes American interests or does not reflect American principles and ideas."¹⁰ Thus, Republicans argued that to protect American interests and to promote American principles, the United States should act as it sees fit in world affairs and let other countries either follow or stand aside.

The merits of unilateralism can be debated endlessly, and critics may be right that it poses dangers that Republicans refuse to recognize. But in the eyes of many on Capitol Hill, multilateralism too often becomes an obstacle to action, witness the disastrous experience with the United Nations Protection Force in Bosnia and the international community's tepid reaction in 1997 to Iraq's violations of the cease-fire agreement ending the Persian Gulf War. As long as substantial numbers of legislators see international organizations as hindering rather than aiding American foreign-policy interests, the congressional push for a unilateralist strain of internationalism will remain strong.

The New Tug of War

Although critics miss the mark when they complain about congressional aggrandizement and resurgent isolationism, their frustration with Congress is understandable. Congress is more assertive today than was true even during the Reagan and Bush administrations. Part of the reason lies with the Clinton administration's missteps in foreign policy. The death of 18 American Army Rangers in Somalia, the timidity of U.S. policy when confronted with ethnic cleansing in Bosnia, and Clinton's about-face on his campaign pledge to pressure China to improve its human rights record all emboldened the president's critics. Clinton's defenders might fairly argue that he inherited problems far messier and far less amenable to resolution than those that faced his predecessors, but such arguments carry little weight with legislators inclined to rally 'round in victory and to pile on in defeat.

The Clinton administration might not have paid as dearly for its missteps if not for the 1994 elections. So long as Democrats were the majority party in Congress, administration officials knew that the congressional leadership would help them pass legislation they needed and derail legislation they opposed. Once Republicans took control of the House and Senate, however, Clinton discovered what Presidents Reagan and Bush had learned before him: foreign policy is much harder to conduct when the other party controls Congress. When control of government is divided, presidents are hit with a double whammy. Not only do they face a congressional majority that is more likely to disagree with them on the substance of policy, they can no longer use appeals to party loyalty to persuade the congressional leadership to blunt rank-and-file challenges to their policies.

As important as the Clinton administration's miscues and the return of divided government are to understanding the intensification of congressional activism on foreign policy in the 1990s, they tell only part of the story. At a deeper level, we are witnessing a fundamental change in executive–legislative relations on foreign policy. With the end of the Cold War, the norms and beliefs that once limited congressional activism are crumbling. The result is the development of what Jeremy Rosner, a former senior director on the staff of the National Security Council under President Clinton, aptly calls "the new tug of war" for the control of foreign policy.[11] Neither Bill Clinton's departure from the White House nor the return of unified government will return executive–legislative relations to their traditional Cold War pattern.

The reason for the new tug of war lies in an observation Alexis de Tocqueville made more than 150 years ago. Commenting on Congress's surprising strength in foreign policy at that time, he speculated that it stemmed from the country's isolation from external threat. "If the Union's existence were constantly menaced, and if its great interests were continually interwoven with those of other powerful nations, one would see the prestige of the executive growing, because of what was expected from it and of what it did."[12] The rise of the imperial presidency in the two decades after the end of World War II proved Tocqueville right. As Americans became convinced in the late 1940s that hostile communist states threatened the United States and the rest of the free world, they increasingly came to agree on two basic ideas: the United States needed to resist communist expansion, and achieving this goal demanded strong presidential leadership. Most legislators shared these two basic beliefs (and helped promote them); those who disagreed risked punishment at the polls. As a result, the president's say in foreign policy grew markedly in the 1950s and 1960s while that of Congress faded significantly.

What Tocqueville identified as the fundamental dynamic of executive–legislative relations in foreign affairs also holds true in reverse. When Americans believe that they face few external threats, they are more inclined to disagree over the objectives of U.S. foreign policy and less inclined to see a need for strong presidential leadership. This has profound consequences for executive–legislative relations. Congress will reflect these substantive disagreements, arguments that members should defer to presidential leadership will sound less persuasive, and members will have less to lose (and perhaps something to gain) by challenging the White House.

The declining perception of external threat largely explains why the United States experienced a resurgence of congressional activism on foreign policy in the 1970s and 1980s after a nearly two-decade-long slumber. The tragic course of the Vietnam War convinced many Americans (and many members of Congress) that communist revolutions in the third world posed no direct threat to core U.S. security interests, just as detente persuaded many people that Brezhnev's Soviet Union posed less of a threat than did Stalin's and Khrushchev's. Both developments encouraged the resurgence of congressional activism and complicated the foreign-policy efforts of presidents from Nixon to Reagan.

The collapse of the Soviet Union and the end of the Cold War further accelerated this same basic trend. Although the United States still faces threats to its national security, none has captured public or congressional attention as did the Soviet threat. With no threat of similar magnitude looming on the horizon, legislators are more likely to disagree with the White House over what constitutes America's vital interests, and voters are less likely to punish them for criticizing the administration. The result is much greater congressional activism and with it greater constraints on the president.

None of this is to say that the United States is poised to return to the second half of the nineteenth century, a time when Congress so dominated foreign policy that it has been called the era of "congressional government," "congressional supremacy," and "government-by-Congress." By no measure has the end of the Cold War made the president irrelevant, a twenty-first century Gulliver ensnared in the land of the Lilliputians. In addition to their constitutional powers, presidents continue to benefit from more than four decades of Cold War legislation that delegated sweeping authorities to act in foreign affairs to the White House. Congressional efforts to reclaim these delegated powers are likely to founder, if only because of the prospect of a presidential veto. And even if efforts to rein in the president's statutory authority should succeed, presidents will continue to enjoy the advantages of "decision, activity, secrecy, and dispatch" that Alexander Hamilton long ago hailed as the great virtues of the presidency.[13]

Facing the Future

What a sustained increase in congressional activism does mean is that future presidents, be they Democrat or Republican, will face tougher challenges from Capitol Hill to their foreign-policy proposals. What should we make of this prospect? Although it is fashionable to deride congressional activism, it has merits that critics frequently overlook. For the same reason that an approaching test encourages students to study, the possibility of congressional activism on an issue encourages administration officials to discharge their duties. Legislators also bring different views to bear on policy debates, views that can provide a useful political scrub for administration proposals. (The Bay of Pigs, Vietnam, and the Iran–contra affair should dispel the notion that the executive possesses a monopoly on wisdom in foreign affairs.) When Capitol Hill is more hawkish than the White House, congressional activism strengthens the president's hand overseas. And congressional debate helps to legitimate foreign policy with the public. This latter virtue should not be underestimated; the success of the United States abroad ultimately depends on the willingness of Americans to accept the sacrifices asked of them.

Yet, if congressional activism is not inherently harmful, neither is it always desirable or beneficial. At a minimum, it makes an already cumbersome decisionmaking process even more so. More people need to be consulted and more potential veto points need to be overcome. Such inefficiency is not inherently dangerous—speed in foreign policy can be an evil as well as a blessing, as the Gulf of Tonkin Resolution attests—but it can aggravate officials in the executive branch and strain relations with America's allies. At its worst, congressional activism may render U.S. foreign policy incoherent as legislators push issues they do not fully understand, pander to their constituents' passions rather than their interests, or seek a role in managing foreign policy that exceeds the institution's capacity.

The foregoing suggests that U.S. foreign policy is best served when a modest level of tension and conflict pervades executive–legislative relations. Put somewhat differently, the U.S. foreign-policy process is best thought of in terms of a *system* in which the differing strengths of the individual branches of government can complement each other and improve the overall quality of decision making. Conversely, when either branch comes to dominate the process its weaknesses also come to the forefront. Thus, the crucial question in the years to come is not whether the president or Congress is better equipped to face the foreign-policy challenges of the twenty-first century but rather how to keep executive–legislative tensions within manageable and productive bounds.

One way would be to fashion a new consensus to replace containment as the cornerstone of U.S. foreign policy. Conflict between Congress and the president might well remain limited if a common understanding of America's role in the world can be re-created. President Clinton tried to chart just such a course during his first term with his efforts to forge a consensus around the doctrine of democratic enlargement. The new doctrine received at best a tepid response, however, as Clinton discovered what social psychologists have long known: Hope is far less effective than fear in promoting group solidarity. However much the United States might benefit from enlarging the community of democratic nations, the prospect of such gains does not provide the same sort of consensual glue as the Soviet threat did during the Cold War. As a result, by the beginning of his second term, President Clinton and his advisers had dropped most references to the idea of democratic enlargement.

If no new foreign-policy consensus appears to be in the offing, strong, proactive presidential leadership on individual policies can help mitigate executive–legislative conflict. Throughout the Cold War, the consensus around containing the Soviet threat often (though not always) relieved presidents of the need to educate Congress and the public about the specifics of their foreign-policy choices. Many times, nothing more was required of the president than to designate a program as "vital" to U.S. security. The result was a certain degree of complacency; unlike domestic policy, where presidential leadership skills were constantly tested, presidents to a great extent became accustomed to commanding on foreign policy.

Such will not be the case in the post–Cold War era. Without the presence of a foreign-policy consensus to provide a safety net, presidents will need to continually define, explain, and persuade both Congress and the public how their policies serve American interests. Presidents who fail to do so will place themselves at the mercy of events. This was a particular problem for President Clinton during his first term. On Somalia, Bosnia, and a host of other foreign-policy issues the administration failed to build support in Congress and the public for its policies *before* trouble arose. As a result, when events moved against the administration, as happened with the deaths of the 18 Army Rangers in Somalia, Congress and the public quickly turned on the White House.

The Clinton administration repeated this same mistake in 1997 when it failed to persuade Congress to give it "fast-track" negotiating authority for international trade agreements. (With fast-track authority, Congress agrees to approve or reject any trade agreement the president negotiates without amendment. This simplifies trade negotiations because other countries no longer have to worry that Congress will rewrite parts of any agreement.) Despite clear warnings that fast-track was in trouble on Capitol Hill, the administration got off to a late start in building support for the legislation. As the deadline for a vote approached, the administration discovered that it lacked the votes it needed to prevail in the House. To help persuade reluctant representatives, President Clinton escalated the stakes by arguing that fast-track legislation was needed because "more than ever, our economic security is also the foundation of our national security."[14] The decision to recast a trade matter as a national security issue—a tried and true strategy of the Cold War era—changed few minds, however. Clinton ultimately recognized that he faced defeat and asked congressional leaders to withdraw the bill from consideration, marking the first time in decades that any president had failed to persuade Congress to support a major trade initiative. A senior White House official summarized in a nutshell why the administration had failed on fast-track: "We figured we always pull these things out in the end and we'd pull this one out too."[15] But the past is not always prologue.

In addition to using their leadership skills to educate and build coalitions among legislators and the broader public, presidents concerned about managing relations with Capitol Hill will need to engage in genuine bipartisan consultations with Congress. For better or worse, the days when presidents could get by with notifying rather than consulting Congress are fading. As a result, it is in the president's interest to consult with members of Congress early on in the policy process before issues become controversial. Of course, Congress can help the consultative process along by designating whom among its members should be consulted. But responsibility for making executive–legislative consultations work ultimately lies with the White House, since consultations can succeed only when presidents are willing to solicit advice.

To its credit, the Clinton administration showed by the beginning of its second term that it had recognized the importance of consulting with Congress. The at times combative language that administration officials had used in 1995 and 1996 to describe congressional proposals gave way to more accommodating rhetoric (at least in public). In early 1997, President Clinton hosted a foreign-policy retreat with congressional leaders, and his national security adviser, Samuel Berger, spoke frequently with Speaker of the House Newt Gingrich and Senate Majority Leader Trent Lott. Newly appointed Secretary of State Madeleine Albright also launched a concerted effort to build bridges to Republican leaders, especially Senator Jesse Helms (R-N.C.), the chair of the Senate Foreign Relations Committee. In addition to these consultations by senior officials, there were also extensive consultations (some mandated by law) at the staff level. For example, administration and congressional staffers met for more than three months in the spring of 1997 to develop a plan to repay U.S. debts to the United Nations and other international organizations.

Of course, bipartisan consultations are not a panacea. They cannot prevent congressional debate on issues that genuinely divide members of Congress. The fate of the Clinton administration's initial proposal to help Mexico respond to a major financial crisis in 1995 is illustrative. The administration won endorsements for its plan from a litany of prominent Republicans, including Bob Dole, Newt Gingrich, Gerald Ford, George Bush, and Henry Kissinger. Yet rank-and-file Republicans rebelled against the proposal, forcing the administration to drop it in favor of a more modest package that did not require congressional approval. This rank-and-file rebellion was all the more remarkable because throughout 1995 House Republicans had displayed a nearly unprecedented degree of party cohesion. Thus, as this incident illustrates, presidents must be prepared for the inevitable frustration that will arise when talks with congressional leaders fail to quiet criticism on Capitol Hill. (Congress's hostile response to the proposed Mexican aid package, like its refusal to grant fast-track authority in 1997, also suggests that an end to divided government will not remove all differences between Capitol Hill and the White House. Indeed, on some issues it may intensify them.)

Whether Congress and the White House will learn to keep their tensions within tolerable bounds remains an open question. At a minimum, post–Cold War presidents will find their leadership skills in foreign policy sorely tested for years to come. Whereas Cold War presidents could often force Congress into line on major issues by arguing that their programs were needed to fight communism, post–Cold War presidents will have no such club. Rather, much as is the case in domestic affairs, they will labor to construct winning coalitions out of the many, and often discordant, voices on Capitol Hill. And at times those voices will be unwilling to follow.

Notes

1. Quoted in Steven Greenhouse, "Christopher Urging Clinton to Veto a Bill to Cut Foreign Aid," *New York Times,* 23 May 1995.

2. Quoted in " 'This Legislation Is the Wrong Way,' " *Congressional Quarterly Weekly Report,* 27 May 1995, p. 1514.

3. Anthony Lewis, "Capitol Power Grab," *New York Times,* 26 May 1995.

4. Ibid.

5. Richard E. Neustadt, *Presidential Power and the Modern Presidents: The Politics of Leadership from Roosevelt to Reagan* (New York: Free Press, 1990), 29.

6. Quoted in " 'This Legislation Is the Wrong Way,' " 1514.

7. Quoted in Thomas W. Lippman and Dan Morgan, "Christopher Attacks GOP Foreign Aid Cuts," *Washington Post,* 13 September 1995.

8. Quoted in Pat Towell, "House Votes to Sharply Rein In U.S. Peacekeeping Expenses," *Congressional Quarterly Weekly Report,* 18 February 1995, p. 535.

9. Quoted in Lee Michael Katz, "New Leader Says U.N. Not Working the Way It Should," *USA Today,* 17 July 1997.

10. Bob Dole, "Shaping America's Global Future," *Foreign Policy* 98 (Spring 1995): 36.

11. Jeremy D. Rosner, *The New Tug of War: Congress, the Executive Branch, and National Security* (Washington, D.C.: Carnegie Endowment for International Peace, 1995).

12. Alexis de Tocqueville, *Democracy in America* (New York: Anchor Books, 1969), p. 126.

13. Alexander Hamilton, "Federalist No. 70," in Alexander Hamilton, James Madison, and John Jay, *The Federalist Papers,* ed. Garry Wills (New York: Bantam Books, 1982), p. 356.

14. Quoted in John M. Broder, "House Postpones Trade-Issue Vote," *New York Times,* 8 November 1997.

15. Quoted in John M. Broder, "Party, Spurned, Repays Clinton with Rebellion," *New York Times,* 11 November 1997.

13

Globalization and Diplomacy: The View from Foggy Bottom

Strobe Talbott

It was the early morning of Monday, October 4, 1993, and there was a new kind of trouble brewing in Moscow. Tanks had surrounded the White House, the giant parliament building on the banks of the Moscow River, where deputies of the Supreme Soviet, some of them heavily armed, were holed up in defiance of President Boris Yeltsin's order to dissolve the legislature and submit to new elections. Just hours earlier, at the urging of the insurgents inside the White House, armed mobs had attacked the Moscow mayor's office and the city's main television station.

I had spent the night camped on the couch in my office on the seventh floor of the State Department. At 3:00 A.M., I went down the corridor to the department's Operations Center, our communications hub, where we had established a round-the-clock task force to monitor the crisis that was coming to a head. Using one of the phone banks in the OpsCenter, I called Deputy Foreign Minister Georgi Mamedov, who was in his own office in the ministry's Stalin-gothic skyscraper on Smolensk Square, less than a mile from the besieged parliament. We had been in frequent touch since the showdown began 24 hours earlier.

Suddenly, in the midst of our conversation, we both fell silent. After a long moment, Mamedov asked: "Are you watching what I'm watching?" I was indeed. We both had our television sets tuned to CNN, which had begun a live broadcast of Russian commandos and armored personnel carriers moving into position to storm the White House. For the next half-hour, Mamedov and I watched transfixed, exchanging occasional impressions as the battle came to its dramatic and bloody denouement. Following a phased assault that gave those inside the White House several opportunities to surrender, government forces retook the building and arrested the leaders of the opposition.

The United States and Russia had come a long way from the era of Cold

War brinkmanship over Berlin and Cuba. Now, the point of crisis was an internal power struggle in Russia, a showdown between a democratically elected leader and a reactionary legislature. Moreover, rather than being waged in secret behind the Kremlin walls, the struggle was being broadcast live to a worldwide audience of tens of millions.

Here was the famous "CNN effect" at its most emblematic. Just as the network had made it possible for Mamedov and me to watch an event unfold in real time as we discussed its implications over an open phone line, so the communications revolution had contributed to the transformation of his country and of our world.

From Bretton Woods to Denver

By the 1980s, self-isolating dictatorships from Chile to the Soviet Union had yielded to democratic and free market ideals spread by radio, television, the fax machine, and e-mail. Since then, in addition to undermining the Berlin Wall and shredding the Iron Curtain, the powerful technological forces of the Information Age have helped to stitch together the economic, political, and cultural lives of nations, making borders more permeable to the movement of people, products, and ideas. When President Bill Clinton visited Bucharest in July [1997], his host, Emil Constantinescu, a democratic activist and reformer who had been elected president of Romania seven months before, took him into his study and proudly showed him the desktop computer that gave him access to cyberspace.

For many millions of people, globalization has meant greater freedom and prosperity. But for millions of others, the same process has brought economic disadvantage and social disruption. Striking workers in South Korea and Argentina have opposed changes that their national leaders insisted were necessary to meet the demands of the global economy. The unexpected victory of the Socialist Party in [the 1997] French legislative elections stemmed in part from voters' apprehensions about globalization. In the United States, political figures such as Ross Perot and Pat Buchanan have tapped into similar anxieties.

Not all those who are within reach of television consider themselves better off as a result—in fact, often quite the contrary. There are satellite dishes in the slums of the world's megacities, and the signals they suck in from Hollywood and Madison Avenue can trigger resentment and anger: The communications revolution has the potential to foment revolutions of a different sort.

Globalization itself is neither inherently good nor bad. Governments cannot block its effects on their citizens without also cutting them off from its opportunities and benefits. But they can shape it to their national and international advantage.

While this task is an increasingly important and explicit theme in U.S. diplomacy in the post–Cold War era, it is not new. In the economic realm, it goes back at least to the immediate aftermath of World War II and the creation of the World Bank and the International Monetary Fund at Bretton Woods. Three decades later, in 1975, the leaders of France, Italy, Japan, the United Kingdom, the United States, and West Germany took another step forward together. They met in the picturesque French farming town of Rambouillet to discuss how they could increase trade, coordinate monetary policies, and reduce their vulnerability to rising oil prices. This was the first of what became, with the addition of Canada the following year in London, the annual summit of the Group of Seven major industrialized democracies.

When the successors of those leaders met for the 22nd time in Denver [in 1997], they were joined by Boris Yeltsin—the first time that the president of the Russian Federation participated in the summit from beginning to end. Just as the cast of characters at Denver had grown since Rambouillet, so had the agenda. Transnational threats such as climate change, the spread of infectious disease, and international organized crime received almost as much attention as the economic aspects of interdependence. Patterns of energy consumption, child vaccination rates, and drug treatment programs—once thought to be almost exclusively domestic issues—had become topics of international concern and targets of concerted action.

While other nations have long paid close attention to the U.S. government's monetary and fiscal policies, there are now growing international implications to U.S. domestic actions in countless other areas. The European Union initially objected to the proposed merger between the Boeing and McDonnell Douglas corporations, arguing that it would undermine competition in the global aircraft market. Senior Mexican officials have said publicly that the new U.S. immigration law that went into effect [in 1997] violates the rights of Mexicans living in the United States. Regulatory agencies around the world often take their cue from the U.S. Food and Drug Administration in approving or banning foodstuffs and medications, with consequences for thousands of companies and millions of consumers.

By the same token, the internal policies of other nations have a growing impact on the United States. The extent to which Mexico enforces the environmental provisions of the North American Free Trade Agreement (NAFTA) will affect the quality of air and water in Arizona, California, New Mexico, and Texas. The extent to which China is prepared to protect intellectual property rights will provide, or cost, jobs for American workers. Columbia's ability and willingness to crack down on narcotics production will affect the balance of forces in the war against illegal drugs in the United States. And conversely, only if the United States can reduce its domestic demand will Colombia and other nations on the supply side of the international narcotics trade succeed in their part of the struggle.

The Imperative for Change

Global interdependence is affecting the way virtually all governments think about international relations and practice diplomacy. The more engaged in and affected by the process, the more they must change. For the United States, therefore, the imperative for change is especially powerful, and it is felt most acutely in the [Department of State].

The Department of State is a proud institution, and it comes by its pride honestly. But the susceptibility of an institution to reform is inversely proportional to its venerability, and the State Department is no exception. [The department is] located in a neighborhood of Washington called Foggy Bottom, a designation that has become a sometimes affectionate, sometimes sardonic nickname for the department itself, with unflattering implications for the mindset of the 13,000 people who work there and in our 249 posts abroad.

Even as the State Department strives to overcome the inertia that is built into a large organization with a long history, it must also do more—and better—with less financial support from the nation it serves. Since 1985, in real dollar terms, the international affairs budget of the United States has plummeted by 50 percent. It has also declined in relative terms. In 1984, foreign affairs spending amounted to 2.5 percent of the federal budget; today [1997] it constitutes roughly 1 percent. [Since 1993], we have had to close 32 embassies and consulates around the world. Although the budget agreement between the White House and Congress for 1998 partially [restored] these damaging cuts, we will be operating under severe limitations for the foreseeable future. Only by leveraging our resources and being smarter in the way we marshal them can the State Department meet the challenges posed to American diplomacy by globalization and interdependence.

Going Global

The bilateral, government-to-government approach that has traditionally been the staple of American diplomacy is often insufficient to address threats like terrorism, narcotics trafficking, and environmental degradation, which are almost always regional—and very often global—in scope. These new challenges will yield only to an internationally coordinated, long-term effort.

In response to these changing realities, at the beginning of his administration, President Clinton created the position of undersecretary of state for global affairs, which was given responsibility for several of the State Department's bureaus dealing with cross-cutting "functional" areas: the protection of the environment, the promotion of democracy and human rights, the management of population and migration issues, and law enforcement. The effect has been to elevate the attention those goals receive in the policymaking process and in diplomacy.

At the beginning of the second term, Vice President Al Gore announced a broader plan for reform and consolidation of the nation's foreign affairs agencies that is also in part a response to globalization. By integrating the Arms Control and Disarmament Agency and the U.S. Information Agency into the Department of State, and by laying the ground for the partial consolidation of State and the U.S. Agency for International Development (USAID), we will be better able to weave the core missions of these agencies into the fabric of U.S. foreign policy.

The multitude, magnitude, and complexity of transnational issues and the collaborative arrangements through which we are working to address them also require that we rethink the way we recruit and train the department's human resources. We are stepping up our efforts to hire people who already have experience in areas such as international finance, labor, environmental science, and law enforcement. We are broadening what might be called the core curriculum in the training of entry-level officers. The Foreign Service Institute, the department's center for instruction in languages, area studies, and technical skills, has introduced a survey course that covers issues like narcotics trafficking and refugee flows, as well as classes on subjects such as the expanding global market for U.S. environmental technologies.

Meanwhile, our diplomats abroad, while still giving priority to U.S. relations with individual host governments, are nurturing regional and transregional relationships to a greater extent than ever. Our embassies in Lima and Quito have worked with the governments of Argentina, Brazil, and Chile to resolve the border conflict between Ecuador and Peru. Our embassy in Pretoria has devoted much of its energy to working with the South African government on peace in Angola and Congo. And whatever our other differences with Beijing, we are engaged with the Chinese, together with the Japanese and South Koreans, in an ongoing effort to reduce tensions on the Korean peninsula.

New Policies, New Partners

Globalization has also increased the need for other departments and agencies of the U.S. government to play an active role in pursuit of American interests abroad—and for the State Department to cooperate more systematically with them. That cooperation has been particularly close on matters of economics, defense, and law enforcement.

- **Economics.** As trade and international investment have become more important to the U.S. economy, the department and the U.S. government's economic agencies have expanded and deepened their collaboration. The agreements reached [since 1995] at the World Trade Organization to eliminate tariffs and increase worldwide trade in information technology and telecommunications represent one such collaborative effort. Working with the Department of Commerce, the Office of the U.S. Trade Representative, and the Federal Communications Commission, State Department officials at home and abroad have played a crucial role, meeting with local representatives of U.S. companies to refine our negotiating strategy and pressing foreign officials in more than 60 countries to accept U.S. positions.

While American diplomats are helping to write the rules and build the institutions that govern the global economy, they are also aggressively advocating the interests of U.S. businesses around the world. The department works with the Export-Import Bank and other federal agencies to ensure that American firms compete on a level playing field. In 1995 our embassies and the Department of Commerce helped NYNEX [now Bell Atlantic] win a $1.5 billion undersea fiber-optic cable project that will link countries in Africa, Asia, and Europe and is expected to support nearly $650 million in U.S. exports and several thousand American jobs.

- **Defense.** There is nothing new about vans shuttling back and forth across the Potomac between Foggy Bottom and the Pentagon. Still, the end of the Cold War has brought a new dimension to the cooperation between the State and Defense Departments. We are working far more closely together to promote the institutions and habits of democracy around the world. Through peacekeeping operations in areas that are critical to U.S. interests and through new security arrangements like the Partnership for Peace, we are encouraging the subordination of military forces to civilian command, respect for international borders, protection of minority rights, and free movement of people.

  When the United States sent troops as part of an international coalition to restore democracy to Haiti in 1994, the U.S. government created an innovative, unified political-military operations plan. Its purpose was to ensure that the civilian and military aspects of the operation were implemented in concert and with equal precision. As a result, when the peacekeepers disarmed members of the Haitian military, USAID had programs in place to help the demobilized soldiers develop the skills they would need to reintegrate into civilian society.

- **Law enforcement.** The burgeoning threats of international organized crime and narcotics trafficking require our diplomats to join forces as never before with U.S. law enforcement authorities. Political officers have worked with Justice Department personnel stationed in key regional embassies like Moscow and Bangkok to negotiate bilateral extradition treaties, as well as agreements that help governments share information on criminal investigations. And consular officers stationed at every American diplomatic post have cooperated in person and via computer with agents from the Drug Enforcement Administration (DEA), the FBI, the

Immigration and Naturalization Service, and the intelligence community to track suspected drug smugglers, terrorists, and criminals and deny them entry into the United States.

In Budapest, we have opened an International Law Enforcement Academy to help the new democracies of the former Soviet bloc establish the rule of law that is essential to a healthy democracy. The academy, which is funded and managed by the State Department, brings together experts from the FBI, the DEA, Customs, the Secret Service, the Internal Revenue Service, the Bureau of Alcohol, Tobacco, and Firearms, and the Department of Energy to share the latest anticrime techniques and technology with their counterparts from Central Europe, the New Independent States of the former Soviet Union, and Western Europe. Later [in 1997], we will establish a similar institution in Central America.

Taken together, these new forms of cooperation have significantly raised the number of U.S. government personnel stationed overseas who are not employed by the traditional foreign affairs agencies. In fact, 63 percent of those now under the authority of our ambassadors and other chiefs of mission are not State Department employees. As globalization moves forward, that number is likely to grow, as will the challenge of coordinating the American government's presence abroad.

Working "Multi-Multilaterally"

Paradoxically, while globalization induces international cohesion and empowers international enterprises, it also accentuates the limitations of national power. Governments are often too cumbersome to respond effectively to transnational threats—including when those threats are manifest within their own borders. Partly as a result, political authority is devolving from the top down and from the center outward, to local and regional governments, and to community organizations working at the grassroots.

Therefore, many governments, including the U.S., have sought to leverage scarce resources and improve their ability to address transnational threats by forming coalitions with "nonstate actors"—multinational corporations, nongovernmental organizations (NGOs), and international institutions like the United Nations, the World Bank, and the International Monetary Fund. These coalitions allow the United States to work not only multilaterally, but multi-multilaterally, through several organizations and institutions at the same time.

In Bosnia, nine agencies and departments of the U.S. government are cooperating with more than a dozen other governments, seven international organizations, and 13 major NGOs—from the Red Cross to the International Crisis Group to the American Bar Association—to implement the Dayton Peace Accords.

In the Middle East, the United States chairs the Multilateral Working Group on Water Resources, a group of 47 countries and international organizations that are working to ensure that the region's shared dependence on a scarce resource does not become a threat to political stability. The governments of Israel, Japan, Oman, South Korea, and the United States have established the Middle East Regional Desalination Center in Muscat to support research to reduce the cost of desalination.

An interagency Food Security Working Group co-chaired by the Department of State, Department of Agriculture, and USAID is looking at new ways to apply American knowledge, technology, resources, and influence to ensure that there will be adequate food to meet the demands of the next century. Under this group's auspices, the U.S. National Oceanic and Atmospheric Administration is leading an international initiative that brings together governments, private companies, and NGOs to begin experimental forecasting of seasonal climate patterns, so that crop planting can be adjusted to anticipated annual rainfall, thereby helping to reduce the severity of food emergencies.

The organizational chart for these kinds of collaborative efforts is a patchwork of boxes connected by overlapping and intersecting solid and dotted lines. It often falls to the State Department to coordinate the work of the other agencies of the U.S. government to make sure that their endeavors serve an overarching and coherent strategy. The department also works to integrate the American governmental effort into what other governments—and, increasingly, NGOs and others—are doing in the same areas.

The End of Foreign Policy

In the context of the many global problems facing the United States today, and also in the context of their solutions, the very word "foreign" is becoming obsolete. From the floor of the stock exchange in Singapore to the roof of the world over Patagonia where there is a hole in the ozone layer, what happens there matters here—and vice versa. That is not only a fact of life and a useful shorthand definition of globalization itself, it is also a key selling point for those of us, inside the government and out, who are trying to make foreign policy less foreign, and more relevant, to the American people.

In the absence of a compelling, unifying threat like the one posed by the Soviet Union during the Cold War, the need for American engagement in the world seems less obvious. Largely as a result, the interest of the American public and media in world affairs has waned markedly in the last decade.

In an effort to reverse this trend, the department has, over the past three years, sponsored 40 "town meetings" at which our diplomats have discussed topics from the Middle East peace process to advancing human rights. In her first 20 weeks in office, Secretary of State Madeleine Albright traveled outside

Washington 15 times to talk about foreign policy with the American people in schools, at presidential libraries, and from the deck of an aircraft carrier. She—like President Constantinescu of Romania—has also made use of the World Wide Web, where the secretary's and the department's home pages average 1.7 million hits a month.

All this "outreach," as we call our public-education programs, is far more than special pleading for the State Department or its budget. It is a matter of making the case on the home front for American engagement and activism abroad.

. . . The United States [now] faces a number of critical decisions, each of which will be, in a larger sense, a decision about how our country will respond to the opportunities and challenges of globalization. We must persuade Congress

- that expanding the NATO alliance to include several of the new democracies of Central and Eastern Europe will enhance the stability of a region in which more than 500,000 Americans lost their lives in this century
- that extending NAFTA to other nations in Latin America will create jobs in the United States and spur economic growth
- that accepting binding limits on greenhouse gas emissions . . . is essential for the long-term ability of the planet to sustain its environment.

Opponents of these and other initiatives often argue that they compromise or dilute our national sovereignty. In fact, the opposite is true. Well-crafted international commitments and a comprehensive strategy of international engagement enhance rather than dilute our mastery of our own fate as a nation, which is the most pertinent definition of sovereignty. NATO, NAFTA, the Chemical Weapons Convention, the Partnership for Peace, and our participation in the United Nations—different as they are in composition and function—all have one thing in common: They help the United States to channel the forces of interdependence, bending them to the advantage of our own citizens and of other nations that share our interests and values.

When we agree to abide by common rules of the road, we gain the commitment of others to live by mutually acceptable standards in areas like labor law, intellectual property rights, environmental protection, aviation safety, and public health. In so doing, we also establish the means to measure compliance meaningfully, fairly, and enforceably.

Other nations are willing to adhere to these standards not just because they seek access to the U.S. market, or because they want to be on good terms with a major world power. They do so because they recognize that a system of equity and openness based on those standards is key to their own ability to benefit from the phenomenon of globalization. And that means working together to guide the evolution of the phenomenon itself in the direction of equitable economic development, manageable levels of population growth, sustainable use of our natural resources, and the spread and consolidation of democracy.

[Several] years after the end of the Cold War, it can be said that, in a sense, we still live in a bipolar world. But the dividing line today is not an iron curtain between East and West. Rather, it is between the forces of stability and instability, integration and disintegration, prosperity and poverty. The United States has a central role to play in that new struggle, just as it did in the old one. And once again, success will require full use of America's diplomatic resources around the world—and in Foggy Bottom.

14

Civil-Military Relations: Causes of Concern

Eliot A. Cohen

[In July 1996 the Foreign Policy Research Institute, located in Philadelphia, held a conference designed to address the state of readiness of American defense forces in the post–Cold War era. Chaired by John F. Lehman, former secretary of the Navy, and directed by Harvey Sicherman, president of the Foreign Policy Research Institute, the conference addressed three broadly defined areas of concern: "demilitarizing the military," "involuntary disarmament," and the reduced civilian control of the military. Eliot A. Cohen, a leading defense intellectual, led the discussion of civil-military relations. This chapter reports his observations —eds.]

There is no crisis in American civil-military relations if crisis means the kind of collision between civil and military authority that would breed a coup d'état or other manifestation of a breakdown of civilian control of the military, such as systematic and open disobedience of orders. But, to a remarkable degree, members of the Defense Task Force agreed that deep and pervasive difficulties plague American civil-military relations, that these problems merit attention and exploration, and that dramatic and possibly painful actions are required to resurrect the relationship between the armed forces and civil society that the Founders envisioned and that makes sense for a twenty-first-century democracy. The three core problems discussed at length were the politicization of the military, the growing divide between civil society and those who wear the uniform, and the centralization of military power in the Joint Staff and in the chairman of the Joint Chiefs of Staff (JCS).

Note: Notes have been deleted.

A Politicized Military

As one participant put it, when hearing military officers speak about President Bill Clinton, he felt tempted to turn Voltaire's apocryphal defense of free speech on its head: "I agree with everything that you say and am appalled by the fact that you say it." The first two years of the Clinton administration were marked by an extraordinary display of open disdain and hostility by the military for the new president. The ill-advised nature of his manpower policies (particularly his effort to lift the ban on homosexuals serving in uniform), the general disregard for things military that characterized junior staffers in the White House, a proclivity to see the military as a tool of domestic and international social work rather than strategic action, and the president's own evasion of the Vietnam-era draft explained this behavior on the part of officers but in no way made it acceptable. On many occasions senior military officers not only tolerated their subordinates' making contemptuous remarks about the commander in chief—itself an offense subject to court-martial under the Uniform Code of Military Justice—but amplified and reinforced such comments. Military officers also were increasingly willing to announce their political affiliation (almost invariably with the Republican Party) or to display their political beliefs in such ways as driving cars with anti-Clinton bumper stickers onto military bases, in defiance of tradition and the norms of military service.

Yet most conference participants argued that the politicization of the military reflects something more profound than the reaction of the officer corps to a particular politician. As one put it, "There has been a long-term, secular trend towards politicization of the U.S. officer corps." To some extent that mirrors similar trends within other professional groups in American society. The current conception of the military officer still reflects an image drawn from the austere portrait of the "professional" put forward in the 1950s. Professionals, according to the social science literature of the time, were defined by three characteristics: corporateness (that is, a sense of collective identity), responsibility (to society at large and not simply to a particular client or customer), and education (both throughout their careers and at a high intellectual level). Society viewed the professional as someone whose technical expertise and detachment from politics made him both unique and difficult to manage, and much ink was spent on the subject of how professionals defined their relationships with those around them.

Over time, this purist model of the professional has changed and eroded. As doctors and lawyers have become politicized and demythologized, so too have military officers shed the image of pure and apolitical expertise once ascribed to them. Like other interest groups, albeit a particularly important one, they lost a sense of uniqueness and learned how to play the game. Indeed, it is not uncommon for officers to describe themselves as a governmental interest group and to justify (if somewhat abashedly) their collective actions in such terms.

Politicization sprang from other sources as well. In the last thirty years, the American military has become remarkably sophisticated regarding politics, in part through a professional military education that stresses the importance of the political dimension of warfare. A revival of the study *On War,* Carl von Clausewitz's classic text examining the relationship between war and politics, followed on the heels of the Vietnam War as officers struggled to understand why they lost a war in which they seemingly held the trump cards of fire-power, mobility, and resources. In his introduction to *On Strategy,* one of the earliest critiques of the military's efforts in Vietnam and a major contribution to the Clausewitz revival, Colonel Harry Summers recalled his conversation with a North Vietnamese officer during the final armistice negotiations. When Summers remarked to his counterpart that the Vietnamese never beat the Americans in a single battle, the North Vietnamese colonel paused for a moment and said: "That's true. It's also irrelevant." More than one officer came away from that war convinced of the necessity of entering the next with a far more sophisticated appreciation of policy than that brought to bear in Vietnam. At the same time, the rejection of the military by some segments of American society after the war dismayed members of the officer corps, who consequently came to believe that domestic politics also required their attention.

Yet Vietnam merely accelerated trends that originated during World War II and the early Cold War, when officers found themselves engaged in the murky areas where politics and war overlapped. Programs ranging from courses in American and international politics at the war colleges to internships in government exposed officers to politics in various forms. Today military officers serve on congressional staffs and are present throughout the federal government, even in such seemingly non-defense-oriented bureaucracies as the Office of Management and Budget (OMB). Indeed, General Colin Powell, perhaps the shrewdest political general since Eisenhower, describes his year as a White House Fellow serving in OMB as his introduction to the bureaucratic politics that he would play so well during his time in Washington.

Seared by its experience in Vietnam, the officer corps reacted by seeking to manipulate political leaders and processes so that any commitment to conflict would be made under circumstances that it approved. An early case in point was General Creighton Abrams's successful creation of the Total Force in the 1970s—in particular, an army dependent on reserve mobilization to conduct any sizable war. With the tacit acquiescence of the civilian leadership, the military in effect created a system that could not go to war without some kind of national mobilization, even though the army's leadership traditionally mistrusted the reserve components.

To some extent, political awareness is desirable in an officer corps. But when military officers lose their self-restraint about both political identification and actual participation in politics—including behind-the-scenes manipulation of any branch of government—a boundary has been crossed. The military is a unique calling that bears special responsibilities for the security of the nation and poses particular threats when deformed by open partisanship. When officers do not hesitate to refer to themselves as another interest group, when they willingly identify themselves by party affiliation and feel free to comment in public, and in front of their subordinates, about the faults of their civilian superiors, corrective action is needed.

The Gap between Society and the Military

Since 1940, military service has shaped the early careers of millions of American young men, particularly those who have gone on to become business and political leaders. The end of the draft in the early 1970s created a noticeable gap between civilian and military elites. That gap widened with the dramatic shrinkage of the military in the wake of the Cold War, a shrinkage likely to continue. At first glance, this development might not seem terribly important. After all, throughout most of U.S. history the military was small and in many cases unrepresentative of American society. The great difference today is that the United States is, and will remain, a superpower for whom military might is central to national policy. That was not the case in times of peace before World War II.

The gap between the military and society is exacerbated by the military's increasing tendency to recruit from narrower segments of the population. Some 25 percent of new entrants into the military now come from military families. Of greater concern, in the view of some, is the increased role of the military academies as providers of officer candidates. Whereas during the Cold War West Point, Annapolis, and the Air Force Academy produced only 10 percent of new officers, today they produce roughly one-quarter. In the view of many, the services would be happy not only to restrict as much officer intake as possible to the service academies but to force new officers to serve for extended periods of time. The demands of efficiency, in particular the desire to reduce training expenses and turnover, lead the military to press for long-term service contracts.

Increasingly, some military leaders also see a growing gap between military and societal values. The U.S. Marine Corps, perhaps the least civilianized of all the armed services, has changed its basic training programs to instill values in recruits that it believes American society has failed to provide. Military leaders routinely remark . . . that the military has coped with problems that still bedevil the rest of American society: drug and alcohol abuse, and even in large measure race relations. As sociologist Charles Moskos has put it, the army is the only institution in which black men routinely give white men orders and no one thinks twice about it. The army's success on issues involving the sexes is less clear. The military has struggled, with varying success, to open to women careers that traditionally embodied masculine qualities. Still, that the military has come to see itself as an organization with better values and more functional social behavior than civil society marks yet another departure from the past, when the armed forces saw themselves more as a reflection of society and less as its superior.

Different issues are inherent on the civilian side of the relationship. Fewer politicians, let alone their staff assistants, have any military experience; yet they will be required to make decisions about the employment and structuring of military forces. . . . The current ignorance gives rise to two equally problematic trends: a growing number of political elites who have little appreciation for the military's needs and are inclined to view it in terms of stereotypes of discipline and inflexibility, and, no less troubling, the emergence of a political class that unthinkingly defers to this alone of all public institutions, without subjecting it to critical but informed scrutiny.

The Rise of a Centralized Military Staff

Since the turn of the century, there has been steady movement toward the centralization of military authority in large staffs. The creation of a chief of staff of the army and a chief of naval operations was followed during World War II by the creation and later institutionalization of the Joint Chiefs of Staff. The Defense Department Reorganization Act of 1958 further strengthened the chairman of the JCS and the Joint Staff, and the Goldwater-Nichols legislation of 1986 took another large step in that direction. Today, the chairman of the JCS serves as a de facto commander of the American armed forces, operating under the supervision of either the president or the secretary of defense. The Joint Staff has taken over many of the prerogatives of the service staffs, both civilian and military, and has even strayed into the legitimate territory of the Office of the Secretary of Defense (OSD). These developments have generated several problems:

A reduction of sources of military advice for civilian authority. The president and secretary of defense need more than one senior military advisor. Any one advisor, being human, may have the prejudices and distorted perceptions that naturally can accumulate during a career. While Goldwater-Nichols does not prohibit civilians from seeking advice from the other chiefs, it tacitly discourages such a move. As a result, during the war in the Persian Gulf, the secretary of defense was forced to resort to unusual channels to elicit more options than he was receiving from the Joint Staff.

An attenuation of long-range thinking. The perspective of the Joint Staff and the regional and functional commanders in chief (CINCs) is short term; their understandable concern with immediate operational issues leads them to discount future problems and focus on current activity. In the past, the services provided a long-range perspective, but their weakened bureaucratic clout and exclusion from military planning activities have undercut their ability to make contributions in this area.

A weakening of competition. The United States has benefited greatly from the armed services' competition with one another for sources and missions. In all other walks of life, the United States has traditionally appreciated the merits of competition. Yet in the Pentagon the trend has been toward centralized control and allocation of resources. Particularly as technology allows the services to compete for roles and missions (in the area of deep strike, for example), it makes sense to enhance rather than diminish the competitiveness that has been so valuable in the past.

A diminution of civilian control. Goldwater-Nichols did little to enhance the quality or power of the staff in the Office of the Secretary of Defense, but its tremendously strengthened the roles and career tracks of Joint Staff officers. As a result, the weight of influence within the Pentagon has shifted decidedly in favor of the Joint Staff, which has an increasingly strong hand in bargaining with OSD and sometimes takes positions at variance with it.

To be sure, some of the results of the Goldwater-Nichols legislation have been favorable. "Jointness" is not merely a fad of the moment, but an undeniable trend in military operations brought about by changing technology. When shipboard systems (missiles as well as aircraft) can precisely strike the same targets as land-based ballistic missiles or aircraft, increased coordination of effort is clearly needed. As certain common systems—intelligence-gathering satellites, for example—gain importance, so too does the need for Department of Defense–wide management of them. Moreover, some of the parochialism and obstructionism of the services conceivably has diminished in the face of the growing power of the chairman of the JCS, the Joint Staff, and the theater CINCs. Nonetheless, like all orthodoxies, that of jointness requires critical examination and a dispassionate review of its impact on long-term strategic thinking and civilian control.

Solutions

The ills besetting civil-military relations in the United States are the deeply rooted product of historical developments dating back several decades or longer. Remedies will take time to have an effect. More important, they will require tough and imaginative civilian leadership, because they will be opposed by important (though by no means all) segments of military opinion and will be relatively unattractive politically. The military opinion will be bolstered by civilian allies, including military retirees (who can speak far more freely than those in uniform) and that large group of civilians who occasionally confuse unthinking support of military traditions and practice with patriotic support for the armed forces.

Reforming the military academies. It should be a basic principle of the American armed forces that the officer corps be as widely recruited as possible. Therefore, for both practical and symbolic reasons, the military academies should be modeled along the lines of Sandhurst. That is, officers would complete their undergraduate educations at any acceptable civilian college or university and then attend a military academy for nine months to a year of military training. This system would preserve the valuable traditions and character-building qualities of the academies, while dispensing with their cliquish and self-absorbed nature. The services would still be pressed to maintain active ROTC presences on campuses, including those that might produce small numbers of high-quality officers.

The service academies currently wrestle with two contradictory missions: the training of young officers and the provision of a liberal education. They cannot be expected to do both well, for the two purposes are somewhat at odds with each other. This proposed reform would allow officers to receive their normal, liberal education elsewhere, leaving the academies free to focus on military training.

Recruitment schemes for the citizen-soldier. Soldiers and civilians alike applaud the concept of the citizen-soldier, but the time has come to reconsider what that term means. It is neither accurate nor adequate to say that professional soldiers have the full rights of all other citizens, thereby making them citizen-soldiers. Rather, citizen-soldiers are best understood to be short-term or temporary service personnel whose primary careers are in the civilian rather than the military world. Ideally, such personnel would comprise a large part of the armed services. The services should therefore be required to develop and advertise programs similar to those operated with some success by the army, which attract young men and women for short (twenty-four month) stints of service in return for college tuition or other benefits. Similar plans would be designed to attract older men and women to the reserves, which would be revamped to take advantage of the many talents in the civilian sector.

Now more than ever, the National Guard and the reserves embody the concept of the citizen-soldier, whose centrality to the national defense was enshrined in the Constitution and remains important today. The guard and reserves have much to offer the armed services by bringing the maturity and expertise of civilians to bear on military problems, as seen in the notable success of the army reserve civil-affairs units. Moreover, the reserves have a tremendous range of programs, from the extremely successful reliance of the air force on reserve air crew and support personnel to operate the logistics fleet, to the far less successful incorporation of naval reservists into the fleet.

Many future units may focus on the realm of information technology, where expertise often commands salaries that the military cannot match. Overall, a general review of reserve policy seems called for, particularly as some reserve units (army civil-affairs units, for example) have begun to be extremely active, to the point of being overstretched, while others (combat divisions in the National Guard) seem to have little function at all.

Professional military education. The conference members also argued for increasing the military educational system's attention to problems in civil-military relations. Too few officers, even at senior levels, have reflected on, not only such well-known cases of civil-military friction as Douglas MacArthur's dismissal from command in Korea, but the legislative and philosophical underpinnings of the U.S. military establishment.

Moreover, as the nature of warfare itself changes, so too does the nature of military professionalism. In an age when the direction of firepower increasingly takes place from a distance, the very concept of officership must be reassessed. To a remarkable degree, current regulations, organizational forms, and rank structures reflect a bygone era, in which the roles and relationships of both commissioned and noncommissioned officers were very different from what they are today. A first-order reexamination of what officership means is thus in order. To this end, the curricula of the staff and war colleges need to be reviewed, including the material that deals with civilian control of the military. The clichéd notion that civilian control consists of giving the military unambiguous (and unchanging) goals, providing resources, and stepping aside—a notion particularly prevalent following the Persian Gulf War—needs to be replaced with a more discriminating, if less comfortable, view.

Military familiarization programs. Lastly, it is desirable to institute programs that would improve the quality of civilian leadership by educating civilians about military organizations and modern warfare. These programs would be intended for legislators, journalists, and other "opinion leaders" (to include civic leaders and people in business), to help them develop sound criteria for evaluating contemporary defense matters. Formats for such an enterprise could include the following:

- lectures on the organization and function of the Department of Defense
- visits to a variety of facilities, including training installations
- participation in simulations and exercises
- academic work (through case studies, seminars, and site visits) in the field of military history

Currently, the Department of Defense offers many groups visits to ships or military facilities, such as the National Training Center at Fort Irwin, California. But these opportunities, though valuable, are episodic (that is, undertaken without a coherent plan of instruction) and are not selectively targeted. A military installation's standard "pitch" for civilian outsiders is generally intended to highlight the sophistication and excellence of its people and machines, not to promote critical evaluation.

A serious program of military instruction would be quite different. It could be a part-time course during two years that would require roughly the same level of participation as reserve duty—say, a weekend a month plus a two-week stint of "active duty." These visitors to military installations would receive more than the standard dog and pony show, and they would be exposed to a variety of opposing views on a range of military matters (for example, the future of the aircraft carrier, or manned aircraft, or women in combat). Innovative use of educational technologies, such as CD-ROM-based instruction like that pioneered by the Air Command and Staff College at Maxwell Air Force Base, would enable participants to absorb quickly many of the basic details of military equipment, organization, and procedure on their own. Participation in such a program would be selective and begun on a small scale.

If Nothing Is Done

. . . It is worth speculating about the direction of American civil-military relations without the kinds of measures indicated above to correct current adverse trends. An ever more inbred military elite would evolve, recruited largely from families of military personnel and increasingly educated at the service academies. Confronted (as appears likely) by a steadily shrinking defense budget, this group would not retire into frosty isolation but would attempt to influence the political process directly. Military officers might, within the bounds of the law (but just barely), attempt to throw support to the political party most favorable to their interests.

At the same time, a political elite generally ignorant of military affairs would divide into three groups: The first, and largest, would simply be indifferent to defense matters and would be inclined to regard military expenditure as wasteful unless proven otherwise. Another group would view the military with suspicion, believing its notions to be both retrograde and at odds with those of society on a variety of issues, most notably homosexuality. And a third group would regard the military with unthinking admiration as the embodiment of virtues shunned by the rest of society.

Oddly enough, this last group could prove to be the most dangerous. Democratic society normally produces a certain amount of healthy suspicion of the military—a distaste for the hierarchy, subordination of self, and adherence to discipline that military life requires. Unrestrained deference to military authority and expertise, on the other hand, can lead to gross errors in both foreign and defense policy. The horrifying experience of World War I, when deference to military authority was at an all-time high, offers an important warning. The generals repeatedly resorted to strategies of appalling blood-shed, not merely out of arrogance, but because of the adulation from journal-ists and politicians, who made them into gods of war rather than what they were—fallible men, albeit well-educated, patriotic, and determined. By the end of that conflict, mutual confidence at the top and throughout society had broken down, politicians mistrusted their military subordinates, and more than one military leader was willing to endorse the theory of the "stab in the back."

Healthy civilian control of the military requires a political leadership that understands how uncertain of a business war is, and that recognizes that even the best-trained and most dedicated military professionals can err. Such politi-cians can exert effective civilian control because they appreciate military vir-tues, can discern which military officers are the best, and can weigh the relative importance of political and military requirements. On the other side of the equation, civil-military relations require officers who understand and accept the preeminence of political considerations in the conduct of war, and who can cope with civilian intrusion into their realm whether or not they like it. And at the very top, a dialogue must exist between statesmen and generals, unequal though that dialogue may be. Overall, healthy civil-military relations need a military with standards distinct from those of general society and a society that appreciates the need for the difference, even if it does not always approve of the military's views.

Left uncorrected, the trends in American civil-military relations could breed certain pathologies. The most serious possibility is that of a dramatic civil-military split during a crisis involving the use of force. In the recent past, such tensions did not result in open division; for example, Franklin Roosevelt insisted that the United States invade North Africa in 1942, though the chiefs of both the army and the navy vigorously opposed such a course, favoring instead a buildup in England and an invasion of the continent in 1943. Back then it was inconceivable that a senior military officer would leak word of such a split to the media, where it would have reverberated loudly and destruc-tively. To be sure, from time to time individual officers broke the vow of professional silence to protest a course of action, but in these isolated cases the officers paid the accepted price of termination of their careers.

In the modern environment, such cases might no longer be isolated. Thus, presidents might try to shape U.S. strategy so that it complies with military opinion, and rarely in the annals of statecraft has military opinion alone been an adequate guide to sound foreign policy choices. Had Lincoln followed the advice of his senior military advisors there is a good chance that the Union would have fallen. Had Roosevelt deferred to General George C. Marshall and Admiral Ernest J. King there might well have been a gory debacle on the shores of France in 1943. Had Harry S Truman heeded the advice of his the-ater commander in the Far East (and it should be remembered that the Joint

Chiefs generally counseled support of the man on the spot) there might have been a third world war.

Throughout much of its history, the U.S. military was remarkably politicized by contemporary standards. One commander of the army, Winfield Scott, even ran for president while in uniform, and others (Leonard Wood, for example) have made no secret of their political views and aspirations. But until 1940, and with the exception of periods of outright warfare, the military was a negligible force in American life, and America was not a central force in international politics. That has changed. Despite the near halving of the defense budget from its high in the 1980s, it remains a significant portion of the federal budget, and the military continues to employ millions of Americans. More important, civil-military relations in the United States now no longer affect merely the closet-room politics of Washington, but the relations of countries around the world. American choices about the use of force, the shrewdness of American strategy, the soundness of American tactics, and the will of American leaders have global consequences. What might have been petty squabbles in bygone years are now magnified into quarrels of a far larger scale, and conceivably with far more grievous consequences. To ignore the problem would neglect one of the cardinal purposes of the federal government: "to provide for the common defense" in a world in which security cannot be taken for granted.

15

Information Age Intelligence

Bruce D. Berkowitz

Most experts agree that U.S. intelligence needs reform. Indeed, at times it seems that everyone wants to have a hand in reforming the intelligence community. . . . [as several] studies have been conducted by official and unofficial organizations on how to improve U.S. intelligence. . . .

All these efforts are well intentioned and many of their recommendations may have merit. But they fall short. For the most part, they propose only incremental changes—moving one organization into another, tweaking the chain of command between organizations, and taking steps to improve efficiency or responsiveness. Marginal reform is not enough. Intelligence is information. No technology is improving as fast as information technology, and no part of our society is changing faster than the way we deal with information.

Most people are familiar with at least some indicators of the technical and economic side of the information revolution: the processing capacity of microchips doubles nearly every 18 months; information technology stocks were largely responsible for the remarkable rise in the stock market [in recent years]; each of the three major U.S. broadcast networks has been the target of a merger or acquisition; and the richest man in the United States is a . . . college dropout who made his fortune selling software.

Moreover, it is not just the technology that is changing. How people use and interact with information has also changed. "Channel surfing" is more than a cliché—it describes how people use information today. People now expect to receive information immediately, and in a form that they can easily use. They are reluctant to accept "wisdom" from authority figures. In an age of media conglomerates, 500-channel cable services, and the Internet, people usually have many sources of information from which to choose. They often prefer to evaluate data themselves. . . .

American society reflects these technological and social changes. So does the private sector economy. Does the U.S. intelligence community reflect these changes as well?

During most of this century, the intelligence community led the world in developing information technology. Intelligence organizations were deeply involved in the development of telegraph and telephone networks, modern computers, and space-based communications and surveillance systems. The intelligence community also established new forms of analysis and areas of expertise. For example, World War II intelligence organizations were the training grounds for many postwar experts in regional politics and macroeconomics.

Intelligence organizations also had a subtle influence over the way people used information. The Office of Strategic Services (OSS) made an art form of tailored reporting for high-level users; when President Harry Truman abolished the OSS, he spared its analytical shops because he liked the reports. Similarly, the process of drafting National Intelligence Estimates, originally developed in the early 1950s, represented one of the first methods for establishing the "best math" within an organization, predating professional facilitators, red-teaming, brainstorming, and other methods currently in corporate vogue. Even modern media archetypes and icons have their roots in intelligence: Consider the typical television news set, designed to resemble an intelligence command and control center.

Yet several signs suggest that the intelligence community is no longer the leader in the information world, and it may have fallen behind significantly in some respects. The underlying problem is that the intelligence community has failed to keep up with changes in how modern society uses information and how information technology develops in modern society. As a result, our model for intelligence is out-of-date. This reality is what current efforts at intelligence reform are failing to recognize.

The Current Approach to Reform

Besides various efforts to make sure that the intelligence community obeys the law and complies with oversight requirements, the Clinton administration . . . concentrated on two areas of intelligence reform: making the intelligence organization more efficient and responsive and defining roles, missions, and priorities within the intelligence community. . . .

Much of the administration's intelligence reform effort [was] devoted to saving money and improving customer service. . . . The . . . administration's other approach to intelligence reform [was] to rethink what the intelligence community should do and who within the community should do it. . . . Unfortunately, President Clinton's plans for intelligence [were] reminiscent of the worst aspects of Jimmy Carter's energy policy and Hillary Rodham Clinton's plans for health care. The president's plans [described] a world in which the demands are great, resources are limited, and the solution is a centralized bureaucracy with better planning to make the best of a bad situation. . . .

An Alternate Agenda for Reform

The Clinton administration's approach to reform—efficiency studies, stream-lining, better prioritization and planning—. . . implies that there is nothing wrong with a traditional, centralized intelligence system (administration officials pre-fer to say "integrated") that better management could not fix. As it stands, this program is likely to produce a more efficient, smoother-running intelligence community, perfectly optimized for the intelligence consumer of . . . 1950.

Consider [that] Congress needed more than a year to negotiate an agree-ment with the White House to establish the Commission on the Roles and Capabilities of the U.S. Intelligence Community. The commission required another year to complete its study. . . . Implementation of its recommendations . . . [had] to wait until after the 1996 elections. Add more time for hearings, legislation, contracting, building hardware, and hiring people, and it soon [be-came] clear that few results [would] appear [quickly].

Compare this with "reform" in the world of information services outside government. Recently, Microsoft was planning to compete with online ser-vices such as CompuServe, Prodigy, and America Online. Just as the company was about to introduce its own online service, it decided that the market had completely changed; the real opportunity was not in charging fees for exclu-sive online services, but in taking advantage of the Internet as a "content provider" and software developer. Microsoft decided that it was so far behind such competitors as Sun Microsystems and Netscape—six to 10 months!—that it needed to take drastic action.

So Microsoft scrapped its plans and developed a new strategy. To imple-ment it, the company retooled its planned online service, the Microsoft Net-work, to be an Internet-based operation providing information and services on the World Wide Web. It updated its Windows operating system and applica-tions such as Microsoft Office so that they would work efficiently through the Web and bought entire companies that had Internet experience, such as Ver-meer Technologies. Furthermore, demonstrating the industry's fast pace and flexibility, Microsoft even licensed its software browsers to CompuServe and America Online—its would-be competitors in online services. The entire process took about a year.

The intelligence community needs to move this fast, too, but the traditional organization is not up to the task. Today's model for intelligence—how it is organized and how it operates—is an artifact from an earlier age. Even the name "Central Intelligence Agency" is reminiscent of the New Deal era, when large, powerful, national bureaucracies were the accepted way of getting things done efficiently. When the CIA was established, the notion of a central-ized bureaucracy for producing information was at least as plausible as, say, a centralized bureaucracy for economic planning. In addition, centralization offered economies of scale at a time when information technology was expensive. (Remember "time sharing" and waiting for "off-peak rates" with the computer system in the basement?) A centralized organization was also the best way at the time to make sure critical information did not slip through the cracks. Appointing an "intelligence ombudsman" would be a great step forward—if one wanted an intelligence organization that worked like the Norwegian socialist bureaucracy of the mid-twentieth century. It makes less sense in a world moving toward fluid, distributed, networked information organizations.

Rather than rewriting organization charts or identifying national intelligence priorities that are apt to be passé within a few years, intelligence reform needs to describe what a twenty-first century intelligence service should look like. At a minimum, this vision should define the general principles that will determine which activities the intelligence community will undertake; create an organizational approach that will readily adapt as requirements for information change and as the ability of the outside world to meet these requirements improves; and provide a concept for producing intelligence based on how government officials and people in general really use information today.

Finding the Niche

Identifying intelligence missions and their priority is only part of the intelligence planning process and, in the Information Age, probably the less important part. The more important part is to identify the specific areas in which the intelligence community enjoys a comparative advantage over others.

Return to first principles and ask why the United States needs an intelligence community at all. That is, why do Americans need a government-funded, government-managed organization to collect and analyze information for national security? Most information U.S. officials use is, and always will be, from open sources—newspapers, journals, broadcast media, or, for that matter, the routine exchange of information that goes on during their everyday business. The reason for an intelligence apparatus is to find and interpret information related to national security that the government needs but cannot obtain from the media or other commercial sources. This information generally falls into the following categories:

- expertise that the private sector cannot maintain because it would be unprofitable;
- information that the private sector will not or cannot collect because it would be unprofitable or too technologically demanding;
- information that the private sector cannot or will not collect because of legal constraints or risks; and
- tailored products providing this specialized information (combined with other sources, as appropriate) to U.S. officials.

Many organizations are ready to provide information. The question for intelligence planners is "What types of information can be provided only by the intelligence community?" When the question is put this way, it soon becomes clear that one is aiming at a moving target. In the Information Age, the non-government, unclassified, commercial sector keeps getting better. Thus, the special niche of the intelligence community needs to be capable of changing continuously, too.

Consider one current example. As recently as five years ago, only the intelligence community could build reconnaissance satellites capable of producing intelligence-quality imagery. Not so today. Private companies like Earth Watch and Space Imaging are building surveillance satellites that are potentially so sophisticated that the government feels the need to regulate them: Officials fear that national security could be put at risk if this space imagery were freely available.

If commercial companies are able and willing to build such satellites, we need to ask why the intelligence community should do the same. Are there still certain types of imagery that only the government can produce? If so, how important is the information that this specialized imagery provides? Is it worth the marginal cost and additional risk to maintain a dedicated, government-operated collection system to gather it? Could private industry, properly regulated, provide that specialized information?

Satellite imagery is an exotic example, but the same is true in other areas. In the world of human-source reporting, commercial information services are expanding to meet new demands and opportunities. Witness the growth of CNN, CNBC, and even MTV. In earlier years, the only way to have a person on the scene to report from such places as Rwanda or Tajikistan was to put a foreign service officer or CIA operative there. Now Peter Arnett reports from Baghdad, Christiane Amanpour covers Sarajevo, and Tabitha Soren offers the latest news from the world's under-25 generation.

The same also applies for intelligence analysis. Consider economic intelligence, for example. In its early days, the CIA was one of the few organizations that could carry out good international economic analyses; it had unique data and expertise. Now many organizations throughout the world gather economic information and provide analysis—Dow Jones, McGraw-Hill, Dun & Bradstreet, to name just a few. Even so, many experts argue that the intelligence community should increase its efforts at providing economic intelligence (claiming trade policy is more important in the post–Cold War era), without explaining just what the intelligence community can do that hundreds of thousands of economic and financial analysts around the world cannot do better.

As the capabilities of the private sector improve, the intelligence community will need to move on to the next frontier of technology or expertise that the private sector has yet to fill. While one challenge for intelligence reform is to keep up with these changes, fundamentally the greater challenge will be to establish an organization that can adapt with the times.

Creating Adaptable Organizations

Some collection systems the intelligence community operates date from the early 1970s, when Americans were balancing their checkbooks with Bomar Brains, the most popular pocket calculator of the time. Today Bomar is gone and long-forgotten, and consumers now keep track of their spending with personal computers and personal finance software like Quicken. Although the intelligence community has, admittedly, made upgrades over the years, something unusual must be going on for an organization to cling to quarter-century-old information technology.

One reason why the intelligence community cannot deal effectively with the Information Revolution is that intelligence requirements and the intelligence community's comparative advantage are both fluid, but the traditional intelligence bureaucracy remains static. In addition, organizations responsible for developing and applying technology, such as the National Reconnaissance Office (NRO) and the National Security Agency (NSA), have created organizational dogma, and dogma always resist change. Once such organizations carve out a place for themselves (and their technologies) in the budget, they can be difficult to dislodge. The fact that these organizations often operate at a classified level further insulates them. As a result, the intelligence community often locks into specific technologies, even when new and possibly better ideas have come along.

For example, recently the House Intelligence Committee reportedly proposed adopting smaller, less expensive satellites that require less time to develop, build, and launch. The NRO, backed by the Senate Intelligence Committee, wanted to stay with its existing large systems. According to news reports, the House committee lost (a commission was appointed to study the issue). The same problem also occurs in analytical organizations, except that the disagreements are usually over methodologies rather than technologies.

Ironically, the [Clinton] administration's efforts to improve efficiency by consolidating agencies [would] make this problem worse. Consolidation narrows the base for new ideas. If the intelligence community is performing missions that no one else can (as should be the case), then, logically, we need multiple organizations within the community to develop a variety of ideas for carrying out those missions. It is unlikely that such a competitive market will exist anywhere else.

Similarly, if mission priorities are codified in national policy, then the technology that the intelligence community buys will likely be overly specialized. Experience suggests that any such system will be used for a completely different mission a few years from now. For example, of the three most expensive space systems now being operated by the intelligence community, none is currently being employed primarily for the mission originally used to justify its development—which is exactly what one should expect with information technology. Fine-tuning the intelligence infrastructure to support one particular user, such as the military, will limit the flexibility that has invariably proved necessary in the past.

A parallel situation applies to intelligence personnel. In the old days, one could hire analysts or technicians, give them civil service tenure, and move them along into progressively more responsible positions within their specialization. The intelligence community had a continuing need for expertise in such areas as Soviet conventional forces and strategic missiles. The topic changed incrementally. This is not so today.

Throughout American society, the supply and demand for job skills are much more fluid and chaotic than in the past. So, while IBM, AT&T, and Sears have been releasing employees they no longer need, Oracle, MCI, and Wal-Mart have been hiring employees to address new markets. Many companies have been hiring and firing simultaneously in order to retool for changing markets.

The same is true of the intelligence community, and it needs at least as much flexibility as private corporations. Many requirements for specialized information are likely to change quickly. Traditional civil service tenure is probably suited only for employees with the most general, long-term skills. As the skills the intelligence community requires become even more specialized, it will need more flexible arrangements for engaging its employees' services.

A New Model for Intelligence

Though the ways in which people use information have changed dramatically, most discussions about intelligence still use a model of the intelligence process that dates from the 1940s. This traditional model of the "intelligence cycle" is linear and single-tracked: Intelligence managers survey their consumers and define requirements. These requirements are used to assign collection responsibilities. Technicians and case officers then process the collected data. Analysts use the data to develop their products, which are then coordinated, edited, and delivered to the consumer. No one believes that intelligence really operates this way, but the concept still underlies most intelligence planning.

The military is already demonstrating an alternate model, showing how it is possible to create a continuous link connecting intelligence consumers directly to intelligence collectors. These concepts go by such names as "Sensor to Shooter" and "Dominant Battlefield Awareness." They envision a dispersed intelligence network rather than a linear hierarchy. Even commanders at the lowest levels of the military chain will, under these plans, determine the information they need and interact directly with collection system operators. Intelligence officers assigned to the commanders will integrate this information into a tailored product suited to the immediate need.

It should be possible to do the same in the nonmilitary world, but we will need to rethink the entire intelligence process. We could, for example, move most of the analysts in organizations such as the CIA's Directorate of Intelligence out of Langley, Virginia, and put them in the offices of their customers (perhaps leaving behind a smaller staff that could carry out long-term research on subjects that the commercial sector and academia cannot cover). These "super analysts" could receive their assignments directly from customers, deal with human and technical intelligence collectors and commercial information sources to obtain their data, and prepare tailored products.

This kind of approach would better serve the way officials in government deal with information in the real world. Like most people in modern society, government officials often act as their own analysts, partly because they are responsible for their decisions, and partly because information consumers of all kinds are less likely to accept authority. The attitude is "Don't tell me what to think; give me enough information for me to make up my own mind." Moreover, officials will shop for intelligence and will discard the "best coordinated wisdom" for what they believe to be correct, for whatever reason.

This attitude is blasphemy according to traditional thinking, which argues for a sharp line between analysts and policymakers to guarantee the objectivity of intelligence. In the real world, however, isolating analysts in this way simply makes them irrelevant.

The great fear that intelligence may be "politicized" if analysts are too close to policymakers is, in fact, another example where U.S. intelligence has not kept up with how society as a whole uses information. No one expects corporate officials, for example, simply to accept a forecast from an unseen, supposedly objective conclave of economic gurus. Rather, we know that economists often disagree and expect company officials to decide whose analysis is most on the mark. We then hold the officials responsible for their decisions.

Similarly, the Information Age solution to the politicization of intelligence is to maintain as many competing centers of analysis as possible. We can then allow political officials to be the final arbiters (as they will be in any case) and hold them responsible when they adopt one view over another. The . . . effort to "streamline" the intelligence community by reducing the number of analysts and analytical organizations [would] not only save relatively little money (analysts account for a tiny portion of the intelligence budget), but it [would] impede this competition of ideas.

In the fast-paced world of information support, it will be hard for the traditional planning process to keep pace. That is why the intelligence community needs new approaches to organization and management. No centralized—or "integrated"—planning process will be able to keep up with the rapidly changing requirements of intelligence consumers in the next century. Intelligence planning needs to become less, not more, centralized, as most would-be reformers currently propose. Intelligence officials can still exert control to make sure customers are satisfied. But they will need more flexible, and often less direct, methods in order to manage and monitor a process that must become more decentralized.

For instance, intelligence planners could use some indirect, market-style approaches to make the planning of intelligence collection systems more flexible and more responsive to the needs of intelligence consumers. Instead of funding the agencies that currently build and operate collection systems (e.g., NRO, NSA), the DCI [Director of Central Intelligence] could provide funds or vouchers to agencies that consume intelligence. These agencies could then decide for themselves what kinds of intelligence they thought was essential and how this information should be provided. They could, for example, buy their own dedicated satellite or sensor; the resulting system might be less capable, but the consumer might be willing to make the sacrifice in exchange for greater control and better service. The DCI could develop standards that would ensure interoperability and act as a broker for agencies that want to collaborate.

Or, consider how an intelligence manager might use indirect measures to make analysis more responsive. [During the first Clinton administration] the intelligence community received a request from U.S. ambassador to the United Nations Madeleine Albright to find rumored mass gravesites of civilians killed in Bosnia. It responded in the traditional way: It apparently assigned additional imagery analysts to the problem. It probably would have been more efficient to put such an assignment "up for bids." Intelligence managers could have offered a bounty to whomever could find the sites, using whatever means they thought would be effective.

Even if intelligence managers do not want to loosen the reins this far, the technology exists so that, at a minimum, every consumer should be able to speak directly to an analyst while managers monitor every request for support and allocate assets in real time as needed. Intelligence products should meet the information needs of consumers in the private sector—which is to say, whatever the consumer wants. This could be a one-word response over a telephone, a multivolume technical study, a briefing, or a point paper.

Some of these ideas may seem radical, but most already have precedents. The intelligence community currently tailors products for high-level officials, because these consumers know what they want and have the necessary clout to get it. Technology makes it possible to provide this level of service more widely, if the community is able to change its modus operandi. . . . The groundwork for a new model of intelligence must be laid now, lest real reform be delayed once again.

16

Trade Policy Decisionmaking: Competing Explanations

Stephen D. Cohen, Joel R. Paul, and Robert A. Blecker

What makes the U.S. trade policymaking process tick? What explains the behavior of the U.S. government as it formulates and implements foreign trade policy? . . . There does not appear to be any single or permanent variable or official operating procedure that can be used to explain all of the major trade decisions made throughout U.S. history or even in the post–World War II era. In the words of a classic study of U.S. foreign trade politics, even "the theory of self-interest as a complete and all-embracing explanation of behavior breaks down when we realize that self-interest is itself a set of mental images and convictions."[1]

Substance and process are linked in the making of public policy. The purpose of this chapter is to verify the complementarity between these two aspects of U.S. trade policy. The nature of how trade policy is made—process—should be consistent with our central thesis about the substance of trade policy being the end product of a process of reconciling economic and political factors, domestic and foreign. . . .

The Inevitable Diversity of Trade Policymaking

The absences of fixed procedures and patterns of behavior are not surprising given the nature of U.S. trade policy. There is a constantly changing cast of policymakers who are coping with constantly changing circumstances and an ever-expanding agenda of substantive issues with varying degrees of importance. Balances of power among competing groups and ideas are also constantly shifting so that different constituencies have different degrees of power in Washington, D.C., at different times. The bottom line is that there is no

---

Note: Some notes have been deleted or renumbered.

single identifiable set of forces serving as the constant, underlying source of trade policymaking decisions. . . . The key to understanding the functioning of the trade policymaking system is to recognize that varying circumstances associated with any given decision dictate that different actors will be in charge, different behavioral patterns will dominate, and different constituencies and perceptions will be given priority treatment. . . .

The Government as Reactive Decisionmaker

By law, government officials are in charge of creating and conducting trade policy. However, this does not automatically mean that they possess sufficient freedom of action to be an autonomous, independent, and activist force in trade policymaking. One theoretical approach to trade policy decisionmaking is to identify the most important force shaping the actions of trade officials. . . . Three of the major identifiable influences on policymakers are discussed here: domestic political forces (interest group politics), global political and economic structures (international regime constraints), and the state of the economy (market conditions).

Interest Group Politics

Private sector activism is brought to bear to some degree on virtually every U.S. trade policy decision. The occasions when the U.S. government imposes trade barriers on a major imported product are dramatic and attract a relatively large amount of publicity. All things considered, a somewhat exaggerated, oversimplified viewpoint emerges that portrays U.S. trade policymaking as being ultimately controlled by organized domestic political forces demanding and receiving protection from import competition. U.S. trade policy is viewed by this theory as being less shaped by resolute, activist politicians than by a Darwinian struggle among special interest groups. The sources of policy are the outcomes of the raw exercises of political power by these groups and the success of their intellectual efforts to convince legislative and executive branch officials that their interests are synonymous with the national interest. Carried to its logical conclusion, this model portrays the U.S. government as a "disinterested referee," providing but not controlling a venue for interest group lobbying. In the end, governmental agencies are seen to be acting as conduits between private sector trade demands and foreign governments.

Some scholars assert that "money talks" and that "policy outcomes on any particular issue are a function of the varying ability of groups to organize and give their interests prominence in the policy process."[2] Examples of this extreme interpretation occasionally materialize but on such a limited basis that this theory is open to the criticism that it can be nothing better than a partial explanation. Overall, the direct impact of special interest groups on U.S. trade policy in the 1990s is laced with nuance. Extensive empirical evidence of a widespread, lobbying-induced protectionist bias in contemporary U.S. trade policy is not currently available. . . .

Interest group politics, like all other models of trade policymaking, is not ubiquitous in the policymaking process. A continuously changing mix of variables seems to determine on a case-by-case basis exactly what will be official responsiveness to the input of interest group lobbying.[3] Sometimes the U.S. trade policymaking process is very responsive to such pressure, sometimes the opposite phenomenon occurs, and sometimes there is a halfway response. No known model can accurately predict which of these responses will occur. Powerful private sector pressure groups seeking either erection of import barriers or relaxations of export controls are regularly rejected by policymakers because of economic ideology or national security reasons. Even in decisions where the interest group politics model dominates, no reliable prediction of the outcome of policy substance is possible.

International Regime Constraints

Another model of trade policymaking argues that trade policy decisions are ultimately grounded in interrelationships and interactions among sovereign states, all of which are using international economic relations to maximize their wealth and influence. Larger states will also be looking to use trade relations to increase their power on global issues. A major variant of this approach is the notion that the discipline of international regimes encourages countries to cooperate and constrain aggressive behavior. U.S. trade officials, like their foreign counterparts, regularly subordinate domestic considerations to international standards of trade behavior, most of which are codified in the General Agreement on Tariffs and Trade. . . . Perhaps the principal reason that countries generally conform to GATT's antiprotectionist provisions, which are less than absolutely binding, is to discourage other countries from imposing their own trade barriers. Some argue that international regimes make cooperation rational in what is essentially a confrontational world. Since trade is a continuous process and not a one-shot event to be won, long-term efforts to cooperate within the framework of liberal trade–oriented rules can ensure the maximization of wealth for everyone. This consideration is likely to be at the back of the minds of U.S. trade officials when they point to GATT-imposed obligations as justification for not responding to domestic pressures for implementation of protectionist measures. . . .

Another argument associated with the global structures model is the theory that a country's position in the global economic order decisively shapes its international commercial policy. Most notable and demonstrable are the two instances of international political and economic hegemons, Great Britain in the nineteenth century and the United States in the twentieth. At the height of their global power, both countries identified their interests with creating and supporting liberal (nonrestrictive) trade regimes.

Market Conditions

Yet another approach to explaining policy substance is to emphasize market conditions. One version of this theory argues that changing international market conditions can make it "economically irrational for a government to continue prevailing policy."[4] This approach would explain the need for radical changes in U.S. trade policy in 1971 and 1985 when exchange rate distortions caused a deterioration both in the level of U.S. industrial competitiveness and in the trade balance. The market conditions model is appropriate to explain the tendency for governments to be relatively resistant to protectionist pressures during periods of high domestic economic growth and low unemployment. It also explains their tendency to be predisposed to imposing protectionist measures during periods of slow or negative growth, a propensity best illustrated by the beggar-thy-neighbor policies employed during the depression years of the 1930s. . . .

The Government as Active Decisionmaker

When U.S. governmental entities convene to formulate general policy or to make a specific decision, they cannot escape being influenced by a varying mix of external stimuli: the previously described constraints as well as perceived opportunities. Decisionmakers cannot and do not act in a value-free vacuum. . . .

The substance of trade policy is often a direct by-product of what a number of officials collectively determine is best for the country, favored constituencies, the global economy, and their personal situations—not necessarily in that order. Few persons aspire to the senior levels of U.S. trade policymaking for the money. Their usual motivation is self-confidence in having intellectual and problem-solving abilities that are well above average. They also tend to possess a conscious or subconscious enjoyment of the exercise of power. For these reasons, U.S. trade officials view themselves as capable of making reasoned and calculated choices, not as being prisoners of externally imposed constraints.

There is no standard operating procedure by which the U.S. government formulates and implements trade policy. The choice of exactly which of several possible organizational procedures is utilized can have implications for policy substance. The delicate balance among the four components of trade policy—domestic and international economics plus domestic and international politics—can be tilted in one direction or the other depending on which government entities are involved and which have leadership roles. . . .

The Presidential Fiat Model

The simplest, most dramatic model of U.S. trade policymaking consists of the relatively rare phenomenon of the president taking an early and dominant role. Presidents are usually too preoccupied with national security and domestic social and economic issues to get deeply involved in the arcane minutiae common to most trade dilemmas. When they do get involved, presidents usually come in at the very end of the process to approve a recommendation from their cabinet or, less frequently, to mediate an irreconcilable dispute. Only on rare occasions, typically in response to dramatic unfolding events, have presidents intervened at the onset of an international trade issue by making a forceful declaration of policy intent that immediately and unequivocally dictated the nature of subsequent U.S. actions. Staff work and interagency consultations are minimal to nonexistent prior to a presidential fiat. In this case, the president speaks first, and then the bureaucracy is ordered into action to provide the support necessary to implement the president's publicly stated position. . . .

Examples of the presidential fiat model in the international trade realm include President Nixon's ordering his senior economic aides to join him at Camp David on an August weekend in 1971 where he guided and approved dramatic overnight decisions that reversed several major domestic and international economic policies. The so-called New Economic Policy, among other things, immediately invoked a 10 percent surcharge on all import duties and suspension of convertibility of dollars held by foreign central banks into gold—after only a cursory calculation of the likely international impact and repercussions of these measures. A second example is the personal anger and shock at the Soviet invasion of Afghanistan that led Jimmy Carter immediately to order an economic retaliation by banning the export of 17 million metric tons of wheat previously ordered by the Soviet government—a move that financially hurt U.S. farmers as well as Soviet consumers.

A few weeks after the 1993 inauguration, the Clinton administration issued a detailed blueprint for enhanced government support for and involvement in the effort to strengthen the U.S. high-technology sector, an endeavor aimed in large measure at increasing U.S. international competitiveness. This technology initiative originated in the White House because it was a direct outgrowth of Clinton's and Vice President Al Gore's personal economic philosophy that was graphically spelled out in their campaign promises to alter economic policies.

Presidents are far more likely—except in the weeks immediately prior to a close race for reelection—to respond to deeply held, preexisting values, ideologies, and concerns for the country's broader, longer-term interests than they are to crass political manipulations. Since each Oval Office incumbent possesses a different mix of personal beliefs and experiences, there is no predictable, preordained tilt in trade policy substance when the presidential fiat model is utilized. President Bush took the lead in articulating his administration's position on China's MFN status. His unwavering opposition to imposing conditions on the extension of MFN tariff treatment appeared to be based on deeply held personal convictions directly related to his earlier experience as ambassador to China.

The Bureaucratic Politics Model

The presence of top-down leadership in the form of active presidential involvement in U.S. trade policy decisionmaking has been and still is the exception rather than the rule. Since presidential time and energies normally are concentrated in other policy sectors, most trade policy decisions are made at or below the cabinet level by an interagency group, sometimes numbering in excess of twenty. Participating agencies in interagency trade policy deliberations have steadily grown in number as the impact of the growing trade sector has impinged on more policy jurisdictions.

Interagency trade committees and working groups in the U.S. government operate mainly as meetings of institutionalized interests possessing different perspectives. They seldom have the benefit of an unambiguous, self-evident strategy to guide selection of optimal policy decisions that everyone deems to maximize the national interest, the definition of which may also escape agreement. Decisionmakers are usually confronted with the need to reconcile conflicting policy proposals that normally emerge in the absence of a specific directive from the president. . . . No executive branch trade policy official . . . represents the country as a whole and has responsibility for the entire policy spectrum. All trade officials work for bureaucratic entities that have been established for and work on behalf of specifically defined institutional constituencies, not the country as a whole. In the trade area, these focal points include domestic economic price stability, the industrial sector, the environment, foreign policy, agriculture, jobs and wages, and human rights. An important part of job performance evaluation for employees of line departments and agencies is how well individuals represent their chosen constituency in interagency meetings. . . .

In most cases, institutional attitudes toward trade issues are consistent and predictable. Certain agencies invariably view trade policy as a tool of foreign relations efforts to influence the attitudes and actions of other countries, friendly and unfriendly. The foreign affairs bureaucracies, namely the State Department and the National Security Council, typically support liberal import policies because an open trading system would best promote a stable system and harmonious relations among like-minded countries. Conversely in the export sector, these two agencies plus the Defense Department typically support illiberal export controls as a means of exacting a price overseas for what is deemed undesirable or dangerous foreign behavior. Officials in the foreign affairs bureaucracies are not totally insensitive to the well-being of domestic workers and companies. However, they know that they are not paid to worry primarily about this constituency and that no one else in the trade bureaucracy can be expected to speak out on behalf of the global political environment—one of several perfectly legitimate concerns in making "good" trade policy.

It is necessary to examine the institutional "essence" of the coordinator of U.S. trade policy, the office of the U.S. Trade Representative, to understand its sometimes paradoxical behavior. Its primary mission is to successfully negotiate reciprocal trade liberalization agreements with other countries. Engaging in trade acts that would anger other governments is hardly conducive to encouraging such agreements. Nevertheless, the USTR takes a hard line on demanding reductions in overseas barriers to U.S. goods, and on occasion it sides with the protectionist faction in import policy debates. USTR's bureaucratic behavior is rooted in the mutually accepted concept that it was born of congressional initiative and that it could be terminated by Congress if it loses touch with domestic constituencies. Translation: It must occasionally recognize the need to limit the injury inflicted on U.S. producers by severe import competition—to provide a safety net for the adverse effects of reduced U.S. import barriers. Furthermore, most USTR officials feel that they alone have the primary role of creating executive branch consensus on policy and not the task of imposing a particular point of view.[5]

The growing linkage between domestic economic performance and the foreign trade sector means that in terms of sheer numbers, the contemporary U.S. trade policymaking process is dominated by so-called domestic agencies with specific, sometimes competing, jurisdictions. The macroeconomic agencies—the Treasury Department, the Council of Economic Advisers, and the Office of Management and Budget—generally advocate liberal trade positions but for reasons that differ from those of the foreign policy bureaucracies. The economic policy agencies are dominated by professionally trained, free market-oriented economists. They tend to equate their mission to enhance the overall U.S. economy with a relatively unrestrained flow of imports, a trend that maximizes competition and price stability within the domestic economy.

The perception of its having an institutional predisposition to tolerating increased imports was the reason the Treasury Department was stripped of its authority over investigating allegations of dumping and foreign governmental subsidies. The Commerce Department, viewed as being institutionally more sympathetic to the domestic industries that are affected by these unfair foreign practices, was given this responsibility in the 1980 reorganization of the U.S. trade policymaking apparatus.

The bureaucratic perspectives of Commerce and Agriculture are simple: Both departments advocate policies that will strengthen and benefit what are arguably vital sectors of the economy. For the Commerce Department, this means industry and services; for the other department, this means the agricultural community. When they confront individual trade decisions, however, their mission is complicated by the dichotomy in both of their constituencies: Some subsectors are internationally competitive and export-oriented, and some are relatively inefficient and import-sensitive. The result is that these departments sometimes vigorously support liberal trade policy options, but selectively recommend exceptions in the form of limited import restraints on specific goods. There is much less ambiguity on the export side: Both Commerce and Agriculture are wholeheartedly supportive of export expansion. They dislike domestically imposed controls and take an activist stand against trade barriers maintained by U.S. trading partners.

When participating in trade policy deliberations, officials of the Environmental Protection Agency are sensitized to the physical and legal need to temper economic considerations whenever necessary to assure conformity with domestic environmental protection laws. For them, the U.S. national interest is not measured primarily in terms of financial considerations and conformity with international trade agreements to avoid imposition of new trade barriers.

Clear-cut examples of bureaucratic politics abound in the record of U.S. trade policy. The trifurcated approach long taken by the executive branch toward trade relations with Japan is symptomatic of the "internal harmony" that exists among an institutional mind-set, a constituency's interest, and perception of what course of action would most likely serve the national interest. The macroeconomic agencies, for the most part, believe that retaliatory import barriers would, on a net basis, hurt the U.S. economy and are a far less desirable means of reducing the bilateral deficit than free market forces. The national security agencies soft-pedal economic priorities because their primary goal here is to prevent commercial squabbles from damaging political relations with a key ally. Last, the "trade warriors" of the USTR and the Commerce Department retain their long-held advocacy of a hard-line trade policy to belatedly force Japan's (allegedly) unfair important and export practices into conformity with U.S. norms for proper trade behavior. A schism between those bureaucracies inclined to favor liberal trade and those leaning toward protectionism is virtually inevitable when the executive branch—regardless of who is president—is deciding on whether to restrict imports under an escape clause proceeding (presidential discretion is allowed because no unfair trade practices are involved) or whether to renew a voluntary export restraint agreement. . . .

Contradictory facts hampered the decision as to whether to extend for another five-year period the voluntary export restraint agreements, negotiated in the mid-1980s on behalf of the U.S. steel industry and due to expire in fall 1989. Parts of the bureaucracy felt that the steel industry had received too much protection for too long. The opposing faction urged continued import restraints on the grounds that many foreign steel producers had not abandoned unfair trade practices (dumping and governmental subsidies) and that the domestic industry had taken great strides in nearly completing efforts to become most productive and internationally competitive. So ambivalent was the situation that President Bush was called upon to break the resulting cabinet deadlock. His decision to prolong the restraints for two and one-half years makes sense only in arithmetic terms: It was the midway point between the two major policy recommendations—no extension of the restraints and a full five-year extension. . . .

Bureaucratic wrangling over trade policy priorities and definitions of the national interest is not ubiquitous in interagency decisionmaking exercises. Occasionally there is easy consensus. This was the case when the decision was made to retaliate against Japan when it was seen to be violating conditions agreed upon in the 1986 semiconductor agreement.[6] On other occasions, a single agency or a single policymaker so dominates an issue that others quietly back off. Letting Treasury Secretary John Connally take the lead in setting international economic policy strategy in the wake of the New Economic Policy pronouncement exemplifies this situation.

Congress and the Interbranch Politics Model

The relatively large percentage of U.S. trade policy that consists of the executive branch dutifully carrying out the spirit and letter of laws written by the legislative branch is one of the unique aspects of the U.S. political system. Unlike in a parliamentary form of government, the president as head of the executive branch has little legal scope to act on his own in conducting trade policy. He depends on Congress for legal authority to commit the United States to most trade agreements. If the president flagrantly disregards strong congressional trade sentiments, he risks a reprimand in the form of passage of statutory language that he opposes.

Any effort to model trade decisionmaking strictly within the executive branch (or the private sector) would ignore important realities. The cumulative effect of numerous statutory provisions devised by Congress is that an administration has limited discretion to act as it sees fit in the realm of foreign trade. The modern-day partnership between Congress and the administration and the fusion of their distinctive institutional perspectives embody a uniquely complex, multifaceted trade policymaking process. Presidents administer trade policy and tend to embrace a liberal trade policy that complements the role of world statesman. Members of Congress write trade laws and tilt toward giving thorough hearing to the demands of voters back home. Each remains uneasy about and at times distrustful of the perceived bias in the other's trade policy inclinations.

The Omnibus Trade and Competitiveness Act of 1988 contains numerous provisions designed by Congress to modify the executive branch's trade policy behavior. Key provisions seek to increase the likelihood of presidential retaliation against discriminatory foreign trade practices and to enhance U.S. industrial competitiveness. Passage of these initiatives reflected a uniquely congressional sentiment that certain trade policy changes—mainly in the form of greater presidential resolve to attack foreign trade barriers—had become necessary. These initiatives in turn were part of the larger trend of congressional efforts dating back to the 1930s to fine-tune the substance of contemporary U.S. trade policy.

Fearful of repeating its excessive acceptance in 1930 of interest group demands for protectionism, Congress since 1934 has used a network of statutory provisions to establish what it considers to be an economically progressive, politically responsive system of import policymaking. Congress has seen fit to relinquish some of its constitutional power to the executive branch and to the independent International Trade Commission. By design, Congress has seen to it that the executive branch takes most of the heat in carrying out the delicate task of determining how to respond to the unending procession of private sector demands for trade actions that favor their interests. . . .

To this day, Congress pursues its trial-and-error effort to codify into U.S. trade laws just the right tension between broad pursuit of trade liberalization and the conditional availability in appropriate situations of protectionist measures and retaliatory sanctions. Congress is an unabashed advocate of "fair" trade, a pleasant-sounding concept lacking both opponents and precise meaning. The trade legislation it has passed since 1934 is characterized by an intricate set of counterweights and shock absorbers. Congress has long encouraged the executive branch to pursue a basically liberal trade policymaking posture. But at the same time that trade barriers are being reduced, a "fair" hearing about eligibility for legislated relief mechanisms is guaranteed to those domestic sectors that are losers from the inflow of imports. Furthermore, U.S. exporters are made happy by congressional efforts to force the administration to be more aggressive than it might otherwise be in threatening grave consequences for trading partners that discriminate against U.S. commerce. In effect, the post-1934 trade policy system has utilized an intricate system of congressionally designed political pulleys and levers to sustain a precarious balance of power unofficially and informally designed to block the reemergence of the once-dominant protectionist coalition.

A system of counterweights also has been inserted in export policy. On the one hand, the executive branch has been delegated authority to impose U.S. export controls and sanctions on unfriendly countries. Simultaneously, however, Congress has pushed offsetting relief in the form of efforts to increase the access of U.S. goods to friendly foreign markets. An examination of the evolution of U.S. export legislation demonstrates patterns similar to those that characterize import legislation: modest interbranch differences in trade philosophy and congressional efforts to restrict the executive branch's freedom of maneuver in a manner consistent with Congress's perception of the national interest. Not wishing to usurp the administration's power to decide when to impose export controls for national security and foreign policy purposes, Congress has progressively put the burden of proof on those executive branch officials advocating export restrictions. Over the years, the Export Administration Act (previously named the Export Control Act) repeatedly has been amended in response to complaints by major exporting companies that they have lost billions of dollars of overseas sales to foreign competitors operating under much more relaxed export control systems. As part of a philosophical effort to dictate the right range of executive branch behavior, recent versions of export control legislation have ordered progressive reductions in the list of controlled items and have required that the overseas availability of an item be taken into account when an export license is being reviewed.

The interbranch politics model of trade policymaking is visible in three different permutations. The first is the harmonious variant in which the two branches bargain cooperatively with one another. No bill submitted under the so-called fast-track authority has yet been defeated. Since this procedure calls for an all-or-nothing, yea-or-nay, no-amendments vote on legislation to ratify proposed trade liberalization agreements, informal interbranch negotiations have always been conducted prior to the administration's submission of such legislation. Administrations have made the concessions and adjustments necessary to assure congressional passage *before* formally submitting such legislation. A second example of harmonious interbranch relations is the tactic frequently used by the U.S. government since the 1970s to goad Japan into responding to trade concession demands. In its role as "bad cop," a seemingly furious Congress threatens to run wild and pass highly protectionist, anti-Japanese trade legislation. This prospect encourages the Japanese to cut a preemptive deal with the more reasonable, less protectionist "good cop" as played by the administration.

Interbranch politics on other occasions become adversarial in nature. Occasionally, Congress passes trade legislation actively opposed by the administration. President Carter's imposition in 1980 of import duties on petroleum was thrown out by legislation banning it. The restrictive provisions in the 1974 trade bill governing extension of MFN status to countries not yet receiving it were deemed excessive by the Ford administration and almost resulted in a presidential veto of this major piece of otherwise acceptable legislation. At other times, Congress has delayed or refused to pass trade legislation submitted by the administration.

A detailed examination of U.S. trade policymaking reveals a third variant of the interbranch model: executive branch positions and attitudes being modified in *anticipation* of congressional action that would go against administration desires. The Reagan and Bush administrations secured a tightening in voluntary export restraints under the Multifiber Arrangement by pointing to the need to sustain presidential vetoes of several textile quota bills. The latter seem to have been passed mainly to induce such an administrative tightening of imports, not with the expectation of being enacted into law. The Reagan administration chose the protectionist option of imposing higher tariffs in an escape clause decision involving shakes and shingles from Canada. Because this action was taken in the midst of free trade agreement negotiations between the two countries, it appeared on the surface to be a case of bad timing. This decision makes sense, however, when one learns that it came, not coincidentally, on the very day that the House was voting on protectionist amendments very much opposed by the administration.[7]

Conclusion

The convergence of economics, politics, and laws that defines the substance of U.S. trade policy is also at the core of its formulation. Through the use of conceptual models and case studies, we have sought to demonstrate in this chapter the inherent diversity and inconsistency that characterize the policy-making actions of the executive and legislative branches as they go about the daunting task of seeking to maximize economic logic within the constraints of political reality. Process affects substance—especially in a policy sector that perpetually must reconcile domestic and external economic and political priorities. . . . The lack of precision by which trade policy decisions are arrived at is not a weakness that can be overcome by better organizational arrangements or by new scholarly models. Diversity and inconsistency are inherent in any U.S. policy that is short on absolute or permanent truths. Given U.S. political and economic ideologies, there may well be merit in having a trade policymaking system so flexible and diverse that it discourages the potentially destabilizing prospects of fixed ideas, unassailable power centers, and permanent winners and losers.

Notes

1. Raymond A. Bauer, Ithiel de Sola Pool, and Lewis A. Dexter, *American Business and Public Policy* (Chicago: Aldine-Atherton, 1972), p. 226.

2. G. John Ikenberry, David A. Lake, and Michael Mastanduno, eds., "The State and American Foreign Economic Policy," *International Organization,* 42 (Winter 1988), 7. Also see Mancur Olson, *The Rise and Decline of Nations* (New Haven: Yale University Press, 1982).

3. Interest groups today are most likely to "capture" the bureaucracy with a protectionist request if the cost of such an action is so scattered over a wide enough group that no one is seriously and noticeably impacted; hence, no major oppositional lobby-

ing effort is likely to be instigated. I thank my colleague, Renee Marlin-Bennett, for this observation.

4. John S. Odell, *U.S. International Monetary Policy: Markets, Power, and Ideas as Sources of Change* (Princeton: Princeton University Press, 1982).

5. Not-for-attribution interview with USTR official, summer 1994.

6. Stephen D. Cohen, *Cowboys and Samurai: Why the United States Is Losing the Battle with the Japanese, and Why It Matters* (New York: HarperBusiness, 1991), p. 62.

7. Not-for-attribution interview with U.S. trade official, spring 1987.

Part III

Decisionmakers and Their Policymaking Positions

Foreign-policy choices are often made by a remarkably small number of individuals, most conspicuous of whom is the president. As Harry S Truman exclaimed, "I make American foreign policy."

Because of the president's power and preeminence, it is tempting to think of foreign policy as determined exclusively by presidential preferences and to personalize government by identifying a policy with its proponents. "There is properly no history, only biography," is how Ralph Waldo Emerson dramatized the view that individual leaders are the makers and movers of history. This *hero-in-history* model finds expression in the practice of attaching the names of presidents to the policies they promulgate (for example, the Truman Doctrine, the Kennedy Round, the Clinton Doctrine), as if the men were synonymous with the nation itself, and of routinely attributing foreign-policy successes and failures to the administration in which they occur.

The conviction that the individual who holds office makes a difference is one of the major premises underlying the electoral process. Thus, each new administration seeks to distinguish itself from its predecessor and to highlight policy departures as it seeks to convey the impression that it has engineered a new (and better) order. The media's tendency to label presidential actions "new" abets those efforts. Hence leadership and policy are portrayed as synonymous, and changes in policy and policy direction are often perceived as the result of the predispositions of the leadership.

Clearly, leaders' individual attributes exert a potentially powerful influence on American foreign policy, and no account of its sources would be complete without a discussion of them. Indeed, the conventional decisionmaking model maintains that policymakers—notably the president and his principal advisors—devise strategies and implement plans to realize goals "rationally," that is, in terms of calculations about national interests based upon the relative costs and benefits associated with alternative goals and means. Many scholars have questioned the accuracy of this popular model. In fact, it would be misleading and simplistic to ascribe too much influence to the individuals responsible for the conduct of American foreign policy or to assume that influence is the same for all leaders in all circumstances. That individuals make a difference is unassailable, but it is more useful to ask (1) under what circumstances the idiosyncratic qualities of leaders exert their greatest impact; (2) what types of institutional structures and management strategies different leaders are likely to follow; and (3) what policy variations are most likely to result from different types of leaders. These questions force us to examine how individual characteristics find expression in foreign-policy outcomes and how policy-making roles leaders occupy may circumscribe their individual influence.

When we consider the mediating impact of policymakers' roles, we draw attention to the fact that many different people, widely dispersed throughout the government, contribute to the making of American foreign policy. In Part II we examined some of the departments and agencies of government involved in the process. Here, in Part III, the concern is with decisionmakers and how the roles created by the government's foreign-policy organizational structures influence the behavior of the policymakers occupying these roles, and, ultimately, American foreign policy itself. As a rival hypothesis to the hero-in-history image of political leadership, *role theory* posits that the positions and the processes, rather than the characteristics of the people who decide, influence the behavior and choices of those responsible for making and executing the nation's foreign policy. Furthermore, changes in policy presumably result from changes in role conceptions, rather than from changes in the individuals who occupy these roles.

Role theory also leads us to other perspectives on how policymakers make foreign policy-choices. Considerable evidence drawn from foreign-policy case studies points toward the pressures for conformity among those responsible for choosing among competing foreign-policy alternatives, which may lead to less than optimal choices. Furthermore, the principal actors in the foreign affairs government often compete with one another as they consider competing policy alternatives, with their bargaining position dictated by organizational references rather than national interests. In particular, the *bureaucratic politics model* of decision making stresses the importance of the roles individuals occupy in large-scale organizations and the struggles that occur among their constituent units. Proponents of the model claim it captures the essence of the highly politicized foreign-policy decision making process more accurately than does the model of rational behavior, which assumes that the government operates as a single, unitary actor.

Graham Allison's book *Essence of Decision,* a study of the 1962 Cuban missile crisis, is the best-known effort to articulate and apply the bureaucratic politics model. Allison developed two alternate strands of the model. One, which he calls the *organizational process* paradigm, reflects the constraints that organizational procedures and routines place on decisionmakers' choices. The other, which he calls *governmental politics,* draws attention to the "pulling and hauling" that occurs among the key bureaucratic participants in the decision process.[1]

How, from the perspective of organizational processes, do large-scale bureaucracies affect policy making? One way is by devising *standard operating procedures* (SOPs) for coping with policy problems when they arise. For example, the Clinton administration's Bottom-Up Review, its design for reshaping the American military for the post–Cold War world, proposed developing a force structure to enable the United States to fight two major regional conflicts (MRCs) simultaneously (or nearly simultaneously). Once all of the routines (SOPs) necessary for coping with simultaneous regional conflict are put into place, they effectively will both mold and limit the range of viable policy choices for policymakers. Rather than expanding the number of policy alternatives in a manner consistent with the logic of rational decision making, then, organizational routines shape what is possible—and what is not.

Governmental politics, the second strand in the bureaucratic politics model as articulated by Allison, draws attention to the way individuals act in organizational settings. Not surprisingly, and as role theory predicts, the many participants in the deliberations that lead to foreign-policy choices often define issues and favor policy alternatives that reflect their organizational affiliations. "Where you stand depends on where you sit" is a favorite aphorism reflecting these bureaucratic (role) imperatives. Furthermore, because the players in the game of governmental politics are responsible for protecting the nation's security, they are "obliged to fight for what they are convinced is right."[2] The consequence is that "different groups pulling in different directions produce a result, or better a resultant—a mixture of conflicting preferences and unequal power of various individuals—distinct from what any person or group intended."[3]

Sometimes, too, these bureaucratic conflicts can lead to policy stalemates, as witnessed by the Clinton administration as it sought a response to the conflict in Bosnia in 1993. Despite the new president's criticism during the 1992 presidential campaign of the Bush administration's timid response to the violence and warfare in the former Yugoslavia, bureaucratic (role) differences quickly surfaced, pitting the Department of State and the chairman of the Joint Chiefs of Staff, who favored diplomatic action, against the national security advisor and the secretary of defense, who favored military action.[4] Policy development was thus stalled for a considerable time. The example is consistent with the logic of the bureaucratic politics model, suggesting that sometimes the explanation for why states make the choices they do lies not in their behavior vis-à-vis one another but rather in the disputes within their own governments. Furthermore, rather than presupposing the existence of a unitary actor, as the rational model does, the bureaucratic politics model suggests that "it is necessary to identify the games and players, to display the coalitions, bargains, and compromises, and to convey some feel for the confusion" in the policymaking process.[5]

Decisionmakers' and Policymakers' Roles as Influences on American Foreign Policy

In virtually every situation in which the United States has contemplated the use of force in the post–Cold War years—in the Persian Gulf, Somalia, Bosnia, Rwanda, and Haiti—policymakers and critics alike have worried about the specter of Vietnam and the "lessons" it provides. In part this is because the protracted series of decisions that took the United States into Vietnam and, eventually, out of it on unsatisfactory terms after years of fighting and the loss of tens of thousands of lives, is fertile ground for probing how American foreign policy is made and implemented.

Part III of this book begins with an account informed by role theory and bureaucratic politics of how the United States became involved in and conducted the prolonged war in Southeast Asia. "How Could Vietnam Happen?" asks James C. Thomson, Jr., almost rhetorically. The failure in Vietnam, Thomson contends, was the failure of America's policymaking process, not of it leadership. Vietnam shows that some of the most catastrophic of America's foreign-policy initiatives are the result not of evil or stupid people, but of misdirected behaviors encouraged by the nature of the policymaking system and the roles and bureaucratic processes embedded in the way the government's foreign-policy system is organized. Thomson's argument, however disturbing, provides insight into the milieu of decision making and identifies many syndromes crucial to understanding how the roles created by the decisionmaking setting influence the kinds of decisions that leaders make and that bureaucracies are asked to implement.

Mark M. Lowenthal shows that many of the determinants of behavior characteristic of Vietnam decision making are still very much alive. He examines the relationship between leaders and "careerists" (foreign-policy professionals who provide continuity from one administration to the next) as it relates to the production and consumption of intelligence, that is, the information presumed to be necessary for rational decision making. Noting that "there has been much soul-searching in the executive and Congress concerning the organization and role of the intelligence community" in the post–Cold War world, Lowenthal worries that too little attention has been given to fundamental questions about the relationship between the producers and consumers of intelligence. "A major problem is that the consumer-producer relationship resembles that of two closely related tribes that believe, mistakenly, that they speak the same language and work in the same manner for agreed outcomes. Reality . . . suggests something wholly different. Indeed, one is often reminded of George Bernard Shaw's quip about Britons and Americans being divided by a common tongue."

Lowenthal's insights about the intelligence process again illustrate that the reasons for the choices states make often lie not in their behavior vis-à-vis one another but within their own governments. He explains inter alia why the assumptions of intelligence consumers (policymakers) and producers (bureaucrats) often differ, why political leaders sometimes (often?) ignore the intelligence they receive, how (and why) intelligence consumers shape the information they get, and how (and why) intelligence producers shape what they give. In the end, Lowenthal concludes, "the production and use or disuse of intelligence as part of the policy process is the net result of several types of mind-sets and behavior within and between two groups that are more disparate than most observers realize."

Lowenthal's analysis is particularly useful in showing how policymaking roles shape the behavior of individuals who occupy them. Christopher M. Jones's "Trading with Saddam: Bureaucratic Roles and Competing Conceptions of National Security," which draws explicitly on Allison's earlier work, takes Lowenthal's perspective a step further and shows how bureaucratic organizations' missions predict their policy stands. The case examined is, like Vietnam, a troubling one: the sale of high-technology goods to Iraq in the period between 1984 and Iraq's invasion of Kuwait in 1990. Jones shows how, with the consent of the U.S. government, American companies "enhanced the capability of Saddam Hussein's war machine, which the United States and its allies later faced on the battlefield." Furthermore, "U.S. technology aided Iraq's unconventional weapons programs, violating a long-standing American goal of preventing the proliferation of weapons of mass destruction to Third World states."

How could this happen? It happened because both "the Reagan and Bush administrations established broad, conciliatory policies toward Iraq that afforded executive agencies wide discretionary power in determining the nature and extent of American trade to Iraq." In this environment, the Commerce Department, following its mandate to promote international trade, became a vigorous proponent of technology sales to Iraq. It usually prevailed in the interoganizational policy process because it was able to build a "'winning' coalition in favor of liberal export controls" with the State Department that blocked the Defense Department's objections. As Jones explains, "each agency's separate organizational mission led it to embrace a different conception of national security and, therefore, different reasons for supporting either trade promotion or trade control."

As noted above, "where you stand depends on where you sit" is a central proposition in the bureaucratic politics model. The aphorism purports to explain why participants in the deliberations that lead to foreign-policy choices often define issues and favor policy alternatives that reflect their organizational affiliations. Jones shows that it applies to organizations. Does it also apply to individuals, including those at the highest levels of government? Steve Smith concludes the answer is "yes" in his "Policy Preferences and Bureaucratic Position: The Case of the American Hostage Rescue Mission." As the title suggests, Smith examines the process that led the Carter administration to the fateful decision to attempt a covert, paramilitary rescue of American diplomats held hostage by Iran beginning in late 1979. As with Vietnam and high-tech sales to Iraq, this is a tale of policy shortcomings—of policy failure. How did it happen?

Smith does not attempt a complete answer to this question, but he does show that the key participants in the decision process "acted in accordance with what the bureaucratic politics approach would suggest: namely, that the National Security Adviser, the Secretary of Defense, the Chairman of the Joint Chiefs of Staff and Director of the CIA would support military action . . . ; the Secretary of State, and in his absence his deputy, would oppose it; those individuals who were bureaucratically tied to the President (the Vice-President, the Press Secretary and the Political Adviser) would be fundamentally concerned with what was best for the Carter presidency; and President Carter, although clearly more than just another bureaucratic actor, would act in a way that reflected bureaucratically-derived as well as personal influences."

Smith's analysis is compelling not only as a study of an important episode in American foreign policy but also as an illustration of the logic of the bureaucratic politics model. It is also important because it shows the pitfalls as well as promises of the perspective and why we must examine not only policymaking roles but also policymakers themselves. Smith's conclusions are important in this respect: "Role, in and of itself, cannot explain the positions adopted by individuals. . . . Yet role occupiers do become predisposed to think in certain, bureaucratic ways, and for a variety of psychological reasons they tend to adopt mind-sets compatible with those of their closest colleagues. In addition, individuals are often chosen for a specific post because they have certain kinds of world-views." In the final analysis, then, to understand the impact of decisionmakers and their policymaking positions on American foreign policy, we must understand both.

Stephen D. Krasner's "Are Bureaucracies Important?: A Re-examination of Accounts of the Cuban Missile Crisis" provides insight into why and how we might distinguish between individual and role explanations of American foreign policy. His chapter is a thoughtful critique of Allison's bureaucratic politics perspective on the 1962 Cuban missile crisis. Krasner argues that emphasizing bureaucratic roles as all-powerful determinants of policy outcomes exaggerates their importance. Indeed, Krasner's reexamination of the facts surrounding the Cuban missile crisis reveals that, while bureaucracies do exert an impact on foreign policy, decisionmakers nonetheless have a capacity for rational choice, and that the choices they make—rather than those made by bureaucratic organizations—ultimately matter most. Hence, the individuals elected by and responsible to the people they represent do matter, and how those leaders define their decisionmaking roles can prove decisive.

James Goldgeier in his "NATO Expansion: The Anatomy of a Decision," supports Krasner's argument about the crucial importance of individuals in molding policy and illustrates the limitation on bureaucracies in shaping it. Based on extensive interviews with officials knowledgeable or involved in the NATO expansion decision, Goldgeier demonstrates that the bureaucracies, and individuals in those bureaucracies, can shape debate over an issue and can "pull" and "haul" to promote different positions, but they cannot determine policy. Instead, the issue of whether NATO membership would formally expand or whether the Partnership for Peace (PFP) option would continue to be pursued ultimately depended on President Clinton. Not until Clinton made a series of speeches in Brussels, Prague, and Warsaw were bureaucratic differences settled. As Clinton stated, "The question is no longer whether NATO will take on new members but when and how."

The NATO case illustrates the importance of individuals in other ways. For example, Anthony Lake, the national security advisor at the time, and other foreign-policy principals were able to move Clinton to make statements that seemingly committed the United States to NATO expansion. They in turn used his remarks as the basis for establishing a working group that set forth an "action plan," thus demonstrating the influence that individuals are sometimes able to exercise in the face of bureaucratic resistance. Particularly interesting is how Richard Holbrooke, assistant secretary of state for European affairs, became the "enforcer" of the NATO expansion decision within the interagency process. Invoking the president's wishes with the argument "Either you are on the president's program or you are not," he was able to crystallize the president's key role in the policy choice.

The last two readings in this book look beyond the bureaucratic politics approach and the role of individuals in bureaucratic organizations. Instead, both focus on the role of individual cognition (or world views) in shaping behavior and, ultimately, foreign policy. Although roles and bureaucratic context do matter, prior experiences and personality predispositions are crucial in determining policymakers' decision style and policy choice, as the two chapters demonstrate.

In his "A Fortuitous Victory: An Information Processing Approach to the Gulf War," Alex Roberto Hybel contends that the Bush administration's decision to go to war against Saddam Hussein in 1991 was less rational than it might first appear. The principal reason rests on the fact that President Bush early on had determined his course. Bush and his national security advisor, Brent Scowcroft, "created a rigid decisionmaking hierarchy, designed to discourage the voicing of ideas that challenged their views." Hence, the process of "groupthink" came to permeate the policymaking environment.

Hybel also examines three different theories from cognitive psychology—attribution theory, cognitive consistency theory, and schema theory—in his effort to understand the decisions Bush made. He notes that Bush relied heavily on two analogies to shape his policy choice and hence to steer his advisers along his preferred path. In particular, the 1938 Munich episode—where the western powers appeased Hitler's expansion into the Sudetenland—proved critical to his thinking. The policy imperative suggested by the analogy was clear: A forceful response to Saddam was necessary ("aggressors cannot be appeased"). A second analogy also loomed large for Bush, namely Vietnam. If force was to be used against Saddam, it had to be overwhelming and decisive, not like the tentative application and calculated escalation of military force believed to have robbed U.S. military forces of victory on the battlefield in that war.

Even as their own cognitive processes were informed by historical analogies, Hybel argues that Bush and Scowcroft believed "that Saddam was a rational calculator, one who never lost sight of the realities of power politics." By relying on the Munich and Vietnam analogies while still maintaining that Saddam Hussein's actions were "rational," Bush and Scowcroft had to strive to minimize the cognitive inconsistency in their views. To do so, Hybel argues, "they excluded from their analysis information and options that might have encouraged questions about their core preconceptions and values." More generally, Hybel's analysis demonstrates that schema theory and cognitive consistency theory can sometimes be treated not as distinct psychological theories of decisionmaking behavior, "but as closely interconnected theoretical frameworks." It also shows that there is a close relationship between the structure of foreign-policymaking processes and the outcomes produced. Rather than encouraging rationality, the Bush system "discouraged the systematic analysis of information and careful appraisal of alternative courses of action."

Analyses of presidents' personalities and their backgrounds in policy decisions are often less dramatic than with Bush's behavior leading to the Persian Gulf War. Yet, analyses of presidential style rooted in personality factors demonstrate their impact across a range of phenomena. Political scientist Alexander George, for example, describes three different approaches presidents have evolved for managing the tasks of mobilizing available information, expertise, and analytical resources for effective policy making they all face: the *formalistic, competitive,* and *collegial* models. What approach a president chooses and how it operates in practice will be shaped by the president's personality: by his cognitive style (analogous to world view), by his sense of efficacy and competence, and by his general orientation to political conflict.[6]

Margaret G. Hermann and Thomas Preston build on these ideas in the concluding chapter of this book. Their essay, "Presidents, Leadership Style, and the Advisory Process," shows how a presidents' leadership styles—their degree of involvement in the policy process, their belief that they can control decision making, and their sensitivity to the political context—will "shape the way specialization, centralization, and coordination are defined in any particular president's administration."

Based on variations in leadership styles, they propose an eightfold typology of presidential advisory systems that encapsulates the kinds of relations we should expect to find between different presidents and their advisers. They then apply their ideas to the advisory systems Presidents Bush and Clinton devised. They hypothesize that Bush would follow two types of advisory systems—one that emphasized "strategizing" with advisers, another that emphasized "consulting" with them—with Bush's sensitivity to the political context an important determinant of which model would apply when. In the case of Clinton, they hypothesize that the president would want an advisory system that permitted him to coordinate the action, a choice driven by his need to be at the center of the policymaking process and his sensitivity to the political context and to the art of the possible. In both instances they conclude that the presidents' actual behavior conforms to expectations. Thus, they show, first, that "differences in leadership style are related to differences in the way the executive branch of government works," and, second, that "how presidents try to deal with institutional constraints is often shaped by who they are."

Notes

1. Graham T. Allison, *Essence of Decision: Explaining the Cuban Missile* (Boston: Little, Brown, 1971). The Allison models have been subjected to considerable criticism over the years, although they continue to be the point of departure for discussing the dynamics of bureaucratic policy making on foreign affairs. For a recent, detailed critique of the models, see Jonathan Bendor and Thomas H. Hammond, "Rethinking Allison's Models," *American Political Science Review* 86 (June 1992): 301–322. For a recent discussion of the Allison models in foreign-policy analysis, and particularly bureaucratic foreign-policy processes, see Deborah J. Gerner, "The Evolution of the Study of Foreign Policy," in Laura Neack, Jeanne A.K. Hey, and Patrick J. Haney, eds., *Foreign Policy Analysis: Continuity and Change in Its Second Generation* (Englewood Cliffs, NJ: Prentice-Hall, Inc., 1995), 17–32.

2. Allison, 145.

3. Allison, 145.

4. It is worth noting that bureaucratic position did not necessarily predict policy position for some individuals in this instance, a source of criticism of this model and thus weakening its explanatory power. Steve Smith explores a similar line of inquiry in his study of the Carter administration's decision in 1980 to launch a military rescue mission, which is reprinted in chapter 20 of this book.

5. Allison, 146.

6. Alexander L. George, *Presidential Decisionmaking in Foreign Policy: The Effective Use of Information and Advice* (Boulder, CO: Westview Press, 1980); and Alexan-

der L. George, "The President and the Management of Foreign Policy: Styles and Models," in Charles W. Kegley, Jr. and Eugene R. Wittkopf, eds., *The Domestic Sources of American Foreign Policy: Insights and Evidence* (New York: St. Martin's, 1988), 107–186.

17

How Could Vietnam Happen?
An Autopsy

James C. Thomson Jr.

As a case study in the making of foreign policy, the Vietnam War will fasci-
nate historians and social scientists for many decades to come. One question
that will certainly be asked: How did men of superior ability, sound training,
and high ideals—American policymakers of the 1960s—create such a costly
and divisive policy?

As one who watched the decision-making process in Washington from 1961
to 1966 under Presidents Kennedy and Johnson, I can suggest a preliminary
answer. I can do so by briefly listing some of the factors that seemed to me to
shape our Vietnam policy during my years as an East Asia specialist at the
State Department and the White House. I shall deal largely with Washington
as I saw or sensed it, and not with Saigon, where I . . . spent but a scant three
days, in the entourage of the vice president, or with other decision centers, the
capitals of interested parties. Nor will I deal with other important parts of the
record: Vietnam's history prior to 1961, for instance, or the overall course of
America's relations with Vietnam.

Yet a first and central ingredient in these years of Vietnam decisions does
involve history. The ingredient was *the legacy of the 1950s*—by which I mean
the so-called "loss of China," the Korean War, and the Far East policy of
Secretary of State Dulles.

This legacy had an institutional by-product for the Kennedy administration:
In 1961 the U.S. government's East Asian establishment was undoubtedly the
most rigid and doctrinaire of Washington's regional divisions in foreign affairs. This was especially true at the Department of State, where the incoming
administration found the Bureau of Far Eastern Affairs the hardest nut to
crack. It was a bureau that had been purged of its best China expertise, and of
far-sighted, dispassionate men, as a result of McCarthyism. Its members were
generally committed to one policy line: the close containment and isolation of

mainland China, the harassment of "neutralist" nations which sought to avoid alignment with either Washington or Peking, and the maintenance of a network of alliances with anticommunist client states on China's periphery.

Another aspect of the legacy was the special vulnerability and sensitivity of the new Democratic administration on Far East policy issues. The memory of the McCarthy era was still very sharp, and Kennedy's margin of victory was too thin. The 1960 Offshore Islands TV debate between Kennedy and Nixon had shown the president-elect the perils of "fresh thinking." The administration was inherently leery of moving too fast on Asia. As a result, the Far East Bureau (now the Bureau of East Asian and Pacific Affairs) was the last one to be overhauled. Not until Averell Harriman was brought in as assistant secretary in December 1961 were significant personnel changes attempted, and it took Harriman several months to make a deep imprint on the bureau because of his necessary preoccupation with the Laos settlement. Once he did so, there was virtually no effort to bring back the purged or exiled East Asia experts.

There were other important by-products of this "legacy of the fifties":

The new administration inherited and somewhat shared a *general perception of China-on-the-march*—a sense of China's vastness, its numbers, its belligerence; a revived sense, perhaps, of the Golden Horde. This was a perception fed by Chinese intervention in the Korean War (an intervention actually based on appallingly bad communications and mutual miscalculation on the part of Washington and Peking; but the careful unraveling of the tragedy, which scholars have accomplished, had not yet become part of the conventional wisdom).

The new administration inherited and briefly accepted *a monolithic conception of the communist bloc.* Despite much earlier predictions and reports by outside analysts, policymakers did not begin to accept the reality and possible finality of the Sino–Soviet split until the first weeks of 1962. The inevitably corrosive impact of competing nationalisms on communism was largely ignored.

The new administration inherited and to some extent shared *the "domino theory" about Asia.* This theory resulted from profound ignorance of Asian history and hence ignorance of the radical differences among Asian nations and societies. It resulted from a blindness to the power and resilience of Asian nationalisms. (It may also have resulted from a subconscious sense that, since "all Asians look alike," all Asian nations will act alike.) As a theory, the domino fallacy was not merely inaccurate but also insulting to Asian nations. . . .

Finally, the legacy of the fifties was apparently compounded by an uneasy sense of a worldwide communist challenge to the new administration after the Bay of Pigs fiasco. A first manifestation was the president's traumatic Vienna meeting with Khrushchev in June 1961; then came the Berlin crisis of the summer. All this created an atmosphere in which President Kennedy undoubtedly felt under special pressure to show his nation's mettle in Vietnam—if the Vietnamese, unlike the people of Laos, were willing to fight.

In general, the legacy of the fifties shaped such early moves of the new administration as the decisions to maintain a high-visibility SEATO (by sending the secretary of state himself instead of some underling to its first meeting in 1961), to back away from diplomatic recognition of Mongolia in the summer of 1961, and, most important, to expand U.S. military assistance to South Vietnam that winter on the basis of the much more tentative Eisenhower commitment. It should be added that the increased commitment to Vietnam was also fueled by a new breed of military strategists and academic social scientists (some of whom had entered the new administration) who had developed theories of counterguerrilla warfare and were eager to see them put to the test. To some, "counterinsurgency" seemed a new panacea for coping with the world's instability.

So much for the legacy and the history. Any new administration inherits both complicated problems and simplistic views of the world. But surely among the policymakers of the Kennedy and Johnson administrations there were men who would warn of the dangers of an open-ended commitment to the Vietnam quagmire?

This raises a central question, at the heart of the policy process: Where were the experts, the doubters, and the dissenters? Were they there at all, and if so, what happened to them?

The answer is complex but instructive.

In the first place, the American government was sorely *lacking in real Vietnam or Indochina expertise*. Originally treated as an adjunct of Embassy Paris, our Saigon embassy and the Vietnam Desk at State were largely staffed from 1954 onward by French-speaking Foreign Service personnel of narrowly European experience. Such diplomats were even more closely restricted than the normal embassy officer—by cast of mind as well as language—to contacts with Vietnam's French-speaking urban elites. For instance, Foreign Service linguists in Portugal are able to speak with the peasantry if they get out of Lisbon and choose to do so; not so the French speakers of Embassy Saigon.

In addition, the *shadow of the "loss of China"* distorted Vietnam reporting. Career officers in the department, and especially those in the field, had not forgotten the fate of their World War II colleagues who wrote in frankness from China and were later pilloried by Senate committees for critical comments on the Chinese Nationalists. Candid reporting on the strengths of the Viet Cong and the weaknesses of the Diem government was inhibited by the memory. It was also inhibited by some higher officials, notably Ambassador Nolting in Saigon, who refused to sign off on such cables.

In due course, to be sure, some Vietnam talent was discovered or developed. But a recurrent and increasingly important factor in the decisionmaking process was the *banishment of real expertise*. Here the underlying cause was the

"closed politics" of policymaking as issues become hot: The more sensitive
the issue, and the higher it rises in the bureaucracy, the more completely the
experts are excluded while the harassed senior generalists take over (that is,
the secretaries, undersecretaries, and presidential assistants). The frantic skim-
ming of briefing papers in the back seats of limousines is no substitute for the
presence of specialists; furthermore, in times of crisis such papers are deemed
"too sensitive" even for review by the specialists. Another underlying cause
of this banishment, as Vietnam became more critical, was the replacement of
the experts, who were generally and increasingly pessimistic, by men described as "can-do guys," loyal and energetic fixers unsoured by expertise. In
early 1965, when I confided my growing policy doubts to an older colleague
on the NSC staff, he assured me that the smartest thing both of us could do
was to "steer clear of the whole Vietnam mess"; the gentleman in question
had the misfortune to be a "can-do guy," however, and [was subsequently]
highly placed in Vietnam, under orders to solve the mess.

Despite the banishment of the experts, internal doubters and dissenters did
indeed appear and persist. Yet as I watched the process, such men were effectively neutralized by a subtle dynamic: *the domestication of dissenters.* Such
"domestication" arose out of a twofold clubbish need: on the one hand, the
dissenter's desire to stay aboard; and on the other hand, the nondissenter's
conscience. Simply stated, dissent, when recognized, was made to feel at
home. On the lowest possible scale of importance, I must confess my own
considerable sense of dignity and acceptance (both vital) when my senior
White House employer would refer to me as his "favorite dove." Far more
significant was the case of the former undersecretary of state, George Ball.
Once Mr. Ball began to express doubts, he was warmly institutionalized: He
was encouraged to become the inhouse devil's advocate on Vietnam. The
upshot was inevitable: The process of escalation allowed for periodic requests
to Mr. Ball to speak his piece; Ball felt good, I assume (he had fought for
righteousness); the others felt good (they had given a full hearing to the dovish
option); and there was minimal unpleasantness. The club remained intact; and
it is of course possible that matters would have gotten worse faster if Mr. Ball
had kept silent, or left before his final departure in the fall of 1966. There was
also, of course, the case of the last institutionalized doubter, Bill Moyers. The
president is said to have greeted his arrival at meetings with an affectionate,
"Well, here comes Mr. Stop-the-Bombing. . . ." Here again the dynamics of
domesticated dissent sustained the relationship for a while.

A related point—and crucial, I suppose, to government at all times—was
the "effectiveness" trap, the trap that keeps men from speaking out, as clearly
or as often as they might, within the government. And it is the trap that keeps
men from resigning in protest and airing their dissent outside the government.
The most important asset that a man brings to bureaucratic life is his "effectiveness," a mysterious combination of training, style, and connections. The

most ominous complaint that can be whispered of a bureaucrat is "I'm afraid Charlie's beginning to lose his effectiveness." To preserve your effectiveness, you must decide where and when to fight the mainstream of policy; the opportunities range from pillow talk with your wife, to private drinks with your friends, to meetings with the secretary of state or the president. The inclination to remain silent or to acquiesce in the presence of the great men—to live to fight another day, to give on this issue so that you can be "effective" on later issues—is overwhelming. Nor is it the tendency of youth alone; some of our most senior officials, men of wealth and fame, whose place in history is secure, have remained silent lest their connection with power be terminated. As for the disinclination to resign in protest: While not necessarily a Washington or even American specialty, it seems more true of a government in which ministers have no parliamentary back-bench to which to retreat. In the absence of such a refuge, it is easy to rationalize the decision to stay aboard. By doing so, one may be able to prevent a few bad things from happening and perhaps even make a few good things happen. To exit is to lose even those marginal chances for "effectiveness."

Another factor must be noted: As the Vietnam controversy escalated at home, there developed *a preoccupation with Vietnam public relations as opposed to Vietnam policymaking.* And here, ironically, internal doubters and dissenters were heavily employed. For such men, by virtue of their own doubts, were often deemed best able to "massage" the doubting intelligentsia. My senior East Asia colleague at the White House, a brilliant and humane doubter who had dealt with Indochina since 1954, spent three-quarters of his working days on Vietnam public relations: drafting presidential responses to letters from important critics, writing conciliatory language for presidential speeches, and meeting quite interminably with delegations of outraged Quakers, clergymen, academics, and housewives. His regular callers were the late A. J. Muste and Norman Thomas; mine were members of the Women's Strike for Peace. Our orders from above: Keep them off the backs of busy policymakers (who usually happened to be nondoubters). Incidentally, my most discouraging assignment in the realm of public relations was the preparation of a White House pamphlet entitled *Why Vietnam,* in September 1965; in a gesture toward my conscience, I fought—and lost—a battle to have the title followed by a question mark.

Through a variety of procedures, both institutional and personal, doubt, dissent, and expertise were effectively neutralized in the making of policy. But what can be said of the men "in charge"? It is patently absurd to suggest that they produced such tragedy by intention and calculation. But it is neither absurd nor difficult to discern certain forces at work that caused decent and honorable men to do great harm.

Here I would stress the paramount role of *executive fatigue.* No factor seems to me more crucial and underrated in the making of foreign policy. The physical and emotional toll of executive responsibility in State, the Pentagon, the White House, and other executive agencies is enormous; that toll is of course compounded by extended service. Many . . . Vietnam policymakers [had] been on the job for from four to seven years. Complaints may be few, and physical health may remain unimpaired, though emotional health is far harder to gauge. But what is most seriously eroded in the deadening process of fatigue is freshness of thought, imagination, a sense of possibility, a sense of priorities and perspective—those rare assets of a new administration in its first year or two of office. The tired policymaker becomes a prisoner of his own narrowed view of the world and his own clichéd rhetoric. He becomes irritable and defensive—short on sleep, short on family ties, short on patience. Such men make bad policy and then compound it. They have neither the time nor the temperament for new ideas or preventive diplomacy.

Below the level of the fatigued executives in the making of Vietnam policy was a widespread phenomenon: *the curator mentality* in the Department of State. By this I mean the collective inertia produced by the bureaucrat's view of his job. At State, the average "desk officer" inherits from his predecessor our policy toward Country X; he regards it as his function to keep that policy intact—under glass, untampered with, and dusted—so that he may pass it on in two to four years to his successor. And such curatorial service generally merits promotion within the system. (Maintain the status quo, and you will stay out of trouble.) In some circumstances, the inertia bred by such an outlook can act as a brake against rash innovation. But on many issues, this inertia sustains the momentum of bad policy and unwise commitments—momentum that might otherwise have been resisted within the ranks. Clearly, Vietnam [was] such an issue.

To fatigue and inertia must be added the factor of internal confusion. Even among the "architects" of our Vietnam commitment, there [was] persistent *confusion as to what type of war we were fighting* and, as a direct consequence, *confusion as to how to end that war.* (The "credibility gap" [was], in part, a reflection of such internal confusion.) Was it, for instance, a civil war, in which case counterinsurgency might suffice? Or was it a war of international aggression? (This might invoke SEATO or UN commitment.) Who was the aggressor—and the "real enemy"? The Viet Cong? Hanoi? Peking? Moscow? International communism? Or maybe "Asian communism"? Differing enemies dictated differing strategies and tactics. And confused throughout, in like fashion, was the question of American objectives; your objectives depended on whom you were fighting and why. I shall not forget my assignment from an assistant secret. y of state in March 1964: to draft a speech for Secretary McNamara which would, inter alia, once and for all dispose of the canard that the Vietnam conflict was a civil war. "But in some ways, of course," I mused, "it *is* a civil war." "Don't play word games with me!" snapped the assistant secretary.

Similar confusion beset the concept of "negotiations"—anathema to much of official Washington from 1961 to 1965. Not until April 1965 did "unconditional discussions" become respectable, via a presidential speech; even then the secretary of state stressed privately to newsmen that nothing had changed, since "discussions" were by no means the same as "negotiations." Months later that issue was resolved. But it took even longer to obtain a fragile internal agreement that negotiations might include the Viet Cong as something other than an appendage to Hanoi's delegation. Given such confusion as to the whos and whys of our Vietnam commitment, it is not surprising, as Theodore Draper has written, that policymakers [found] it so difficult to agree on how to end the war.

Of course, one force—a constant in the vortex of commitment—was that of *wishful thinking*. I partook of it myself at many times. I did so especially during Washington's struggle with Diem in the autumn of 1963 when some of us at State believed that for once, in dealing with a difficult client state, the U.S. government could use the leverage of our economic and military assistance to make good things happen, instead of being led around by the nose by [foreign dictators]. If we could prove that point, I thought, and move into a new day, with or without Diem, then Vietnam was well worth the effort. Later came the wishful thinking of the air-strike planners in the late autumn of 1964; there were those who actually thought that after six weeks of air strikes, the North Vietnamese would come crawling to us to ask for peace talks. And what, someone asked in one of the meetings of the time, if they don't? The answer was that we would bomb for another four weeks, and that would do the trick. And a few weeks later came one instance of wishful thinking that was symptomatic of good men misled: In January 1965, I encountered one of the very highest figures in the administration at a dinner, drew him aside, and told him of my worries about the air-strike option. He told me that I really shouldn't worry; it was his conviction that before any such plans could be put into effect, a neutralist government would come to power in Saigon that would politely invite us out. And finally, there was the recurrent wishful thinking that sustained many of us through the trying months of 1965–1966 after the air strikes had begun: that surely, somehow, one way or another, we would "be in a conference in six months," and the escalatory spiral would be suspended. The basis of our hope: "It simply can't go on."

As a further influence on policymakers I would cite the factor of *bureaucratic detachment*. By this I mean what at best might be termed the professional callousness of the surgeon (and indeed, medical lingo—the "surgical strike" for instance—seemed to crop up in the euphemisms of the times). In Washington the semantics of the military muted the reality of war for the civilian policymakers. In quiet, air-conditioned, thick-carpeted rooms, such terms as "systematic pressure," "armed reconnaissance," "targets of opportunity," and even "body count" seemed to breed a sort of games-theory detachment. Most memorable to me was a moment in the late 1964 target planning when the question under discussion was how heavy our bombing should be, and how extensive our strafing, at some midpoint in the projected pattern of systematic pressure. An assistant secretary of state resolved the point in the following words: "It seems to me that our orchestration should be mainly violins, but with periodic touches of brass." Perhaps the biggest shock of my return to Cambridge, Massachusetts, was the realization that the young men, the flesh and blood I taught and saw on these university streets, were potentially some of the numbers on the charts of those faraway planners. In a curious sense, Cambridge [was] closer to this war than Washington.

There is an unprovable factor that relates to bureaucratic detachment: the ingredient of *cryptoracism*. I do not mean to imply any conscious contempt for Asian loss of life on the part of Washington officials. But I do mean to imply that bureaucratic detachment may well be compounded by a traditional Western sense that there are so many Asians, after all; that Asians have a fatalism about life and a disregard for its loss; that they are cruel and barbaric to their own people; and that they are very different from us (and all look alike?). And I *do* mean to imply that the upshot of such subliminal views is a subliminal question whether Asians, and particularly Asian peasants, and most particularly Asian communists, are really people—like you and me. To put the matter another way: Would we have pursued quite such policies—and quite such military tactics—if the Vietnamese were white?

It is impossible to write of Vietnam decision making without writing about language. Throughout the conflict, words [were] of paramount importance. I refer here to the impact of *rhetorical escalation* and to the *problem of oversell*. In an important sense, Vietnam [became] of crucial significance to us *because we . . . said that it [was] of crucial significance*. (The issue obviously relates to the public relations preoccupation described earlier.)

The key here is domestic politics: the need to sell the American people, press, and Congress on support for an unpopular and costly war in which the objectives themselves [were] in flux. To sell means to persuade, and to persuade means rhetoric. As the difficulties and costs . . . mounted, so [did] the definition of the stakes. This is not to say that rhetorical escalation is an orderly process; executive prose is the product of many writers, and some concepts—North Vietnamese infiltration, America's "national honor," Red China as the chief enemy— . . . entered the rhetoric only gradually and even sporadically. But there [was] an upward spiral nonetheless. And once you have *said* that the American Experiment itself stands or falls on the Vietnam outcome, you have thereby created a national stake far beyond any earlier stakes.

Crucial throughout the process of Vietnam decision making was a conviction among many policymakers: that Vietnam posed a *fundamental test of America's national will*. Time and again I was told by men reared in the tradition of Henry L. Stimson that all we needed was the will, and we would then prevail. Implicit in such a view, it seemed to me, was a curious assumption that Asians lacked will, or at least that in a contest between Asian and Anglo-Saxon wills, the non-Asians must prevail. A corollary to the persistent belief in will was a *fascination with power* and an awe in the face of the power America possessed as no nation or civilization ever before. Those who doubted our role in Vietnam were said to shrink from the burdens of power, the obligations of power, the uses of power, the responsibility of power. By implication, such men were soft-headed and effete.

Finally, no discussion of the factors and forces at work on Vietnam policy-makers can ignore the central fact of *human ego investment.* Men who have participated in a decision develop a stake in that decision. As they participate in further, related decisions, their stake increases. It might have been possible to dissuade a man of strong self-confidence at an early stage of the ladder of decision; but it is infinitely harder at later stages since a change of mind there usually involves implicit or explicit repudiation of a chain of previous decisions.

To put it bluntly: At the heart of the Vietnam calamity [was] a group of able, dedicated men who [were] regularly and repeatedly wrong—and whose standing with their contemporaries, and more important, with history, depended, as they [saw] it, on being proven right. These [were] not men who [could] be asked to extricate themselves from error.

The various ingredients I have cited in the making of Vietnam policy . . . created a variety of results, most of them fairly obvious. Here are some that seem to me most central:

Throughout the conflict, there [was] *persistent and repeated miscalculation* by virtually all the actors, in high echelons and low, whether dove, hawk, or something else. To cite one simple example among many: In late 1964 and early 1965, some peace-seeking planners at State who strongly opposed the projected bombing of the North urged that, instead, American ground forces be sent to South Vietnam; this would, they said, increase our bargaining leverage against the North—our "chips"—and would give us something to negotiate about (the withdrawal of our forces) at an early peace conference. Simultaneously, the air-strike option was urged by many in the military who were dead set against American participation in "another land war in Asia"; they were joined by other civilian peace-seekers who wanted to bomb Hanoi into early negotiations. By late 1965, we had ended up with the worst of all worlds: ineffective and costly air strikes against the North, spiraling ground forces in the South, and no negotiations in sight.

Throughout the conflict as well, there [was] *a steady give-in to pressures for a military solution* and only minimal and sporadic efforts at a diplomatic and political solution. In part this resulted from the confusion (earlier cited) among the civilians—confusion regarding objectives and strategy. And in part this resulted from the self-enlarging nature of military investment. Once air strikes and particularly ground forces were introduced, our investment itself had transformed the original stakes. More air power was needed to protect the ground forces; and then more ground forces to protect the ground forces. And needless to say, the military mind develops its own momentum in the absence of clear guidelines from the civilians. Once asked to save South Vietnam, rather than to "advise" it, the American military could not but press for escalation. In addition, sad to report, assorted military constituencies, once involved in Vietnam, . . . had a series of cases to prove: for instance, the utility not only of air power (the Air Force) but of supercarrier-based air power (the Navy). Also, Vietnam policy . . . suffered from one ironic by-product of Secretary McNamara's establishment of civilian control at the Pentagon: In the face of such control, interservice rivalry [gave] way to a united front among the military—reflected in the new but recurrent phenomenon of JCS unanimity. In conjunction with traditional congressional allies (mostly Southern senators and representatives) such a united front would pose a formidable problem for any president.

Throughout the conflict, there [were] *missed opportunities, large and small, to disengage ourselves from Vietnam on increasingly unpleasant but still acceptable terms.* Of the many moments from 1961 onward, I shall cite only one, the last and most important opportunity that was lost: In the summer of 1964 the president instructed his chief advisers to prepare for him as wide a range of Vietnam options as possible for postelection consideration and decision. He explicitly asked that all options be laid out. What happened next was, in effect, Lyndon Johnson's slow-motion Bay of Pigs. For the advisers so effectively converged on one single option—juxtaposed against two other, phony options (in effect, blowing up the world, or scuttle-and-run)—that the president was confronted with unanimity for bombing the North from all his trusted counselors. Had he been more confident in foreign affairs, had he been deeply informed on Vietnam and Southeast Asia, and had he raised some hard questions that unanimity had submerged, this president could have used the largest electoral mandate in history to deescalate in Vietnam, in the clear expectation that at the worst a neutralist government would come to power in Saigon and politely invite us out. . . .

In the course of these years, another result of Vietnam decision making [was] *the abuse and distortion of history.* Vietnamese, Southeast Asian, and Far Eastern history [was] rewritten by our policymakers, and their spokesmen, to conform with the alleged necessity of our presence in Vietnam. Highly dubious analogies from our experience elsewhere—the "Munich" sellout and "containment" from Europe, the Malayan insurgency and the Korean War from Asia—[were] imported in order to justify our actions. And [later] events [were] fitted to the Procrustean bed of Vietnam. Most notably, the change of power in Indonesia in 1965–1966 has been ascribed to our Vietnam presence; and virtually all progress in the Pacific region—the rise of regionalism, new forms of cooperation, and mounting growth rates—has been similarly explained. The Indonesian allegation is undoubtedly false (I tried to prove it, during six months of careful investigation at the White House, and had to confess failure); the regional allegation is patently unprovable in either direction (except, of course, for the clear fact that the economies of both Japan and Korea . . . profited enormously from our Vietnam-related procurement in these countries; but that is a costly and highly dubious form of foreign aid).

There is a final result of Vietnam policy I would cite that holds potential danger for the future of American foreign policy: *the rise of a new breed of American ideologues who saw Vietnam as the ultimate test of their doctrine.* I have in mind those men in Washington who have given a new life to the missionary impulse in American foreign relations: who believe that this nation, in this era, has received a threefold endowment that can transform the world. As they see it, that endowment is composed of, first, our unsurpassed miliary might; second, our clear technological supremacy; and third, our allegedly invincible benevolence (our "altruism," our affluence, our lack of territorial aspirations). Together, it is argued, this threefold endowment provides us with the opportunity and the obligation to ease the nations of the earth toward modernization and stability: toward a full-fledged *Pax Americana Technocratica.* In reaching toward this goal, Vietnam [was] viewed as the last and crucial test. Once we . . . succeeded there, the road ahead [was seen to be] clear. . . .

Long before I went into government, I was told a story about Henry L. Stimson that seemed to me pertinent during the years that I watched the Vietnam tragedy unfold—and participated in that tragedy. It seems to me more pertinent than ever. . . .

In his waning years Stimson was asked by an anxious questioner, "Mr. Secretary, how on earth can we ever bring peace to the world?" Stimson is said to have answered: "You begin by bringing to Washington a small handful of able men who believe that the achievement of peace is possible.

"You work them to the bone until they no longer believe that it is possible.

"And then you throw them out—and bring in a new bunch who believe that it is possible."

18

Tribal Tongues: Intelligence Consumers, Intelligence Producers

Mark M. Lowenthal

In the aftermath of the Cold War and the Gulf War there has been much soul-searching in the executive and Congress concerning the organization and role of the intelligence community: How should it be organized? Which issues should it be covering? What are the emerging issues that should be addressed now? These are of course important questions. But they tend to bypass more fundamental issues within the intelligence community that are of a more per-manent—and thus, perhaps—more important nature because they deal with how the community functions and fulfills its role on a daily basis. One of these is the relationship between the intelligence consumers and the intelligence producers.

Most analyses of the U.S. intelligence process pay lip service to the con-sumer–producer relationship. Although occasional serious forays on the sub-ject exist, such as Thomas Hughes's *The Fate of Facts in the World of Men,*[1] most either ignore or downplay the importance of this relationship as a sig-nificant shaper of intelligence *throughout* the so-called intelligence process, starting with collection and ending with its final consumption.

A major problem is that the consumer–producer relationship resembles that of two closely related tribes that believe, mistakenly, that they speak the same language and work in the same manner for agreed outcomes. Reality, when viewed from either perspective, suggests something wholly different. Indeed, one is often reminded of George Bernard Shaw's quip about Britons and Americans being divided by a common tongue.

We All Want the Same Thing

Most policymakers (i.e., consumers) work on the assumption of basic support throughout the government for their various policy initiatives, including sup-

---

Note: Some notes have been deleted or renumbered.

port by the intelligence community. The first problem lies in the very word *support*. For policymakers, this means a shared and active interest and, if necessary, advocacy. This runs counter, however, to the intelligence community's long-standing position not to advocate any policy. Rather, the intelligence community tends to see itself, correctly or not, as a value-free service agency, although at its upper levels the line begins to blur.

Second, the intelligence community, like all other parts of the permanent government bureaucracy, has a "we/they" view of its political masters. The intelligence community is part of the *permanent* government; those making policy are politically driven *transients,* even when nominated from within the professional ranks of agencies. Indeed, with the exception of the uniformed military, nowhere else in the entire foreign policy and defense apparatus can there be found as many career officials at such senior levels as in the intelligence community. They can sometimes be found at the level equivalent to deputy secretary and clearly predominate at and below the level equivalent to assistant secretary.

Compounding this professional versus political, "we/they" conflict is the fact that consumers can and do advocate policy initiatives that run athwart intelligence community preferences. For example, the political demands for visibly intrusive arms-control monitoring methods, regardless of their minimal contribution to verification, pose real dangers for counterintelligence. The need to go public with information in order to justify policy initiatives or to brief foreign officials in order to build international support for policies often poses dangers to intelligence sources and methods. Such confrontations must often be resolved at the cabinet level and, although there will be some cutting and pasting to accommodate intelligence concerns, the overall policy will generally prevail. This is as it should be within the U.S. system of government. At the same time, it deepens the "we/they" syndrome.

Finally, the two groups have very different interests at stake. A successful policy is what the consumers were hired to create and execute. The intelligence community's reputation, however, rests less on the success of any policy than on its ability to assist in the formation of that policy and to predict potential outcomes—both good and bad. The producers are only vulnerable if the policy is perceived as failing because the intelligence support was in some way lacking. Ironically, the intelligence community is rarely given credit if the policy succeeds. In part, this is a self-fulfilling outcome given the distance the producers cultivate from the process; in part, it is the natural bureaucratic phenomenon of scrambling for honors.

The Value of a Free Commodity: Priceless or Worthless?

Intelligence products arrive in the consumers' limousines, pouches, and in-boxes every morning and evening. They are part of the established routine.

These products are, for their readers, basically cost-free subscriptions that were never ordered and never have to be paid for, perks of the job. High-level policy consumers have no real sense of either budgetary or mission/manpower cost to their departments or agencies for the very existence of these products, even if some of the products come from entities that they control. Thus, the secretary of defense will rarely be faced with a significant trade-off between required intelligence programs for the Defense Intelligence Agency and the National Security Agency versus next year's weapons procurement, nor will the secretary of state have to juggle the Bureau of Intelligence and Research's budget against prospective embassy closings.

Intelligence production, for the consumers, exists somewhere beyond their ken, as if unseen gnomes labor to produce the papers that magically arrive. If the analyses are good, all the better; if they are not, consumers are unlikely to advocate redirecting some of their resources to improving them.

Moreover, the very regularity with which these products appear has a lulling effect. The standard items—the *National Intelligence Daily,* the *Secretary's Morning Summary*—are essentially newspapers. Anyone who has read yesterday's edition or watched last night's 11:00 P.M. news can predict what is likely to be covered in this morning's edition. Indeed, while these publications are all lumped together as part of the "current intelligence" emphasis of the intelligence community, in reality they represent items that can safely be given to customers the next day. They are not urgent warnings or long-awaited breakthroughs, items that scream "read me now." Rather, they are part of the daily routine.

To break through this lulling effect, intelligence has to be able to prove to its consumers that it brings "value added" to the steady drone of information, analysis, and opinion that comes from both within and beyond the intelligence community. But one bureau or agency's memo looks much like another's, unless you bother to read them and assess them. How do you assure that, if only one will be read, it's yours? In reality, the unstated value added that intelligence producers bring is their sources. But, for very good reasons, raw intelligence is rarely presented to consumers. The intelligence is given context and comment, analysis that again makes it look like everyone else's.

How does the producer break out of this trap? One way is simply packaging, designing products that *do* scream for attention when there is a truly important piece of intelligence or a fast-breaking event about which the producers know first. The second is establishing a track record, although this still depends on whether the consumer reads intelligence analyses and remembers who was right and who was wrong.

In the end, consumers incur no real and regular penalty for ignoring this daily flow of information. In managing their day, high-level consumers establish methods to cut down on reading extraneous material. At the very highest levels, a large portion of daily intelligence products probably falls into this category. These consumers assume that their subordinates will read what they must within their areas of responsibility and that truly urgent items will come to their attention.

Consumer Behaviors that Matter

In reality, the intelligence consumer does more than just consume. He or she is not some eager, expectant eye and mind waiting at the end of the intelligence process. The consumer helps set the agenda, from intelligence priorities, to collection, to format.

Agenda

Consumers have their own sets of priorities and preferences, issues in which they are deeply interested, those in which they must take an interest by their nature, and those they would just as soon ignore. If they bother to communicate these preferences to the intelligence producers (a rare enough occurrence), and the producers respond accordingly, then the entire intelligence process has already been influenced. Although producers will not cease to try to cover all the issues that *they* believe are important, only those intelligence officers with a taste for abuse and a desire to be ignored will try to force these on an unwilling consumer. This can put producers in an awkward position, especially if the subject in question is one they feel quite strongly deserves attention. It can also run athwart the intelligence community's "warning function," namely, the requirement that it look ahead for issues—especially sleepers—that have the potential to become grave concerns.

Collection

The most senior consumer, the president, can also determine what gets collected and what does not for reasons of policy beyond the preferences of the intelligence producers. The U.S. policy in the shah's Iran of having no contact with the mullahs,[2] or President Jimmy Carter's termination of U-2 flights over Cuba, both come to mind.

"What Don't I Know?"

To the producer, the ideal consumer is one who knows what he doesn't know. Unfortunately, this quality can be hard to come by. It is understandable that senior officials dislike admitting areas of ignorance within their fields of responsibility. Those who do, however, have a clear advantage, especially if they are wiling to take steps, among them requested analyses and briefings, to remedy the situation. Similarly, it is important for the consumers to distinguish between what they must know, what they'd like to know, and what is simply enjoyable but unnecessary. Failure to do this well, and continually, can lead to one of two traps—either consuming too much time on some subjects or too little on others. Given the primacy of time management, this should be a crucial skill for the harried consumer. Once this skill is acquired, and its results communicated to the producers, it again establishes priorities and agendas.

Dealing with Uncertainty

Neither producers nor consumers like intelligence gaps. At best they are annoying; at worst they can be both crucial and frightening. They do exist, however, and are often responsible for uncertainties in estimates and analyses. As strange as it may seem, such uncertainties appear to be very difficult to convey, at least in English. "If/then" constructions can become long laundry lists covering all the possibilities, without regard to likelihood; "on the one hand/on the other hand" often creates octopuses of sentences—too many hands spoil the analyses. The absence of an easily used subjunctive really hurts.

Unfortunately, consumers often interpret these very real problems of limited sources and uncertain outcomes as pusillanimity on the part of producers. "They have a best guess," consumers suppose, "they're just hedging so they won't be wrong." The inability on the part of producers to convey adequately the cause and nature of uncertainty and ambiguity tends to alienate a largely dubious audience.

"Shooting the Messenger"

This consumer behavior is as old as recorded history—if the messenger brings bad news, kill him. Unfortunately, it still happens. The messenger is not killed; he is first berated and then, on subsequent occasions, ignored. In part this consumer behavior stems from the darker side of the "we-all-want-the-same-thing" syndrome. Once consumers have figured out that they and their intelligence people do *not* all necessarily want the same thing, they become suspicious of the producers. Do they have their own agenda for their own dark reasons? If they are not actively supporting me, are they working against me? Unfortunately, the delivery of "bad news," usually some piece of intelligence or an analysis that questions preferred or ongoing policies, fits this more paranoid view all too well.[3]

What, however, is the producer's alternative? Suppress the intelligence and risk having the consumer blind-sided or even badly embarrassed, a sure blow to credibility? Better to err on the side of caution and risk opprobrium, knowing full well that this, too, can harm credibility. Either way, the outcome largely rests on the intelligence's reception by the consumers, on their maturity, experience, and willingness to be challenged by people who are not a threat to their policies.

The Consumer as Analyst

Consumers are, by and large, a self-confident group. They have achieved fairly exalted and responsible positions through either the trial by fire of long professional careers or through the hurly-burly of private enterprise or partisan politics. No matter the route, they assume that it is not just connections and luck that have brought them to their current positions. This self-assurance is all to the good, although it can lead to some aberrant behavior.

The first such behavior has to do with issues of long standing regarding which the consumer believes that he or she knows as much, if not more, than the intelligence analysts. Certainly, assistant secretaries of state for Europe, the Near East, and so on, are likely to have spent a large portion of their professional careers on these issues, and they probably know some of the key players in the region on a personal basis. Interestingly, the same perception eventually [took] hold of senior officials [who dealt] with Soviet issues, regardless of their previous experience. At least two factors [were] at work here. First, the long-standing nature of the U.S. rivalry with the Soviets [lent] an air of familiarity, whether deserved or not. Second, after about two years in office, the average secretary of state [had] met with his Soviet counterpart more than half a dozen times and probably [felt] he [had] greater insight into Soviet thinking than [did] "ivory tower" analysts who [had] only seen the Soviet Union from 150 miles up.[4] The [end of the Cold War] may have tempered the first attitude, now that the familiar signposts of relations have gone. This probably results, however, in increased emphasis on the second attitude, the value of high-level, face-to-face contacts over analysis by those more remote from events.

For this type of reaction the "value-added" question becomes paramount. What can the producer bring to the issue that is new, insightful, and useful? Here, the natural inclination, if not necessity, to hedge analyses works against the producer and only serves to reinforce the prejudice of the consumer.

The second "consumer-as-analyst" behavior manifests itself during those periods of intense activity usually misnamed crises. Suddenly, the premium for current intelligence rises dramatically; consumers will often cry out for the "raw intelligence." There is the sudden assumption that at moments like these, trained intelligence analysts will somehow get in the way, that they will, perhaps inadvertently, distort the incoming information. Ideally, the intelligence officers should resist, offering to come back in several minutes with some sort of analysis or context along with the raw intelligence. Quite simply, consumers are probably less well suited at these moments to serve as their own analysts. Their ability to assess objectively and dispassionately what is happening is usually inverse to the importance of the issue, its intensity, and the amount of time they have been dealing with it. This is not to say that consumers have nothing of analytical value to bring to the process, including during crises. They should not, however, act to cut off the contributions of professional expertise. At worst, they will get an alternative point of view that they are always free to reject.

The Assumption of Omniscience

For the United States as a global power, it is difficult to find many issues or regions that are not of at least some minimal interest. For the consumer this translates into the erroneous assumption that somewhere in the labyrinths of the intelligence community there is at least one analyst capable of covering each issue that comes along.

The source of this assumption is most likely a conceit derived from the expectation that U.S. interests must be matched by U.S. capabilities, that intelligence managers must know that *all* bases should be covered. Interestingly, this runs counter to the often-heard criticism (and accepted folk wisdom) that the intelligence community has traditionally spent too much time and effort on the Soviet target, to the disadvantage of less sexy albeit no less important issues.

Unfortunately, there is no safe way for the producers to correct the assumption of omniscience. The intelligence community is loath to admit that it is not true and is fearful of the criticism that will ensue if this is discovered. Yet, in a world of unlimited issues and limited intelligence resources, gaps are unavoidable. How resources are allotted either to close or to allow gaps remains a murky process based on past experience and known or—more likely—perceived consumer interest. Too often this process degenerates into a debate over the size of the intelligence budget, raising the suspicion among consumers (and congressional overseers) that cries of insufficient coverage are in reality pleas for more resources that will be redirected to areas that the intelligence community sees fit. Were the producers, however, to address the issue forthrightly and ask consumers, say down to the assistant secretary level, for a list of issues that had to be covered and those that could be given shorter shrift, it is unlikely that they would get consensus. Here again the "free commodity" issue is at work, only now consumers would be asked to give up something that they had always received, even if they had never had any great use for it.

Inevitably, one of the issues that has long been considered below the threshold will suddenly require attention. With a little luck there may be an analyst somewhere who has at least passing familiarity with it. This is the moment when the producers hope to shine, to prove the "value added" they bring to the process. If they succeed, however, they also reinforce the omniscience assumption, which sooner or later will be found, painfully, to be false.

The Absence of Feedback

Intelligence consumers have neither the time nor the inclination to offer much feedback on what they are getting or not getting. This stems from several sources. First, the throwing of bouquets is not a habit in government nor should it be expected.[5] Second, there is rarely enough time. As soon as one problem is solved or crisis ended, it is time to move on to the next. But the absence of feedback enforces the producers' image of top consumers as "black holes," into which intelligence is drawn without any sense of the reception or effect. The result is to deny the producers any guidance as to how they are doing.

At the same time, it must be admitted that, despite calls on their part for feedback, many in the intelligence community are quite content with the status quo. They do not favor "report cards"; they fear that they will only hear the negative and not receive any praise; they are concerned lest feedback becomes a means by which consumers would try to affect the content of intelligence to elicit greater support for policies. None of this needs to happen if the feedback process is honest and regularized.

There also would be genuine benefits. The intelligence community is made up of analysts who largely enjoy their work and who believe, as individuals, that the issues they cover are worthy of attention. At the working level, however, they exist in relative isolation, without any reference point as to how well their work fulfills its purported purposes among the consumers. Analysts will continue to work on what they believe to be relevant and important unless or until consumers offer guidance as to preferences, needs, and style. In short, producers need to be told how best to shape their products and focus for the consumers, but the initiative for doing so remains with the consumers.[6]

Feedback is also an area where Congress, in its oversight role, can be helpful. Congress has, in the past, reviewed important policy issues for which intelligence was a major factor and has offered objective assessments of the quality of intelligence and the uses to which it was put by consumers. The Senate Select Committee on Intelligence, for example, offered a critique of the famous Team A–Team B competitive Soviet analysis and called the exercise worthwhile but flawed in its execution. This same committee also found that President Jimmy Carter's release of Central Intelligence Agency analysis of Soviet oil prospects was largely driven by his own political needs. Similarly, the House Permanent Select Committee on Intelligence offered a scathing review of intelligence on Iran prior to the fall of the shah. The same committee's review of intelligence prior to the Mariel exodus from Cuba concluded that U.S. surprise on that occasion was not due to lack of intelligence warnings.

Such a service is quite useful and can be done by Congress objectively and without partisan rancor. However, the two Select Committees on Intelligence also have limits on their time and cannot provide this sort of review regularly. Congress is an intelligence consumer as well, although it is not privy to the full extent of the analyses that flow to policymakers in the executive. Thus, Congress can supplement feedback from consumers but cannot fully substitute for it.

Producer Behaviors that Matter

Just as the consumer does more than consume, the producers do more than simply collect, analyze, and produce. Their behavior also affects the product and the perceptions held by the consumers.

Current versus Long-Term Intelligence

All intelligence agencies, managers, and analysts are constantly tugged between the need for current intelligence and the desire to write long-term intelligence. Thomas Hughes portrayed the struggle as one of "intelligence butchers" (current intelligence, done in short, sharp chops of material) versus "intelligence bakers" (long-term intelligence, done in prolonged melding and blending). As cute as Hughes's model is, it gives the mistaken impression that the choice of which type of intelligence to emphasize lies with the producers. This tends not to be so. Rather, it is the very nature of how foreign and defense policy is handled by consumers that drives the choice. Intelligence producers claim not to be bothered by this consumer preference for current intelligence, but this too is not entirely correct.

Current intelligence (i.e., tonight, tomorrow, this week) will always dominate. That is the very nature of the U.S. policy process. It is very "now" oriented, creating a series of difficult choices among issues all crying for attention. Indeed, there is very little sense of completion, because each issue laid to rest has too many successors waiting for attention as well. The drive of current events even tends to distort the notion of "long-term" analysis, which becomes the next ministerial meeting, the next arms-control round, the next summit, next year's budget process at best.

Much lip service is given by both producers and consumers to the need for long-term intelligence. Yet nothing in their daily lives indicates what use they would make of such intelligence if it existed. For consumers it would represent luxury items, things to be read when or if the press of current business allowed. For producers it would mean just a chance to be more wrong at a greater distance from the events—a constant concern.

Some will argue that the intelligence community already produces long-term analyses in the form of the National Intelligence Estimates (NIEs). But what is the function of the NIEs? In theory they represent the best judgment of the entire intelligence community on major issues, as conveyed by the director of central intelligence to the president. Some NIEs are done at the request of consumers, most often a fast-track or Special NIE (SNIE, pronounced "snee"). Other NIEs are done at the suggestion of an intelligence organization or are initiated by national intelligence officers, who perceive a need among consumers.

But beyond their impressive name and theoretical status, do NIEs really influence long-term policies? Or are they, in the scathing words of the House Permanent Select Committee on Intelligence, "not worth fighting for"? It is difficult to find many NIEs that have substantially influenced ongoing policy debates. Various intelligence agencies participate earnestly in the NIE game largely to keep track of their brethren and to preserve their own points of view. NIEs are important simply because they exist and not because of any great value that they regularly add to the process. More often they serve either as databases for budget justifications (in the case of the annual NIE on Soviet programs) or as the source of self-serving and often misleading quotations for use by consumers during policy debates.

Although both producers and consumers constantly cry out for more long-term and less current intelligence, it remains unclear that the outcry has any substance beyond a general and unsubstantiated belief that, if it were produced, long-term intelligence would give greater coherence to policy.

Portraying Uncertainty

One of the most difficult problems that producers face on a daily basis is the need to portray uncertainty. Every issue that is analyzed has gaps, unknown areas, competing plausible outcomes. As much as producers would like to be able to predict with finality, they both know that it is rarely possible and tend to write so as to cover, at least minimally, less likely outcomes so as not to be entirely wrong.

Portraying this in writing can be difficult. In the absence of a widely used subjunctive tense, producers use other techniques: "perhaps, although, however, on the one hand/on the other hand, maybe." There is nothing intrinsically wrong with any of these, although their net effect can be harmful for several reasons.

First, their use becomes habitual, creating written safety nets that allow the producers to keep all their bets covered. Second, and perhaps more important, they strike the consumer, especially with repetition, as "weasel words," efforts by the producers to avoid coming down on one side or another of any issue.

Producers do not spend enough time or effort explaining why these uncertainties remain. Consumers, being thus uninformed, tend to revert to their omniscience syndrome and see pusillanimity instead.

The Perceived Penalty for Changing Estimates

Producers do not like to be wrong, but they realize they are fallible. They also, however, do not like having to make changes in estimates, fearful of the cost to their credibility with the consumers. Wide swings are especially anathema; better to adjust one's estimates gradually, to bring the consumers along slowly to the new view. Thus, if for years the estimate has said "*T* is most likely," and producers now believe that "*Z* is most likely," few will want to jump directly from *T* to *Z*. Instead, they would rather move slowly through *U, V, W, X,* and *Y,* preparing the consumer for the idea that *Z* is now correct.

In this case, the perception may be worse than the reality. Most consumers, if properly prepared as to why there is a change (new data, new sources, new models, and so on), are likely to accept it unless changes become so regular a phenomenon as to raise serious questions.[7] Again, it is largely an issue of communications, of adequately explaining the uncertainties inherent in any estimate and the factors that have led to the change. Unfortunately, the outcome is so dreaded that the process rarely takes place.

Miracles versus Saints

One of the necessary premiums put on all intelligence writing (with the exception of some NIEs) is brevity. Less is more when dealing with overly busy readers. Unfortunately, this runs counter to the desire burning within nearly every analyst to tell as much of the story as possible, to give the reader background, context and, in part, to show off. (For example: "You can't really understand the FMLN insurgency in El Salvador unless you go back to the Spanish land grants of the sixteenth century." A plausible point, but not an analysis that any busy reader is likely to read.)

Analysts tend not to err on the side of brevity. It becomes, therefore, the task of the intelligence production managers to edit material down to a suitable length. Analysts must be admonished to "just tell the miracles, and not the lives of all the saints involved in making them happen."

The miracles versus saints problem, however, also poses a difficult managerial decision. Analysts cannot write about the miracles with any facility until they have mastered the lives of the saints. Managers therefore have to be flexible enough to allow their analysts the time to study and even to write about the saints, if only for use in background papers sent to other analysts. But this time must not be allowed to conflict with ongoing demands for written products, including those about the very miracles in question. It's a tough call, but one that has a payoff later on.

Jaded versus Naive

Given a choice between appearing jaded or naive on a given subject, the average intelligence professional will choose to appear jaded at least nine times out of ten. No one wants to appear to be the new kid on the block. Instead, analysts act as though they have seen it all and done it all before. This is especially troublesome in group meetings with peers, where appearances matter.

What this means, in terms of analysis, is that few situations are treated as being truly new, regardless of their nature. But some situations *are* new or different and do require analysis that has not been done before. A nuclear power plant blows up catastrophically; the Chinese sell intermediate-range ballistic missiles; or the Soviet Union allows its Eastern European satellites to remove their communist governments. By taking the jaded approach analysts force themselves, first of all, to play catch-up to situations that are ongoing, having initially wasted time playing them down. Moreover, they allow themselves to appear less than perspicacious before their consumers and now must spend time explaining away their previous stance, for which there may be little justification beyond mind-set.

The fix here is apparently simple—approach issues with a more open mind. But how can this be implemented? It cannot be institutionalized or even easily taught. It largely depends on production managers who continually ask skeptical questions, forcing their analysts to rethink. It is not easy, but it is achievable.

"Covering the World"

This is the producers' version of the agenda issue. At most times there will be more issues crying out for attention than resources available to cover them all adequately. Producers, however, do not want to let any one of these issues slip, in part out of concern that they will choose the wrong ones and not be ready if they become more important or if consumer interest is suddenly piqued. Interestingly, this behavior on the part of producers only reinforces the consumers' belief in the intelligence community's omniscience. Feedback from consumers is an essential ingredient in making choices. If this is absent, however, then the intelligence producers must decide, knowing they cannot cover everything. They must also be able to distinguish, which they sometimes do not, between issues genuinely requiring serious attention and those that do not. They may also find, as noted earlier, that there are important issues that consumers do not want to address. Here, the producers are torn, their professional responsibilities and best judgment at odds with the political realities. Overall, producers tend to side with covering more than less.

Reporting "No Change"

Although the intelligence community cannot cover everything, it does keep track of more issues than most of its consumers can or want to deal with. Because of the limits on space in written products and the consumers' time, much goes unreported. But a second filtering process also takes place. On issues that are not "front burner" but are still of some interest, analysts will choose not to report developments or, more significantly, the lack of developments. The absence of activity is taken to mean the absence of any need to report.

There is value, however, to reporting periodically (admittedly at long intervals) on these issues and nondevelopments. If the analysts or managers know that the Ruritanian nuclear program is of interest but that nothing new has happened in the last six months, there is nothing wrong with reporting that to consumers. What is the effect of such a report? First, it shows the consumer that the producers are alert, that they are tracking areas of interest beyond the self-evident. Second, it allows consumers to check off that issue on their mental lists. They can assume, probably correctly, that the producers will alert them to any change. For the moment, they need not worry about it. There is, however, a cost to such reporting, in that it tends to reinforce the consumers' omniscience assumption. Still, the net effect remains a positive one, albeit infrequent.

The Absence of Self-Analysis

This is the flip side of the absence of consumer feedback. Like everyone else in the government, intelligence analysts and officials are busy people. As soon as one crisis ends they move on to the next with very little reflection on what worked and what did not. Nor do they spend much time trying to sort out why certain analyses in certain situations work well and others do not, why warnings and indicators flag proper attention in some cases but not others, why the synergism of collection resources works for this topic or region and not for that.

Admittedly, genuine critical self-examination is difficult. The payoff for having it done more regularly, not by "outside" reviewers in the intelligence community but by the analysts and their supervisors themselves, is a much clearer insight into their institutional behaviors and processes that can greatly improve their work and their ability to serve the consumers.

Conclusion

The production and use or disuse of intelligence as part of the policy process is the net result of several types of mind-sets and behavior within and between two groups that are more disparate than most observers realize. Moreover, the disparity is more likely to be appreciated by one group, the intelligence producers, than it is by the intelligence consumers. As argued here, the consumers play a much greater role *throughout* the intelligence process and at all stages in that process than is customarily realized. Certain aspects of the gap between these two groups will never be bridged. Other aspects, like the issue of supporting policy, *should* never be bridged. Nonetheless, there remains much that can be done—even within current structures and processes—to improve communications between the two groups.

Notes

1. Thomas Hughes, *The Fate of Facts in the World of Men* (New York: Foreign Policy Association, 1976).

2. See Gary Sick, *All Fall Down* (New York: Penguin Books, 1985), pp. 36, 64, 91, 104–105.

3. Needless to say, not *all* paranoia is unjustified. There have undoubtedly been instances in which intelligence analysts have tried to work against policies with which they disagreed. Most analysts, however, and certainly their senior supervisors know the severe penalty for being caught in such a compromising position and would most often prefer to avoid it, even at the risk that the policy will go forward. Most often, the cost to future credibility far outweighs the value of stopping one specific policy initiative.

4. During the first U.S.–Soviet ministerial meeting of the Bush administration, the deputy national security adviser, Robert Gates, who had spent a considerable part of his intelligence career as a Soviet analyst, was in Moscow for the first time. President Mikhail Gorbachev reportedly kidded Gates, asking him if the Soviet Union looked different from the ground than it did from satellites.

5. Feedback is so rare that, when it occurs, the effect can often be comical. When one senior official noted his pleasure over a piece of intelligence analysis, the initial reaction among those responsible was, first, elation, quickly followed by doubts. Was this memo so good, they wondered, or was it that all of the others that received no such notice were so bad?

6. The President's Foreign Intelligence Advisory Board (PFIAB), a group of outside experts that reviews both intelligence analysis and operations, provides such guidance. It was PFIAB, for example, that suggested the Team A–Team B competitive analysis. However, PFIAB meets infrequently, reportedly once a month, and remains somewhat removed from the daily needs of producers. It cannot substitute entirely for direct producer feedback.

7. There have been cases, however, in which wide swings did hurt credibility. In the mid-1970s U.S. intelligence estimates of the portion of Soviet gross national product devoted to defense went from 6 to 7 percent in the mid-1970s to 10 to 15 percent, leading some consumers to question the validity of the new estimates as well. Critics in Congress suspected that the change was created to support the Ford administration's larger defense budget. . . . When the intelligence community repeated its estimate a year later, . . . Carter administration officials purposely excluded some of the premises that they saw driving the new estimates. . . .

19

Trading with Saddam: Bureaucratic Roles and Competing Conceptions of National Security

Christopher M. Jones

In the aftermath of the Persian Gulf War, America's prewar courtship of Iraq became the subject of intense scrutiny by congressional committees, scholars, and journalists. Of the many troubling revelations to emerge from these inquiries, none was more disturbing than the government's decision to authorize advanced technology sales by American manufacturers to Iraq between March 1985 and the invasion of Kuwait in August 1990. The U.S. Department of Commerce approved "without condition" nearly 800 export licenses to Iraq, allowing American companies to sell $1.5 billion in products with both civilian and military applications.[1] These dual-use products included high-speed computers, electron beam welders, lasers, quartz crystals, oscilloscopes, image-enhancement systems, biological agents, and precision machine and measurement tools. Much of the technology was either shipped directly or diverted to ballistic missile sites, government agencies, and research centers involved in the development of biological, chemical, and nuclear weapons.[2]

This export policy clearly had dangerous implications. First, American companies, with the consent of the federal government, enhanced the capability of Saddam Hussein's war machine, which the United States and its allies later faced on the battlefield. Following the war, the military significance of U.S. exports was confirmed by government officials, United Nations weapons inspectors, and private researchers.[3] One analyst noted there was evidence to suggest U.S. technology may have "helped build the SCUD missile that killed American troops in [Saudi Arabia]."[4] The best evidence of the military threat, however, was the high priority American officials placed on wartime bombing raids against Iraqi installations identified as both recipients of U.S. technology and sites of unconventional weapons programs. Indeed, one facility was attacked by American cruise missiles as late as January 1993, illustrating that Iraq's capabilities were still a concern two years after the war.[5]

Second, U.S. technology aided Iraq's unconventional weapons programs, violating a long-standing American goal of preventing the proliferation of weapons of mass destruction to Third World states. While the United States was only one of a number of countries that sold Iraq dual-use technology,[6] American products played a central role in Saddam Hussein's clandestine nuclear program. For instance, the United States was Iraq's primary supplier of advanced, high-speed computers, which are essential for designing atomic weapons and simulating nuclear tests.[7] Further, postwar United Nations inspections uncovered American computers and sophisticated technology at over twenty sites confirmed to be involved in the development of weapons of mass destruction.[8] By August 1990, this equipment coupled with material from other states brought Iraq "no more than 18 months from the acquisition of a crude nuclear weapon."[9]

Of the theories available for understanding foreign-policy behavior, Allison and Halperin's bureaucratic politics paradigm[10] provides a compelling explanation for why this dangerous export policy was maintained for over five years. The framework views the actions of government as political resultants. These resultants emerge from a foreign-policy process, characteristic of a game, where multiple players, holding different conceptions of national security, struggle, compete, and bargain over the nature and conduct of policy. The policy stands taken by the decisionmakers are largely determined by their bureaucratic roles and interests. The final outcome either represents a compromise among the actors or reflects outright the policy preferences of the players who won the political game.

Allison and Halperin's framework encourages organizations to be treated as policy actors. In these instances, an agency's mission and essence become strong predictors of its policy stand on a particular issue. Further, Allison and Halperin distinguish among decision games, policy games, and action games. They identify "the activity of players leading to decision by senior players as decision games, activities leading to policy as policy games, and activities that follow from or proceed in the absence of decisions by senior players as action games."[11] These insights are important in explaining American prewar technology sales to Iraq. In essence, the case is an instance of an action game where three organizations within the executive branch fought over the implementation of a vague and unmonitored policy.

The White House and the Congress set the stage for this action game and the bureaucratic politics that pervaded it. The Reagan and Bush administrations established broad, conciliatory policies toward Iraq that afforded executive agencies wide discretionary power in determining the nature and extent of American trade to Iraq. Congress was responsible for developing the export licensing process or the "action-channel"—"a regularized means of taking government action on a specific issue"[12]—whereby the Departments of Commerce and State, on one side, and the Department of Defense, on the other, struggled over the sale of dual-use technology to Iraq. In case after case, the Defense Department warned that export licenses for advanced, dual-use products should be denied due to the likelihood of military end use. The Pentagon's objections were challenged repeatedly by the Commerce Department, which enjoyed the support of the State Department. The three agencies' policy positions were based unequivocally on their distinct bureaucratic roles. The organizational mission and essence of each created different conceptions of national security and, therefore, different reasons in favor of or against export controls.

This chapter shows how the White House and Congress provided a conducive environment for both the technology sales to Iraq and the bureaucratic politics that surrounded the export licensing process. It then demonstrates how key actors' policy stands and supporting arguments were directly related to their traditional bureaucratic missions and interests. Prewar dual-use exports to Iraq are treated as a whole, as the behavior of the relevant institutions was remarkably consistent over time.

The White House

With one exception, high-level officials in the Reagan and Bush administrations did not intervene within the export licensing process as it related to dual-use items intended for Iraq. Rather, both administrations adopted broad conciliatory policies toward Iraq, though for different reasons. Once the general direction was set, the White House became inattentive to the details of export control policy. This context permitted bureaucratic politics to determine licensing decisions from March 1985 to August 1990.

By early 1982 the Iran–Iraq War appeared to be turning against Iraq. This situation alarmed the Reagan administration, which feared the prospect of Iran's Islamic fundamentalist government in control of more Middle East territory and oil. Consequently, the Reagan White House, without departing from an official position of neutrality, initiated a policy "tilt" toward Iraq. Geoffrey Kemp, the National Security Council's Middle East section chief at the time, explains the logic behind the decision:

> The memory of the hostages was quite fresh; the Ayatollah was still calling us the Great Satan and attempting to undermine governments throughout the Gulf states. It wasn't that we wanted Iraq to win the war, we did not want Iraq to lose. We really weren't naive. We knew [Saddam Hussein] was an S.O.B., but he was our S.O.B.[13]

Thus, the main motivation behind the tilt was to restore the war's earlier stalemate, which diminished the military power of both Khomeini and Hussein.

Former Secretary of State George Schultz describes the strategy as " a limited form of balance-of-power policy," where American "support of Iraq increased in rough proportion to Iran's military successes: plain and simple."[14]

In reality, however, American assistance had several dimensions and intensified over time. In March 1982 Iraq was removed from the State Department's list of states sponsoring terrorism. This action occurred despite evidence Iraq continued to aid terrorist groups. The change in the State Department list also allowed Iraq to buy millions of dollars worth of American food and products—including dual-use technology after March 1985—with loan guarantees sponsored by two U.S. government agencies, the Commodity Credit Corporation and the Export-Import Bank. In fact, Vice President Bush personally lobbied the chairman of the Export-Import Bank on two occasions to increase the amount of credits. In 1982 the Reagan administration also launched Operation Staunch, an American-led effort to encourage other states to participate in an arms embargo of Iran. Two years later the Iraqis began receiving U.S. intelligence data and satellite imagery to track Iranian troops movements and plan bombing missions. Last, diplomatic relations were reestablished in November 1984 after a seventeen-year suspension.[15] The significance of this action was apparent four months later when advanced technology sales to Iraq, which previously had been denied, "started to go through as if someone had turned a switch."[16]

The tilt was maintained as Iraq supported terrorist groups, sought to acquire nuclear weapons technology, and attacked Iranian troops with chemical agents. More surprisingly, the policy continued after the conclusion of the Iran–Iraq War—the original pretext for the approach—and in the face of Saddam Hussein's two chemical weapons attacks on Iraqi Kurds in 1988. In fact, the policy, which did not undergo review in the final months of the Reagan administration, remained on "automatic pilot"[17] nine months into the Bush presidency. The failure to name political appointees in foreign affairs, rapidly changing events in Europe, and time-consuming problems like the Tiananmen Square Massacre delayed a review. As former Secretary of State James Baker recalls, "none of us considered policy toward Iraq to be an urgent priority."[18]

When President Bush's policy—National Security Directive (NSD) 26— finally emerged on October 2, 1989, it simply changed the pretext of the Reagan approach. In the absence of the Iran–Iraq War, America's tilt toward Saddam Hussein would no longer be based on preventing an Iranian victory, but rather on influencing the behavior of Iraq through economic and political incentives.[19] To promote regional stability and good relations with Iraq, the Bush administration followed the same strategy of accommodation its predecessor did. It encouraged trade, provided Export-Import and CCC loan guarantees, and opposed U.S. trade sanctions when Iraq's behavior worsened. After the Persian Gulf War, President Bush consistently justified the policy with the argument: "We tried to bring Iraq into the family of nations through commerce and failed."[20]

Unfortunately, it appears President Bush and his top aides were not fully informed about the nature of U.S.–Iraqi trade in 1989 and 1990. This inattention was apparent in the summer of 1992 when Bush twice denied that American technology had enhanced Saddam Hussein's unconventional weapons capability.[21] It was again evident a few months later, when the national security advisor and the acting secretary of state made similar claims.[22] And further evidence of high-level unfamiliarity with the details of prewar export policy emerged during the 1992 presidential campaign. For instance, President Bush stated on October 19: "The nuclear capability [in Iraq] has been searched by the United Nations and there hasn't been one single scintilla of evidence that there's any U.S. technology involved in it."[23] Bush later admitted some dual-use technology might have reached Iraq, but he dismissed its significance, arguing his policy was in place. He remarked on October 28:

> We had a policy on dual use. We had a policy to screen, to be sure that key [dual-use] elements did not go to nuclear weapons or for arms. Now, if a Tandy computer or an IBM personal computer ends up somewhere in a nuclear program, too bad, but the policy was not to do that.[24]

NSD 26 was indeed in place. However, declassified sections reveal its ambiguity. For instance, one portion reads: "We should pursue, and seek to facilitate, opportunities for U.S. firms to participate in the reconstruction of the Iraqi economy, particularly in the energy area, where they do not conflict with our nonproliferation and other significant objectives."[25] It appears the Bush administration wanted to encourage U.S. trade with Iraq *and* prevent Saddam Hussein from acquiring weapons of mass destruction. Given the nature of dual-use technology, however, these may have been mutually exclusive goals. Further, the Bush policy did not provide the bureaucrats responsible for issuing export licenses with guidelines for making decisions. A 1989 State Department memorandum illustrates the disarray surrounding the implementation of NSD 26: "The problem is not that we lack a policy on Iraq. We have a policy. However, the policy has proven very hard to implement when considering proposed exports of dual-use commodities to ostensibly non-nuclear end users, particularly state enterprises."[26]

The ambiguity of NSD 26 was further exacerbated by the paucity of senior-level concern about Iraq in general and with the details of export licensing in particular. First, "the National Security Council (NSC) never met once to discuss Iraq from the time NSD 26 was signed until the invasion of Kuwait."[27] Lower echelons of the NSC system, namely the deputies' and policy coordinating committees, did meet on Iraq, but only when Saddam Hussein's behavior became ominous a few months before the war.[28] Second, the White House blocked only one dual-use export to Iraq. The intervention occurred in July 1990 when, after considerable publicity and pressure from Republican senators, the White House stopped the shipment of industrial furnaces.[29] In other cases the NSC did not provide the necessary policy coordination or intervention to mitigate the intense bureaucratic rivalry surrounding most licensing decisions. Like the Reagan years, the absence of senior-level attention in the Bush administration allowed advanced U.S. technology to reach Iraq's unconventional weapons programs. Former Secretary of State James Baker writes: "We should have given Iraqi policy a more prominent place on our radar screen at an earlier date."[30]

The Action-Channel

Despite Iraq's use of chemical weapons and its development of biological and nuclear armaments, Congress did not pass trade sanctions or conduct a review of export control policy before the invasion of Kuwait. Its main contribution was to legislate the rules for the export licensing process or "action game." According to the Export Administration Act, most dual-use industrial goods controlled for national security purposes are on the Commodity Control List (CCL) and, therefore, fall under the jurisdiction of the Commerce Department's Bureau of Export Administration (BXA). Nuclear-related, dual-use items on the Nuclear Referral List (NRL) also require export licenses from the Commerce Department. Only a small portion of dual-use goods are not directly controlled by BXA. These products fall exclusively on the Munitions List (ML), which is supervised by the State Department. Some ambiguous dual-use goods can appear on both the CCL and the ML, since the lists lack mutually exclusive categories. While this overlap can be a source of contention between the Commerce and State Departments, there is no evidence it played a role in prewar technology sales to Iraq.

BXA can operate along two action-channels. A decision on whether to approve a particular export license is made either unilaterally by the Commerce Department or through an interagency review process where, after consultations, the Commerce Department has the final say. The review process, which was frequently activated in the case of prewar sales to Iraq,[31] brings together diverse actors and interests and is, therefore, the action-channel where bureaucratic politics are most prevalent.

In terms of dual-use goods, interagency reviews are initiated when specific applications for export licenses raise policy or technical questions that exceed the expertise of the Commerce Department. Interestingly, BXA determines whether an application requires referral to other agencies for their review and recommendation. This fact allows the Department of Commerce to determine what actors become involved in the national security licensing process under its authority. Given the State Department's wealth of foreign-policy and country-specific expertise, it is frequently brought into the process when goods are controlled for foreign-policy purposes (e.g., regional stability, terrorism, and embargoes). In national security cases (as distinct from foreign-policy cases), the Energy and Defense Departments are often consulted due to their knowledge of nuclear and military critical technologies.[32]

In terms of national security cases, the goal of the interagency review and licensing processes is to fulfill "the national security objective" as set forth originally by the Export Control Act of 1949 and maintained in the current Export Administration Act (EAA). Specifically, that objective is "to restrict the export of goods and technology which would make a significant contribution to the military potential of any other country or combination of countries which would prove detrimental to the national security of the United States."[33] This goal has remained constant, but subsequent legislation—the Export Administration Acts of 1969 and 1979 and the EAA Amendments of 1981, 1985, and 1988—incorporated additional objectives. The agencies involved in export control policy not only interpret the original national security objective differently, but they also have become associated with particular definitions of national security encompassed in the newer objectives. These disparate conceptions of national security, which are further enhanced by distinct organizational missions and interests, are difficult to balance and often lead to acute policy differences.

In fact, conflict between bureaucracies can become so intractable that formal dispute resolution mechanisms are necessary. The Export Administration Review Board (EARB) is a three-tier structure designed to resolve interagency disputes involving national security cases and proscribed destinations. "Although the EARB's process for resolving disputed licenses has worked fairly successfully for exports to proscribed destinations, as late as 1990 there was no parallel system for exports to nonproscribed countries or for proliferation cases."[34] This shortcoming is not only serious, but is directly relevant to the case under study. With regard to export controls for national security purposes, Iraq was a "nonproscribed country" before the Persian Gulf War. If the Commerce Department granted an export license for a dual-use item to a nonproscribed destination, then only a direct intervention from the White House could stop its delivery. Such senior-level intervention was rare. In fact, it occurred only once, when in July 1990, as noted, the White House permanently blocked the shipment of industrial furnaces to Iraq. Its decision to override the Commerce Department's approval was out of concern the furnaces might be used to develop components for nuclear weapons and missiles.

The Defense Department

Within the interagency review process, the Department of Defense was the most vigorous opponent of American prewar technology sales to Iraq. Its policy stand and corresponding arguments regarding export controls were directly related to its organizational mission. Charged with ensuring the defense and security of the United States and its allies, the Pentagon's position on dual-use exports was motivated by a military conception of national security. It believed U.S. technology would contribute to Iraq's armed forces and, therefore, be harmful to regional stability and American security interests. The Defense Technology Security Agency (DTSA), a small unit with expertise in militarily critical technologies, waged the Pentagon's bureaucratic battles with Commerce and State over the sale of dual-use technology. Despite DTSA's success in controlling dual-use exports to the Soviet Union and Eastern Europe during the Cold War, it failed with Iraq.

DTSA's powerlessness emanated from a number of bargaining disadvantages. First, unlike the Department of Commerce, which was working on behalf of American companies, trade associations, and foreign importers interested in U.S.–Iraqi trade, the Defense Department had no natural constituency to back its position. Even the Pentagon's many congressional allies were reluctant to intervene with U.S. trade and jobs at stake. In fact, the Defense Department's long-standing reputation of being overzealous in blocking the sale of dual-use technology limited its support on Capitol Hill.

Second, DTSA had no specific statutory export control authority. It was only granted a consulting role. Although it was customary for the Pentagon to review dual-use exports to proscribed destinations and "to nonproscribed destinations that [might] pose a risk of diversion to a proscribed destination,"[35] it had no automatic right to review exports to nonproscribed states like prewar Iraq. Third, DTSA's participation in the export licensing process was contingent upon it being referred a case to review independently or through an interagency review process. To avoid Pentagon objections, however, the Commerce Department often sought technical reviews from other agencies. For instance, the Departments of Energy and State were consulted more often than the Defense Department on the risk of nuclear proliferation to Iraq.[36] Fourth, even when the Pentagon participated in the review process, it rarely shaped the final decision. Stephen Bryen, deputy undersecretary of defense for trade security (1981–1988), comments: "It was routine for our recommendations [on Iraq] to be ignored. [The Commerce Department] disregarded five years of thorough technical and intelligence evaluations by Defense and the CIA."[37] Last, although DTSA registered objections to particular export licenses, it could not veto a sale. Barring White House intervention, the Commerce Department had the final authority.

DTSA employed a number of arguments to promote and defend its position on denying dual-use exports to Iraq. These justifications, like its policy stand, were motivated by the Pentagon's organizational mission and military conception of national security. Its most widely cited justifications for exports controls were legal arguments related to nonproliferation and, second, the military threat posed by the technology. As Bryen stated: "We have a law called the Nuclear Nonproliferation Act, and if you have knowledge that a technology could be used to build nuclear weapons and intelligence to back it up . . . , then you don't sell it."[38] On military grounds, the Defense Department opposed many dual-use exports, arguing the products could be used to manufacture unconventional weapons. DTSA supported the claim by referencing its own Military Critical Technologies List (MCTL), a classified document used to determine whether certain dual-use exports threaten national security. In the case of Iraq, the products the Pentagon sought to control were consistent with MCTL categories and, therefore, viewed as militarily significant.

Two notable cases were the authorized sales of a hybrid analog computer system and an image enhancement system. In the first case, a November 1986 memorandum warned that the sale of a hybrid computer to Iraq's Saad 16 missile facility should not be approved "because of the high likelihood of military end use and the association of the involved companies in sensitive military applications." It also cautioned that "the computer could be used to monitor wind-tunnel tests for ballistic missiles."[39] In the second case, which occurred in 1987, the Pentagon attempted to block the export license for an image enhancement system, arguing: "We believe that the real purpose of this equipment [is] to assist the Iraqis in targeting sites far from the Iraqi borders, giving them eyes in the day and the night thousands of miles from their territory. That, to us, . . . [is] a very dangerous thing to be doing."[40]

Besides the nonproliferation and potential military use arguments, the Pentagon at times employed other reasons for controlling dual-use exports to Iraq. For instance, it raised the possibility of Iraqi deception. As Assistant Secretary of Defense Richard Perle wrote in July 1985:

> Iraq continues to actively pursue an interest in nuclear weapons; a large number of Warsaw Pact nationals in Iraq make diversion a real possibility; and in the past, Iraq has been somewhat less than honest in regard to the intended end use of high technology equipment.[41]

An additional argument was how the Commerce Department's promotion of American technology made it difficult for the United States to convince its allies to limit their own dual-use exports to Iraq. Bryen reports the comments of the Germans and Italians when the Pentagon approached them regarding missile technology: "they pointed the finger right back at us and . . . said you people are exporting the same kinds of goods . . . Why don't you stop your own companies?"[42] Finally, DTSA raised other issues in making its case against advanced technology sales: concern for the regional balance of power, the repressive nature of the Iraqi regime, and the reputation of some exporting companies in contributing to weapons projects elsewhere.

When prewar exports to Iraq are examined as a whole, a common pattern

arises. The Defense Department embraced the original "national security objective" and consistently argued Iraq should be denied American dual-use
technology. The Commerce Department, on the other hand, repeatedly overrode the Pentagon's objections and approved sales "without condition." Indeed, DTSA was interested in expanding its domain in export control policy
as a means of promoting its conception of national security. However, the fact
its "rejection rate for Iraqi cases (it was allowed to see) was 40 percent, compared to 5 percent for the Soviet Union,"[43] indicates the Defense Department
was truly concerned about the type of technology being sold.

The Commerce Department

The Commerce Department repeatedly favored the sale of a wide array of
dual-use products to Iraq. Therefore, it held an export policy position diamet-
rically opposed to the Pentagon's. The policy stand and corresponding arguments in favor of liberal export controls embraced by Commerce were directly
related to its organizational mission. Specifically, the department's role is to
promote the nation's economic standing through international trade. This mission, besides motivating its position on export controls, was responsible for
the department's *active promotion* of Iraqi-American trade, of which dual-
use technology was a large part. Although Congress separated the Commerce
Department's export control and trade promotion functions between its BXA
and its International Trade Administration (ITA), the two units worked in tandem in this particular case. ITA vigorously promoted trade with Iraq, while
BXA issued the necessary export licenses. Such interbureau cooperation
leaves little doubt about the Commerce Department's organizational essence,
that is, "the view held by the dominant group in the organization of what [its]
missions and capabilities should be."[44]

ITA viewed the prewar sale of American products (including high technology items) to Iraq as both a fulfillment of its mission and a benefit to the
country's trade balance. Before March 1985 until the invasion of Kuwait, ITA
was engaged in a number of activities designed to facilitate contact between
U.S. companies and Iraqi importers. It sponsored trade fairs, missions, and
shows, for instance. From 1982 through 1984, ITA supported the participation
of more than twenty major U.S. companies in the annual Baghdad International Trade Fair. Then from 1985 through 1989, ITA "sponsored its own
official U.S. pavilion" at those same annual trade expositions. Moreover, the
number of participating companies increased each year. Last, the Commerce
Department scheduled special events like the 1990 Executive Aerospace Trade
Mission to Iraq.[45]

Besides promotional activities, the ITA provided information and open encouragement to potential American exporters. For example, it worked actively

on behalf of U.S. corporations by disseminating trade data, providing ad hoc counseling, and, in some instances, lobbying potential Iraqi importers. In ITA's official publication, *Business America,* Iraq was touted consistently as "the last major untapped market in the Near East for American goods and services."[46]

Many of the exports ITA promoted clearly had dual uses and were of a sophisticated nature. In 1987, Thomas Sams, ITA's country desk officer for Iraq, wrote encouragingly: "Computers and software offer good export sales opportunities for the United States. Since 1980, the Iraqi government has been firmly committed to the expanded use and application of computers and related technology."[47] It is now known this "expanded use and application" was devoted in large part to developing weapons of mass destruction. Surprisingly, the Commerce Department even dismissed direct warnings from U.S. companies that their products had both civilian and military uses. Regarding a sale of industrial furnaces to Iraq, for example, Henry M. Rowan, chairman of Inductotherm Industries Inc., writes:

> The [Commerce] Department was adamant that our doubts were unfounded— that the Iraqis did not have nuclear designs—and strongly encouraged our exports. An expert sent by the department to our office even left a brochure, *Helpful Hints to Exporters.* And when Baghdad approved our $11 million contract . . . , a State Department representative in Baghdad sent a telex saying, "Hooray for you!"[48]

Despite ITA's promotional role, it was BXA that ensured American products ultimately reached Iraq. That is, it successfully fought the Commerce Department's bureaucratic battles with the Pentagon over the sale of dual-use products to Iraq, and it issued the necessary export licenses. BXA was aided in its confrontations with the Defense Department by a number of bargaining advantages. These assets included the preponderance of formal authority under the EAA, an absence of White House intervention, State Department support within the interagency review process (discussed below), and a strong business constituency to reinforce its policy stand and interests within the larger policymaking arena. The constituency embraced the seventy-six member U.S.–Iraq Business Forum, Iraq's American lobbyists, and companies interested in exporting to Iraq.

In terms of the bureaucratic politics that pervaded the export licensing process, BXA's major disadvantage was its lack of technical expertise regarding militarily critical technologies and foreign policy. This limitation frequently forced BXA into the interagency review process, where the Pentagon challenged the Commerce Department's policy stand and parochial interests. Nevertheless, Commerce was often able to mitigate its bargaining disadvantage by blocking the DTSA's participation in the review process. Its usual justification for not referring the Defense Department an export license was that another agency was a more appropriate source of expertise. Former Undersecretary of Commerce Paul Freedenberg comments: "[Licenses] were made available to the intelligence community and were aired fully before the State Department. It would depend on [the nature of] the particular license if the Defense Department had an automatic right to see it."[49] Also, BXA was reluctant to consult the Pentagon on many dual-use exports to Iraq, fearing DTSA's well-known delays as well as its attempts to gain "turf" in export control policy.

In case after case, BXA employed a number of consistent arguments to support its policy stand against export controls on Iraq. These justifications, like its policy stand, were derived from its dominant organizational mission and economic conception of national security. Two arguments were particularly popular. First, the Commerce Department maintained there was no legal basis for prohibiting most sales of dual-use technology to Iraq. As Freedenberg observed, "one of the problems you had was you didn't have an international agreement on controlling technology to Iraq the way you did in controlling technology to the Soviet Union. And that meant that if the U.S. was going to turn something down, we also had to get our allies to turn it down."[50] Second, it was argued there was no reason to believe the Iraqis would not use the dual-use technology for its stated purpose. In support of this second claim, the Commerce Department emphasized the need for reconstruction after the Iran–Iraq War and for economic development in general. Moreover, BXA often referenced Iraqi assurances the technology would be used for peaceful purposes and the "insufficient documentation," it claimed, the Pentagon used to support its policy stand.[51] However, the department's position in favor of liberal export controls for Iraq ultimately hinged on one all-encompassing argument: the need to protect America's economic interests, including its jobs, market share, and trade balance. In short, if U.S. companies were not going to reap the profits available in Iraq, other countries surely would.

The Commerce Department repeatedly favored and promoted dual-use exports to Iraq between 1985 and 1990. Its behavior within the licensing and review process was consistent with its organizational mission and economic conception of national security. Embracing newer national security objectives introduced by the Export Administration Acts of 1969 and 1979, the Commerce Department believed liberal export controls on U.S. technology to Iraq would benefit the country's balances of trade and payments and, therefore, its security. When it was revealed American trade significantly enhanced Saddam Hussein's military arsenal, the department maintained "it merely implemented policy."[52] Yet, its extensive authority to license dual-use exports and the absence of senior-level oversight leaves little doubt the Commerce Department, in most cases, was *making* policy.

The State Department

Within the interagency licensing and review process, the State Department repeatedly joined the Department of Commerce in favoring prewar technology sales to Iraq. Like the Pentagon and Commerce Department, its policy stand and supporting arguments were directly related to its organizational role. Specifically, the State Department conducts U.S. foreign relations. There is a consensus among the members of the organization that this duty should be fulfilled through reporting, representation, and negotiation. Consistent with this organizational mission and essence, the department's policy stand on dual-use exports to Iraq was motivated by a diplomatic conception of national security. In its view, technology sales facilitated good relations with Iraq and promoted U.S. foreign-policy interests.

Regardless of whether it was licensing or simply reviewing a dual-use export to Iraq, the State Department consistently opposed export controls for national security purposes. First, in the few instances where dual-use goods fell on the Munitions List instead of the Commodity Control List, the State Department did not hesitate to authorize the necessary licenses. For example, its Office of Defense Trade Controls authorized Iraq's purchase of sixty Hughes MD 500 Defender helicopters in 1982 and forty-eight Bell-214 helicopters in 1984. It was later reported the Bell helicopters, originally intended for "recreation," had gone to the armed forces; and many of the Hughes Defenders were used to train military pilots.[53] Second, the State Department approved the sale of militarily useful items to other countries that were assisting Saddam Hussein's unconventional weapons programs. One such supplier, Brazil, was allowed to buy American rocket motor casings and supercomputer parts.[54] Third, in the vast majority of the cases where the State Department did not have licensing authority over dual-use items, it fully supported the Commerce Department. Because of its foreign-policy expertise and intragovernmental clout, the State Department was a great ally to the Commerce Department in its political battles with the Pentagon. In a 1986 memorandum the State Department complained the Defense Department's assessment of the Iraqi threat "differed radically from all other agencies."[55] This backing was important to Commerce since, despite its formal authority, it would have had difficulty maintaining its policy stand without support from other actors.

In addition to its reluctance to advocate national security controls for Iraq, the State Department generally did not recommend trade restrictions for foreign-policy purposes. According to the Export Administration regulations, possible foreign policy and nonproliferation controls include crime control, antiterrorism, regional stability, embargoed countries, biological organisms, nuclear nonproliferation, missile technology controls, and chemical weapons. Although chemical weapons controls were placed on Saddam Hussein's regime in 1987, Iraq easily qualified for a number of other restrictions given its known association with terrorists and its development of weapons of mass destruction. Moreover, although the State Department chairs the Policy Coordinating Committee on Missile Technology Proliferation, it refused to label Iraq a "country of concern."

Besides its behavior related to export licensing and review, the State Department's actions in the general area of U.S.–Iraqi relations facilitated the flow of advanced, dual-use technology. For instance, it certified to Congress that Saddam Hussein had stopped supporting terrorist groups when it removed Iraq from its list of states sponsoring terrorism in 1982. This move paved the way for American trade and loans. Second, it actively lobbied the Commodity Credit Corporation and Export-Import Bank to extend loan guarantees to Iraq. Third, despite evidence of Iraq's unconventional weapons programs and human rights violations, the department repeatedly and actively opposed the imposition of trade sanctions against Iraq, thereby allowing the continued purchase of American dual-use technology. Even when Saddam Hussein's behavior became particularly aggressive between March and July of 1990 with threats against Israel and Kuwait, the State Department failed to express its displeasure to the Commerce Department and White House in any meaningful way.

The Department of State occasionally employed the Commerce Department's economic rationale to justify its own policy stand in favor of liberal export controls. Regarding the 1984 sale of helicopters, for example, a department memorandum read: "Increased American penetration of the extremely competitive civilian aircraft market [in Iraq] would serve U.S. interests by improving our balance of trade, and lessening unemployment in the aircraft industry."[56] However, the State Department's policy arguments were more commonly motivated by a diplomatic conception of national security consistent with its bureaucratic role: maintaining good relations and promoting U.S. foreign-policy interests.

For instance, the State Department argued Iraq was important to U.S. interests in the Persian Gulf and, therefore, should not be ignored or castigated. Marshall W. Wiley, a foreign service officer, observed: "Iraq plays an important political and geographical role in addition to being an important trading partner for us, and we can't push all these considerations to the side and shut our eyes to them because of some perceived human rights violations."[57] The State Department also did not want the United States to be isolated in such an important region. It therefore saw relations with Iraq as more feasible and tolerable than ties with Iran. Another common justification was that business ties could improve U.S.–Iraqi relations, moderate Saddam Hussein's behavior, and enhance regional stability. Richard W. Murphy, President Reagan's senior Middle East diplomat, commented after leaving his post: "We didn't support sanctions when they first came up, because we thought we were getting somewhere in private channels."[58] Furthermore, the Department of State asserted trade with Iraq was consistent with the general policy direction set by Reagan and Bush.[59] Last, the State Department supported its policy stand by offering weak evidence that Iraq was becoming a more cooperative actor in certain areas. Citing Iraq's participation in two disarmament conferences and its discussion of a new constitution with greater concern for human rights, Assistant Secretary of State John Kelly told a congressional committee in April 1990: "We believe there is still a potentiality for positive alterations in Iraqi behavior."[60]

It was not until July 25, 1990, just days before the Iraqi invasion of Kuwait, that the Department of State proposed a change in U.S. export policy toward Iraq. This belated recommendation came in the form of a memorandum from Secretary of State James Baker to Secretary of Commerce Robert Mosbacher.[61] The department's previously consistent policy stand in favor of dual-use exports to Iraq was motivated directly by its distinct organizational role and a diplomatic conception of national security. Even though it recognized Saddam Hussein "was working hard at chemical and biological weapons and new missiles,"[62] the State Department was inclined not to "rock the boat" diplomatically, viewing good relations with Iraq as a way to promote larger U.S. foreign-policy interests.

Conclusion

The government's decision to authorize dual-use technology sales to Iraq between March 1985 and August 1990 was the result of an implementation process pervaded by bureaucratic politics. The major actors within this process, the Departments of Commerce, Defense, and State, held policy positions on dual-use exports to Iraq based directly on their distinct bureaucratic roles. Each agency's separate organizational mission led it to embrace a different conception of national security and, therefore, different reasons for supporting either trade promotion or trade control. These differing stands, perceptions, and arguments largely explain the bureaucratic conflict surrounding prewar technology sales. These interagency differences were further exacerbated by the nature of the U.S. export control system: multiple actors, lack of clear control criteria for dual-use items, ambiguity surrounding the Pentagon's "consulting role," the Commerce Department's conflicting missions, and an absence of clear definitions for key concepts (e.g., national security, military critical, and dual-use). Moreover, this conflict and ambiguity persisted in the absence of a dispute resolution mechanism, sufficient attention and coordination from the White House, and congressional action. In the end, the Pentagon never had a chance. The Departments of Commerce and State, motivated by different conceptions of national security and aided by several bargaining advantages, built a "winning" coalition in favor of liberal export controls and, therefore, determined the final action.

Students of foreign-policy analysis should not be surprised by the capacity of the bureaucratic politics paradigm to capture the episode in this study. Even critics of the theory concede its explanatory power in instances marked by senior-level inattention and inaction.[63] Further, the technical nature of export control policy activates executive branch players (in this case, government organizations) that lie at the center of Allison and Halperin's work. Yet, if the bureaucratic politics paradigm is so useful in understanding the approval of prewar technology sales to Iraq, why has it yielded such a small number of published case studies? Are not many foreign-policy decisions shaped by the presence of multiple actors, differing interests, overlapping jurisdictions, and politics?

Unfortunately, the bureaucratic politics approach encounters problems as an explanatory tool because decision making often does not satisfy the conditions present in the Iraq case. Instead, foreign-policy issues often extend beyond technical policy areas to involve nonbureaucratic actors within and beyond the executive branch. In many instances, the bureaucratic politics approach cannot adequately capture the foreign-policy process, because it underestimates the power of the president and virtually ignores the role of legislative and nongovernmental actors. For example, Congress and interest groups are treated as marginal players and are rarely featured in case study applications of the theory.

As a result of these shortcomings, scholars have long needed to devote attention to the development of a *political* decisionmaking approach that recognizes the true diversity of actors, interests, and processes capable of shaping foreign policy. One possibility is a "governmental politics paradigm" encompassing multiple analytic models. On one level, the models might share a common set of assumptions capturing the *general* characteristics of governmental politics: fragmented power, multiple actors, role-determined policy stands, differing interests, and politically generated outcomes. On another level, each model could be differentiated by a specific *type* of governmental politics defined by particular actors, forms of politics, action-channels, and several other procedural characteristics. These assumptions might vary with the salience of the issue or the locus of decision making. For instance, there might be separate models to explain foreign policy made by (1) the president and senior-level advisors, (2) bureaucracies, (3) the executive and legislative branches, and (4) executive, legislative, and private sector actors. With further refinement, such a framework might preclude the need for foreign-policy behavior to meet certain, rigid conditions in order to be well-explained by a political model of decision making.

Notes

1. Commerce Department records indicate the value of dual-use technology actually delivered to Iraq was $500 million, because military cargo trucks worth roughly

$1 billion were not shipped. House Committee on Government Operations, *Strengthening the Export Licensing System,* 102nd Cong., 1st sess., 1991, H. Rept. 102–137, 17, n. 45; *hereafter* U.S. House 1991.

2. See Gary Milhollin, "Licensing Mass Destruction—U.S. Exports To Iraq: 1985–1990," (June 1991) in Senate Committee on Banking, Housing, and Urban Affairs, *United States Export Policy Toward Iraq Prior to Iraq's Invasion of Kuwait,* 102nd Cong., 2d sess., 1992, S. Hrg. 102-996, 102–120; *hereafter* U.S. Senate 1992.

3. See testimony in U.S. Senate 1992.

4. Milhollin Report in U.S. Senate 1992, 104.

5. See Michael R. Gordon, "Raids in 2 Regions," *New York Times* 19 January 1993, Section A.

6. See U.S. Senate 1992, 72, and Douglas Jehl, "Who Armed Iraq? Answers the West Didn't Want to Hear," *New York Times* 18 July 1993, Section E.

7. Testimony of Kenneth R. Timmerman, U.S. Senate 1992, 33–35.

8. Ibid., 35.

9. Testimony of David A. Kay, U.S. Senate 1992, 42.

10. Graham T. Allison and Morton H. Halperin, "Bureaucratic Politics: A Paradigm and Some Policy Implications," *World Politics* 24 (Spring supplement 1972): 40–80. See also Graham T. Allison, *Essence of Decision: Explaining the Cuban Missile Crisis* (Boston, MA: Little, Brown, 1971).

11. Allison and Halperin 1972, 46.

12. Allison 1971, 169.

13. Judith Miller and Laurie Mylroie, *Saddam Hussein and the Crisis in the Gulf* (New York: Times Books/Random House, 1990), 143.

14. George P. Schultz, *Turmoil and Triumph* (New York: Charles Scribner's Sons, 1993), 237.

15. For an overview of the Reagan policy, see Bruce W. Jentleson, *With Friends Like These: Reagan, Bush, and Saddam 1982–1990* (New York: W. W. Norton & Company, 1994), 42–48.

16. Kenneth R. Timmerman, *The Death Lobby: How the West Armed Iraq* (New York: Houghton Mifflin Company, 1991), 202.

17. This phrase is from Elaine Sciolino, *The Outlaw State: Saddam Hussein's Quest for Power and the Gulf Crisis* (New York: John Wiley & Son, 1991), 172.

18. James A. Baker III with Thomas M. DeFrank, *The Politics of Diplomacy: Revolution, War & Peace, 1989–1992* (New York: G. P. Putnam & Sons, 1995), 263.

19. See declassified sections of NSD 26 in U.S. Senate 1992, 427.

20. Gerald F. Seib, "Attention Refocuses on U.S. Courtship of Iraq, Illustrating How An Issue Can Be Rekindled," *Wall Street Journal,* 12 May 1992, Section A.

21. See U.S. Senate 1992, 10.

22. Brent Scowcroft, "We Didn't Coddle Saddam," *Washington Post,* 10 October 1992, Section A, and Lawrence Eagleburger, "Administration Hides Nothing on Iraq," *New York Times,* 21 October 1992, Section A.

23. U.S. Senate 1992, 10.

24. ABC News Nightline, "Arming Saddam: Cover-Up or Witchhunt?," aired 28 October 1992, 3 (transcript).

25. Declassified portion of NSD 26 in U.S. Senate 1992, 427.

26. Declassified memorandum in U.S. Senate 1992, 368.

27. Sciolino 1991, 173.

28. See Baker 1995, 269–270, and U.S. Senate 1992, 400.

29. See Michael A. Wines, "White House Blocks Furnace Export to Iraq," *New York Times,* 20 July 1990, Section A.

30. Baker 1995, 273.

31. Of the 1,133 proposed exports to Iraq between 1985 and 1990, the Pentagon reviewed 704 or about 62 percent. See U.S. Senate 1992, 415–416.

32. See National Academy of Sciences, *Finding Common Ground* (Washington, DC: National Academy Press, 1991), 72–86; *hereafter* NAS 1991.

33. NAS 1991, 63.

34. NAS 1991, 99.

35. NAS 1991, 80.

36. See Milhollin Report in U.S. Senate 1992, 108–109.

37. Murray Waas, "What Washington Gave Saddam for Christmas," in Michah L. Sifry and Christopher Cerf, eds., *The Gulf War Reader* (New York: Times Books/Random House, 1991), 91.

38. ABC News Nightline, "Doing Business with Saddam," aired 6 February 1991, 5 (transcript).

39. Elaine Sciolino, "Documents Warned in '85 of Iraqi Nuclear Arms," *New York Times,* 5 July 1992, Section A.

40. ABC News Nightline, "World Class Leadership," aired 9 June 1992, 1 (transcript).

41. Defense Department memorandum in U.S. Senate 1992, 408.

42. ABC News 1991, 7–8.

43. ABC News 1991, 4. Commerce Department records dispute this figure, see U.S. Senate 1992, 416.

44. Morton H. Halperin, *Bureaucratic Politics and Foreign Policy* (Washington, DC: The Brookings Institution, 1974), 28.

45. On the role of ITA, see Mark Roth, "Post-War Opportunities May Be Open To Some U.S. Firms," *Business America,* 9 August 1982, 32–33; U.S. Department of Commerce, "The Baghdad International Fair Is A Good Marketing Vehicle," *Business America,* 7 July 1986, 25; U.S. Department of Commerce, "Trade Watch: Iraq," *Business America,* 13 August 1990, 1; Mark Roth, "Market Improving But Financing Is Key To Sales," *Business America,* 4 March 1990, 52; and William Safire, "Country of Concern," *New York Times,* 14 October 1990, Section A.

46. Karl S. Reiner, "U.S. and Iraqi Trade Officials Discuss Improvement in Commercial Relations," *Business America,* 4 February 1985, 22.

47. Thomas A. Sams, "Trade Agreement Will Boost Sales Prospects," *Business America,* 28 September 1987, 28.

48. Henry M. Rowan, "Left Holding the Bag in Iraq," *New York Times,* 14 October 1992, Section A. Also see testimony in U.S. Senate 1992, 91–94.

49. ABC News 1991, 8. See also Timmerman 1991, 347–348.

50. ABC News 1991, 7.

51. See Sciolino 1991, 153–154.

52. Timmerman 1991, 211.

53. Jentleson 1994, 44.

54. U.S. House 1991, 27 and 44–46.

55. U.S. Senate 1992, 91.

56. U.S. Senate 1992, 74.

57. Joe Conason, "The Iraq Lobby: Kissinger, the Business Forum & Co.," in Micah L. Sifry and Christopher Cerf, eds., *The Gulf War Reader* (New York: Times Book/Random House, 1991), 83.

58. Michael Wines, "U.S. Aid Helped Hussein's Climb; Now Critics Say, the Bill Is Due," *New York Times* 13 August 1990, Section A.

59. See Jentleson 1994, 137.

60. Jentleson 1994, 160, and Henderson 1991, 187.

61. State Department memorandum in U.S. Senate 1992, 382.

62. 1989 State Department memorandum in U.S. Senate 1992, 409–414.

63. See, for example, Stephen D. Krasner, "Are Bureaucracies Important? (Or Allison Wonderland)," *Foreign Policy* 7 (1972): 168. [Krasner's article is reprinted in Chapter 21 of this book—eds.]

20

Policy Preferences and Bureaucratic Position: The Case of the American Hostage Rescue Mission

Steve Smith

Within two days of the seizure by student revolutionaries of the American embassy in Tehran on 4 November 1979, planning began on a possible rescue mission. Initial estimates of the probability of success were "zero," given the severe logistic problems involved in getting to the embassy in Iran and back out of the country without losing a large number of the hostages as casualties. Nevertheless, as negotiations dragged on with very little promise of success, and as the 1980 American presidential election campaign approached, the decision was made to undertake a very bold rescue mission. Photographs of the charred remains of the burnt-out helicopters in the Dasht-e-Kavir desert provide the most vivid image of the failure of that mission.

The decisions about the mission were taken at three meetings on 22 March, 11 April, and 15 April 1980 by a very small group of people (on average, there were nine participants). Since 1980, the hostage rescue mission has received considerable coverage in the press and in the memoirs of the participants in that decision-making process. As such, it is an excellent case study for one of the most widely cited but rarely tested theories of foreign policy behavior: the bureaucratic politics approach.

The Theoretical Background

The dominant theories of why states act as they do derive from the basic assumption of rationality. Most theories of foreign policy are based on the premise that states act in a more or less monolithic way: Foreign policy is,

---

Note: Some notes have been deleted or renumbered.

accordingly, behavior that is goal-directed and intentional. Of course, many practitioners and academics quickly move away from the monolith assumption, but they can rarely command the kind of detailed information that would enable them to assess precisely what the factions are and how the balance of views lies in any decision-making group. It is, therefore, very common to talk of states as entities and to analyze "their" foreign policies according to some notion of a linkage between the means "they" choose and the ends these must be directed toward. Since practitioners and academics do not literally "know" why State X undertook Action Y, it becomes necessary to impute intentions to the behavior of states. The rationality linkage makes this task much easier; hence the popularity of the idea of the national interest, which incorporates very clear and powerful views on what the ends of governments are in international society and, therefore, on how the behavior can be linked to intentions. The most important attack on this viewpoint has been the "bureaucratic politics approach," most extensively outlined by Graham Allison in his *Essence of Decision*.[1] According to this approach, foreign policy is the result of pulling and hauling between the various components of the decision-making process. Foreign policy may, therefore, be better explained as the outcome of bureaucratic bargaining than as a conscious choice by a decision-making group. As Allison puts it, the outcome of the decision-making process is not really a result but "a resultant—a mixture of conflicting preferences and unequal power of various individuals—distinct from what any person or group intended."[2] The critical point is that these conflicting preferences are determined, above all, by bureaucratic position. Foreign policy, according to this perspective, is therefore to be explained by analyzing the bureaucratic battleground of policymaking, rather than imputing to something called the state a set of motives and interests. On the bureaucratic battleground, the preferences of the participants are governed by the aphorism . . . "where you stand depends on where you sit."[3] . . .

The decision of the United States government to attempt a rescue of the 53 American hostages held in Iran offers an excellent opportunity . . . to test . . . Allison's claims about bureaucratic position and policy preference. . . .

The planning process for the rescue mission began on 6 November 1979, just two days after the hostages were seized in Tehran. During the winter and spring the planning continued, focusing on the composition and training of the rescue force, on the precise location of the hostages and the nature and location of their captors, and on the enormously complex logistic problems involved in mounting the mission. These preparations continued in secret alongside an equally complex process of negotiation for the release of the hostages with the various elements of the Iranian government (including a secret contact in Paris). Bargaining was also under way with the United States's allies, in an attempt to persuade them to impose sanctions on Iran. As noted above, there were three key meetings at which the rescue plan was discussed (on 22 March, 11 and 15 April 1980), although the actual decision to proceed, taken on 11 April and confirmed on 15 April, was in many ways only the formal ratification of what had by then become the dominant mode of thinking among President Carter's most senior advisors. There were two schools of thought in the initial reaction to the seizure of the hostages: first, that the United States should impose economic sanctions on Iran; second, that it should make use of international public opinion and international law to force the Iranian government to release the hostages. As these measures appeared less and less likely to succeed, the U.S. government became involved in attempts to persuade its allies to join in economic sanctions—a move that succeeded just two days before the rescue mission.

President Carter's initial reaction to the seizure was to stress the importance of putting the lives of the hostages first. He declared on 7 December 1979, "I am not going to take any military action that would cause bloodshed or cause the unstable captors of our hostages to attack or punish them." Yet leaks from the White House indicated that military plans were being considered. By late March 1980, President Carter and his advisers were becoming convinced that negotiations were not going to be successful, a view confirmed by the secret source in the Iranian government. At a meeting held on 22 March at Camp David, the president agreed to a reconnaissance flight into Iran to find an initial landing site for the rescue force (Desert One). The plan called for eight RH-53 helicopters from the aircraft carrier *Nimitz* to fly nearly 600 miles, at a very low altitude and with radio blackout, from the Arabian Sea to Desert One. There, they would meet the rescue force of 97 men (code named "Delta Force") who would have arrived from Egypt via Oman on four C-130 transport aircraft. The helicopters would refuel from the C-130s and then take Delta Force to a second location (Desert Two) some 50 miles southeast of Tehran, where Central Intelligence Agency (CIA) agents would meet them and hide the rescue force at a "mountain hideout." Delta Force would remain hidden during the day before being picked up by CIA operatives early the next night and driven to a location known as "the warehouse" just inside Tehran. From there they would attack the embassy and the Foreign Ministry where three of the hostages were held, rescue the hostages, and take them to a nearby soccer stadium, where the helicopters would meet them and transfer them to a further airstrip at Monzariyeh, to be taken to Egypt by the C-130s. The planning process had meant that very definite deadlines had emerged: By 1 May there would only be 16 minutes of darkness more than required for the mission; by 10 May, the temperature would be so high that it would seriously hamper helicopter performance. 1 May appeared to be the latest feasible date for the mission, and by late March the planners were recommending 24 April for the mission (primarily because a very low level of moonlight was expected that night). But the rescue mission failed. It never got beyond Desert One. Of the eight helicopters assigned to the mission, one got lost in a duststorm and returned to the *Nimitz* and two suffered mechanical breakdowns. This left only five helicopters in working order at Desert One, whereas the plan had called for six to move on to Desert Two. The mission was subsequently aborted, and, in the process of maneuvering to vacate Desert One, one of the helicopters hit a C-130, causing the death of eight men.

It is critical, in any discussion of the applicability of the bureaucratic politics approach, to focus on the actual decisions that led to this mission and to review the positions adopted by the participants. . . . We know that the three meetings of 22 March, 11 and 15 April were the decisive ones, and we know who took part and what they said. The key meeting in terms of the actual decision was on 11 April, when the "go-ahead" was given. The meeting on 22 March was important because at it President Carter gave permission for aircraft to verify the site for Desert One. The meeting of 15 April was important because Cyrus Vance, the secretary of state, presented his reservations about the decision. As Zbigniew Brzezinski, President Carter's national security adviser, pointed out: "In a way, the decision [on 11 April] had been foreshadowed by the discussion initiated at the March 22 briefing at Camp David. From that date on, the rescue mission became the obvious option if negotiations failed—and on that point there was almost unanimous consent within the top echelons of the Administration."[4] A virtually identical set of people were present at those meetings. On 22 March, there attended President Carter, Walter Mondale (the vice president) Cyrus Vance (the secretary of state), Harold Brown (the secretary of defense), David Jones (the chairman of the Joint Chiefs of Staff), Stansfield Turner (the director of the CIA), Zbigniew Brzezinski (the national security adviser), Jody Powell (the press secretary), and David Aaron (the deputy national security adviser). On 11 April, the same participants convened, except that Warren Christopher, the deputy secretary of state, replaced Cyrus Vance, and Carter's aide Hamilton Jordan replaced Aaron. The final meeting on 15 April was attended by the same people who attended on 11 April, except that Vance replaced Christopher.

In order to outline the positions adopted by the participants in this decision-making group, the participants can be divided into four subgroups: President Carter, "hawks," "doves," and "presidential supporters." (These terms are only intended as analytical shorthand.) . . . Although there is a risk of fitting evidence to a preconception, the conclusion . . . is that these groups acted in accordance with what the bureaucratic politics approach would suggest: namely, that the national security adviser, the secretary of defense, the chairman of the Joint Chiefs of Staff, and the director of the CIA would support military action . . . ; the secretary of state, and in his absence his deputy, would oppose it; those individuals who were bureaucratically tied to the president (the vice president, the press secretary, and the political adviser) would be fundamentally concerned with what was best for the Carter presidency; and President Carter, although clearly more than just another bureaucratic actor, would act in a way that reflected bureaucratically derived as well as personal influences.

President Carter

The key to understanding President Carter's position lies in the interaction between his desire to avoid the blatant use of American military power and the great pressure on him to satisfy his public and "do something." From the earliest days of the crisis, he was attacked in the press and by the Republican party for failing to act decisively. 1980 was, of course, a presidential election year, the president's public opinion rating was poor, and he was being challenged strongly for the Democratic party's nomination. His promise not to campaign for the election so long as the hostages were in Iran made his situation worse. He was advised by his campaign staff that decisive action was needed (especially after the fiasco of the morning of the Wisconsin primary, on 1 April, when the president announced that the hostages were about to be released). That inaccurate assessment was seen by many as a reflection of his lack of control over events; it was also portrayed as manipulating the issue for his own political ends.

Another factor which added to the president's frustration was the desire to make the allies go ahead with sanctions against Iran. It later turned out that the allies' belief that the U.S. administration was planning military action was their main incentive to join in the sanctions, in the hope of forestalling it. But the critical moment came when the president felt that the only alternative to military action was to wait until, possibly, the end of the year for the release of the hostages by negotiation. That was the impression he gained in the early days of April: Information coming out of Tehran indicated that the release of the hostages would be delayed for months by the parliamentary elections due to be held in Iran on 16 May. Indeed, by the time the rescue mission was undertaken, the favorite estimate of how long the new government in Iran would take to negotiate was five or six months. So, as a result of fear that the hostages might be held until the end of 1980, President Carter determined on a change in policy: "We could no longer afford to depend on diplomacy. I decided to act."[5] In fact, the president threatened military action on 12 and 17 April, unless the allies undertook economic sanctions. This action (which, he said, had not been decided on yet) would involve the interruption of trade with Iran. (This was widely interpreted as meaning a naval blockade or the mining of Iranian harbors.) Of course, this was a deliberate smokescreen: Accordingly, when on 23 April the European countries agreed to the imposition of sanctions on Iran, the White House let it be known that this would delay any military action until the summer!

Yet the desire of the president for drastic action is only part of the story. It is evident that he was also extremely concerned to limit the size of the operation, in order to avoid unnecessary loss of life. At the briefing with the mission commander, Colonel Beckwith, on 16 April, Carter said: "It will be easy and tempting for your men to become engaged in gunfire with others and to try and settle some scores for our nation. That will interfere with your objective of getting our people out safely. In the eyes of the world, it is important that the scope of this mission be seen as simply removing our people." William Safire has argued that the reason why the mission was unsuccessful was precisely because Carter wanted the rescue to be a humanitarian rather than a combat mission and stipulated only a small force with very limited backup.[6] Hence, in explaining President Carter's position on the rescue mission, two factors seem dominant: a personal concern to ensure that the mission was not to be seen as a punitive military action and a role-governed perception that American national honor was at stake. . . .

Carter's actions were, of course, a response to a number of factors. The bureaucratic politics approach draws our attention to certain of these: specifically, his desire for reelection and his perception of his responsibility as the individual charged with protecting American national honor. Clearly, Carter's personality was an important factor . . . , but the bureaucratic politics approach seems much more useful in identifying the kinds of considerations that would be important to Carter than concentrating on notions of what would be most rational for the American nation. This is not to imply that bureaucratic factors are the only important ones in explaining what Carter did; but it is to claim that a bureaucratic perspective paints a far more accurate picture of what caused Carter to act as he did than any of the rival theories of foreign policymaking.

The Hawks

The leading political proponents of military action throughout the crisis were Brzezinski and Brown. Drew Middleton wrote, "For months, a hard-nosed Pentagon view had held that the seizure of the hostages itself was an act of war and that the United States was, therefore, justified in adopting a military response."[7] Indeed, just two days after the hostages were taken, Brzezinski, Brown, and Jones began discussing the possibilities of a rescue mission. Their discussions led to the conclusion that an immediate mission was impossible, but Brzezinski felt that "one needed such a contingency scheme in the event . . . that some of the hostages either were put on trial and then sentenced to death or were murdered. . . . Accordingly, in such circumstances, we would have to undertake a rescue mission out of a moral as well as a political obligation, both to keep faith with our people imprisoned in Iran and to safeguard American national honor." In fact, Brzezinski felt a rescue mission was not enough: "It would [be] better if the United States were to engage in a generalized retaliatory strike, which could be publicly described as a punitive action and which would be accompanied by the rescue attempt. If the rescue succeeded, that would be all to the good; if it failed, the U.S. government could announce that it had executed a punitive mission against Iran."[8] This punitive action, he thought, could take the form of a military blockade along with airstrikes. In the earliest days of the crisis, Brzezinski, Turner, Jones, and Brown began to meet regularly in private and discuss military options; Brzezinski alone took (handwritten) notes. It was this group which directed the planning for the mission (which used military and CIA personnel) and gave the eventual plan its most detailed review. Similarly, it was Brzezinski who pressed for the reconnaissance flight into Iran, agreed on 22 March, and the same group of four who proposed the rescue plan at the 11 April meeting, led by Brown and Jones. But it is clear from the available evidence that Brzezinski was the political force behind military action.

As early as February, Brzezinski felt increasing pressure from the public and from Congress for direct action to be taken against Iran. Brzezinski thought there were three choices: to continue negotiations, to undertake a large military operation, or to mount a small rescue mission. What swung him away from his earlier first choice, a punitive military operation, was the consideration that, after the Soviet intervention in Afghanistan in December 1979, any military action might give the Soviet Union additional opportunities for influence in the Persian Gulf and Indian Ocean: "It now seemed to me more important to forge an anti-Soviet Islamic coalition. It was in this context that the rescue mission started to look more attractive to me."[9] As negotiations failed, Brzezinski sent a memorandum to Carter on 10 April in which he argued that a choice must be made between a punitive military action or a rescue mission. Given his fears about the spread of Soviet influence, Brzezinski recommended the latter option, concluding, "We have to think beyond the fate of the 50 Americans and consider the deleterious effects of a protracted stalemate, growing public frustration, and international humiliation of the U.S."[10] At both the 11 April and 15 April meetings, Brzezinski spoke forcefully in favor of the mission.

Brown and Jones were the main advocates of the actual rescue plan. . . . These two men presented the plan to the 11 April meeting and conducted the detailed private briefing with Carter on 16 April; it was Harold Brown who gave the detailed account, and defense, of the mission to the press after its failure. It was also Brown who spoke against the Christopher/Vance position at the 11 April and 15 April meetings. Finally, both Brown and Brzezinski spoke very strongly in justification of the mission after its failure, stating that it had been morally right and politically justified. Brzezinski was said to be "downright cocky about it [the mission] in private and insisting that military action might be necessary in future."[11] He also warned America's opponents: "Do not scoff at America's power. Do not scoff at American reach."[12]

Turner, the director of the CIA, was also very much in favor of the mission, so much so that it appears that he did not voice the very serious doubts about the mission which had been expressed in a report by a special CIA review group, prepared for him on 16 March 1980. According to this report, the rescue plan would probably result in the loss of 60 percent of the hostages during the mission: "The estimate of a loss rate of 60 percent for the AmEmbassy hostages represents the best estimate." The report also estimated that the mission was as likely to prove a complete failure as a complete success. Yet it was exactly at this time that the review of the plan was undertaken by Brzezinski's small group. To quote Brzezinski again: "A very comprehensive review of the rescue plan undertaken by Brown, Jones, and me in mid-March led me to the conclusion that the rescue mission had a reasonably good chance of success though there probably would be some casualties. *There was no certain way of estimating how large they might be* [emphasis added]."[13] Turner was involved in the detailed briefings of the president; at the meeting of 11 April he even said, "The conditions inside and around the compound are good." The evidence does not suggest that he made his agency's doubts public at any of these meetings, either in the small group or in the group of nine.

To sum up: The positions adopted by those classified here as "hawks" could have been predicted in advance. What is striking about the evidence is the consistency with which these four men—Brown, Brzezinski, Jones, and Turner—proposed policies that reflected their position in the bureaucratic network. . . . To the extent that the bureaucratic politics approach explains the policies adopted by these individuals, it illustrates the weaknesses of rationality-based theories of U.S. foreign policy.

Presidential Supporters

The next group to consider are those who do not fit into the traditional "hawks–doves" characterization of U.S. government. These are individuals whose primary loyalty is to the president and who would therefore be expected to adopt positions that promised to bolster the president's domestic standing. Unlike those groups discussed so far, the first concern of this group is not the nature of U.S. relations with other states, but, rather, the domestic position of the president. Mondale, Powell, and Jordan seem to have been neither "hawks" nor "doves" in their views of the Iranian action; rather, their policy proposals show that their concern was first and foremost with the effect of the crisis on the Carter presidency. This can be seen very clearly in Jordan's memoirs,[14] which reveal both a loyalty to Carter and an evaluation of the rescue mission in terms of how it helped Carter out of a domestic political problem. "I knew our hard-line approach would not bring the hostages home any sooner, but I hoped that maybe it would buy us a little more time and patience from the public." The rescue mission was "the best of a lousy set of options." Throughout his memoirs, at every juncture of the mission's planning, failure, and consequences, Jordan's position is consistently one in which he advocates what he believed would benefit the president. This determined his reaction to Vance's objections (Vance was failing to support the president when he needed it, thereby putting Carter in an uncomfortable position), to the failure of the mission (Congress's reaction would be to concentrate on the lack of consultation, and it might accuse Carter of violating the War Powers Resolution), and to Vance's resignation and his replacement by Ed Muskie (the former created a problem for Carter, the latter was a vote of confidence in Carter's political future).

The evidence also unambiguously supports the contention that Mondale and Powell were motivated above all by an awareness of the president's domestic standing and their perceptions of how it might be improved. Brzezinski notes that Powell, Mondale, and Jordan "were feeling increasingly frustrated and concerned about rising public pressures for more direct action against Iran."[15] All of them seemed to think that direct action was needed to stem this public pressure, *especially* after the Wisconsin primary announcement on 1 April. As Powell put it on 1 April: "We are about to have an enormous credibility problem. The combination of not campaigning and that early-morning announcement has made skeptics out of even our friends in the press." Salinger argues that Carter's "campaign for reelection registered the frustrations of the American public. While his political fortunes had risen after the taking of the hostages, he was beginning to slip in the polls and had lost a key primary in New York to Senator Kennedy. Jimmy Carter was now in the midst of a fight for his political life, and it looked as if he was losing. A military operation that freed the hostages would dramatically alter the odds."[16] The position of the "presidential supporters" was summed up in Mondale's contribution to the 11 April meeting, when he said, "The rescue offered us the best way out of a situation which was becoming intolerably humiliating." . . .

The "presidential supporters," then, proposed policies which reflected their own bureaucratic position. Mondale, Powell, and Jordan had no vast bureaucratic interests to represent, nor was their chief concern the relationship between U.S. foreign policy and other states. Each of them owed their influence to their position vis-à-vis President Carter (as, of course, did Brzezinski), and their concern was to act so as to aid his presidency, above all his domestic political fortunes. In contemporary press reports, it was these three men who voiced concern about the president's relations with Congress and his chances of reelection. This was in contrast to both the "hawks" and the "doves" who were far more concerned with Carter's relations with Iran, the Soviet Union, and U.S. allies. As in the case of the "hawks," the policy preferences of the "presidential supporters" seem to have been predominantly determined by their bureaucratic role.

The Doves

The evidence that bureaucratic role determines policy stance is strongest of all in the case of the "doves": Cyrus Vance, the secretary of state, and Warren Christopher, the deputy secretary of state. Not only did the two men take virtually identical stands on the subject of the rescue mission, but, as will be discussed below, Christopher did not know what Vance's position was when he attended the 11 April meeting.

From the earliest days of the crisis Vance had advised against the use of military force. At the meeting on 22 March, Vance agreed that a reconnaissance flight should go ahead in case a rescue mission should prove necessary (in the case of a threat to the hostages' lives), but argued against "the use of any military force, including a blockade or mining, as long as the hostages were unharmed and in no imminent danger. In addition to risking the lives of the hostages, I believed military action could jeopardize our interests in the Persian Gulf. . . . Our only realistic course was to keep up the pressure on Iran while we waited for Khomeini to determine that . . . the hostages were of no further value. As painful as it would be, our national interests and the need to protect the lives of our fellow Americans dictated that we continued to exercise restraint." After this meeting, Vance felt there was no indication that a decision on the use of military force was imminent, and on 10 April he left for a long weekend's rest in Florida.

But on the very next day the meeting was held that made the decision to go ahead with the rescue mission. Jody Powell explained to the press later that Cyrus Vance was on a well-earned vacation and that "Vance was not called back because it would have attracted too much attention when the operation had to remain secret." There is no evidence as to why the meeting was called in his absence, but it is clear that Vance did not know that the mission was being so seriously considered and that everyone else involved knew that Vance would disagree. Tom Wicker argues that Vance was deliberately shunted aside from the critical meeting in order to weaken his (and the State Department's) ability to prevent the mission from proceeding.[17] All the Carter, Brzezinski, and Jordan memoirs say is that Vance was on "a brief and much needed vacation" (Carter), "on vacation" (Brzezinski), and "in Florida on a long overdue vacation" (Jordan). In many ways the exclusion of Vance can be interpreted as a symptom of what Irving Janis calls "groupthink"; other symptoms can also be determined in this case study of the phenomenon, which refers to the tendency for groups to maintain amiability and cohesiveness at the cost of critical thinking about decisions.[18]

The president opened the meeting of 11 April by saying that he was seriously considering undertaking a rescue mission, and he invited Brown and Jones to brief those present on the planned mission. At this point, Jordan turned to Christopher and said: "What do you think?" "I'm not sure. Does Cy know about this?" "The contingency rescue plan? Of course." "No, no—does he realize how far along the President is in his thinking about this?" "I don't know . . . I assume they've talked about it." When the briefing finished, Christopher was first to speak. He outlined a number of alternatives to a rescue mission: a return to the U.N. for more discussions, the blacklisting of Iranian ships and aircraft, the possibility of getting European support for sanctions against Iran. Brown immediately dismissed these as "not impressive," and he was supported by Brzezinski, Jones, Turner, Powell, and Jordan, all of whom wanted to go ahead. Christopher was alone in his opposition to the plan. He declined to take up a formal position on the rescue mission since he had not been told about it in advance by Vance; he therefore felt that Vance had either accepted the plan or had felt that the State Department could not really prevent its going ahead. . . . His impression was reinforced when Carter informed the meeting that Vance "prior to leaving for his vacation in Florida, had told the President that he opposed any military action but if a choice had to be made between a rescue and a wider blockade, he preferred the rescue." Christopher knew that Vance had opposed the use of military force, but it is logical to assume that he felt all he could do was to offer nonbelligerent alternatives (they were, after all, State Department people being held hostage) to any use of military force, but remain silent on the actual mission; particularly as it had been strongly suggested that Vance had *already* agreed to it. In support of this conclusion, it is interesting to note that Christopher did not contact Vance on holiday to tell him what had happened. . . .

Vance's reaction to the news was "that he was dismayed and mortified."[19] Vance writes: "Stunned and angry that such a momentous decision had been made in my absence, I went to see the President."[20] At this meeting Vance listed his objections to the mission, and Carter offered him the opportunity to present his views to the group which had made the original decision in the meeting to be held on 15 April. Vance's statement at that meeting focused on issues almost entirely dictated by his bureaucratic position. He said, first, that to undertake the mission when the United States had been trying to get the Europeans to support sanctions on the explicit promise that this would rule out military action would look like deliberate deception; second, the hostages, who were State Department employees, were in no immediate physical danger; third, there were apparently moves in Iran to form a functioning government with which the United States could negotiate; fourth, that even if it succeeded, the mission might simply lead to the taking of more American (or allied) hostages by the Iranians; fifth, it might force the Iranians into the arms of the Soviet Union; and, finally, there would almost certainly be heavy casualties (he cited the figure of 15 out of the 53 hostages and 30 out of the rescue force as a likely death toll).

After Vance's comments, Brown turned to him and asked him when he expected the hostages to be released; Vance replied that he did not know. No one supported Vance: His objections were met by "a deafening silence." Although Vance said later that, after the meeting, a number of participants told him that he had indeed raised serious objections, no one mentioned them at the time—an example of "groupthink?" Carter noted that Vance "was alone in his opposition to the rescue mission among all my advisers, and he knew it."[21] In their memoirs, Carter and Brzezinski put Vance's subsequent resignation down to tiredness: "He looked worn out, his temper would flare up, his eyes were puffy, and he projected unhappiness. . . . Cy seemed to be burned out and determined to quit" (Brzezinski); "Vance has been extremely despondent lately . . . for the third or fourth time, he indicated that he might resign . . . but after he goes through a phase of uncertainty and disapproval, then he joins in with adequate support for me" (Carter). Even worries expressed by Vance about the details of the plan at the 16 April briefing were dismissed on the grounds that they reflected his opposition to the raid in principle. On 21 April, Vance offered his resignation to Carter; it was accepted, with the agreement that it would not be made public until after the rescue mission, whatever the outcome. Vance duly resigned on 28 April. The press reports about his resignation suggested that opposition to the mission was only the last incident in a long line and that Vance's resignation stemmed from his battle with Brzezinski over the direction of U.S. foreign policy. As a White House aide said, it had been "clear for some time that Mr. Vance was no longer part of the foreign policy mainstream in the Carter administration."

That Vance and Christopher opposed the rescue mission is not, in itself, proof of the applicability of the bureaucratic politics approach. What is critical is that their opposition was generated *not* simply from their personal views, but more as a result of their bureaucratic position (although there is a problem in weighting these). These factors warrant this conclusion. First, Christopher, without knowing Vance's position on the rescue mission, and having been told (erroneously) that Vance supported it, still outlined alternatives. In fact, his opposition to the mission was on the same grounds as Vance's, even though he was led to believe that his superior had given the go-ahead. Second, Vance's statement at the 15 April meeting very clearly reflected State Department concerns. The response of Brown and Brzezinski did not address the problems Vance had outlined (for example, the position of the allies), but stressed issues such as national honor and security. These are role-governed policy prescriptions. Third, Vance was not opposed to a rescue mission as such, but only to one at a time when negotiation was still possible; his objection did not simply reflect a personal attitude toward violence. . . .

Conclusion

In the three key meetings that led to the decision to undertake the hostage rescue mission, the evidence presented here suggests that the participants adopted positions that reflected their location in the bureaucratic structure. The influence of bureaucratic structure makes it possible to explain the change in policy that occurred between the 22 March meeting and that of 11 April. In each case, the same group proposed a rescue mission, and the same group (Vance on 22 March, Christopher on 11 April) opposed it. The change came about because the "presidential supporters" and President Carter himself felt that the situation had altered significantly. While this alteration was due in part to external events (the breakdown of negotiations), the evidence . . . suggests that an even stronger reason was the extent of domestic criticism of Carter's inaction (especially after the Wisconsin primary fiasco). The "presidential supporters" felt it was "time to act." For similar reasons, Cyrus Vance's inability to change the rescue decision at the 15 April meeting is also explicable from a bureaucratic political standpoint. In the event, of course, his doubts were only too clearly vindicated. What this case study shows, therefore, is the limitations of an attempt to explain foreign policy decision making as if the state were monolithic and as if "it" had interests. Such an approach makes policymaking appear rational, and this is a major reason for the popularity of such a perspective; but the case of the hostage rescue mission amply demonstrates the limitations of such conceptions of rationality, in that the key decisions are more powerfully explained by the bureaucratic politics perspective.

However, this conclusion requires some qualification since it raises fundamental problems about the precise claims advanced by proponents of the bureaucratic politics approach. . . . The question that must be addressed is whether bureaucratic position alone leads to the adoption of certain policy positions. As it stands, the bureaucratic politics approach is rather mechanical and static; it commits one to the rather simplistic notion that individuals will propose policy alternatives because of their bureaucratic position. Two problems emerge when this is applied to a case study such as this one. The first is that the bureaucratic politics approach lacks a causal mechanism; it cannot simply be true that occupying a role in a bureaucratic structure leads the occupant to hold certain views. The second relates to the wider issue of belief systems, in that certain individuals are "hawkish" irrespective of their precise position in a bureaucracy. The latter problem is most clearly illustrated by the case of Brzezinski, since it is arguable that whatever position he had occupied in Carter's administration, he would have adopted roughly similar views. Together, these problems force us to focus on one issue, namely, the exact meaning of the notion of role in the context of the bureaucratic politics approach.

This issue had been dealt with . . . in the work of Alexander George and of

Glenn Snyder and Paul Diesing.[22] George is concerned with the ways in which U.S. decision makers use (and abuse) information and advice in the policy process. He examines in some depth the ways in which individuals and bureaucracies will select information to assist their rather parochial goals. In other words, through his study of the use of information, George arrives at precisely the same kind of concern that this study has led to, namely, the relationship between individuals and their policy advocacy. More salient, in their comprehensive survey of crisis decision making, Snyder and Diesing discuss the psychological makeup of those groups of individuals named in their study (as in this) "hawks" and "doves." They believe that "hard and soft attitudes are more a function of personality than of governmental roles," and they offer a very useful summary of what the world views of hard- and soft-liners are. As such, the works of George and of Snyder and Diesing are the best available discussions of the impact of role on belief and of belief on information processing. . . .

While it is clear that it is simplistic to assume that bureaucratic position *per se* causes policy preference, it is equally clear that bureaucratic position has some impact. Role, in and of itself, cannot explain the positions adopted by individuals; after all, the very notion of role implies a certain latitude over how to play the role. Further, a role does not involve a single goal, and there is therefore significant room for maneuver and judgment in trading off various goals against each other. Thus, for example, it is not a sufficient explanation of Vance's position just to say that he was secretary of state. There was a complex interplay between his role, his personality, the decision under consideration, and other personal and bureaucratic goals. Yet role occupiers do become predisposed to think in certain, bureaucratic, ways, and for a variety of psychological reasons they tend to adopt mind-sets compatible with those of their closest colleagues. In addition, individuals are often chosen for a specific post *because* they have certain kinds of world views. So for reasons of selection, training, and the need to get on with colleagues, it is not surprising that individuals in certain jobs have certain world views. . . . Thus, while it is clearly the case that Brzezinski was a hawk, it is neither accurate to say that this was because he was national security adviser (since this would not in and of itself cause hawkishness), nor to say that his views were simply personal (since it is surely the case that, had he been secretary of state, he would have had to argue for courses of action other than those he did argue for—given the State Department's concern with getting the allies to agree on sanctions).

This case study therefore leaves us with some critical questions unanswered. On the one hand, the empirical findings are important in that they illustrate the weaknesses of the rational actor approach as an explanation of foreign policy behavior. States are not monoliths, and we might impute very misleading intentions to them if we assume that decisions are rational in this anthropomorphic way. The evidence indicates that the bureaucratic politics approach is very useful in explaining the decision to make an attempt to rescue the hostages. The linkage between the policy preferences of those individuals who made the decision and their bureaucratic position is a more powerful explanation of that decision than any of the alternatives. But . . . the bureaucratic politics approach overemphasizes certain factors and underemphasizes others. On the other hand, the theoretical implications of this case study force us to consider the issue of the sources of the beliefs of decision makers. The "hawks–doves" dichotomy is brought out very strongly in this case study; and yet the bureaucratic politics approach as it stands is not capable of supporting a convincing mechanism for linking position and world view. . . . What is needed is to link the concept of individual rationality with the structural influence of bureaucratic position. . . . This [chapter], therefore, points both to the utility of the bureaucratic politics approach and to its theoretical weaknesses. The very fact that bureaucratic position was so important in determining policy preference over the decision to attempt to rescue the hostages makes the clarification of the nature of bureaucratic role all the more important. . . .

Notes

1. Graham Allison, *Essence of Decision* (Boston: Little, Brown, 1971).

2. Allison, *Essence of Decision,* p. 145.

3. See Allison, *Essence of Decision,* p. 176.

4. Zbigniew Brzezinski, *Power and Principle* (London: Weidenfeld & Nicolson, 1983), p. 493.

5. [Jimmy] Carter, *Keeping Faith* [(London: Collins, 1982)], p. 506.

6. W. Safire, *International Herald Tribune,* 29 April 1980, p. 5.

7. Drew Middleton, "Going the Military Route," *New York Times Magazine,* 17 May 1981, p. 103.

8. Brzezinski, *Power and Principle,* pp. 487–488.

9. Brzezinski, *Power and Principle,* p. 489.

10. Brzezinski, *Power and Principle,* p. 492.

11. *The Times,* 1 May 1980, p. 16.

12. *International Herald Tribune,* 28 April 1980, p. 1.

13. Brzezinski, *Power and Principle,* pp. 489–490.

14. [Hamilton Jordan, *Crisis: The Last Year of the Carter Presidency* (New York: G. P. Putnam's Sons, 1982), pp. 248–289.]

15. Brzezinski, *Power and Principle,* p. 490.

16. [Pierre] Salinger, *America Held Hostage* [(New York: Doubleday, 1981)], p. 235. See also *Newsweek,* 5 May 1980, pp. 24–26, for a discussion of the domestic context.

17. Tom Wicker, "A Tale of Two Silences," *New York Times,* 4 May 1980, p. E.23.

18. See Irving Janis, *Groupthink,* 2nd ed. (Boston: Houghton Mifflin, 1982). . . .

19. Brzezinski, *Power and Principle,* p. 493.

20. [Cyrus] Vance, *Hard Choices* [(New York: Simon & Schuster, 1983)], p. 409.

21. Carter, *Keeping Faith,* p. 513.

22. Alexander George, *Presidential Decision-Making in Foreign Policy: The Effective Use of Information and Advice* (Boulder, Colo.: Westview, 1980); and Glenn Snyder and Paul Diesing, *Conflict Among Nations* (Princeton, N.J.: Princeton University Press, 1977).

21

Are Bureaucracies Important?
A Reexamination of Accounts of the
Cuban Missile Crisis

Stephen D. Krasner

Who and what shapes foreign policy? In recent years, analyses have increasingly emphasized not rational calculations of the national interest or the political goals of national leaders but rather bureaucratic procedures and bureaucratic politics. Starting with Richard Neustadt's *Presidential Power,* a judicious study of leadership published in 1960, this approach has come to portray the American president as trapped by a permanent government more enemy than ally. Bureaucratic theorists imply that it is exceedingly difficult if not impossible for political leaders to control the organizational web which surrounds them. Important decisions result from numerous smaller actions taken by individuals at different levels in the bureaucracy who have partially incompatible national, bureaucratic, political, and personal objectives. They are not necessarily a reflection of the aims and values of high officials. . . .

. . . Analyses of bureaucratic politics have been used to explain alliance behavior during the 1956 Suez crisis and the [1962] Skybolt incident, Truman's relations with MacArthur, American policy in Vietnam, and now most thoroughly the Cuban missile crisis in Graham Allison's *Essence of Decision: Explaining the Cuban Missile Crisis,* published in 1971 (Little, Brown & Company). Allison's volume is the elaboration of an earlier and influential article on this subject. With the publication of his book this approach to foreign policy now receives its definitive statement. The bureaucratic interpretation of foreign policy has become the conventional wisdom.

My argument here is that this vision is misleading, dangerous, and compelling: misleading because it obscures the power of the president; dangerous because it undermines the assumptions of democratic politics by relieving high officials of responsibility; and compelling because it offers leaders an

excuse for their failures and scholars an opportunity for innumerable reinter-
pretations and publications.

The contention that the chief executive is trammeled by the permanent government has disturbing implications for any effort to impute responsibility to
public officials. A democratic political philosophy assumes that responsibility
for the acts of governments can be attributed to elected officials. The charges
of these men are embodied in legal statutes. The electorate punishes an erring
official by rejecting him at the polls. Punishment is senseless unless high
officials are responsible for the acts of government. Elections have some impact only if government, that most complex of modern organizations, can be
controlled. If the bureaucratic machine escapes manipulation and direction
even by the highest officials, then punishment is illogical. Elections are a farce
not because the people suffer from false consciousness, but because public
officials are impotent, enmeshed in a bureaucracy so large that the actions of
government are not responsive to their will. What sense to vote a man out of
office when his successor, regardless of his values, will be trapped in the same
web of only incrementally mutable standard operating procedures?

The Rational Actor Model

Conventional analyses that focus on the values and objectives of foreign policy, what Allison calls the rational actor model, are perfectly coincident with
the ethical assumptions of democratic politics. The state is viewed as a rational
unified actor. The behavior of states is the outcome of a rational decisionmaking process. This process has three steps. The options for a given situation
are spelled out. The consequences of each option are projected. A choice is
made which maximizes the values held by decision makers. The analyst
knows what the state did. His objective is to explain why by imputing to
decision makers a set of values which are maximized by observed behavior.
These values are his explanation of foreign policy.

The citizen, like the analyst, attributes error to either inappropriate values
or lack of foresight. Ideally the electorate judges the officeholder by governmental performance which is assumed to reflect the objectives and perspicac-
ity of political leaders. Poor policy is made by leaders who fail to foresee
accurately the consequences of their decisions or attempt to maximize values
not held by the electorate. Political appeals, couched in terms of aims and
values, are an appropriate guide for voters. For both the analyst who adheres
to the rational actor model and the citizen who decides elections, values are
assumed to be the primary determinant of government behavior.

The bureaucratic politics paradigm points to quite different determinants of
policy. Political leaders can only with great difficulty overcome the inertia
and self-serving interests of the permanent government. What counts is mana-

gerial skill. In *Essence of Decision,* Graham Allison maintains that "the central questions of policy analysis are quite different from the kinds of questions analysts have traditionally asked. Indeed, the crucial questions seem to be matters of planning for management." Administrative feasibility, not substance, becomes the central concern.

The paradoxical conclusion—that bureaucratic analysis with its emphasis on policy guidance implies political nonresponsibility—has most clearly been brought out by discussions of American policy in Vietnam. Richard Neustadt on the concluding page of *Alliance Politics . . .* muses about a conversation he would have had with President Kennedy in the fall of 1963 had tragedy not intervened. "I considered asking whether, in the light of our machine's performance on a British problem, he conceived that it could cope with South Vietnam's. . . . [I]t was a good question, better than I knew. It haunts me still." For adherents of the bureaucratic politics paradigm, Vietnam was a failure of the "machine," a war in Arthur Schlesinger's words "which no President . . . desired or intended."[1] The machine dictated a policy which it could not successfully terminate. The machine not the Cold War ideology and hubris of Kennedy and Johnson determined American behavior in Vietnam. Vietnam could hardly be a tragedy for tragedies are made by choice and character, not fate. A knowing electorate would express sympathy, not levy blame. Machines cannot be held responsible for what they do, nor can the men caught in their workings.

The strength of the bureaucratic web has been attributed to two sources: organizational necessity and bureaucratic interest. The costs of coordination and search procedures are so high that complex organizations *must* settle for satisfactory rather than optimal solutions. Bureaucracies have interests defined in terms of budget allocation, autonomy, morale, and scope which they defend in a game of political bargaining and compromise within the executive branch.

The imperatives of organizational behavior limit flexibility. Without a division of labor and the establishment of standard operating procedures, it would be impossible for large organizations to begin to fulfill their statutory objectives, that is, to perform tasks designed to meet societal needs rather than merely to perpetuate the organization. A division of labor among and within organizations reduces the job of each particular division to manageable proportions. Once this division is made, the complexity confronting an organization or one of its parts is further reduced through the establishment of standard operating procedures. To deal with each problem as if it were *sui generis* would be impossible given limited resources and information processing capacity, and would make intraorganizational coordination extremely difficult. Bureaucracies are then unavoidably rigid; but without the rigidity imposed by division of labor and standard operating procedures, they could hardly begin to function at all.

However, this rigidity inevitably introduces distortions. All of the options to a given problem will not be presented with equal lucidity and conviction unless by some happenstance the organization has worked out its scenarios for that particular problem in advance. It is more likely that the organization will have addressed itself to something *like* the problem with which it is confronted. It has a set of options for such a hypothetical problem, and these options will be presented to deal with the actual issue at hand. Similarly, organizations cannot execute all policy suggestions with equal facility. The development of new standard operating procedures takes time. The procedures which would most faithfully execute a new policy are not likely to have been worked out. The clash between the rigidity of standard operating procedures which are absolutely necessary to achieve coordination among and within large organizations, and the flexibility needed to spell out the options and their consequences for a new problem and to execute new policies is inevitable. It cannot be avoided even with the best of intentions of bureaucratic chiefs anxious to faithfully execute the desires of their leaders.

The Costs of Coordination

The limitations imposed by the need to simplify and coordinate indicate that the great increase in governmental power accompanying industrialization has not been achieved without some costs in terms of control. Bureaucratic organizations and the material and symbolic resources which they direct have enormously increased the ability of the American president to influence the international environment. He operates, however, within limits set by organizational procedures.

A recognition of the limits imposed by bureaucratic necessities is a useful qualification of the assumption that states always maximize their interest. This does not, however, imply that the analyst should abandon a focus on values or assumptions of rationality. Standard operating procedures are rational given the costs of search procedures and need for coordination. The behavior of states is still determined by values although foreign policy may reflect satisfactory rather than optimal outcomes.

An emphasis on the procedural limits of large organizations cannot explain nonincremental change. If government policy is an outcome of standard operating procedures, then behavior at Time T is only incrementally different from behavior at time T-1. The exceptions to this prediction leap out of [such] events . . . [as Nixon's] visit to China and [his] new economic policy. Focusing on the needs dictated by organizational complexity is adequate only during periods when policy is altered very little or not at all. To reduce policymakers to nothing more than the caretakers and minor adjustors of standard operating procedures rings hollow in an era rife with debates and changes of the most fundamental kind in America's conception of its objectives and capabilities.

Bureaucratic analysts do not, however, place the burden of their argument on standard operating procedures, but on bureaucratic politics. The objectives of officials are dictated by their bureaucratic position. Each bureau has its own interests. The interests which bureaucratic analysts emphasize are not clientalistic ties between government departments and societal groups, or special relations with congressional committees. They are, rather, needs dictated by organizational survival and growth—budget allocations, internal morale, and autonomy. Conflicting objectives advocated by different bureau chiefs are reconciled by a political process. Policy results from compromises and bargaining. It does not necessarily reflect the values of the president, let alone of lesser actors.

The clearest expression of the motivational aspects of the bureaucratic politics approach is the by now well-known aphorism—where you stand depends upon where you sit. Decision makers, however, often do not stand where they sit. Sometimes they are not sitting anywhere. This is clearly illustrated by the positions taken by members of the ExCom during the Cuban missile crisis, which Allison elucidates at some length. While the military, in Pavlovian fashion, urged the use of arms, the secretary of defense took a much more pacific position. The wise old men, such as Acheson, imported for the occasion, had no bureaucratic position to defend. Two of the most important members of the ExCom, Robert Kennedy and Theodore Sorensen, were loyal to the president, not to some bureaucratic barony. Similarly, in discussions of Vietnam in 1966 and 1967, it was the secretary of defense who advocated diplomacy and the secretary of state who defended the prerogatives of the military. During Skybolt, McNamara was attuned to the president's budgetary concerns, not those of the Air Force.

Allison, the most recent expositor of the bureaucratic politics approach, realizes the problems which these facts present. In describing motivation, he backs off from an exclusive focus on bureaucratic position, arguing instead that decision makers are motivated by national, organizational, group, and personal interests. While maintaining that the "propensities and priorities stemming from position are sufficient to allow analysts to make reliable predictions about a player's stand" (a proposition violated by his own presentation), he also notes that "these propensities are filtered through the baggage that players bring to positions." For both the missile crisis and Vietnam, it was the "baggage" of culture and values, not bureaucratic position, which determined the aims of high officials.

Bureaucratic analysis is also inadequate in its description of how policy is made. Its axiomatic assumption is that politics is a game with the preferences of players given and independent. This is not true. The president chooses most of the important players and sets the rules. He selects the people who head the large bureaucracies. These individuals must share his values. Certainly they identify with his beliefs to a greater extent than would a randomly chosen group of candidates. They also feel some personal fealty to the president who has elevated them from positions of corporate or legal to ones of historic significance. While bureau chiefs are undoubtedly torn by conflicting pressures arising either from their need to protect their own bureaucracies or from personal conviction, they must remain the president's people. At some point disagreement results in dismissal. The values which bureau chiefs assign to policy outcomes are not independent. They are related through a perspective shared with the president.

The president also structures the governmental environment in which he acts through his impact on what Allison calls "action channels." These are decision-making processes which describe the participation of actors and their influence. The most important "action channel" in the government is the president's ear. The president has a major role in determining who whispers in it. John Kennedy's reliance on his brother, whose bureaucratic position did not afford him any claim to a decision-making role in the missile crisis, is merely an extreme example. By allocating tasks, selecting the White House bureaucracy, and demonstrating special affections, the president also influences "action channels" at lower levels of the government.

The president has an important impact on bureaucratic interests. Internal morale is partially determined by presidential behavior. The obscurity in which Secretary of State Rogers languished during the China trip affected both State Department morale and recruitment prospects. Through the budget the president has a direct impact on that most vital of bureaucratic interests. While a bureau may use its societal clients and congressional allies to secure desired locations, it is surely easier with the president's support than without it. The president can delimit or redefine the scope of an organization's activities by transferring tasks or establishing new agencies. Through public statements he can affect attitudes towards members of a particular bureaucracy and their functions.

The President as "King"

The success a bureau enjoys in furthering its interests depends on maintaining the support and affection of the president. The implicit assumption of the bureaucratic politics approach that departmental and presidential behavior are independent and comparably important is false. Allison, for instance, vacillates between describing the president as one "chief" among several and as a "king" standing above all other men. He describes in great detail the deliberations of the ExCom implying that Kennedy's decision was in large part determined by its recommendations and yet notes that during the crisis Kennedy vetoed an ExCom decision to bomb a SAM base after an American U-2 was shot down on October 27. In general, bureaucratic analysts ignore the critical effect which the president has in choosing his advisers, establishing their access to decision making, and influencing bureaucratic interests.

All of this is not to deny that bureaucratic interests may sometimes be decisive in the formulation of foreign policy. Some policy options are never presented to the president. Others he deals with only cursorily, not going beyond options presented by the bureaucracy. This will only be the case if presidential interest and attention are absent. The failure of a chief executive to specify policy does not mean that the government takes no action. Individual bureaucracies may initiate policies which suit their own needs and objectives. The actions of different organizations may work at cross-purposes. The behavior of the state, that is of some of its official organizations, in the international system appears confused or even contradictory. This is a situation which develops, however, not because of the independent power of government organizations but because of failures by decision makers to assert control.

The ability of bureaucracies to independently establish policies is a function of presidential attention. Presidential attention is a function of presidential values. The chief executive involves himself in those areas which he determines to be important. When the president does devote time and attention to an issue, he can compel the bureaucracy to present him with alternatives. He may do this as Nixon apparently [did] by establishing an organization under his Special Assistant for National Security Affairs, whose only bureaucratic interest [was] maintaining the president's confidence. The president may also rely upon several bureaucracies to secure proposals. The president may even resort to his own knowledge and sense of history to find options which his bureaucracy fails to present. Even when presidential attention is totally absent, bureaus are sensitive to his values. Policies which violate presidential objectives may bring presidential wrath.

While the president is undoubtedly constrained in the implementation of policy by existing bureaucratic procedures, he even has options in this area. As Allison points out, he can choose which agencies will perform what tasks. Programs are fungible and can be broken down into their individual standard operating procedures and recombined. Such exercises take time and effort but the expenditure of such energies by the president is ultimately a reflection of his own values and not those of the bureaucracy. Within the structure which he has partially created himself he can, if he chooses, further manipulate both the options presented to him and the organizational tools for implementing them.

Neither organizational necessity nor bureaucratic interests are the fundamental determinants of policy. The limits imposed by standard operating procedures as well as the direction of policy are a function of the values of decision makers. The president creates much of the bureaucratic environment which surrounds him through his selection of bureau chiefs, determination of "action channels," and statutory powers.

The Missile Crisis

Adherents of the bureaucratic politics framework have not relied exclusively on general argument. They have attempted to substantiate their contentions with detailed investigations of particular historical events. The most painstaking is Graham Allison's analysis of the Cuban missile crisis in his *Essence of Decision*. In a superlative heuristic exercise Allison attempts to show that critical facts and relationships are ignored by conventional analysis that assumes states are unified rational actors. Only by examining the missile crisis in terms of organizational necessity, and bureaucratic interests and politics, can the formulation and implementation of policy be understood.

The missile crisis, as Allison notes, is a situation in which conventional analysis would appear most appropriate. The president devoted large amounts of time to policy formulation and implementation. Regular bureaucratic channels were short-circuited by the creation of an executive committee which included representatives of the bipartisan foreign policy establishment, bureau chiefs, and the president's special aides. The president dealt with details which would normally be left to bureaucratic subordinates. If, under such circumstances, the president could not effectively control policy formulation and implementation, then the rational actor model is gravely suspect.

In his analysis of the missile crisis, Allison deals with three issues: the American choice of a blockade, the Soviet decision to place MRBMs and IRBMs on Cuba, and the Soviet decision to withdraw the missiles from Cuba. The American decision is given the most detailed attention. Allison notes three ways in which bureaucratic procedures and interests influenced the formulation of American policy: first, in the elimination of the nonforcible alternatives; second, through the collection of information; third, through the standard operating procedures of the Air Force.

In formulating the U.S. response, the ExCom considered six alternatives. These were:

1. Do nothing
2. Diplomatic pressure
3. A secret approach to Castro
4. Invasion
5. A surgical air strike
6. A naval blockade

The approach to Castro was abandoned because he did not have direct control of the missiles. An invasion was eliminated as a first step because it would not have been precluded by any of the other options. Bureaucratic factors were not involved.

The two nonmilitary options of doing nothing and lodging diplomatic protests were also abandoned from the outset because the president was not interested in them. In terms of both domestic and international politics this was the most important decision of the crisis. It was a decision which only the president had authority to make. Allison's case rests on proving that this decision was foreordained by bureaucratic roles. He lists several reasons for Kennedy's elimination of the nonforcible alternatives. Failure to act decisively would undermine the confidence of members of his administration, convince the permanent government that his administration lacked leadership, hurt the Democrats in the forthcoming election, destroy his reputation among members of Congress, create public distrust, encourage American allies and enemies to question American courage, invite a second Bay of Pigs, and feed his own doubts about himself. Allison quotes a statement by Kennedy that he feared impeachment and concludes that the "non-forcible paths—avoiding military measures, resorting instead to diplomacy—could not have been more irrelevant to *his* problems." Thus Allison argues that Kennedy had no choice.

Bureaucratic analysis, what Allison calls in his book the governmental politics model, implies that any man in the same position would have had no choice. The elimination of passivity and diplomacy was ordained by the office and not by the man.

Such a judgment is essential to the governmental politics model, for the resort to the "baggage" of values, culture, and psychology which the president carries with him undermines the explanatory and predictive power of the approach. To adopt, however, the view that the office determined Kennedy's action is both to underrate his power and to relieve him of responsibility. The president defines his own role. A different man could have chosen differently. Kennedy's *Profiles in Courage* had precisely dealt with men who had risked losing their political roles because of their "baggage" of values and culture.

Allison's use of the term "intragovernmental balance of power" to describe John Kennedy's elimination of diplomacy and passivity is misleading. The American government is not a balance of power system; at the very least it is a loose hierarchical one. Kennedy's judgments of the domestic, international, bureaucratic, and personal ramifications of his choice were determined by *who* he was, as well as *what* he was. The central mystery of the crisis remains why Kennedy chose to risk nuclear war over missile placements which he knew did not dramatically alter the strategic balance. The answer to this puzzle can only be found through an examination of values, the central concern of conventional analysis.

The impact of bureaucratic interests and standard operating procedures is reduced then to the choice of the blockade instead of the surgical air strike. Allison places considerable emphasis on intelligence gathering in the determination of this choice. U-2 flights were the most important source of data about Cuba; their information was supplemented by refugee reports, analyses of shipping, and other kinds of intelligence. The timing of the U-2 flights, which

Allison argues was determined primarily by bureaucratic struggles, was instrumental in determining Kennedy's decision:

> Had a U-2 flown over the western end of Cuba three weeks earlier, it could have discovered the missiles, giving the administration more time to consider alternatives and to act before the danger of operational missiles in Cuba became a major factor in the equation. Had the missiles not been discovered until two weeks later, the blockade would have been irrelevant, since the Soviet missile shipments would have been completed. . . . An explanation of the politics of the discovery is consequently a considerable piece of the explanation of the U.S. blockade.

The delay, however, from September 15 to October 14 when the missiles were discovered reflected presidential values more than bureaucratic politics. The October 14 flight took place 10 days after COMOR, the interdepartmental committee which directed the activity of the U-2s, had decided the flights should be made. "This 10 day delay constitutes some form of 'failure,'" Allison contends. It was the result, he argues, of a struggle between the Central Intelligence Agency and the Air Force over who would control the flights. The Air Force maintained that the flights over Cuba were sufficiently dangerous to warrant military supervision; the Central Intelligence Agency, anxious to guard its own prerogatives, maintained that its U-2s were technically superior.

However, the 10-day delay after the decision to make a flight over western Cuba was not entirely attributable to bureaucratic bickering. Allison reports an attempt to make a flight on October 9 which failed because the U-2 flamed out. Further delays resulted from bad weather. Thus the inactivity caused by bureaucratic infighting amounted to only five days (October 4 to October 9) once the general decision to make the flight was taken. The other five days' delay caused by engine failure and the weather must be attributed to some higher source than the machinations of the American bureaucracy.

However, there was also a long period of hesitation before October 4. John McCone, director of the Central Intelligence Agency, had indicated to the president on August 22 that he thought there was a strong possibility that the Soviets were preparing to put offensive missiles on Cuba. He did not have firm evidence, and his contentions were met with skepticism in the administration.

Increased Risks

On September 10, COMOR had decided to restrict further U-2 flights over western Cuba. This decision was based upon factors which closely fit the rational actor model of foreign policy formulation. COMOR decided to halt the flights because the recent installation of SAMs in western Cuba coupled with the loss of a Nationalist Chinese U-2 increased the probability and costs of a U-2 loss over Cuba. International opinion might force the cancellation of the flights altogether. The absence of information from U-2s would be a national, not simply a bureaucratic, cost. The president had been forcefully attacking the critics of his Cuba policy, arguing that patience and restraint were the best course of action. The loss of a U-2 over Cuba would tend to undermine the president's position. Thus, COMOR's decision on September 10 reflected a sensitivity to the needs and policies of the president rather than the parochial concerns of the permanent government.

The decision on October 4 to allow further flights was taken only after consultation with the president. The timing was determined largely by the wishes of the president. His actions were not circumscribed by decisions made at lower levels of the bureaucracy of which he was not aware. The flights were delayed because of conflicting pressures and risks confronting Kennedy. He was forced to weigh the potential benefits of additional knowledge against the possible losses if a U-2 were shot down.

What if the missiles had not been discovered until after October 14? Allison argues that had the missiles been discovered two weeks later the blockade would have been irrelevant since the missile shipments would have been completed. This is true but only to a limited extent. The blockade was irrelevant even when it was put in place for there were missiles already on the island. As Allison points out in his rational actor cut at explaining the crisis, the blockade was both an act preventing the shipment of additional missiles and a signal of American firmness. The missiles already on Cuba were removed because of what the blockade meant and not because of what it did.

An inescapable dilemma confronted the United States. It could not retaliate until the missiles were on the island. Military threats or action required definitive proof. The United States could only justify actions with photographic evidence. It could only take photos after the missiles were on Cuba. The blockade could only be a demonstration of American firmness. Even if the missiles had not been discovered until they were operational, the United States might still have begun its response with a blockade.

Aside from the timing of the discovery of the missiles, Allison argues that the standard operating procedures of the Air Force affected the decision to blockade rather than to launch a surgical air strike. When the missiles were first discovered, the Air Force had no specific contingency plans for dealing with such a situation. They did, however, have a plan for a large-scale air strike carried out in conjunction with an invasion of Cuba. The plan called for the air bombardment of many targets. This led to some confusion during the first week of the ExCom's considerations because the Air Force was talking in terms of an air strike of some 500 sorties while there were only some 40 known missile sites on Cuba. Before this confrontation was clarified, a strong coalition of advisers was backing the blockade.

As a further example of the impact of standard operating procedures, Allison notes that the Air Force had classified the missiles as mobile. Because this classification assumed that the missiles might be moved immediately before an air strike, the commander of the Air Force would not guarantee that a surgical air strike would be completely effective. By the end of the first week of the ExCon's deliberations when Kennedy made his decision for a blockade, the surgical air strike was presented as a "null option." The examination of the strike was not reopened until the following week when civilian experts found that the missiles were not in fact mobile.

This incident suggests one caveat to Allison's assertion that the missile crisis is a case which discriminates against bureaucratic analysis. In crises when time is short the president may have to accept bureaucratic options which could be amended under more leisurely conditions.

Not Another Pearl Harbor

The impact of the Air Force's standard operating procedures on Kennedy's decision must, however, to some extent remain obscure. It is not likely that either McNamara, who initially called for a diplomatic response, or Robert Kennedy, who was partially concerned with the ethical implications of a surprise air strike, would have changed their recommendations even if the Air Force had estimated its capacities more optimistically. There were other reasons for choosing the blockade aside from the apparent infeasibility of the air strike. John Kennedy was not anxious to have the Pearl Harbor analogy applied to the United States. At one of the early meetings of the ExCom, his brother had passed a note saying, "I now know how Tojo felt when he was planning Pearl Harbor." The air strike could still be considered even if the blockade failed. A chief executive anxious to keep his options open would find a blockade a more prudent initial course of action.

Even if the Air Force had stated that a surgical air strike was feasible, this might have been discounted by the president. Kennedy had already experienced unrealistic military estimates. The Bay of Pigs was the most notable example. The United States did not use low-flying photographic reconnaissance until after the president had made his public announcement of the blockade. Prior to the president's speech on October 22, 20 high altitude U-2 flights were made. After the speech there were 85 low-level missions, indicating that the intelligence community was not entirely confident that U-2 flights alone would reveal all of the missile sites. The Soviets might have been camouflaging some missiles on Cuba. Thus, even if the immobility of the missiles had been correctly estimated, it would have been rash to assume that an air strike would have extirpated all of the missiles. There were several reasons, aside from the Air Force's estimate, for rejecting the surgical strike.

Thus, in terms of policy formulation, it is not clear that the examples offered by Allison concerning the timing of discovery of the missiles and the standard operating procedures of the Air Force had a decisive impact on the choice of a blockade over a surgical air strike. The ultimate decisions did rest with the president. The elimination of the nonforcible options was a reflection of Kennedy's values. An explanation of the Cuban missile crisis which fails to explain policy in terms of the values of the chief decision maker must inevitably lose sight of the forest for the trees.

The most chilling passages in *Essence of Decision* are concerned not with the formulation of policy but with its implementation. In carrying out the blockade the limitations on the president's ability to control events became painfully clear. Kennedy did keep extraordinarily close tabs on the workings of the blockade. The first Russian ship to reach the blockade was allowed to pass through without being intercepted on direct orders from the president. Kennedy felt it would be wise to allow Khrushchev more time. The president overrode the ExCom's decision to fire on a Cuban SAM base after a U-2 was shot down on October 27. A spy ship similar to the *Pueblo* was patrolling perilously close to Cuba and was ordered to move further out to sea.

Despite concerted presidential attention coupled with an awareness of the necessity of watching minute details which would normally be left to lower levels of bureaucracy, the president still had exceptional difficulty in controlling events. Kennedy personally ordered the Navy to pull in the blockade from 800 miles to 500 miles to give Khrushchev additional time in which to make his decision. Allison suggests that the ships were not drawn in. The Navy being both anxious to guard its prerogatives and confronted with the difficulty of moving large numbers of ships over millions of square miles of ocean, failed to promptly execute a presidential directive.

There were several random events which might have changed the outcome of the crisis. The Navy used the blockade to test its antisubmarine operations. It was forcing Soviet submarines to surface at a time when the president and his advisers were unaware that contact with Russian ships had been made. A U-2 accidentally strayed over Siberia on October 22. Any one of these events, and perhaps others . . . , could have triggered escalatory actions by the Russians.

Taken together, they strongly indicate how much caution is necessary when a random event may have costly consequences. A nation, like a drunk staggering on a cliff, should stay far from the edge. The only conclusion which can be drawn from the inability of the chief executive to fully control the implementation of a policy in which he was intensely interested and to which he devoted virtually all of his time for an extended period is that the risks were even greater than the president knew. Allison is more convincing on the problems concerned with policy implementation than on questions relating to policy formulation. Neither bureaucratic interests nor organizational procedures explain the positions taken by members of the ExCom, the elimination of passivity and diplomacy, or the choice of a blockade instead of an air strike.

Conclusion

. . . Before the niceties of bureaucratic implementation are investigated, it is necessary to know what objectives are being sought. Objectives are ultimately a reflection of values, of beliefs concerning what man and society ought to be. The failure of the American government to take decisive action in a number of critical areas reflects not so much the inertia of a large bureaucratic machine as a confusion over values which afflicts the society in general and its leaders in particular. It is, in such circumstances, too comforting to attribute failure to organizational inertia, although nothing could be more convenient for political leaders who having either not formulated any policy or advocated bad policies can blame their failures on the governmental structure. Both psychologically and politically, leaders may find it advantageous to have others think of them as ineffectual rather than evil. But the facts are otherwise—particularly in foreign policy. There the choices—and the responsibility—rest squarely with the president.

Note

1. Quoted in Daniel Ellsberg, "The Quagmire Myth and the Stalemate Machine," *Public Policy* (Spring 1971): 218. [For an exemplary treatment of this thesis, see James C. Thomson's essay in Chapter 17 in this book—eds.]

22

NATO Expansion:
The Anatomy of a Decision

James M. Goldgeier

In deciding to enlarge the North Atlantic Treaty Organization (NATO) Bill Clinton's administration followed through on one of its most significant foreign policy initiatives and the most important political-military decision for the United States since the collapse of the Soviet Union. The policy has involved a difficult tradeoff for the administration between wanting to ensure that political and economic reform succeeds in Central and Eastern Europe and not wanting to antagonize Russia, which has received billions of dollars to assist its transition to a democratic, market-oriented Western partner. Skeptics of the NATO expansion policy within the government also worried about its costs, its effect on the cohesiveness of the Atlantic Alliance, and the wisdom of extending security guarantees to new countries. How did President Clinton, often criticized for a lack of attention to foreign policy and for vacillation on important issues, come to make a decision with far-reaching consequences for all of Europe at a time when NATO faced no military threat and in the context of diminishing resources for foreign policy?

This article analyzes the process the U.S. government followed that led to this major foreign policy initiative. I have based my findings largely on interviews I conducted in 1997 with several dozen current and former U.S. government officials, from desk officers deep inside the State and Defense Departments all the way up to President Clinton's top foreign policy advisers. The interviews reveal that the administration decided to expand NATO despite widespread bureaucratic opposition, because a few key people wanted it to happen, the most important being the president and his national security adviser, Anthony Lake. Other senior officials—particularly those in the State Department—became important supporters and implementers of NATO

Note: Some notes have been deleted or renumbered.

expansion, but Lake's intervention proved critical early in the process. Keenly interested in pushing NATO's expansion as part of the administration's strategy of enlarging the community of democracies, Lake encouraged the president to make statements supporting expansion and then used those statements to direct the National Security Council (NSC) staff to develop a plan and a timetable for putting these ideas into action. The president, once convinced that this policy was the right thing to do, led the alliance on this mission into the territory of the former Warsaw Pact and sought to make NATO's traditional adversary part of the process through his personal relationship with Russian president Boris Yeltsin.

Rather than being a story of a single decision, this policy initiative came about through a series of decisions and presidential statements made during three key phases of the process in 1993 and 1994. During the summer and fall of 1993, the need to prepare for Clinton's January 1994 summit meetings in Brussels pushed the bureaucracy into action. The product of this bureaucratic activity was the October 1993 proposal to develop the Partnership for Peace (PFP), which would increase military ties between NATO and its former adversaries. In the second phase, which culminated in his January 1994 trip to Europe, Clinton first signaled U.S. seriousness about NATO expansion by saying the question was no longer "whether" but "when."

The final phase discussed here encompasses the period from April to October 1994, when key supporters of NATO expansion attempted to turn this presidential rhetoric into reality. At the end of this period, the newly installed assistant secretary of state for European affairs, Richard Holbrooke, bludgeoned the bureaucracy into understanding that expansion was presidential policy, and an idea that had been bandied about for a year and a half finally started to become reality.

Phase One: Bureaucratic Debate and Endorsement of the PFP

In the first few months of his administration, President Clinton had not given much thought to the issue of NATO's future. Then, in late April 1993, at the opening of the Holocaust Museum in Washington, he met one-on-one with a series of Central and Eastern European leaders, including the highly regarded leaders of Poland and the Czech Republic, Lech Walesa and Vaclav Havel. These two, having struggled so long to throw off the Soviet yoke, carried a moral authority matched by few others around the world. Each leader delivered the same message to Clinton: Their top priority was NATO membership. After the meetings, Clinton told Lake how impressed he had been with the vehemence with which these leaders spoke, and Lake says Clinton was inclined to think positively toward expansion from that moment.

At the June 1993 meeting of the North Atlantic Council (NAC) foreign ministers in Athens, Greece, U.S. secretary of state Warren Christopher said enlarging NATO's membership was "not now on the agenda." But Christopher understood that NATO needed to assess its future, and with White House endorsement, he pushed his fellow foreign ministers to announce that their heads of state would meet six months later, in January 1994.[1] This announcement set in motion a process back in Washington to discuss the contentious issue of expansion. At the White House, Lake wrote in the margins of Christopher's statement, "why not now?", and his senior director for European affairs, Jenonne Walker, convened an interagency working group (IWG) to prepare for the January 1994 meeting in Brussels and to recommend what the president should do there. The working group involved representatives from the NSC staff, the State Department, and the Pentagon. According to several participants, Walker informed the group at the start that both the president and Lake were interested in pursuing expansion.

On September 21, 1993, nine months into the Clinton administration, Lake gave his first major foreign policy speech, in which he developed ideas on promoting democracy and market economies that Clinton had enunciated during his campaign. Clinton had stressed the theme that democracies do not go to war with one another and thus that U.S. foreign policy strategy should focus on promoting democracy. Lake had helped to develop this approach, which leading campaign officials saw as a foreign policy initiative behind which different wings of the Democratic party could rally. In the 1993 speech, Lake argued that "the successor to a doctrine of containment must be a strategy of enlargement—enlargement of the world's free community of market democracies." And he added, "At the NATO summit that the president has called for this January, we will seek to update NATO, so that there continues behind the enlargement of market democracies an essential collective security."[2]

Although Lake tried rhetorically to push the process along, the bureaucracy greatly resisted expanding the alliance. Officials at the Pentagon unanimously favored the Partnership for Peace proposal developing largely through the efforts of General John Shalikashvili and his staff, first from Shalikashvili's perch as Supreme Allied Commander in Europe and then as chairman of the Joint Chiefs of Staff. PFP proponents sought to foster increased ties to all the former Warsaw Pact states as well as to the traditional European neutrals, and to ensure that NATO did not have to differentiate among its former adversaries or "draw new lines" in Europe. Every state that accepted its general principles could join the PFP, and the countries themselves could decide their level of participation. Many officials viewed the partnership as a means of strengthening and making operational the North Atlantic Cooperation Council (NACC), which had been NATO's first formal outreach effort to the East, undertaken in 1991. From the Pentagon's standpoint, it did not make sense to talk about expansion until after NATO had established the type of military-to-military relationships that would enable new countries to integrate effectively into the alliance. Several participants in the IWG say that Pentagon representatives made clear that both Secretary of Defense Les Aspin and General Shalikashvili opposed expansion and, in particular, feared diluting the effectiveness of NATO. . . .

In addition to concern about NATO's future military effectiveness, the bureaucracy also feared that expansion would antagonize Russia and bolster nationalists and Communists there. Many State Department debates at this time focused on this fear, and views on expansion there were more divided than those in the Pentagon. In September, Yeltsin had written a letter to Clinton and other NATO heads of state backtracking on positive remarks he had made in Warsaw on Polish membership in NATO and suggesting that if NATO expanded, Russia should be on the same fast track as the Central Europeans. Then, in early October, Yeltsin's troops fired on his opposition in Parliament, and it appeared to many that the political situation in Russia was deteriorating.

During this period, a small group at the State Department—including Lynn Davis, the under secretary for arms control and international security affairs, Thomas Donilon, the chief of staff, and Stephen Flanagan, a member of the Policy Planning Staff—advocated a fast-track approach to expansion. This group argued that in January 1994, NATO should lay out criteria, put forward a clear timetable, and perhaps even offer "associate membership" to a first set of countries. At a series of lunches with Secretary Christopher, organized to present him with the pros and cons of expansion, these individuals pressed him to move the process forward as quickly as possible, saying, as one participant recalls, that NATO should "strike while the iron is hot.". . .

Flanagan, Donilon, and Davis worried that without the prospect of membership in a key Western institution, Central and Eastern Europe would lose the momentum for reform. NATO and the European Union (EU) were the premier institutions in Europe, and the EU, absorbed in the internal problems associated with the Maastricht Treaty, would clearly postpone its own expansion. These officials wanted to encourage states such as Poland and Hungary to continue on the path of reform—to adopt civilian control of the military, to build a free polity and economy, and to settle border disputes—by providing the carrot of NATO membership if they succeeded.

This pro-expansion group also drew on compelling arguments from two other government officials. Charles Gati, a specialist on Eastern Europe serving on the Policy Planning Staff, had written a memo in September 1993 arguing that the new democracies were fragile, that the ex-Communists were likely to gain power in Poland, and that if NATO helped Poland succeed in carrying out reforms, it would have a huge impact on the rest of the region. Donilon took this memo straight to Christopher, who found the reasoning impressive. When the ex-Communists did win parliamentary elections in Poland weeks later, Gati's words carried even greater weight.

The other argument came from Dennis Ross, the special Middle East coordinator for the Clinton administration, who had been director of policy planning under Secretary of State James A. Baker III. Given his involvement in the German unification process and the development of the NACC, Ross attended two of the Christopher lunches on NATO. During one, he reminded the group that critics had believed that NATO could not successfully bring in a united Germany in 1990, but it did, and without damaging U.S.–Soviet relations. He suggested that NATO involve Russia in the expansion process rather than confront its former enemy. Ross argued that the previous administration's experience with German unification offered good reason to believe that the current administration could overcome problems with Russia.

Inside the State Department's regional bureaus dealing with Europe and with the New Independent States (NIS), however, bureaucrats expressed tremendous opposition to a fast-track approach and in a number of cases to any idea of expansion. Many who worked on NATO issues feared problems of managing the alliance if Clinton pushed ahead with this contentious issue. Those who worked on Russia issues thought expansion would undermine reform efforts there.

In these State Department debates, the most important proponent of a much more cautious and gradualist approach to expansion was Strobe Talbott, then ambassador-at-large for the NIS [New Independent States]. Talbott proved important for two reasons: As a longtime friend, he had direct access to Clinton, and as a former journalist, he could write quickly, clearly, and persuasively. Christopher asked Talbott and Nicholas Burns—the senior director for Russian, Ukrainian, and Eurasian Affairs at the NSC—to comment on the fast-track approach. He and Burns argued to both Christopher and Lake that Russia would not understand a quick expansion, which would impair the U.S.–Russia relationship and, given the domestic turmoil in Russia in late September and early October, might push Russia over the edge.

One Saturday in mid-October, when Talbott was out of town, Lynn Davis forcefully argued to Christopher at a NATO discussion lunch that NACC and the PFP were simply not enough. When Talbott returned that afternoon and learned about the thrust of the meeting, he quickly wrote a paper reiterating the importance of a gradual approach to expansion. The next day, he delivered a memo to Christopher, stating, "Laying down criteria could be quite provocative, and badly timed with what is going on in Russia." Instead, he suggested, "Take the one new idea that seems to be universally accepted, PFP, and make that the centerpiece of our NATO position." Talbott argued that the administration should not put forward any criteria on NATO membership that would automatically exclude Russia and Ukraine, and that the administration could never manage the relationship if it did not offer Russia the prospect of joining the alliance at a future date. He firmly believed that Clinton should mention neither dates nor names in Brussels.[3]

By Monday morning, October 18, Christopher had decided to support the gradual rather than fast-track approach, which meant that any agreement among leading officials would place the policy emphasis on the PFP. Among Clinton's top foreign-policy advisers, Lake sought to push ahead with expansion, Aspin and Shalikashvili sought to delay consideration of expansion and instead supported the PFP, and Christopher fell somewhere in between, open to gradual expansion but concerned about Russia's reaction. At the White House later that day, Clinton endorsed the consensus of his principal foreign policy advisers that, at the January summit, the alliance should formally present the PFP, and he should announce NATO's intention eventually to expand. This decision reflected the consensus that had emerged from the bargaining within agencies and in the IWG, which had easily agreed on the PFP, but which could not agree on issues such as criteria, a timetable, or "associate membership" status. In the end, the IWG agreed on what its principals in turn could accept: to put forward the PFP and to say something general about NATO's eventual expansion.

The consensus emerged because, as with many decisions, opponents and proponents of expansion had different interpretations of what they had decided, and this ambiguity created support for the decision throughout the bureaucracy. Vociferous opponents of NATO expansion believed the administration's principals had decided to promote the PFP while postponing a decision on enlargement. Those in the middle, who could live with expansion but did not want to do anything concrete in 1994, also saw the October decision as consistent with their preferences. Finally, the decision that Clinton should comment on expansion pleased proponents of near-term enlargement, as they believed such a treatment would help to move the process along on a faster track.

The October 18 meeting would be the last of its kind on NATO expansion for another year. Given the meeting's ambiguous outcome—the foreign policy principals had not given the president a timetable to endorse—confusion reigned concerning the policy's direction. For the moment, the decision to develop the PFP was the Clinton administration's NATO outreach policy.

Yet from the moment the participants went their separate ways observers could tell they interpreted the decision differently. Secretary of State Christopher's entourage, on its way to Budapest to brief the Central Europeans (and then on to Moscow to explain the policy to Yeltsin), said the January summit would send the signal that NATO's door would open at some future date (and apparently even State Department officials on Christopher's plane disagreed about how to present the decision). The senior official conducting the airborne press briefing stated, "We believe that the summit should formally open the door to NATO expansion as an evolutionary process."[4] Meanwhile, Secretary of Defense Aspin and his advisers, attending the NATO defense ministers' meeting in Travamünde, Germany, to gain alliance endorsement of the PFP, emphasized that NATO would not enlarge soon. According to one report, Lake called Aspin in a pique saying the secretary of defense had veered from the script.[5]

Phase Two: The President Speaks

After mid-October, administration officials knew the president would say something about NATO enlargement on his trip to Europe in January. But no one was sure how much he would say and how specific he would be. After all, the bureaucratic wrangling had produced a decision that the president should emphasize the PFP while delivering a vague statement that NATO could eventually take in new members.

The first official statement prior to the summit came from Secretary Christopher at the plenary session of the Conference on Security and Cooperation in Europe (CSCE) in Rome on November 30. Noting that the United States was proposing a Partnership for Peace, he also stated, "At the same time, we propose to open the door to an evolutionary expansion of NATO's membership."[6] Two days later, at the NAC ministerial in Brussels, he said, "The Partnership is an important step in its own right. But it can also be a key step toward NATO membership."[7]

Meanwhile, prominent figures from previous administrations pressured Clinton to be more forthcoming on expansion at the summit. Former secretary of state Henry Kissinger complained in an op-ed piece that the PFP "would dilute what is left of the Atlantic Alliance into a vague multilateralism," and he called for movement to bring Poland, Hungary, and the Czech Republic into some form of "qualified membership." Former national security adviser Zbigniew Brzezinski urged NATO members to sign a formal treaty of alliance with Russia and to lay out a more explicit path to full NATO membership for the leading Central European candidates. Former secretary of state James Baker also made the case for a "clear road map" with "clear benchmarks" for the prospective members.[8]

During this time, Brzezinski had been meeting with Lake to share ideas about his two-track approach to expansion, and he also invited Lake to his home to meet a number of Central and Eastern European leaders. Since the debate at the White House focused more on "whether" than concretely "how," these meetings with Brzezinski helped Lake to clarify his own thinking and emphasized to him the importance of keeping the process moving forward. Significantly, Brzezinski argued that Russia would be more likely to develop as a stable, democratic presence in Europe if the West removed all temptations to reassert imperial control and precluded Russia's ability to intimidate its former satellites.

In late December, Lake's staff members, who were in general opposed to moving expansion onto the near-term agenda, presented him with the draft briefing memoranda for the different stops on the president's upcoming trip to Europe. Several of his staffers say he threw a fit on seeing the initial work, because the memos emphasized the Partnership for Peace. According to Nicholas Burns, Lake wanted a presidential statement in January that would leave no doubt about the policy's direction.

But high-level opposition to any push toward expansion continued to color the agenda. The Pentagon appeared unanimously to share the view that the policy should be sequential; countries would participate in the PFP for a number of years and then the alliance might start addressing the issue of expansion. General Shalikashvili, at a White House press briefing on January 4, emphasized the value of the Partnership for Peace as a way of ensuring that the alliance create no new divisions in Europe, and he suggested postponing discussions of membership to a future date. . . .

But, he added, in words that Clinton would make much more significant a week later, "It is useful to remember that we are talking so much less today about whether extension of the alliance [should take place], but so much more about how and when." Pentagon officials, however, had a much different view of what "when" meant than did proponents of expansion at the NSC and State, believing the PFP should operate for several years before the alliance began thinking about expansion.

Prior to the summit, even Clinton still seemed unsure of how far he wanted to go. The strong showing of nationalists and Communists in the December 1993 Russian parliamentary elections had sent shockwaves through the administration. On January 4, Clinton said in an exchange with reporters at the White House,

> I'm not against expanding NATO. I just think that if you look at the consensus of the NATO members at this time, there's not a consensus to expand NATO at this time and we don't want to give the impression that we're creating another dividing line in Europe after we've worked for decades to get rid of the one that existed before.[9]

This was hardly the signal the Central Europeans had hoped to receive.

Just prior to his trip, Clinton sent Polish-born General Shalikashvili, Czech-born U.S. ambassador to the UN Madeleine Albright, and Hungarian-born State Department adviser Charles Gati to Central Europe to explain the administration's policy and to quell criticisms stemming from this region prior to the summit. Albright argued forcefully to the Central European leaders that the Partnership for Peace would provide the best vehicle for these countries to gain future NATO membership, and she reiterated that it was not a question of whether, but when.

In Brussels, Clinton said that the PFP "sets in motion a process that leads to the enlargement of NATO." According to Donilon, Lake wanted the president to make a more forceful statement in Prague to give a clear impetus to expansion. Sitting around a table in Prague prior to Clinton's remarks, Lake, Donilon, and presidential speechwriter Robert Boorstin wrote the statement that Clinton agreed to deliver. Echoing what Albright had told the Central Europeans, the president said, "While the Partnership is not NATO membership, neither is it a permanent holding room. It changes the entire NATO dialogue so that now the question is no longer whether NATO will take on new members but when and how."[10]

To proponents such as Lake, this statement was a clear victory, and it laid the basis for moving the process along. He wanted the alliance to address the "when" as soon as possible. For expansion skeptics, to whom "when" meant after the PFP had created a new military environment in Europe, the president's words meant nothing specific and reflected, they believed, the outcome of the October 18 decision; they concluded that although the president had stated that expansion was theoretically possible, the administration would not undertake any actual effort to expand the alliance anytime soon. Their failure to recognize the importance of the president's remarks—at least as Lake and other expansion proponents interpreted them—would lead to their surprise later in the year that the process had been moving forward.

Administration critics would later suggest that Clinton supported expansion purely for political purposes, to woo voters of Polish, Czech, and Hungarian descent. Numerous foreign policy officials in the administration, who deny that domestic political considerations came up in their meetings on expansion, hotly disputed this claim. Lake says that although everyone knew the political context of the NATO enlargement debate, he never had "an explicit discussion" with the president about the domestic political implications of expansion.

Domestic politics probably played a more complicated role in this policy decision than a simple attempt to court ethnic votes in key midwestern and northeastern states. First, for several political reasons, Clinton needed to demonstrate U.S. leadership. His administration's policy in Bosnia was failing miserably, and this failure overshadowed every other foreign policy issue at the time. Second, even if ethnic pressures did not drive the decision, Clinton would have alienated these vocal and powerful domestic constituencies had he decided against expanding NATO; Republicans thus would have gained another issue to use in congressional elections later that year. If domestic politics did not drive the decision, they gave it more resonance for the White House, and both parties certainly used the policy for political purposes: Clinton's speeches in places like Cleveland and Detroit in 1995–96 provide clear evidence of the perceived value of NATO expansion to those communities, and the Republicans included NATO expansion as a plank in their Contract with America during the 1994 congressional campaign.

The bureaucratic decision-making process had not advanced much between

October 1993 and the president's trip to Europe in January 1994. But regardless of where the bureaucratic consensus remained, Clinton had opened the door for expansion with his forceful remarks in Brussels and Prague. This is turn gave Lake the impetus he needed, and because of his proximity and access to the president, for the moment he could move the process along without having to gain the backing of the rest of the bureaucracy.

Phase Three: From Rhetoric to Reality

For several months after Clinton's pronouncements in January, neither his advisers nor the bureaucracy paid much attention to NATO expansion, largely because of the crises in Bosnia that winter and because of the attention they paid to getting the PFP up and running. In early spring, the NATO expansion process began moving forward again, at Lake's instigation. In April, Lake held a meeting with his deputy, Samuel R. "Sandy" Berger, and one of his staffers, Daniel Fried, a specialist on Central and Eastern Europe, to discuss how to follow up on the president's January remarks and to prepare for the president's trip to Warsaw that July. Lake asked for an action plan on enlargement, and when Fried reminded him of the bureaucracy's continued strong opposition, Lake replied that the president wanted to move forward and Lake therefore needed an action plan to make it happen.

To write the policy paper, Fried brought in two old colleagues: Burns at NSC and Alexander Vershbow, then in the European bureau of the State Department but soon to become the NSC's senior director for European affairs. . . . Despite his NSC portfolio on Russian affairs, Burns was not opposed to NATO expansion, which pleased Fried; Burns in turn appreciated that Fried accepted a gradual approach and understood that the strategy had to include a place for Russia. Unlike the authors of many policy papers that need approval, or clearance, from key actors at each of the relevant agencies, this troika worked alone, thus sidestepping the need for bureaucratic bargaining. Before the president's Warsaw trip, Lake invited Talbott and State Department Policy Planning director James Steinberg to the White House to discuss the draft paper with Fried and Burns. Talbott sought assurances that the proposed process would be gradual, consistent with the policy he had pushed the previous October.

Many people believe Talbott opposed enlargement during this time, especially because most of the Russia specialists outside government vehemently opposed expanding NATO. Talbott clearly opposed making any immediate moves and emphasized that the process must be gradual and include rather than isolate Russia. But many of Talbott's colleagues say that once he became deputy secretary of state in February 1994 and more regularly considered the broader European landscape and the needs of the Central and Eastern Europeans, he warmed to expansion. (Several of Talbott's colleagues argue that he opposed expansion, lost, and then sought to ensure that both the expansion track and the NATO–Russia track would proceed in tandem.) Talbott encouraged Christopher to bring Richard Holbrooke back from his post as ambassador to Germany to be assistant secretary of state for European affairs in summer 1994, both to fix the Bosnia policy and to work on NATO expansion. By the following year, Talbott had become one of the most articulate Clinton administration spokespersons in favor of the NATO expansion policy.

By summer, the NSC and State Department positions had converged. Thinking in more gradual terms than Lake had been pushing earlier in the year, the troika's views now coincided with the consensus that had developed in the State Department. The efforts to begin figuring out a way to develop a timetable for both the expansion track and the NATO-Russia track led to a major push in summer and fall 1994 to get an expansion policy on firmer footing.

In Warsaw in July, Clinton spoke more forcefully on the issue than many in the bureaucracy would have preferred, just as he had done in Brussels and Prague earlier in the year. In an exchange with reporters after his meeting with Lech Walesa, he said, "I have always stated my support for the idea that NATO will expand. . . . And now what we have to do is to get the NATO partners together and to discuss what the next steps should be."[11] By emphasizing the need to meet with U.S. allies, the president gave a green light to those who wanted a concrete plan.

Two months later, addressing a conference in Berlin, Vice President Al Gore proved even more outspoken, saying,

> Everyone realizes that a military alliance, when faced with a fundamental change in the threat for which it was founded, either must define a convincing new rationale or become decrepit. Everyone knows that economic and political organizations tailored for a divided continent must now adapt to new circumstances— including acceptance of new members—or be exposed as mere bastions of privilege.[12]

Holbrooke apparently had major input on this speech, and one staffer for the Joint Chiefs says the vice president's remarks gave the military its first inkling that the administration's NATO policy had changed since January. Senior military representatives objected to the draft text of Gore's remarks, but to no avail.

Despite his inclination toward expanding the alliance, Clinton understood concerns about Russia's reaction. After all, Clinton's foreign policy had centered in part on U.S. assistance for the Yeltsin government's reform program, and he did not want to undercut Yeltsin before the 1996 Russian presidential election. In late September, Yeltsin came to Washington, and Clinton had a chance to tell him face to face that NATO was potentially open to all of Europe's new democracies, including Russia, and that it would not expand in a way that threatened Russia's interests. At a White House luncheon, Clinton told Yeltsin that he had discussed NATO expansion with key allied leaders, and he made sure Yeltsin understood that NATO would not announce the new members until after the Russian and U.S. 1996 presidential elections. At the same time, Clinton wanted to ensure that any advances in the process that might take place in the meantime—during the NATO ministerials—would not surprise the Russian president.

With Holbrooke coming back to the State Department and with Vershbow and Fried both now special assistants to the president at the NSC, expansion proponents had gained more power within the bureaucracy than they had during the previous autumn. Lake successfully circumvented bureaucratic opposition to get Clinton to make forceful statements that expansion would occur. His troika had continued to update its action plan throughout the summer and fall, and by October 1994 its strategy paper proposed the timeline that the alliance eventually followed: a series of studies and consultations designed to lead to a membership invitation to the first group and a NATO–Russia accord in 1997. But concerns about the military dimension of expansion still existed in the Pentagon, without whose efforts to address the nuts and bolts of expanding the military alliance the decision could not have moved from theory to practice.

For their next task, proponents had to convince skeptics within the administration that the president was serious. . . . For NATO expansion, the enforcer would be Holbrooke, the newly installed assistant secretary of state, whom Christopher had brought back to the department at the urging of Talbott, Donilon, and Under Secretary for Political Affairs Peter Tarnoff.

Holbrooke held his first interagency meeting on NATO expansion at the State Department in late September, almost immediately after taking office. He wanted to make clear that he would set up and run the mechanism to expand NATO, because the president wanted it to happen. Holbrooke knew that most Pentagon officials preferred concentrating on making the PFP work rather than moving ahead with expansion, and he wanted to make sure everyone understood that he was taking charge. His opportunity came at this meeting when the senior representative from the Joint Chiefs of Staff (JCS), three-star General Wesley Clark, questioned Holbrooke's plans to move forward on the "when" and "how" questions of expansion. To the Pentagon's way of thinking, no one had yet made a decision that would warrant this action. Holbrooke shocked those in attendance by declaring, "That sounds like insubordination to me. Either you are on the president's program or you are not."[13]

According to participants, Deputy Assistant Secretary of Defense Joseph Kruzel, one of the key figures in developing the PFP program, argued that the issue had been debated in October 1993 and the decision at that time, the last formal meeting on the subject at the highest levels, was *not* to enlarge. Other Pentagon officials in attendance argued that only the "principals" could make this decision, and thus another meeting needed to be held at the highest level. Holbrooke responded that those taking this view had not been listening to what the president had been saying. The skeptics simply could not believe that Holbrooke was resting his whole case on remarks Clinton had made in Brussels, Prague, and Warsaw. Former defense secretary William Perry still refers to Holbrooke as having "presumed" at that point that the administration had decided to enlarge NATO, whereas Clinton had made no formal decision to that effect.

After this dramatic outburst, Holbrooke asked Clark to set up a meeting to brief this interagency group on what they would need to do to implement the policy. Through this request, Holbrooke enabled the Joint Chiefs of Staff to voice their concerns but also forced them to begin acting on the issue. At the Pentagon two weeks later, a team with representatives from both the Office of the Secretary of Defense (OSD) and the JCS presented to the interagency group the full range of military requirements each country would need to meet to join NATO. The JCS briefer pointed, for example, to the 1,200 Atlantic Alliance standardization agreements the former Warsaw Pact armed forces would have to address to become compatible with NATO. Holbrooke, now playing "good cop," responded by saying that this briefing was exactly what the group needed, and he invited them to work with him to make the process a smooth one. This briefing would, in fact, serve as the basis both for the briefing to the NAC later in the fall and for the NATO study conducted the following year.

Because Pentagon officials did not believe the administration had ever made a formal decision, Perry recalls that he called Clinton and asked for a meeting of the foreign policy team to clarify the president's intentions. At the meeting, Perry presented his arguments for holding back and giving the PFP another year before deciding on enlargement. He wanted time to move forward on the NATO–Russia track and to convince Moscow that NATO did not threaten Russia's interests, before the alliance moved ahead on the expansion track. Instead, the president endorsed the two-track plan that Lake and his staff, as well as the State Department, now pushed—the plan that ultimately led to the May 1997 signing of the NATO–Russia Founding Act and the July 1997 NATO summit in Madrid inviting Poland, Hungary, and the Czech Republic to begin talks on accession to full NATO membership.

The Ambiguity of the Decision

Like so many decision-making processes, the NATO expansion process was not at all clearcut. The best evidence of its ambiguities comes from asking participants a simple question: "When did you believe that the decision to expand NATO had been made?" Their answers demonstrate that what you see depends on where you stand; attitudes toward the decision affected individuals' views of what was happening. Most supporters, including Lake, cite the period between the October 1993 meeting of the principals and Clinton's trip to Europe in January 1994. The answers of opponents, on the other hand, generally range over the second half of 1994, depending on when they finally realized the president was serious. One State Department official who opposed expansion said that when he objected to language circulating in an interagency memo on the issue in August 1994, a colleague told him it was the same language the president had used in Warsaw the previous month. At that point, he says, he understood that the policy had moved from theory to reality. Others, such as Perry, did not start to believe that expansion was on the table until after the Holbrooke interagency meeting in September 1994. In support of this last interpretation, Brzezinski pointed out at the time that until Clinton *answered* the questions "when" and "how," rather than simply *asking* them, the United States had no decisive plan for Europe.[14]

These interpretations vary so widely because the president and his top advisers did not make a formal decision about a timetable or process for expansion until long after Clinton had started saying NATO would enlarge. The when, who, how, and even why came only over time and not always through a formal decision-making process. In January 1994, when the president first said that he expected the alliance to take in new members, no consensus existed among his top advisers on the difficult questions of "when" and "how." Clinton's advisers could as reasonably believe that his remarks amounted to no more than a vague statement that NATO might someday expand as they could believe that the president wanted to begin moving forward *now*. Whereas proponents of expansion took his statements as a signal to begin planning how to put theory into practice, the president did not make an explicit decision in the presence of his top foreign policy advisers until nearly a year later, and some opponents therefore choose to believe that the course was not set until that meeting.

Readers may find it unsatisfying that I have not uncovered either *the* moment of decision or the president's ulterior motive. Truthfully, however, most policies—even those as significant as this one—develop in a more ambiguous fashion. This process was hardly unique to the Clinton administration. White House meetings often result in participants, as well as those they inform, having conflicting understandings of what the administration has decided. Policy entrepreneurs use presidential statements to push forward an issue that remains highly contentious in the bureaucracy. Each step alone seems trivial. But cumulatively, they can result in momentous policies.

As for motive, Walesa and Havel may well have made a huge impression on a president open to emotional appeals. Still, given that Clinton cared so much about the fate of Russian reform, Walesa's appeal to bring Poland and other Central European nations into the West could hardly have been sufficient. Rather, Clinton's motive was probably more complex, and he probably had only a vague idea of when he himself made the formal commitment to expand NATO. For Clinton, the appeal by the Central Europeans to erase the line drawn for them in 1945, the need to demonstrate U.S. leadership at a time when others questioned that leadership, the domestic political consequences of the choice, and his own Wilsonian orientation toward spreading liberalism combined by the second half of 1994—if not earlier—to produce a presidential preference favoring expansion. . . . Once Clinton spoke out in favor of NATO expansion in January 1994, expansion supporters within the administration had what they needed to begin to turn rhetoric into reality.

Notes

1. For information on Secretary Christopher's intervention at the June 1993 NAC meeting, see *U.S. Department of State Dispatch* 4, no. 25, p. 3.

2. Anthony Lake, "From Containment to Enlargement," *Vital Speeches of the Day* 60 (October 15, 1993), pp. 13–19.

3. For quotations from the Talbott memo, see Michael Dobbs, "Wider Alliance Would Increase U.S. Commitments," *Washington Post*, July 5, 1995, pp. A1, 16; Michael R. Gordon, "U.S. Opposes Move to Rapidly Expand NATO Membership," *New York Times*, January 2, 1994, pp. A1, 7.

4. The official is quoted in Elaine Sciolino, "U.S. to Offer Plan on a Role in NATO for Ex-Soviet Bloc," *New York Times*, October 21, 1993, pp. A1, 9.

5. Elaine Sciolino, "3 Players Seek a Director for Foreign Policy Story," *New York Times*, November 8, 1993, pp. A1, 12; Stephen Kinzer, "NATO Favors U.S. Plan for Ties with the East, but Timing is Vague," *New York Times*, October 22, 1993, pp. A1, 8.

6. *U.S. Department of State Dispatch*, December 13, 1993.

7. Ibid.

8. See Henry Kissinger, "Not This Partnership," *Washington Post*, November 24, 1993, p. A17; Zbigniew Brzezinski, "A Bigger—and Safer—Europe," *New York Times*, December 1, 1993, p. A23; and James A. Baker III, "Expanding to the East: A New NATO," *Los Angeles Times*, December 5, 1993, p. M2.

9. Remarks by the president in a photo op with Netherlands prime minister Ruud Lubbers, January 4, 1994, *Public Papers* (1994), pp. 5–6.

10. On the Brussels statement of January 10, 1994, see *U.S. Department of State Dispatch Supplement*, January 1994, pp. 3–4; for the Prague remarks, see Clinton, *Public Papers* Book I (1994), p. 40.

11. For his exchange with reporters in Warsaw after meeting with Walesa on July 6, 1994, see Clinton, *Public Papers* (1994), p. 1206.

12. *U.S. Department of State Dispatch*, September 12, 1994, pp. 597–598.

13. Quoted in Dobbs, "Wider Alliance." Confirmed by author interviews with numerous officials who attended the meeting.

14. Zbigniew Brzezinski, "A Plan for Europe," *Foreign Affairs* 74 (January/February 1995), pp. 27–28.

23

A Fortuitous Victory: An Information Processing Approach to the Gulf War

Alex Roberto Hybel

A Less Than Rational Decision

"War," wrote Karl von Clausewitz, "is the province of chance. In no other sphere of human activity must such a margin be left for this intruder. It increases the uncertainty of every circumstance and deranges the course of events" (1990: 225). The intent of Clausewitz's message is unmistakable—to warn that war should never be initiated before its makers conduct a careful, rational analysis of its potential consequences. Though the analysis does not erase uncertainty totally, it can reduce it to a manageable level.

The ease with which the United States defeated Iraq in 1991 persuaded many analysts that the Bush administration's decision to go to war was rational. In this chapter I take a different stand. I assert that though the effect of a policy is important, rationality is always a function of process, not of result. A rational response to any major problem entails working within a system that enables decisionmakers to gather the information necessary to delineate the nature of the problem, identify and evaluate the goals and their interrelationships, isolate the pertinent alternatives and estimate their probable consequences, and choose the alternative with the highest expected utility. Based on this proposition, I argue that the Bush administration's decisions that the United States would not tolerate the loss of Saudi Arabia to Iraq and that it would use U.S. forces both to protect Saudi Arabia and expel Iraq from Kuwait were not the upshot of a rational process. President George Bush and his National Security Adviser Brent Scowcroft prevented the "rational" execution of these steps during the Gulf crisis. They alone determined that the United States would 1) refuse to tolerate Iraq's attempt to impose its will on Kuwait, and possibly Saudi Arabia, because such change in the status quo would give Saddam Hussein extensive control over the oil market; 2) deploy its forces over Saudi territory, if authorized to do so by the Saudi leaders, to protect it from a possible Iraqi attack; and 3) resort to violence, instead of containment, to expel Iraq from Kuwait. Bush and Scowcroft made their decisions with almost no input from Middle Eastern experts, and without eliciting alternative interpretations and possible solutions of the problem from other top foreign-policy officials.

President Bush and his National Security Adviser Scowcroft obstructed the rational process in three closely interrelated ways. First, they created a hierarchical decisionmaking process that prevented the open discussion of alternative options to the Gulf crisis. Second, under the guardianship of such a hampered decisionmaking system, they relied on two historical analogies to formulate their decisions. They used the 1938 Munich debacle to deduce that appeasement never pacifies tyrants. By viewing Saddam Hussein as another Adolf Hitler, they argued that the only choice left to the United States was to act aggressively. This meant protecting Saudi Arabia and going to war against Iraq, if necessary, to free Kuwait. As Bush and Scowcroft saw the situation, a decision not to protect Saudi Arabia would have been viewed by Saddam as a lack of resolve on the part of the United States and, thus, as an invitation to continue with his policy of expansion. Moreover, a policy of containment would have signaled to Saddam that the United States and its allies lacked the will to make hard choices, and that if he stood fast the alliance would eventually falter.

Before deciding that a military operation against Saddam and his military establishment was a viable option, Bush, Scowcroft, and the principal military leaders revealed their dependence on another very important memory: Vietnam. The central decisionmakers inferred from the Vietnam nightmare that the United States should never get involved in another major conflict unless it was willing to use the military power necessary to win the war swiftly and impressively.

Some decisionmakers are better than others at dealing with uncertainty. Those who are not good at coping with this condition often attempt to impose on reality a structure that makes events or subjects have a clear, coherent meaning. As a result of this process, the decisionmaker tends to conclude that he or she does not need to evaluate a range of alternatives, particularly any alternative that may challenge his or her point of view and induce unwanted uncertainty. Bush and Scowcroft relied on historical analogies not just to define and respond to the Gulf crisis, but also to obstruct the consideration of alternative interpretations and options that could have occasioned uncertainty and, as a result, breed cognitive imbalance.

Groupthink and Decisionmaking Aptitudes

Consequential foreign policies are typically made by individuals who interact as members of a small decisionmaking group. In the United States the president surrounds himself with a small number of individuals who keep him informed about the latest important developments in the international system, suggest and evaluate potential policies, and act as a sounding board for his ideas. Students of foreign-policy making have proposed that the size, membership, and role structure of the group can have a significant effect not just on how policies are formulated, but also on their quality. Irving Janis, for instance, writes:

> The advantages of having decisions made by groups are often lost because of psychological pressures that arise when the members work closely together, share the same values, and above all face a crisis situation in which everybody is subjected to stresses that generate a strong need for affiliation (Janis, 1972: 13).

My intention in this section is not to rehash an argument that has been both praised and criticized. My objective is simply to ascertain whether it is imperative to account for a decisionmaking group's dynamic when analyzing the reasoning process of its principal parties. The constitution of a decision-making group can affect the way in which its members search for and process information, survey objectives and alternatives, examine the risks of a preferred choice, reappraise alternatives, and work out contingency plans (Janis and Mann, 1977). A group that is highly cohesive, emotionally and functionally dependent on its leader, insulated from other groups, and that lacks methodical procedures for search and appraisal, is likely to reflect symptoms of "groupthink." By groupthink, Janis means "a mode of thinking that people engage in when they are deeply involved in a cohesive in-group, when the members' striving for unanimity overrides their motivation to realistically appraise alternative courses of action" (Janis, 1972: 9). A group that reflects the symptoms of groupthink will have its self-appointed mindguards; rationalize collectively; develop illusions of invulnerability and unanimity; believe in its inherent morality; view other groups as adversaries and less capable; tolerate only self-censorship; and pressure internal dissenters to conform. ("A mind-guard protects [officials] from thoughts that might damage their confidence in the soundness of the policies to which they are committed or . . . about to commit themselves" [Janis, 1972: 42].) When such a group is faced with a high stress problem, its tendency will be to conduct a poor information search; process only that information that confirms its members' beliefs and expectations; carry out an incomplete survey of objectives and alternatives; and refuse to examine the risks behind its preferred choice, reappraise alternatives, and work out contingency plans.

Notwithstanding the fact that groupthink, as a theoretical construct, has been challenged by a wide range of analysts, it is helpful to investigate the conditions under which it may come into being. Every president "faces the task of deciding how to organize and manage foreign-policy making in his administration" (George, 1980: 139). How a president organizes and manages his foreign-policy making are functions of his sense of efficacy as it relates to management and decisionmaking tasks, informational needs and ways of acquiring and using information and advice, attitude to the give-and-take of politics, and tolerance for conflict among his advisers. In other words, the central postulate seems to be that the quality of a foreign-policy making process is a function of the group that formulates the policy which, in turn, is a function of the personal characteristics of the president who decides how his advisory group will be structured. This is another way of saying that a president's approach to decision making has a direct effect on the type of advisory group he creates.[1] If this is the case, then it would seem redundant to analyze both a president's reasoning process and the structure of the group that advises him. However, rather than accepting the logic of the challenge just postulated, I will attempt to evaluate its validity by focusing on both the reasoning processes of Bush and his principal advisers and the structure of the group that encompassed them.

Attribution, Schema, and Cognitive Consistency Theories

In the 1950s some analysts proposed that because it is humanly impossible to assess all pertinent information and consider all relevant alternatives and their potential consequences, decisions always fall short of the ideal. Rationality, they noted, is bounded by our own human limitations (Simon, 1957: 3). Since then, the study of foreign-policy making has experienced a critical metamorphosis. After several false starts some analysts decided that it would be preferable to compare the explanatory value of alternative psychological theories with single cases to uncover important explanatory variables and possible relationships rather than attempt to develop an all-encompassing decisionmaking theory. I accept the premise but then move further.

Contemporary cognitive psychologists inform us that the problem solver can be conceptualized as a seeker of attributable cause, analogical schemes, or cognitive consistency.[2] These three cognitive perspectives share rationality as their reference point, but do not ascribe to different decisionmakers the same capabilities for solving problems and preventing their cognitive needs from interfering in their decisionmaking processes. Attribution theory, which depicts the analysts as "naive" scientists, stands closest to the rational decisionmakers. It is defined not by one perspective but by competing models that differ in their descriptions of cognitive processes, information used, and outcomes. All these models, however, assume that individuals formulate causal explanations of behavior that, in turn, help shape their reactions (Larson, 1985: 35–6). Attribution theorists acknowledge that decisionmakers often try to confirm hypotheses by searching for evidence that is consistent with an expectation. This form of behavior, they note, should be ascribed not to an assumed tendency by decisionmakers to focus only on information that confirms the expectations, but to their unawareness that the most effective and systematic manner to gauge the soundness of a proposition is by attempting to falsify it (Larson, 1985: 41).

If the depiction of analysts as naive scientists stands the closest to the rational decisionmakers, the model that characterizes them as "consistency seekers" is located the farthest away.[3] In the 1950s various social psychologists proposed that humans lack the psychological maturity required to carry out the tasks associated with a rational decisionmaking process. When humans process and interpret information, they are not just attempting to understand a problem and formulate a solution; they are also trying to ensure that in the process their beliefs, feelings, and cognitions remain mutually consistent (Jervis, 1976: 382–3).[4] A consistent structure is one in which "All relations among 'good elements' [i.e., those that are positively valued] are positive (or null), all relations among 'bad elements' [i.e., those that are negatively valued] are positive (or null), and all relations among good and bad elements are negative (or null)" (Jervis, 1976: 117). This model thus perceives the mind not as a machine in quest for meaning and validity, but as a veritable inference-making instrument that actively manipulates the information it receives to create a consistent structure out of an ambiguous reality (Steinbruner, 1974).

Faced with uncertainty, contend cognitive consistency theorists, the analyst imposes on reality a structure that makes events or subjects have a clear, coherent, meaning. Through the use of categorical rather than probable judgments, the analyst convinces himself or herself that decision outcomes can be predicted and feels no need to evaluate other alternatives. Such judgment is generally derived from a reinforcing experience. The process is identified as the assumption of a single outcome calculation. Moreover, faced with a problem involving conflicting values, the decisionmaker separates them and makes choices in terms of only one value without estimating how the other values may be affected. This predisposition on the part of the analyst is known as the assumption of value separation (Steinbruner, 1974: 90 and 111).

Between attribution theory and cognitive consistency theory lie schema theory and one of its derivatives, the theory of cognitive scripts (Abelson, 1976: 33–45). According to schema theorists, the decisionmaker, overwhelmed by sensations and information, seeks to understand the world without using inordinate amounts of energy and time. Such an analyst compresses reality by matching present experiences with schemas stored in his or her memory from past events. Schema theory shares with attribution theory the assumption that the individual is not driven by an internal need to maintain a balance between beliefs and actions, but it posits fewer illusions than the latter about his or her analytical capabilities. Instead, schema theory proposes that the individual commits errors when handling information not because he or she does not know better (although this may be true), but because the person's mental capabilities are limited.

A "cognitive script" refers to a sequence of events that tells a story, is known well by decisionmakers, and is recorded in their memories in the form of a stereotype. It is possible to differentiate between two types of scripts. An episodic script is based on the analysis of a single experience defined by a sequence of events. In the early 1950s for instance, analysts at the Department of State stored in their memories the "Yenan Way" script, in which radical agrarian reforms instituted in the People's Republic of China were believed to have contributed to the creation of the Chinese communist system. An episodic script may or may not be generalized to form a categorical script. Having undergone similar experiences, with each being structured by analogous sequences of events, foreign-policy makers "may generalize from the common features to form one categorical script" (Flory and Hybel, 1995: 84). From the Yenan Way script and other related incidents, thus, foreign-policy makers in the 1950s created the categorical script: "radical agrarian reforms are the prelude to the birth of communist regimes" (Hybel, 1990: 65). The designing of a categorical script, however, is not always preceded by several similar past experiences. One single costly incident can pressure foreign-policy makers to transform an episodic script into a categorical one. Lyndon Johnson's determination to ensure that the Dominican Republic in 1965 would not become a "second Cuba" attests to this possibility (Hybel, 1990: Ch. 6).

If it is assumed that the ideal foreign-policy making process involves the systematic collection of information to define the real nature of an international problem, isolation and ranking of values afflicted by the problem, identification of possible alternatives along with their expected costs and benefits, and selection of the alternative with the highest expected utility, then to develop a typology of decisionmaking aptitudes based on the arguments elicited from the different cognitive theories it is necessary to focus on how each responds to the aforementioned tasks. It has been proposed already that of the three cognitive models, attribution theory comes the closest to the ideal assumption, with cognitive consistency theory standing at the opposite end of the spectrum. More specifically, this signifies that when attribution, schema, and cognitive consistency theories are compared, the first implies greater expectations than the other two about an individual's decisionmaking capabilities.

From attribution theory it can be inferred that the decisionmaker first gathers whatever information is needed to describe the nature of the problem and identify the values it affects. The decisionmaker then studies a variety of alternatives by looking at sample data of past events involving the originator of the problem and other actors entangled in similar situations. Subsequently, he or she attempts to find out how the problem maker responded to different policies. In particular, the decisionmaker tries to ascertain whether his or her adversary was prone to respond in the same way regardless of the policy he or she was confronted with or in different ways depending on the policy. If the latter were the case, the decisionmaker must determine how strong was the adversary's tendency to react to the same policy in the same way. Finally, the analyst endeavors to establish whether the present problem maker's past responses to the various policies were unique or concurred with the responses of other past problem makers. The decisionmaking process in this case is not obstructed by the need to maintain mutually consistent beliefs, feelings, and cognitions, nor by a desire to minimize uncertainty to assuage certain insecurities. The principal obstacle is the decisionmaker's own inability to understand that the most rational way to evaluate an adversary's behavioral pattern is by referring not to the cases that fit nicely with an initial expectation but to those that at face value are likely to contest this expectation. In other words, the decisionmaker does not realize that failure by a least likely case to falsify his or her argument will strengthen the soundness of the hypothesis.

Schema theory, with its emphasis on scripts or analogies, posits a different description of the decisionmaking process. Burdened by the need to save energy and time, and by the inability to process vast amounts of information, decisionmakers rely on an analogy to define an international problem. They may use either an episodic or categorical script to define the problem, but in either case the definition results from conclusions inferred from one or more notable analogous situations. The content of the script they use to define the problem, moreover, bounds the range of values they believe are pertinent. Finally, the same or a different script affects the type of alternatives they evaluate and the final policy choice.

Thus, according to schema theory, decisionmakers rely not on a quasi-scientific approach to problem solving, but on analogical reasoning.[5] Their definition of an international problem is the result not of an attempt to contrast competing explanations of past actions by the problem maker and other actors, but of a script or analogy derived from a very narrow set of cases, recorded deep in their memories because of their political, social, economic, or moral significance. These same decisionmakers do not decide on a policy by evaluating past responses by the problem maker and other parties in order to understand what values are at stake and how different alternatives may affect them. Instead, they search for that script or analogy that enables them to capture the relationships between a narrow set of consequential past responses and the response they believe is required by the new problem.[6]

The least rational form of behavior expected from decisionmakers is that explained by cognitive consistency theory. The need for decisionmakers to avert inconsistencies and to give an uncertain situation an unchallenged, well-defined form, pressures them to disregard potentially valuable information. This need, moreover, forces them to evaluate only those alternatives that do not contradict their preconceptions and to disregard the possibility that some of these alternatives may impact negatively on a few of the decisionmakers' values. This faulty process also imposes itself on the policy selection task. The decisionmakers opt for the alternative that most strongly reinforces their preconceptions and avoid any remaining doubts about the outcome. Under cognitive consistency theory, thus, rationality is undercut not by the absence of information about how to garner knowledge, want of intellectual capacity, nor inclination to conserve energy and time on the part of the decisionmakers. The culprit is the decisionmakers' own inability to accept that uncertainty in the international arena is a common phenomenon, their preconceptions some-times are wrong, and their preferred options are not always the best ones.

The three theories, as described, assume that a decisionmaker's aptitude remains constant. The general assumption is that an individual who rational-izes according to the precepts of attribution theory is unlikely to suddenly be dominated by a tremendous need to keep beliefs, feelings, and cognitions mutually consistent, and vice versa. This assumption, although appealing be-cause of its parsimonious nature, may not be backed by the empirical evi-dence. Events with great consequences are bound to have considerable effects on the decisionmaking aptitudes of foreign-policy leaders. John F. Kennedy's decision to topple Fidel Castro's Cuban government in 1961, for instance, can be explained by cognitive consistency theory. The same theory, however, could not be used to explain his actions during the Cuban missile crisis. In 1962 Kennedy sought to ensure that he would not err during the decisionmak-ing process as he had the previous year. Thus, instead of assuming that the decisionmaking aptitudes of foreign-policy makers remain constant through time, this analysis assumes that past experiences, positive or negative, can alter them.

Groupthink, Reasoning by Analogy, and the Drive for Cognitive Consistency

Groupthink in Action

To explain the decisionmaking process adopted by the Bush administration during the Gulf crisis, one must identify the principal decisionmakers, discuss the way they interacted, and establish what led them to conclude that it would be in the interest of the United States to use its forces both to protect Saudi Arabia and free Kuwait.

The way a problem is initially defined has a decisive effect on the way it is treated. Ideally, the leader of the decisionmaking group will encourage the presentation and discussion of the problem and its reevaluation as the mem-bers of the group gain new information. President Bush and National Security Adviser Scowcroft created a foreign-policy process that, at first glance, con-veyed the impression that they both wanted other decisionmakers to express freely their views. Many of these leaders knew each other well and treated one another in an informal and friendly manner. "When the principals met, Bush liked to keep everyone around the table smiling—jokes, camaraderie, the conviviality of old friends" (Woodward, 1991: 302). But the nature of the decisionmaking process was more complex. Bush and Scowcroft created a rigid decisionmaking hierarchy, designed to discourage the voicing of ideas that challenged their views. Secretary of State James Baker III, for instance, though conscious of his high standing in the decisionmaking structure, knew that he could question the president only so far. He understood that his "inner circle" membership would be revoked if he did not ultimately acquiesce in the "dominant view."[7] Similarly, the chairman of the Joint Chiefs of Staff, General Colin Powell, came to accept that as Bush's principal military adviser he had a smaller role than he previously had as Reagan's national security adviser, and that Bush was very conscious of each adviser's status (Woodward, 1991: 225).

The inflexibility of the decisionmaking structure was reflected in the way the members of the group responded to the views advanced by Bush and Scowcroft. When Bush and his foreign-policy advisers gathered for the first time to assess the strategic and economic implications of Iraq's invasion of Kuwait, the president did not begin the meeting by asking his counselors to present their own interpretations of the situation in the Middle East. Instead, he started by observing that it would be disastrous to the United States and the world economy if Saddam were to gain control of Kuwait's, and possibly Saudi Arabia's, oil production. None of the other participants volunteered an alternative perspective, or questioned the president's interpretation (Drew, 1991: 184). At the second meeting, Scowcroft, not wanting Bush to appear to be trying to restrict the context within which the problem in the Middle East was addressed, took it upon himself to argue that it was impossible for the United States to tolerate Iraq's action. Ideally, Scowcroft's remark would have been seen and understood as a viewpoint to be evaluated. But this was not the interpretation that resulted. Every participant recognized that Scowcroft was speaking for Bush, and that the president was determined to do something that would show Iraq and the world that the United States had the power and will to act.

Analogical Reasoning and Cognitive Consistency in Action

The presence of a decisionmaking system that does not evoke openness does not automatically preclude some form of rationality, so long as the leader of the group and his closest adviser adhere to a quasi-rational process. Bush's and Scowcroft's approach to the problem in the Middle East was not the result of the type of decisionmaking method depicted by attribution theory, whereby they followed "statistical rules of inference in interpreting evidence concerning various patterns of covariation to formulate causal explanations" about

Saddam's behavior (Larson, 1985: 36). Specifically, the American president
and the national security adviser did not try to understand Saddam's action by
assessing whether their initial assumptions about Saddam's intent were correct, gauging the degree to which the Iraqi leader's decision to invade Kuwait
could be linked to one factor instead of another, and establishing how many
other political leaders had resorted to invasion when confronted with the same
conditions faced by Iraq.

To know one's adversary is one of the central tenets of good foreign-policy
making. Saddam's decision to invade Kuwait took Bush by surprise. Prior to
the invasion, Bush and Scowcroft had regarded Saddam as a rational decisionmaker who would not attack Kuwait. They viewed him as a power-hungry
leader who would exploit every available opportunity to increase his and his
country's strength, but whose experience in the 1980s against Iran had been
so costly that it would restrain him from actually launching a major attack
against Kuwait. They believed, in short, that Saddam was a rational calculator,
one who never lost sight of the realities of power politics.

It is not uncommon, even for highly competent analysts, to base their analyses of adversaries on incorrect assumptions. However, any rational analyst,
upon learning that his or her original inference was inaccurate, will seek to
find the source of this mistake by attempting to learn more about the subject
of the original evaluation. Bush and Scowcroft did not fit this profile. Part of
the problem with their initial assumption was that they arrived at it without
considering the possibility that the Iraqi leader might not rank his values or
approach risk-taking as they assumed he would. Specifically, Bush and Scowcroft did not take into account that though rationality is related to the way
values are ranked, the concept itself does not dictate the order in which they
must be ranked. Furthermore, they did not reflect on the fact that the leaders
of weak states, or states that have endured bad experiences but still have a
great deal at stake, sometimes are willing to accept costs and risks that would
be unacceptable to leaders of more powerful states or states that have been
quite successful in their international endeavors (George and Smoke, 1974:
221). Iraq's invasion of Kuwait did not inspire Bush and Scowcroft to reassess
their initial assumption about Saddam. Bush had no qualms about letting his
political allies in the Arab world know that he had relied on their expertise
to derive his own assumption about Saddam. At one point he even jokingly
admonished Prince Bandar, Saudi Arabian ambassador to the United States,
for telling him that Saddam was "okay." But this comment did not reflect a
renewed desire to know more about the Iraqi leader. The president did not ask
Middle East experts to attend any of the main meetings to present their views
about Saddam and suggest how the Iraqi leader might respond to some of the
options being considered by top officials in the Bush administration. Secretary
of Defense Richard Cheney, in fact, was one of the few high-ranking officials
who felt that it would be of some value to hear what the experts on Middle

Eastern affairs had to say. Their advice, however, typically came after a major decision had already been made by the principal leaders.

Almost immediately after the invasion of Kuwait, Bush concluded, first, that the incident had altered markedly the balance of power in the Middle East and, second, that the United States could not tolerate any further changes in the status quo. Afraid that if Washington failed to protect Saudi Arabia, Saddam would view it as a sign of weakness on the part of the United States and, thus, as an open invitation to march into Saudi territory, the president decided that his only choice was to deploy U.S. forces on a large scale. To reach this conclusion, he relied on the lessons he had inferred from the 1938 Munich debacle and on his belief that Saddam was a rational leader. From the 1938 incident, which had a dramatic effect on his life and that of millions of other people of his era, he surmised that unchallenged tyrants view the absence of opposition to their attempts to aggrandize their powers as a weakness to be exploited.[8] As he stated in a speech he delivered on August 8, 1990: "Appeasement does not work. As was the case in the 1930s" (Woodward, 1991: 277). Scowcroft's thinking process was also swayed by his confidence in the lesson he derived from the same earlier case. It was not grandstanding that led the national security adviser to remark during a foreign-policy meeting that the United States did not "have the option to appear not to be acting" and to add at a later meeting that although it would be hard to act against Iraq, ultimately "it's our job." Like Bush, Scowcroft believed the United States should not try to appease Saddam for, as the Second World War had proven, appeasement did not work on tyrants. A tyrant responded only to pressure, exercised with great determination and force.

Bush's determination to defend Saudi Arabia with U.S. forces was reinforced by his belief that the action would not imperil the lives of U.S. troops. He recognized that an attack on Saudi Arabia by Iraq during the early stages of the troop deployment could result in a high number of U.S. casualties, and that the unfolding of such a scenario would undermine both his reputation and that of the United States. But he also assumed that Saddam, as a rational decisionmaker, would understand that such an attack would force the United States to use whatever power it needed to offset the initial costs and punish the offender. The secretary of state did not share this belief. Though unwilling to disclose his own opinion, Baker feared that the Iraqi leader might launch an attack on Saudi Arabia before the United States had deployed enough of its troops to resist a major assault (Woodward, 1991: 262).

In short, Bush and Scowcroft, instead of attempting to contrast competing explanations of past actions by Saddam with those of other political leaders, as portrayed by attribution theory, relied on the single analogy that the Iraqi leader, like Hitler, was a tyrant, and that the only thing tyrants respect is power and its effective use. Equally as important, Bush and Scowcroft used the Munich analogy not just to reason but also to maintain personal cognitive consistency. Their unwillingness to tolerate uncertainty also materialized as they refused to consider the possibility that their initial assessment of Saddam as a rational actor might have been faulty. These phenomena would surface a second time as the Bush administration began to consider what measures to take to liberate Kuwait.

On October 30, 1990, the president met with the national security adviser, the secretaries of state and defense, and the chairman of the Joint Chiefs of Staff. Scowcroft began the meeting by noting that the United States was "at a Y" in the road," and could continue to deter-and-defend, or could begin to prepare for an attack. The next speaker, General Powell, made it clear that if the president wanted to take the offensive route, the troops in the Middle East would have to be doubled. The chairman added that General H. Norman Schwarzkopf, the Central Command Commander, had requested such an increase and that he (Powell) supported it. Secretary of Defense Cheney concurred with the advice and went further. In his own mind, he noted, it was not a question of whether to take the offensive route; the president should want that option and should order its implementation immediately. Bush's response was succinct: "If that's what you need, we'll do it" (Woodward, 1991: 320). He gave his formal approval the following day.

What persuaded the president to resort to force instead of giving containment a chance? The decision to reject an alternative is not always associated with the belief that one's own policy would be more effective. In Bush's case, it was. Bush had doubted from the beginning that containment would be enough to persuade Saddam to pull out of Kuwait. In his own mind, containment was part of a process; it was a necessary but not sufficient step.[9] Containment was begun more than two months before the Pentagon had achieved the military strength it would need to protect Saudi Arabia from an Iraqi attack. Its implementation helped the Bush administration buy time as U.S. troops were moved to the Middle East to protect Saudi Arabia, and to signal to the world that the United States was willing to give Saddam the opportunity to come to his senses and recognize that his only choice was to pull his troops out of Kuwait. The value of containment, however, was perceived as being limited. Bush reasoned that Saddam would not be persuaded by containment, for he would assume that if he waited long enough the allied forces would ultimately give up. It was not mere coincidence, therefore, that Bush ordered the doubling of U.S. troops in the Middle East just as the Pentagon was telling him that it had enough forces in Saudi Arabia to protect it from an Iraqi attack. At that moment, the president could have decided in favor of waiting until his administration was in a better position to determine whether containment would be enough to pressure Saddam out of Kuwait.

Bush's decision to opt for an offensive strategy instead of waiting to see whether containment would bend Saddam had its origin in the same analogy he had used to justify ordering the protection of Saudi Arabia. From the Munich debacle he had inferred that tyrants respect only those who have power and are willing to use it. The United States had shown its determination to use power to protect Saudi Arabia, but that was not enough. Having attained its first objective, the United States needed to prove that its resolve extended to the use of force to free Kuwait. Such an end could be achieved only by, first, increasing the number of U.S. forces in the region and, second, going to war if necessary. The first step would signal Saddam that his only choice was to pull out of Kuwait. The United States, however, had to be prepared to resort to violence just in case the Iraqi leader did not heed the warning.

The Munich analogy, though deeply ingrained in Bush's memory, did not dominate fully his thinking process. The president and his advisers, especially those who worked under the Pentagon's banner, were convinced that the United States could not afford to be dragged into another Vietnam-type quagmire. Powell's reluctance to send troops to the Middle East was always based on his fear that the military would be made once again the scapegoat for a poorly considered policy. When Powell realized that the president was serious about going to war, he made sure that if he received the order to attack, U.S. troops would achieve the assigned objectives swiftly and at the lowest possible cost.

This belief was not Powell's alone. For quite some time officials at the Pentagon had been arguing that the United States' principal error in the Vietnam war was to assume that if it applied force gradually the enemy would be "inspired to sue for peace at an early level of escalation." The war taught them that the other side took advantage of gradualism to strengthen its military and political stand. The lesson: if the United States had to fight a war, it had to use as much firepower as was necessary to quickly destroy the enemy's fighting capability and will (Klare, 1991: 474). This doctrine was verbalized by Schwarzkopf in November 1990 when he stated: "If we go to war, I am going to use every single thing that is available to me to bring as much destruction to Iraqi force as rapidly as I possibly can in the hopes of winning victory as soon as possible" (Klare, 1991: 474).

Powell and Schwarzkopf had the full support of their civilian boss. Sometime in November, Cheney told Prince Bandar: "The military is finished in this society if we screw this up" (Woodward, 1991: 324). Cheney's days as Gerald Ford's chief of staff were not so distant for him to have forgotten how difficult it had been for the military to rebuild its image in the years immediately after the end of the Vietnam War. The Pentagon's determination to avert another Vietnam was shared by the president. Vietnam had taught him that if a president chose to go to war he had to be prepared to let the military make its own decisions and use the force necessary to win it decisively and promptly. As he explained to a group of congressional leaders on November 30: "We don't need another Vietnam War. World unity is there. No hands are going to be tied behind backs. This is not a Vietnam. . . . I know whose

backside's at stake and rightfully so. It will not be a long, drawn-out mess"
(Woodward, 1991: 300).

Power Over Rationality

To question the absence of a rational decisionmaking process by an administration that defeated its enemy decisively in a very short time might seem
absurd. One could also add that such a challenge does not take into account
that the severity of the situation in the Middle East pressed the Bush administration to respond rapidly. And finally, one could note that the Bush administration was fully aware that a war with Iraq, if not handled properly, could
cause some twenty thousand U.S. casualties, including the death of seven
thousand soldiers, the loss of approximately one hundred and fifty U.S. planes
over a thirty-day period, and the killing of two thousand Iraqi civilians.[10]

Although these challenges seem reasonable, they fail to take into account
that concern about the quality of the decisionmaking process within the Bush
administration was voiced by many of its principal representatives. Powell,
who as the leader of the JCS played a central role in the planning and execution of the military operation against Iraq, concluded on August 5 as he evaluated the latest decisions that the president had decided to commit U.S. troops
without a clear statement of his goals or a document that laid out the alternatives or the decision. His concern did not diminish with the passage of time.
Around mid-September he became particularly disturbed by the absence of
process that would enable Bush and his advisers to gauge carefully the costs
and benefits of implementing containment for an indefinite period of time.
The policy of containment was favored by many members of the U.S. Congress and military service and by the secretary of state (Woodward, 1991:
300).

Baker, one of Bush's closest political allies and a very disciplined and organized negotiator and decisionmaker, felt that the president had decided to use
the military to protect Saudi Arabia without asking his advisers what they
thought about his choice, and that the level of force had been decided not by
them but by Operation Plan 90-1002. Baker agreed with Bush that Saudi Arabia was important to the United States, but feared that the White House was
in such a hurry to respond that it was not considering the policy's possible
consequences. He was particularly concerned when Bush decided to deploy
U.S. troops in Saudi Arabia. As he remarked in private: "These young men
could be slaughtered if Saddam Hussein attacked" (Woodward, 1991: 262).

Anxiety about the nature of the White House's decisionmaking process
remained strong as the weeks went by. On October 30, just as Bush was getting ready to order that the number of U.S. troops in Saudi Arabia be doubled,
Paul Wolfowitz, who as undersecretary of defense for policy had access to the

war plans, was struck by the absence of a process of writing alternatives and implications so that the principal decisionmakers could analyze them (Woodward, 1991: 320). This uneasiness surfaced once more on Christmas Eve, when Bush, without requesting a thorough and careful analysis of the existing conditions, ordered the Pentagon to warn General Schwarzkopf to be prepared to launch an attack on Iraq shortly after January 15, if Saddam Hussein's troops did not pull out of Kuwait.[11]

This case, more than many others, establishes that success does not prove rationality. The momentous decision of January 16, 1991, was not the outcome of a rational process or even a process similar to that depicted by attribution theory. The process was structured by a decisionmaking system designed to minimize the voicing of alternative perspectives, and was delineated by a president's dependence on historical analogies to define problems and formulate policies, his need to keep a cognitive balance between his perception of Saddam and his belief in the appropriateness of the Munich analogy, and by his confidence that the Iraqi leader would be defeated if the U.S. military was permitted to fight the war it had not been allowed to carry out in Vietnam.

The case also demonstrates, however, that neither Bush nor the military forgot General Douglas MacArthur's advice, subsequently reinforced by the Vietnam War, that it is "fatal to enter any war without the will to win it." The military, in particular, sought to ensure that the absence of a rational decisionmaking process would be fully compensated by the unquestionable commitment to winning the war. This meant having the freedom to use the strategies and instruments necessary to achieve the assigned objectives. Superior military power saved the Bush administration from experiencing the costs that often ensue when an organization opts for satisfying instead of maximizing (March and Simon, 1958).

How leaders reason varies. Some leaders are less able than others to recognize the conflict between highly important beliefs and address rationally the tension it generates. Moreover, even among leaders who are highly adept at resolving conflict between beliefs, some are more competent than others at gathering and processing information, comparing alternative policies, and selecting the most viable one.

This study generated at least three significant conclusions. First, it disclosed that attribution theory did not help explain the decisionmaking strategy of the Bush administration. The administration's decisionmaking process was too much under the control of two leaders with very rigid views to encourage open discussion, and the comparison of Saddam's actions with a sample of data gathered from past actions initiated by similar leaders under equivalent circumstances, to elicit sound estimates and options. Second, it revealed that schema theory and cognitive consistency theory might sometimes function not as independent and distinct arguments, but as closely interconnected theoretical frameworks. Bush and Scowcroft were heavily dependent on the Munich analogy in formulating their definition of the problem created by Iraq's invasion of Kuwait and in making their decision to rely on force to move against Iraq. Bush, Scowcroft, and the military leaders repeatedly referred to the Vietnam War as the script that the United States could least afford to repeat. However, the president and the national security adviser also used the Munich and Vietnam scripts to minimize cognitive inconsistency. By relying rigidly on the Munich and Vietnam analogies, they excluded from their analysis information and options that might have encouraged questions about their core preconceptions and values. And third, this study showed that there was a clear parallel between the structure of the Bush administration's foreign-policy making process and the type of theoretical constructs that best helped explain the reasoning process of its principal leaders. Bush and Scowcroft created a decisionmaking system that, although it fostered camaraderie among its members, it also discouraged the systematic analysis of information and careful appraisal of alternative courses of action. In sum, based on the association observed in this study between cognitive theories and the structure of the decisionmaking process, this study corroborates the contention that leaders who strive to maintain cognitive consistency and rely on scripts to reinforce their preconceptions and impede the consideration of options that challenge them are likely to depend on the support of decisionmaking groups that are highly centralized and hierarchical.

The verdict on the applicability and value of cognitive models to the study of foreign-policy making is unlikely to be resolved for years to come. And yet, notwithstanding this study's empirical limitation, it has proven that much can be gained from the application of alternative cognitive models to one foreign-policy making event. A case does not make a theory, but the use of alternative cognitive theories justifies inquiring what one might learn from their application to different foreign-policy makers addressing different foreign-policy issues at different points in time.

Notes

1. It is very unlikely that a president whose behavior can be explicated by cognitive consistency theory will rely on the advice of an open and highly systematic decisionmaking group.

2. Though the range of theories advanced in cognitive psychology transcends attribution, cognitive consistency, and schema theories, the three are the most reputable and widely used.

3. Studies that come under the attribution theory rubric show that some of their basic postulates contradict one another. For this study I rely on Harold H. Kelley's thesis that in formulating causal explanations, individuals use information to gauge distinctiveness, consistency, and consensus. In using information for these three pur-

poses, the individual conducts an "analysis of variance" that resembles that used by trained social scientists (Kelley, 1967: 194).

4. Cognitive consistency theory should not be confused with cognitive dissonance theory. The former assumes that the individual develops simple rules for processing information in order to maintain consistency. It explains the process that takes place prior to and just at the time the decision is being made. The latter, with its focus on postdecision situations, is built on the assumption that ego-defensive motivations lead the individual to seek strong justification for his or her behavior, to the point that he or she will rearrange beliefs so that they provide more support for the actions chosen.

5. Analogical reasoning is what schema theory explains.

6. One of the most immediate effects of this process is to "obscure aspects of the present case that are different from the past one" (Jervis, 1976: 220).

7. An example of Baker's tendency to give in to Bush's and Scowcroft's view is his decision to accept their demand that he not travel to Baghdad to meet with Saddam Hussein. According to Drew, Scowcroft objected to the meeting partly because he feared that the secretary of state might be too inclined to negotiate an agreement. Baker ultimately agreed to meet with Iraq's foreign minister in Geneva. However, by then there was no chance of reaching any settlement because Bush had made it very clear that he was not "in a negotiating mood" and that Iraq had to "withdraw without condition" (Drew, 1991: 186).

8. The Hitler analogy became very popular during the months preceding Bush's final decision to attack Iraqi troops in Kuwait.

9. As an official in the Bush administration put it, sanctions and diplomacy were nothing more than the political precursors of war; each was a "box to check" (Drew, 1991: 181).

10. The first set of figures was presented in Saudi Arabia on December 1 by General Schwarzkopf to Secretary of Defense Cheney and General Powell. The second set was delivered to President Bush on December 1 by the new Air Force chief, General Merrill McPeak (Woodward, 1991: 349, and 340–41).

11. The formal authorization was not sent until December 29, but by then Schwarzkopf and his superiors in Washington had already agreed on a date and time (Woodward, 1991: 352–54).

References

Abelson, Robert. 1976. "Script Processing in Attitude Formation and Decision Making," in J. S. Carroll and J. W. Payne, eds., *Cognition and Social Behavior.* Hillsdale, N.J.: Lawrence Erlbaum Associates.

Clausewitz, Karl von. 1990. "On the Nature of War," in John A. Vasquez, ed. *Classics of International Relations.* Englewood Cliffs, N.J.: Prentice Hall.

Drew, Elizabeth. 1991. "Washington Prepares for War," in Micah L. Sifry and Christopher Cer, eds., *The Gulf War Reader: History, Documents, and Opinions.* New York: Random House.

Flory, Ingrid and Alex Roberto Hybel. 1995. "To Intervene or Not to Intervene: A Comparative Analysis of U.S. Actions Toward Guatemala and Bolivia in the Early 1950's." *Journal of Conflict Studies* 15: 82–103.

George, Alexander L., and Richard Smoke. 1974. *Deterrence and American Foreign Policy.* New York: Columbia University Press.

George, Alexander L. 1980. *Presidential Decisionmaking in Foreign Policy: The Effective Use of Information and Advice.* Boulder, Colo.: Westview Press.

Hybel, Alex Roberto. 1990. *How Leaders Reason.* Oxford: Basil Blackwell.

Janis, Irving L. 1972. *Victims of Groupthink.* Boston: Houghton Mifflin.

Janis, Irving L., and Leon Mann. 1977. *Decisionmaking: Psychological Analyses of Conflict, Choice and Commitment.* New York: Free Press.

Jervis, Robert. 1976. *Perception and Misperception in International Politics.* Princeton: Princeton University Press.

Kelley, Harold. 1967. "Attribution Theory in Social Psychology," in David Levine, ed., *Nebraska Symposium on Motivation.* Lincoln: University of Nebraska Press.

Klare, Michael T. 1991. "The Pentagon's New Paradigm," in Micah L. Sifry and Christopher Cer, eds., *The Gulf War Reader: History, Documents, Opinions.* New York: Random House.

Larson, Deborah. 1985. *Origins of Containment.* Princeton: Princeton University Press.

March, James, and Herbert Simon. 1958. *Organizations.* New York: Wiley & Sons.

Simon, Herbert. 1957. *Models of Man.* New York: John Wiley & Sons.

Steinbruner, John. 1974. *The Cybernetic Theory of Decision.* Princeton: Princeton University Press.

Woodward, Bob. 1991. *The Commanders.* New York: Simon & Schuster.

24

Presidents, Leadership Style, and the Advisory Process

Margaret G. Hermann and Thomas Preston

As the world becomes more complex and interconnected and its issues less well-defined, presidents face an increasing dilemma in the making of foreign policy: More parts of the government have become involved in the foreign-policy making process and have a stake in the administrations' decisions. As a result, presidents routinely find themselves confronted with an ever increasing number of agencies, institutions, and people who are trying to influence what the United States does in the international arena. Presidents must work to maintain control over their administration's foreign policy as this myriad of other actors seek to define the foreign policy agenda, generate alternative plans, and shape the implementation of decisions. To improve their capacity to coordinate American foreign policy, presidents have been forced over time to increase the size of the White House staff focusing on international issues. The presidency has evolved into a complex organization that requires staffing and managing. This advisory system helps to extend the modern president's capabilities by increasing his or her span of control and by keeping the president abreast of what is happening in specified arenas.

The presidency can be managed in a variety of ways. Presidents usually rely on styles and practices that have served them well before and with which they are comfortable. Indeed, because presidents participate in the selection of members of their advisory systems and set into place the norms that govern the advisory process, what presidents are like often influences what their advisers are like and how their organization tackles foreign policy issues. "Leadership in the modern presidency is not carried out by the president alone, but rather by presidents with their associates. It depends . . . on both the president's strengths and weaknesses and on the quality of the aides' support" (Greenstein, 1988, p. 352). The kinds of people that a president chooses or lets be chosen as well as how he or she configures these people thus have

351

implications for not only how the advisory system itself will function but how successful the president will ultimately be in the struggle for control over the conduct of American foreign policy.

In this chapter we explore how presidents' leadership styles influence the ways in which they structure their advisory systems. The framework we use builds on previous studies of how presidents have organized their relations with their advisers. To illustrate the framework we examine how Presidents Bush and Clinton organized and used advisers in foreign-policy making.

Characteristics of Presidential Leadership Styles

A review of the literature on the leadership styles of American presidents highlights three characteristics that appear to influence the way presidents organize their White House staffs: 1) degree of involvement in the policymaking process, 2) the belief that they can control what happens in decision making, and 3) sensitivity to the political context (see Hermann and Preston, 1994; Preston, 1997). In what follows, we will argue that these characteristics interact to shape the way presidents structure and manage their advisory systems.

Involvement

The degree presidents will want to be involved in the making of foreign policy is reflected in their interest and expertise in foreign-policy making. Presidents are far more likely to participate in the foreign-policy making process if they are interested in foreign policy and have had experience with foreign policy (see, e.g., Crabb and Mulcahy, 1988; George, 1980). Indeed, prior policy experience has been shown to have an effect on presidential style, the nature of advisory interactions, and how forcefully presidents will assert their own positions on policy issues.

Past experience provides presidents with a sense of what actions will be effective or ineffective in specific policy situations as well as helps them differentiate which cues from the environment should be attended to and which are irrelevant. It also influences how much learning must be accomplished on the job, the repertoire of behaviors presidents have at their fingertips, and their confidence when interacting with experts. Such is the case because presidents' sense of efficacy in the foreign-policy arena is likely to be enhanced when they are either interested or believe they have experience in foreign-policy making (George, 1980). The job is both more satisfying and easier with interest and/or experience and there is a tendency to focus on foreign policy when the president can choose what to attend to. With personal engagement in the process comes a desire to be part of what is happening, to be on top of any problem solving that centers around foreign policy. Without this sense of efficacy and comfort, presidents are likely to delegate the authority for foreign policy to others.

Control

The degree to which presidents believe that they can control what happens in the foreign-policy making process is a second important facet of presidential leadership style. This focus on control has implications for the way in which they will organize their advisers and the kinds of advisers they will seek. Generally presidents who are intent on controlling their environments seek to mitigate conflict among their advisers and to achieve their goals by putting in place a structure that they can manipulate and in which they have the most authority (see, e.g., Johnson, 1974; Hess, 1988). They want people around them who are loyal, interested in their goals, and willing to help them implement these goals. Such presidents would like to clone advisers who share their raison d'etre so that their world view permeates the executive branch of government.

Presidents who are not so intent on control often are willing to tolerate conflict among advisers because it stimulates debate and dialogue in the advisory organization, enhancing the opportunities for a range of points of view and options to be raised and discussed. Advisers who represent the "best and the brightest" and some diversity are preferable to having an advisory system of only "those like us." It is possible to tolerate "equals" and to encourage them to have areas of expertise that build on and broaden the president's.

Sensitivity

A third relevant characteristic of presidential leadership style involves presidents' sensitivity to the political context in which foreign policy decisions are made. How important does the president perceive it is to take into account and respond to the domestic and international constraints on what the United States can do in its foreign policy at any point in time? In other words, are constraints to be respected and worked with or to be challenged and worked around (see, e.g., Burke and Greenstein, 1991; Hermann and Kegley, 1995)? Presidents seek different kinds of information from the political environment depending on their answers to these questions.

Presidents willing to challenge perceived constraints often have an idea (cause, ideology, strategy) that they want to further and they search for information that is supportive or consonant with what they want to do. Advocacy and persuasion are the "name of the game." These presidents evidence less sensitivity to the nuance and complexity in their political environments, focusing primarily on distilling the arguments needed to line up a majority on the problem at hand. They are likely to rely upon analogies and stereotypical images of their opponents during policy deliberations and to be quite decisive since they know what they want.

Those who are prone to respect and react to perceived political constraints are interested in information that shows the range of opinion on how to solve a problem and what constituencies hold which opinions—there is a desire to know both consonant and dissonant information to facilitate locating oneself in the political terrain. Being the hub of the communication wheel is important to such presidents as is having advisers who have access to a broad array of constituencies. These presidents have been found to be highly sensitive to their political environments, desiring extensive search for information, considerable discussion about future policy contingencies, and policy debate before arriving at a decision.

Impact of Presidential Leadership Style on the Advisory System

In describing executive and presidential organizations, scholars have emphasized several functions that such organizations serve. The functions revolve around mastery of the task, motivation and control, and coordination and coherence. There is a need within the president's advisory system to solve problems, to motivate, to have some semblance of control, and to arrive at policies that receive support. These functions lead to specialization, centralization, and coordination (Wilensky, 1967). In what follows we will argue that the three characteristics of presidential leadership style discussed above shape the way specialization, centralization, and coordination are defined in any particular president's administration. We propose that presidential involvement in the foreign-policy making process is indicative of specialization of foreign policy. Such involvement suggests that presidents will want to shape the foreign-policy agenda. Presidents' need for control is indicative of the degree of centralization they are likely to desire in the advisory system. This leadership style variable influences how authority is structured in the White House. Sensitivity to contextual information suggests how presidents will go about coordinating policy making and where they will look for support for their policies.

Specialization

Degree of involvement in the foreign-policy making process is used here to denote specialization. We propose that a president's leadership style will have more impact on the centralization and coordination of foreign policy when the president is interested and experienced in the foreign-policy arena. A president involved in foreign-policy making will want to personally organize the White House staff responsible for foreign policy and to have an imprint on the nature of that staff. Moreover, such presidents are likely to pay more attention to foreign-policy issues and be attuned to potential problems and opportunities in the international arena. Shaping foreign policy becomes a central part of such presidents' agendas. Presidents who are less interested and experienced in foreign policy are more likely to react to foreign-policy problems and to allow others to configure the day-to-day operations of the foreign-policy apparatus.

Centralization

Complex organizations include people with different goals and interests—differences that generally cannot be resolved through voting but can be resolved through the establishment of a hierarchy and a pattern of organizational authority. How much control a president wants to exert over his or her advisory system helps to shape the nature of the pattern of authority that develops.

Presidents who perceive themselves as controlling what happens generally want to make the final decisions—that is, to have their preferences prevail. Such presidents view themselves as the ultimate authorities, whose positions cannot be reversed. These presidents are likely to organize authority into a hierarchical system with themselves at the apex of a formal chain of command. Information processing, problem definition, and option generation occur at lower levels of the chain of command and percolate up to the president. The advisory system is organized into a formal and rather inflexible hierarchy. In effect, there is a correct way to do things; the pattern of authority is well-defined.

If, on the other hand, the president's belief that what happens can be controlled is more moderate, or even low, the president is less likely to use a formal hierarchical pattern of authority and often is more comfortable when decisions are made through consensus or concurrence. Who participates in decision making and how structured the process is become determined largely by the situation and problem the president faces. There is a looseness and informality to the pattern of authority that facilitates the president's building of consensus. The president is still on top, but has purposively chosen to involve others directly in decision making and to use more informal channels of authority because there is no need to be in charge of everything that occurs.

Coordination

Presidents have many types of constituencies, both inside and outside the administration, whose concerns they must consider in making policy—for example, the Congress, executive agencies, various interest groups, political parties, public opinion, other national leaders. Presidents differ from one another in how much they take the interests of these constituencies into account and the role they perceive advisers should play with such constituents. Moreover, they have different tolerances for disagreement among their close associates and different tastes in social interaction. Thus, the ways in which presidents coordinate the vast array of people involved in foreign-policy making can vary based on their preferences for managing information, interpersonal interactions, and conflict. Presidents' sensitivity to the political context provides us with information about how they engage in coordination.

As George (1980) observed in examining the foreign-policy making of American presidents, those who were less sensitive or responsive to the political context tended to come to office with an agenda that framed how situations were perceived and interpreted. They were intent on finding that information in the environment that supported their definition of the situation or their position and overlooking evidence that was disconfirmatory (see also Burke and Greenstein, 1991; Crabb and Mulcahy, 1988). Their attention was focused on persuading others of their position. And, indeed, such presidents use their time to build a case and lobby others to their side. They are advocates who seek in advisers those who are also convinced of a particular point of view and able to line up the "votes" or constituencies that are needed to ensure success. These presidents are interested in meeting a situation head-on, in achieving quick resolution of problems, in being decisive, and in advancing their agendas in the process. Their emphasis is on mobilization, implementation, and effective problem solving.

Presidents who are more responsive to the context are more empathetic to their surroundings and intent on ascertaining how relevant constituents are viewing events and in seeking their support. They perceive that politics involves bargaining, trade-offs, and compromise. Flexibility, political timing, and consensus building are viewed as important leadership tools. Such presidents both define the problem and identify a position by checking what important others are advocating and doing. They consider the range of alternative scenarios that is possible in the current context, often "running ideas up the flagpole to see who salutes them." Feedback is critical in helping these presidents modify their behavior to fit the situation. Their focus is on the development of networks, collegial interactions, and the empowerment of others. Relationships are important to these presidents as is mapping the terrain of support and opposition on any issue. That which is doable and feasible at the moment is what is tried.

A Typology of President-Adviser Relations

The three presidential leadership style variables create an eightfold typology of possible advisory systems. This typology is presented in Table 24.1. Each cell of the typology indicates a kind of relationship between the president and his advisers based on the president's leadership style. The terms in the cells give an overall impression of the way in which a president's leadership style can shape the advisory system. The terms describe the role that a president

TABLE 24.1

Typology of Possible Presidential Advisory Systems Based on the President's Leadership Style

		Prior Experience in Foreign-Policy Making	
		High	*Low*
Belief Can Control: High	Sensitivity to Context — Low	Direct (Nixon)	Arbitrate (Truman, Johnson[a])
	Sensitivity to Context — High	Guide (Eisenhower)	Coordinate (Carter, Clinton)

with each set of characteristics is likely to play in the policymaking process and, in turn, the kinds of advisers such a president will choose and how they will be organized.

Table 24.1 indicates where American presidents since Truman fit in this typology based on their prior foreign policy experience (or expertise), their belief that they can control what happens, and their sensitivity to the political context. The presidents are placed in Table 24.1 according to their scores on these variables using a personality assessment-at-a-glance technique (Hermann, 1987a, 1987b). Presidents' scores indicating the extent to which they stated that they could influence events were used to assess their belief that they could control what happens; their scores denoting their ability to differentiate among people and objects in their environment (are things categorized into black/white, either/or categories as opposed to being viewed as more contextualized and nuanced) measured sensitivity to the political context; and previous experience in the foreign-policy arena denoted involvement or concern for foreign policy.

Being categorized as "high" on a leadership style variable in Table 24.1 means that the president's score on that variable was higher than the mean of the nine presidents included in the figure; being categorized as "low" indicates that the president's score was lower than the mean. It quickly becomes evident upon studying Table 24.1 that most U.S. presidents since World War II have wanted to have control of the executive branch of government (some 6 of 9 or 67%). The presidents are more evenly divided with regard to their experience in foreign policy (4 of 9—44%—have had extensive experience) and sensitivity to the political context (5 of 9—56%—are highly sensitive). All but two cells of Table 24.1 are represented among the nine presidents studied here. These nine individuals have varied in their leadership styles.

It is important for us to note, however, that under certain circumstances presidents can move between the cells in Table 24.1. One such situation involves presidents who are normally less engaged by foreign-policy problems. They can be forced by events—e.g., an international crisis, a persistent international problem, a summit meeting, a speech before an international body, a request from another country's leadership—to be involved in the foreign-policy making process. On such occasions, these presidents will exhibit the style of their more involved counterparts. Thus, for instance, as the Vietnam War heated up, Lyndon Johnson had to focus (against his wishes) more of his attention away from his Great Society program and onto the war effort. As a consequence, he became more directive in both the way he set up his advisory system and the people he chose to participate (see Burke and Greenstein, 1991; Crabb and Mulcahy, 1988). Otherwise, Johnson preferred to play the arbiter in foreign-policy making with his advisers (see Clifford, 1991; Kearns, 1976).

As footnoted in Table 24.1, three of the presidents had scores that were at the mean of this group of post-World War II American leaders: Johnson, Reagan, and Bush. These presidents could have been considered either low or high on the particular leadership style characteristic. Johnson and Reagan were at the mean on belief they could control what happens; Bush on sensitivity to the political context. In placing them in a particular cell in Table 24.1, we have taken into account their scores on several other characteristics. If such a president scores high on need for power and self-confidence when compared with the others, his average belief he can control events score is deemed high; otherwise, it is considered low. These two characteristics have been found to reinforce a leader's need to control his or her setting (Hermann, 1987b). Johnson was high in need for power and high in self-confidence when contrasted with the other presidents in Table 24.1 and, therefore, was classified as high on control. The opposite was the case for Reagan, who was low in both need for power and self-confidence in comparison with the others and, thus, was classified as low on control. With regard to sensitivity to the political context, research (Hermann, 1987b) has suggested that leaders are less sensitive if they are also highly distrustful of others and view the world in terms of friends and enemies. Since Bush was low on these two traits, he was classified as high in sensitivity to the political context.

When presidents' scores are at the mean, they have the potential to evidence both types of leadership styles depending on the situation in which they find themselves. Consider what has been written about Ronald Reagan. In both his governorship of California and the presidency, Reagan took charge—setting up programs and priorities—in areas of interest to him and delegated authority in areas that were of little interest to him. In foreign policy, issues related to the East-West conflict and Cold War were important to Reagan; he wanted to have, and took, control over policy making focused on these issues (Cannon, 1982; Kessel, 1984). Otherwise, he appears to have been more willing to share authority. Thus, Reagan's advisory system could be one where he played a monitor role or that of arbiter or director depending on how interested he was in the problem at hand.

Table 24.2 elaborates on the terms in the cells in Table 24.1 to describe the kinds of advisory systems we can expect around presidents with the different leadership styles. These descriptions synthesize the research on presidents with that on organizations, groups, and political leadership in general (see, e.g., Burns, 1978; House, 1990; 't Hart, Stern, and Sundelius, 1997; Hermann, 1993; Nutt, 1990). The information in Table 24.2 suggests that presidents' advisory systems are more hierarchical and formal the higher the president's belief that what happens can be controlled. There is more centralization of authority in the president. Advisers' input to problem definition, option generation, and planning is more valued the more sensitive the president is to the political context, while there is more emphasis on advisers who share the concerns, vision, and ideology of presidents who are less sensitive to the polit-

TABLE 24.2

The Proposed Influence of Presidential Leadership Style on the Selection and Organization of Advisers

			Prior Experience in Foreign-Policy Making	
			High	*Low*
Belief Can Control What Happens				
High	Sensitivity to Context	Low	Interested in framing policy agenda; Interested in focusing on important decisions; Loyalty is important; Procedures well-defined and highly structured; Disagreements allowed on means but not ends	Interested in evaluating not generating options; Select advisers with similar policy concerns; Decision shaped by shared vision; Advisers viewed as implementors and advocates of policy
		High	Interested in planning and anticipating problems; Advisers used as sounding board; Time spent considering options and consequences; Coherence in policy is valued; Advisers represent important constituencies	Seek doable solution that will sell politically; Advisers seen as part of team; Advisers propose and delineate problems and options; Compromise is valued; Seek experts as advisers; Policy by discussion
Low	Sensitivity to Context	Low	Interested in shaping option; Seek advisers with similar vision; Discussion focuses on how to coordinate policy; Groupthink is possible; Advisers provide psychological support	Interested in overseeing policy; Seek advisers who can act on own within particular framework; One or two advisers play gatekeeper role for information and access
		High	Interested in noncontroversial policy; Advisers' input is valued; Sharing of accountability; Seek advisers whom they know; Interested in reactions inside and outside advisory system; Consensus is valued	Advisers have leeway to decide policy; Seek advisers with skills that match position; Seek advisers who are interested in acting independently

ical context. The advisory systems are more open to outside influences the more sensitive and responsive the president is to contextual information.

The Bush and Clinton Advisory Systems

Using the classifications of the last two American presidents—George Bush and Bill Clinton—that we have made based on their leadership styles and our expectations about what their advisory systems should look like, do we find support for our typology in writings about their presidencies? In exploring the Bush administration, we will rely on assessments of his advisory system by those who served with him, journalists, and scholars of the presidency (see, e.g., Bush and Gold, 1988; Campbell, 1991; Dowd and Friedman, 1990; Duffy and Goodgame, 1992; Friedman and Tyler, 1991; Glad, 1995; Green, 1992; Jentleson, 1994; Podhoretz, 1993; Winter, 1995; Woodward, 1991). For the Clinton presidency we will use a similar diverse set of materials (see, e.g., Apple, 1994; Campbell, 1996; Drew, 1994; Dumas, 1993; "Grading the President," 1997; Harris, 1997; Hoagland, 1997; Renshon, 1995; Rockman, 1996; Watson, 1993; Woodward, 1994). How do these authors view the way Bush and Clinton fashioned their advisory organizations?

Bush and His Advisers

Our assessment of George Bush's leadership style suggests that his administration will exhibit two types of advisory systems with regard to foreign policy: one where the emphasis is more on strategizing with advisers and one where the focus is on consulting with advisers. In strategizing with advisers, the focus is generally on choosing an action, not whether or not to act; in consulting with advisers, just the opposite is the case—attention is directed toward defining the problem and considering whether action is needed. The president's views are more likely to frame the agenda in strategizing than in consulting with advisers. The fact that Bush's score on sensitivity to the political context was average among the post–World War II presidents studied here denotes that he will be more or less responsive to the political environment in which he finds himself depending on the current situation, thus the two advisory systems.

Literature on the Bush advisory system lends support to our framework and how Bush is classified. Bush was noted for preferring to spend time on foreign policy; indeed, he appears to have turned over responsibility for domestic policy to his chief of staff, John Sununu. Indeed, "he saw domestic affairs as a field that could pretty much run on its own" (Campbell, 1996, p. 61). Part of Bush's reelection strategy in 1992 was to run "on his reputation as a foreign policy leader" (Glad, 1995, p. 12). His previous experience as the United States delegate to the United Nations, ambassador to China, director of the

Central Intelligence Agency, as well as his world travels as vice president meant that he knew and was known personally by many heads of state and that he had an extensive knowledge of U.S. foreign policy that he could use to his advantage. Considering himself an expert, he wanted to be involved in making American foreign policy.

This same literature also indicates that how Bush used his advisers differed depending on the stress he was experiencing. He became less sensitive to the political context and less inclusive in his advisory system the more he perceived a threat not only to the policies of his administration but to policies important to his political well-being and place in history (Campbell, 1991, 1996; Winter, 1995; Woodward, 1991). Some instances when such change occurred include just prior to the United States' invasion of Panama, after the Iraqi invasion of Kuwait, and around Bush's China policy. In each case, Bush felt his policies were being challenged and his integrity and expertise were being called into question.

For most of the foreign-policy decisions in his administration, Bush followed a consultative approach in the advisory process. He was interested in a collegial environment where the focus was on building a consensus that would be noncontroversial and politically viable (e.g., Campbell, 1991; Glad, 1995; Woodward, 1991). At issue was making decisions that would play well with Congress, the media, and public opinion—"the focus was on managing the reaction" (Woodward, 1991, p. 81). He was concerned with the morale of his advisers, intent on keeping them in a good mood. Bush tended to involve as advisers those whom he had known for a period of time; in fact, "he had known 10 of the 16 people in his cabinet for at least 10 years" (Glad, 1995, fn. 3). He felt comfortable with them and had already established rapport and a mode of interaction. Bush worked with his advisers on what has been called the "art-of-the-impossible"—as Campbell (1996, pp. 57–58) has observed, Bush was pragmatic and interested in arriving at a consensus that was viewed as fair and on which all parties could agree. Such a goal often meant that he was selective in the foreign-policy issues in which he engaged his administration, avoiding "seemingly intractable problems" around which this type of consensus was highly unlikely.

This advisory pattern changed when Bush felt himself backed into a corner. In such circumstances, he personalized the conflict, tending to see the world in black and white terms (those who support us and those who do not) and to become less responsive to environmental cues and more defensive of what he had done or proposed (Campbell, 1991). His interaction with advisers was more strategic. Bush became a man with a mission wanting advisers who also shared his perspective on the problem. Only advisers who had his vision concerning what was happening were included in the inner circle. The focus of discussion was on how to coordinate policy not on what policy should be. For example, questions about options other than the offensive military policy being pushed by Bush after the Iraqi invasion were never considered in meetings at which Bush was present (Woodward, 1991, pp. 300–301). Motivation changed from seeking advisers' input and support to promoting a cause, and attention switched from building concurrence to coordinating strategies for accomplishing a task. As Bush observed during the initial stages of the Gulf crisis: "Let's be clear about one thing: We are not here to talk about adapting. . . . We are not going to plan how to live with this" (Friedman and Tyler, 1991, p. 18).

When Bush perceived a foreign-policy threat to his sense of self-worth, his political reputation, or his policies, he became more riveted on making something happen that would deal with the situation and save him face. At such times Bush's certainty about his expertise increased—he knew what to do and what was right. His reasoning often was couched "in harsh and vindictive terms" (Campbell, 1996, p. 63). Problems were defined in moral terms and driven less by the polls and what people wanted than by the challenge to his integrity and expertise. At these times, Bush went from an advisory system that involved consultation with advisers and the building of consensus to one that focused on strategy and implementation with advisers providing moral and tactical support.

Clinton and His Advisers

Our assessment of Bill Clinton's leadership style suggests that he will organize his advisory system for foreign policy so that he coordinates what happens. As noted in Table 24.1, Clinton has a high need to control his environment, that is, to be at the center of the policymaking process, and is very responsive to the political context and what is possible at any point in time. But he is less interested in foreign policy and, thus, less consistently engaged in foreign-policy making. When he is engaged, Clinton wants to take charge and consider the political ramifications of the options being considered.

Literature on Clinton and his foreign-policy advisory system lends support to our classification of him. Building from his campaign promise that he would "focus like a laser beam" on domestic problems and politics, Clinton has spent most of his presidency dealing with domestic issues. Indeed, he gave the foreign-policy advisers of his first term the assignment of keeping "foreign policy from distracting the President from his domestic agenda" (Drew, 1994, p. 28). Although he was a Rhodes Scholar and had spent some time abroad as well as had worked as an intern for Senator William Fulbright when the latter was focusing much of his activity on foreign policy, Clinton's interests and experience are more domestic in focus. It is hard to find an evaluation of the Clinton presidency that does not comment about his absorption with domestic problems and his lack of engagement with foreign policy. The following is a sample of such observations: Clinton "has never hidden his unease and bore-dom with the basics of foreign policy" (Hoagland, 1997, p. 5); Clinton has "remained absorbed by domestic policy" (Bennet and Pear, 1997, p. A1); Clinton has seemed "almost oblivious to foreign policy," delegating "the larger world to his foreign policy team" (Greenstein, 1995, p. 139); Clinton has evidenced a "limited foreign affairs attention span"—one gets the sense "that he does not like the stuff because he is not a master of it" (Campbell, 1996, pp. 67–68); Clinton "did not want to be a captive of foreign policy; the idea, in fact, was to keep foreign policy from interfering with domestic busi-ness" (Rockman, 1996, p. 341). Even when Clinton has become involved with foreign policy, it has been with a domestic operation—that of "domestic re-newal." His interest is in foreign economic policy; his top priorities are improving American economic performance and its international competitive-ness. This domestic orientation has led to "a lack of presidential attentiveness to the outside world and a tendency to hold foreign policy hostage to domestic constituencies" (Berman and Goldman, 1996, p. 298).

In both of Clinton's terms in office, he has chosen people with expertise in foreign policy to staff the important cabinet positions (secretaries of state and defense and director of the Central Intelligence Agency) as well as the Na-tional Security Council apparatus within the White House. Their expertise has been meant to compensate in part for Clinton's own lack of experience and interest in foreign policy. At the same time he chose people who were not towering figures in their own right, focusing "on not having people on the White House staff who were independent powers" (Drew, 1994, p. 33). They were good team players; "he didn't want any one person, other than himself, to have a great deal of power" (Drew, 1994, p. 349). Clinton is interested in being the ringmaster and selecting what problems take center stage and who is involved in policy making; he sees himself as the coordinator of U.S. for-eign-policy activity.

For Clinton, policy is made by discussion. "He needs time to talk, to bring people together" (Drew, 1994, p. 56). By his very nature he "wants to get as much information as possible. . . . He wants the satisfaction of knowing that he has reached out to advisers, to groups of people, to friends" (Harris, 1997, p. A8). "Clinton is Mr. Wiggling Antenna, who tries to read every face in the room and smooth down any hard edges . . . that are an obstacle to accommoda-tion" (Wiebe cited in Harris, 1997, p. A8). As several advisers observed, Clin-ton is not sequential in his thinking but circles a problem and is loath to make a decision "until he absolutely has to"—indeed, "when he must make a decision that he is not ready to make, the decision does not get made" (Drew, 1994, p. 67). Some had complained that this process leads Clinton to want to "staff himself in making decisions" (Campbell, 1996, p. 75) and if he is not attentive to the problem from the very beininng, as is the case with foreign policy, his policies are likely to appear indecisive and reactive as he gets himself up to speed.

Clinton also is intent on coming up with policy that is doable, that is politically feasible. "He is a consummate politician" (Burton cited in Harris, 1997, p. A8) who understands and revels in the horse-trading, cajolery, log-rolling, and persuasiveness that are pivotal in achieving workable compromises. Thus, he often tests ideas to check who reacts how, as well as being interested in exploring "a variety of perspectives" (Rockman, 1996, p. 352) and keeping a "balance around the table" (Drew, 1994, p. 69). This preference often means that Clinton will want the advise of those who are more politically inclined as well as those who are more expert on a particular topic. Such a practice in the Clinton advisory system automatically makes foreign policy look more domestic in orientation given the president's own interests and those of the large majority of his advisers. The focus is on reconciling differences and coming "to a consensus which will push the country forward" (Harris, 1997, p. A8) and on taking incremental steps that permit some movement—half a loaf, instead of an empty plate (see Smith, 1993, p. 16).

Interestingly, in much of the literature on Clinton's advisory system comparisons are made between his practices and those of Jimmy Carter. In Table 24.1 the reader will note that Carter's leadership style suggests that his advisory processes should bear a resemblance to those of Clinton. Both are classified as presidents interested in coordinating foreign policy. Both came to office with little experience in foreign policy, both "wanted things to come to [them] and not be filtered through a chief of staff" (Rockman, 1996, p. 352), both were open-minded and interested in gathering information from a variety of sources, both involved their advisers in the policymaking process, and both included on their advisory teams people with a particular expertise and people who were friends and campaign confidants (see, e.g., Campbell, 1996; Drew, 1994; Rockman, 1996).

In Conclusion

As one scholar (Hess, 1988) has observed, presidents' styles, work habits, how they like to receive information, the people they prefer around them, and the way they make up their minds are all key to how the White House is organized. "In the end, an American president is responsible for organizing his own White House and his own administration" (Rockman, 1996, p. 353). And what the president is like shapes the nature of that advisory system. In this chapter, we have focused on how the president's leadership style influences the nature of the foreign-policy advisory system. We have presented a typology of advisory systems that is derived from information about presidents' need to control what happens in the policymaking process, their sensitivity or responsiveness to the political context, and their prior experience and interest in foreign policy issues. An examination of the Bush and Clinton foreign-policy advisory systems has lent some support to the typology—at least, to the ways in which these two presidents were classified. These illustrations suggest that differences in leadership style are related to differences in the way the executive branch of government works. Unfortunately, "obeisance to the view that presidents can do little [because they are institutionally constrained] has limited attention to the relationship between personality, management style, and presidential performance during the last fifteen years" (Campbell, 1996, p. 57). This chapter indicates the importance of reversing this trend. After all, as we have shown, how presidents try to deal with institutional constraints is often shaped by who they are.

References

Apple, R. W., Jr. 1994. "Tight Corner for Comeback Kid," *New York Times,* December 15: A12.

Bennet, James, and Robert Pear. 1997. "A Presidency Largely Defined by the Many Parts of Its Sum," *New York Times,* December 8: A1.

Berman, Larry, and Emily O. Goldman. 1996. "Clinton's Foreign Policy at Midterm." In Colin Campbell and Bert A. Rockman, eds., *The Clinton Presidency: First Appraisals.* Chatham, N.J.: Chatham House.

Berman, Larry, and Bruce W. Jentleson. 1991. "Bush and the Post-Cold War World." In Colin Campbell and Bert A. Rockman, eds. *The Bush Presidency: First Appraisals.* Chatham, N.J.: Chatham House.

Burke, John P., and Fred I. Greenstein. 1991. *How Presidents Test Reality: Decisions on Vietnam, 1954 and 1965.* New York: Russell Sage Foundation.

Burns, James MacGregor. 1978. *Leadership.* New York: Harper & Row.

Bush, George, and V. Gold. 1988. *Looking Forward.* New York: Bantam.

Campbell, Colin. 1991. "The White House and Presidency under the 'Let's Deal' Presidency." In Colin Campbell and Bert A. Rockman, eds., *The Bush Presidency: First Appraisals.* Chatham, N.J.: Chatham House.

Campbell, Colin. 1996. "Management in a Sandbox: Why the Clinton White House Failed to Cope with Gridlock." In Colin Campbell and Bert A. Rockman, eds., *The Clinton Presidency: First Appraisals.* Chatham, N.J.: Chatham House.

Cannon, L. 1982. *Reagan.* New York: G.P. Putnam's Sons.

Clifford, Clark. 1991. *Counsel to the President.* New York: Random House.

Crabb, Cecil V., Jr., and Kevin V. Mulcahy. 1988. *Presidents and Foreign Policy Making.* Baton Rouge, La.: Louisiana State University Press.

Dowd, Maureen, and Thomas L. Friedman. 1990. "The Fabulous Bush and Baker Boys," *New York Times Magazine,* May 6.

Drew, Elizabeth. 1994. *On the Edge: The Clinton Presidency.* New York: Touchstone.

Duffy, M., and D. Goodgame. 1992. *Marching in Place: The Status Quo Presidency of George Bush.* New York: Simon & Schuster.

Dumas, E., ed. 1993. *The Clintons of Arkansas: An Introduction by Those Who Know Them Best.* Fayetteville, Ark.: University of Arkansas Press.

Friedman, Thomas L., and Patrick Tyler. 1991. "From the First, U.S. Resolve to Fight: The Path to War, Bush's Critical Decisions," *New York Times,* March 3: A18–A19.

George, Alexander L. 1980. *Presidential Decisionmaking in Foreign Policy: The Effective Use of Information and Advice.* Boulder, Colo.: Westview Press.

Glad, Betty. 1995. "How George Bush Lost the Presidential Election of 1992." In Stanley A. Renshon, ed., *The Clinton Presidency: Campaigning, Governing, and the Psychology of Leadership.* Boulder, Colo.: Westview Press.

"Grading the President: Redefining American Leadership." 1997–98. *Foreign Policy* No. 109.

Green, F. 1992. *George Bush: An Intimate Portrait.* New York: Hippocrene Books.

Greenstein, Fred I. 1995. "Political Style and Political Leadership: The Case of Bill Clinton." In Stanley A. Renshon, ed., *The Clinton Presidency: Campaigning, Governing, and the Psychology of Leadership.* Boulder, Colo.: Westview Press.

Greenstein, Fred I. 1988. "Nine Presidents: In Search of a Modern Presidency." In Fred I. Greenstein, ed., *Leadership in the Modern Presidency.* Cambridge, Mass.: Harvard University Press.

Harris, John F. 1997. "Winning a Second Term; Waiting for a Second Wind," *Washington Post National Weekly Edition,* January 20: A8.

't Hart, Paul, Eric K. Stern, and Bengt Sundelius, eds. 1997. *Beyond Groupthink: Political Group Dynamics and Foreign Policymaking.* Ann Arbor: University of Michigan Press.

Hermann, Margaret G. 1987a. "Handbook for Assessing Personal Characteristics and Foreign Policy Orientations of Political Leaders," *Mershon Occasional Papers,* Spring.

Hermann, Margaret G. 1987b. "Workbook for Developing Personality Profiles of Political Leaders from Content Analysis Data," *Mershon Occasional Papers,* Summer.

Hermann, Margaret G. 1993. "Leaders and Foreign Policy Making." In Dan Caldwell and Timothy McKeown, eds., *Diplomacy, Force, and Leadership: Essays in Honor of Alexander George.* Boulder, Colo.: Westview Press.

Hermann, Margaret G., and Charles W. Kegley, Jr. 1995. "Rethinking Democracy and International Peace: Perspectives from Political Psychology," *International Studies Quarterly* 39: 511–533.

Hermann, Margaret G., and Thomas Preston. 1994. "Presidents and Their Advisers: Leadership Style, Advisory Systems, and Foreign Policymaking," *Political Psychology* 15: 75–96.

Hess, Stephen. 1988. *Organizing the Presidency.* Washington, D.C.: Brookings Institution.

Hoagland, Jim. 1997. "Crisis-Managing in a Fog," *Washington Post National Weekly Edition,* December 1: 5.

House, Robert J. 1990. "Power and Personality in Complex Organizations." In Barry M. Staw and L. L. Cummings, eds., *Personality and Organizational Influence.* Greenwich, Conn.: JAI Press.

Jentleson, Bruce. 1994. *With Friends Like These: Reagan, Bush, and Saddam, 1982–1990.* New York: W. W. Norton.

Johnson, Richard T. 1974. *Managing the White House: An Intimate Study of the Presidency.* New York: Harper & Row.

Kearns, Doris. 1976. *Lyndon Johnson and the American Dream.* New York: Harper & Row.

Kessel, John H. 1984. "The Structure of the Reagan White House," *American Journal of Political Science* 28: 231–258.

Nutt, Paul C. 1990. *Making Tough Decisions: Tactics for Improving Managerial Decision Making.* San Francisco: Jossey Bass.

Podhoretz, J. 1993. *Hell of a Ride: Backstage at the White House Follies, 1989–1993.* New York: Simon & Schuster.

Preston, Thomas. 1997. "Following the Leader: The Impact of U.S. Presidential Style Upon Advisory Group Dynamics, Structure, and Decision." In Paul 't Hart, Eric K. Stern, and Bengt Sundelius, eds., *Beyond Groupthink: Political Group Dynamics and Foreign Policymaking.* Ann Arbor: University of Michigan Press.

Renshon, Stanley A. 1995. *The Clinton Presidency: Campaigning, Governing, and the Psychology of Leadership.* Boulder, Colo.: Westview Press.

Rockman, Bert A. 1996. "Leadership Style and the Clinton Presidency." In Colin Campbell and Bert A. Rockman, eds., *The Clinton Presidency: First Appraisals.* Chatham, NJ: Chatham House.

Smith, S. A. 1993. "Compromise, Consensus, and Consistency." In E. Dumas, ed. *The Clintons of Arkansas: An Introduction by Those Who Know Them Best.* Fayetteville, Ark.: University of Arkansas Press.

Watson, J. 1993. "The Clinton White House," *Presidential Studies Quarterly* 23: 429–436.

Wilensky, Harold. 1967. *Organizational Intelligence.* New York: Basic Books.

Winter, David G. 1995. "Presidential Psychology and Governing Styles: A Comparative Psychological Analysis of the 1992 Presidential Candidates." In Stanley A. Renshon, ed. *The Clinton Presidency: Campaigning, Governing, and the Psychology of Leadership.* Boulder, Colo.: Westview Press.

Woodward, Bob. 1991. *The Commanders.* New York: Simon & Schuster.

Woodward, Bob. 1994. *The Agenda: Inside the Clinton White House.* New York: Simon & Schuster.

Index

Page numbers in *italics* indicate tables and illustrations.

About the Contributors

Genevieve Anton is a reporter for the *Gazette,* Colorado Springs, Colorado.

Bruce D. Berkowitz is a writer and consultant in Alexandria, Virginia.

Richard Bernstein is a book critic for the *New York Times.*

Robert A. Blecker is associate professor of economics at The American University.

Eliot A. Cohen is professor and director of strategic studies at the Paul H. Nitze School of Advanced International Studies, The Johns Hopkins University.

Stephen D. Cohen is professor of international relations in the School of International Service at The American University.

Anthony J. Eksterowicz is associate professor of political science at James Madison University.

Louis Fisher is senior specialist in separation of powers at the Congressional Research Service of the Library of Congress.

James M. Goldgeier is assistant professor of political science at The George Washington University.

Glenn P. Hastedt is professor of political science at James Madison University.

Margaret G. Hermann is professor in the Department of Political Science and the Maxwell School of Citizenship and Public Affairs, Syracuse University.

Ole R. Holsti is George V. Allen Professor of Political Science at Duke University.

Samuel P. Huntington is the Albert J. Weatherhead III University Professor at Harvard University.

Alex Roberto Hybel is the Susan Eckert Lynch Professor of Government at the Connecticut College.

Christopher M. Jones is assistant professor of political science at Northern Illinois University.

Geoffrey Kemp is the director of regional strategic programs at The Nixon Center.

Stephen D. Krasner is Graham H. Stuart Professor of International Relations at Stanford University.

James M. Lindsay is professor of political science at the University of Iowa.

Mark M. Lowenthal is president of Open Source Solutions USA, Inc., in Fairfax, Virginia.

James M. McCormick is professor of political science at Iowa State University.

Ross H. Munro is the director of the Asian Program at the Foreign Policy Research Institute in Philadelphia.

John Mueller is professor of political science and Director of the Watson Center for the Study of International Peace and Cooperation at the University of Rochester.

Joel R. Paul is professor of law and director of international legal programs at the University of Connecticut School of Law.

Thomas Preston is assistant professor of political science at Washington State University.

William B. Quandt is the Henry E. Byrd Jr. Professor of Government and Foreign Affairs at the University of Virginia.

James N. Rosenau is university professor of international affairs at The George Washington University.

Steve Smith is professor and head of the department of international politics at the University of Wales, Aberystwyth.

Ronald Steel is professor of international relations in the School of International Relations at the University of Southern California.

Warren P. Strobel is the White House and former State Department correspondent for the *Washington Times.*

Strobe Talbott is U.S. deputy secretary of state.

Jeff Thomas is a business editor for the *Gazette,* Colorado Springs, Colorado.

James C. Thomson Jr. is professor in the Department of History and in the College of Communications at Boston University.

Eugene R. Wittkopf is R. Downs Poindexter Distinguished Professor of Political Science at Louisiana State University.